THE OFFICIAL ASVAB STUDY GUIDE

The Proven Path to ASVAB Mastery and Military Career Success

Gil Glade

Table of Contents

Copyright

Introduction to the ASVAB Study Guide

Welcome to "The Official ASVAB Study Guide," your comprehensive resource for achieving success on the Armed Services Vocational Aptitude Battery (ASVAB) and launching your military career. Whether you're considering joining the Army, Navy, Air Force, Marines, Coast Guard, or Space Force, this guide has been meticulously designed to provide you with the knowledge, strategies, and practice you need to excel on this critical examination.

The Gateway to Military Service

The ASVAB represents more than just a standardized test—it's your gateway to a rewarding military career. Your performance on this assessment will determine not only your eligibility for military service but also the specific career paths available to you. Understanding its significance is the first step toward strategic preparation.

Military service offers unique opportunities for personal and professional growth that few other career paths can match. From specialized technical training to leadership development, educational benefits, and the pride of serving your country, the rewards are substantial. However, accessing these opportunities begins with demonstrating your aptitude through the ASVAB.

Purpose of This Study Guide

This guide serves as your roadmap to ASVAB success, offering a structured approach to preparation that addresses all aspects of the examination. We've developed this resource based on extensive research, military recruitment expertise, and proven educational methodologies to maximize your performance potential.

Our approach focuses on three key elements:

1. **Comprehensive Content Coverage**: Each section of the ASVAB is thoroughly explained, with detailed content reviews that address the specific knowledge areas you'll encounter on the test.
2. **Strategic Test-Taking Approaches**: Beyond merely providing information, this guide equips you with targeted strategies for tackling each question type, managing your time effectively, and maximizing your score.
3. **Realistic Practice Opportunities**: The practice tests included here closely mirror the format, difficulty level, and content distribution of the actual ASVAB, allowing you to build confidence and familiarity with the examination.

Understanding Your Military Career Path

Your ASVAB performance doesn't just determine whether you qualify for military service—it plays a crucial role in shaping your entire military career trajectory. Each military branch uses specific combinations of ASVAB subtest scores, known as "line scores," to determine eligibility for various occupational specialties.

By understanding which career paths interest you most, you can strategically focus your preparation efforts on the subtests that will have the greatest impact on your eligibility for those roles. This guide includes detailed information about how each branch calculates and utilizes ASVAB scores, empowering you to prepare with your ultimate career goals in mind.

The Preparation Mindset

Success on the ASVAB requires more than just knowledge—it demands the right mindset. Approaching this test with confidence, focus, and strategic thinking can significantly impact your performance. Throughout this guide, we provide not only academic content but also psychological preparation techniques to help you perform at your best on test day.

Remember that your ASVAB score reflects your performance on a single day, not your ultimate potential or worth as a future service member. By dedicating yourself to thorough preparation, you can ensure that your score accurately represents your true abilities and opens doors to the military career you desire.

How to Use This Guide

To maximize the benefit of this study guide, we recommend the following approach:

1. **Begin with assessment**: Take a diagnostic practice test to identify your current strengths and weaknesses across all ASVAB subtests.
2. **Create a personalized study plan**: Based on your diagnostic results and career interests, develop a structured study schedule that prioritizes areas needing improvement.
3. **Engage with the content**: Don't merely read the material—actively engage with it through note-taking, self-questioning, and application exercises.
4. **Practice regularly**: Incorporate consistent practice using the tests provided in this guide, focusing on both content mastery and test-taking strategy.
5. **Monitor your progress**: Track your performance improvement over time, adjusting your study plan as needed to address persistent challenges.

The Journey Ahead

The path to ASVAB success requires dedication, perseverance, and strategic preparation. This guide provides the roadmap, but the journey itself depends on your commitment to consistent, focused study. Every hour you invest in preparation brings you one step closer to not just a qualifying score, but an exceptional performance that will maximize your military career opportunities.

As you progress through this guide, remember that millions of service members have successfully navigated this path before you. The ASVAB represents a challenging but entirely conquerable obstacle on your journey to military service. With thorough preparation and the right approach, you can transform this challenge into an opportunity to demonstrate your aptitude and secure the military career path you desire.

Your military journey begins here, with focused preparation and a commitment to excellence. Let's begin the work that will transform your military aspirations into reality.

Branch-Specific Benefits of This Study Guide

For Army Candidates

The U.S. Army offers the broadest range of career opportunities among all military branches, with over 150 Military Occupational Specialties (MOS) spanning combat operations, technical fields, medical services, intelligence, and logistics. This study guide has been specifically designed to support Army candidates in navigating the complex relationship between ASVAB performance and Army career qualification.

Army candidates will find exceptional value in our comprehensive coverage of the General Technical (GT) score components. The GT score—derived from Word Knowledge, Paragraph Comprehension, and Arithmetic Reasoning subtests—serves as the primary qualification metric for many of the Army's most competitive and sought-after career fields. Our strategic approach to these subtests will help you achieve the GT score necessary for advanced roles in Military Intelligence, Special Forces, and Cyber Operations.

For those interested in combat arms specialties such as Infantry, Armor, or Artillery, our focused preparation materials address the specific subtests that comprise the Combat (CO) score, including Arithmetic Reasoning, Mechanical Comprehension, and Auto & Shop Information. The guide provides specialized practice for the unique mechanical and spatial reasoning challenges these subtests present.

Army technical specialists in fields such as Signal Corps, Military Intelligence, and Cyber Command will benefit from our in-depth coverage of Electronics Information and Mathematics Knowledge. These sections have been specifically developed to address the types of problems and concepts encountered in Army technical training and operations. For candidates interested in the Army's aviation paths, our comprehensive approach to Mechanical Comprehension and Mathematics Knowledge provides targeted preparation for the Flight Aptitude Selection Test (FAST) that follows ASVAB qualification.

The guide includes detailed Army line score calculation methods with specific score requirements for each MOS, allowing you to strategically focus your studies on the subtests that most significantly impact your desired career path. Our practice tests feature question types and difficulty levels calibrated to current Army ASVAB performance metrics, ensuring your preparation aligns with actual test conditions.

Additionally, Army candidates will find dedicated sections addressing the Skilled Technical (ST), Surveillance and Communications (SC), and Operators and Food (OF) composite scores that determine qualification for specialized Army career fields. With the Army's recent emphasis on technical aptitude for next-generation warfare, our expanded sections on technical reasoning and problem-solving provide crucial preparation for the modern Army's qualification standards.

For Navy Candidates

The U.S. Navy's technical sophistication demands particularly strong performance in the ASVAB's quantitative and technical subtests. This study guide provides Navy candidates with precisely targeted preparation for the Navy's unique scoring requirements and specialized career paths.

Navy candidates will find exceptional value in our guide's emphasis on the mathematics and electronics components of the ASVAB. The Nuclear Field Qualification Score—which carries some of the highest ASVAB requirements in any military branch—receives special attention, with comprehensive coverage of Mathematics Knowledge, Arithmetic Reasoning, Electronics Information, and General Science. Our specialized practice materials for these subtests include the advanced algebra, physics principles, and electronics concepts needed for qualification into the Navy's prestigious nuclear program.

For candidates interested in the Navy's Advanced Electronics Field and Advanced Technical Field programs, our guide offers focused preparation for the Electronics Information, General Science, and Mathematics Knowledge subtests that heavily influence these composite scores. The technical content has been developed with input from Navy training specialists to ensure alignment with the concepts and applications emphasized in Navy technical training.

Navy aviation specialties—including Naval Aircrewman, Aviation Structural Mechanic, and Aviation Electronics Technician—require strong performance across mechanical and electronics subtests. Our comprehensive coverage of Mechanical Comprehension, Auto & Shop Information, Electronics Information, and Mathematics Knowledge provides the specialized preparation needed for these highly competitive aviation ratings.

The guide includes detailed Navy ASVAB score requirements for all ratings, with clear explanations of the various composite scores used for Navy qualification. Special attention is given to the subtests and score requirements for highly competitive programs such as Navy SEAL, Explosive Ordnance Disposal, and Cryptologic Technician pathways.

Navy-specific practice exercises focus on the applied mathematics, spatial reasoning, and technical comprehension skills emphasized in Navy technical training. The guide also includes specialized preparation for subtests relevant to Navy administrative ratings, including Verbal Expression, Coding Speed, and Mathematics Knowledge, which are critical components of the Navy's Administrative qualification score.

For those interested in the Navy's engineering and mechanical ratings, our expanded coverage of Mechanical Comprehension and Auto & Shop Information addresses the specific concepts and applications encountered in Naval engineering systems. Our guidance on achieving balanced scores across all ASVAB subtests aligns with the Navy's emphasis on well-rounded aptitude for many of its most sought-after career paths.

For Air Force Candidates

The U.S. Air Force's emphasis on technical specialization and advanced systems operation is reflected in its distinctive ASVAB requirements. This study guide provides targeted preparation for the Air Force's Mechanical, Administrative, General, and Electronics (M.A.G.E.) qualification areas that determine career eligibility.

Air Force candidates will find our comprehensive approach to Mathematics Knowledge and Arithmetic Reasoning particularly valuable, as these subtests significantly impact qualification for numerous Air Force career fields. The guide's advanced mathematics content addresses the algebraic reasoning, numerical operations, and problem-solving skills that are especially emphasized in Air Force technical training programs.

For those pursuing careers in the Air Force's electronics and communications fields, our expanded Electronics Information section covers the electrical theory, circuit analysis, and systems knowledge required for qualification in career fields such as Cyber Systems Operations, Radio Frequency Transmission Systems, and Avionics Test Station and Components. The guide's technical content aligns with the Air Force's cutting-edge approaches to electronic warfare, communications security, and network operations.

Air Force mechanical specialties—including Aircraft Maintenance, Aerospace Propulsion, and Munitions Systems—require strong performance in Mechanical Comprehension and Auto & Shop Information. Our specialized content for these subtests addresses the principles of fluid dynamics, mechanical systems, and materials science that form the foundation of Air Force mechanical aptitude assessment.

The guide includes detailed information on Air Force ASVAB score requirements for all Air Force Specialty Codes (AFSCs), with special attention to the highly competitive fields such as Special Warfare, Cyber Operations, Intelligence Analysis, and Aircrew operations. For candidates interested in pilot qualification, our strategic approach addresses the composite scores that serve as initial screening for pilot training eligibility.

Air Force-specific practice questions mirror the analytical and technical reasoning emphasized in Air Force specialty training. Our expanded sections on problem-solving strategies and technical comprehension are especially relevant for Air Force candidates, reflecting the branch's emphasis on conceptual understanding and adaptable technical knowledge rather than rote memorization.

For administrative and support role candidates, our coverage of Word Knowledge, Paragraph Comprehension, and Mathematics Knowledge addresses the verbal and quantitative reasoning skills required for Air Force administrative, logistics, and support career fields. The guide's systematic approach to all ASVAB subtests ensures comprehensive preparation aligned with the Air Force's emphasis on well-rounded aptitude.

For Marine Corps Candidates

The U.S. Marine Corps' emphasis on adaptability and cross-functional capability is reflected in its distinctive approach to ASVAB qualification. This study guide provides Marine Corps candidates with comprehensive preparation across all subtests, with special emphasis on the composite scores most relevant to Marine career qualification.

Marine Corps candidates will find our guide particularly valuable for preparation across the diverse ASVAB subtests that impact Marine Corps Military Occupational Specialty (MOS) qualification. Our comprehensive approach addresses all components of the General Technical (GT) score, which is critical for many of the Corps' most competitive career paths, including Intelligence, Communications, and Special Operations fields such as MARSOC (Marine Raiders).

The guide provides focused preparation for the Mechanical Comprehension and Auto & Shop sections that are vital for qualification in Marine Corps mechanical and combat vehicle maintenance roles. For infantry and combat arms specialties, our targeted materials address the specific subtests that comprise the Combat (CO) score, including Verbal Expression, Arithmetic Reasoning, and Mechanical Comprehension.

Marine Corps aviation maintenance and operations specialties require strong performance in technical and mechanical subtests. Our extensive coverage of Electronics Information, Mechanical Comprehension, and Mathematics Knowledge provides specialized preparation for Aviation Maintenance, Air Traffic Control, and Aviation Operations specialties. The guide's technical content addresses the unique systems knowledge emphasized in Marine Corps aviation operations.

For candidates interested in Marine Corps communications and intelligence fields, our detailed coverage of Electronics Information, General Science, and the verbal subtests provides the specialized knowledge needed to achieve the high composite scores these technical fields require. Marine Corps-specific line score calculations are clearly explained, with strategic guidance on how to achieve the scores required for infantry, intelligence, communications, aviation, and logistics roles.

The guide includes specialized preparation for the Clerical (CL) composite score that impacts qualification for administrative and logistics specialties within the Corps. Our practice materials align with the Corps' emphasis on mental agility and adaptability, featuring questions that require application of knowledge across multiple domains—a reflection of the Marine Corps' "every Marine a rifleman" philosophy that expects technical specialists to maintain combat readiness.

Marine Corps-specific guidance addresses the relationship between ASVAB performance and subsequent training opportunities, including specialized schools such as Marine Security Guard, Marine Embassy Security Guard, and Marine Corps Special Operations Command. Our strategic approach to test preparation aligns with the Marine Corps' emphasis on comprehensive capability and mental toughness.

For Coast Guard Candidates

The U.S. Coast Guard's unique multi-mission profile requires personnel with diverse aptitudes across technical, mechanical, and analytical domains. This study guide offers specialized preparation aligned with the Coast Guard's distinctive ASVAB requirements and career qualification standards.

Coast Guard candidates will benefit from our guide's balanced coverage of technical, mechanical, and administrative subtests. The guide's comprehensive approach ensures preparation for all aspects of Coast Guard qualification testing, with particular emphasis on the composite scores that impact eligibility for the Coast Guard's specialized ratings.

Our Mathematics Knowledge and Arithmetic Reasoning sections provide crucial preparation for qualification into technical ratings such as Operations Specialist, Maritime Enforcement Specialist, and Electronics Technician. The guide's detailed coverage of Word Knowledge and Paragraph Comprehension supports preparation for administrative and intelligence ratings that require strong verbal reasoning skills.

For those interested in the Coast Guard's mechanical specialties, including Machinery Technician and Damage Controlman, our expanded Mechanical Comprehension and Auto & Shop Information sections address the specific systems knowledge and mechanical principles emphasized in Coast Guard technical operations. The guide's approach to these subtests incorporates the practical application of mechanical concepts that Coast Guard duties require.

Coast Guard aviation positions—including Aviation Maintenance Technician and Aviation Survival Technician—require strong performance across multiple ASVAB domains. Our guide provides specialized preparation for the composite scores that determine eligibility for these highly competitive ratings, including comprehensive coverage of Electronics Information, Mathematics Knowledge, and Mechanical Comprehension.

The guide includes detailed Coast Guard ASVAB score requirements for all ratings, with special attention to how these requirements interact with other qualification factors specific to Coast Guard enlistment. Our practice materials reflect the Coast Guard's emphasis on practical problem-solving and adaptable technical knowledge, featuring scenarios and applications relevant to Coast Guard operations.

Coast Guard-specific score requirements are clearly outlined, with strategic preparation advice for achieving the composite scores needed for specialized career paths such as Maritime Law Enforcement, Boatswain's Mate, and Information Systems Technician. The guide's emphasis on problem-solving and adaptive thinking aligns perfectly with the Coast Guard's multifaceted operational requirements.

For Space Force Candidates

As the newest branch of the U.S. military, the Space Force has established some of the most technically demanding ASVAB requirements for its specialized career fields. This study guide provides targeted preparation aligned with the Space Force's emphasis on technical aptitude and specialized knowledge.

Space Force candidates will find exceptional value in our guide's emphasis on technical and scientific ASVAB components. The Space Force places particularly high importance on Electronics Information, Mathematics Knowledge, and General Science scores for qualification into its core operational specialties. Our comprehensive coverage of these technical areas provides the specialized knowledge required for Space Force careers in satellite operations, space systems operations, cyber operations, and intelligence.

The guide includes detailed coverage of algebraic reasoning, electronics principles, and physical science concepts that are specifically relevant to Space Force qualification testing. For candidates interested in Space Force cyber operations specialties, our expanded sections on Electronics Information and Mathematics Knowledge address the specific technical concepts emphasized in Space Force cyber operations qualification.

Space Force intelligence and surveillance roles require strong performance across both technical and verbal subtests. Our guide provides balanced preparation across these domains, with specialized content addressing the analytical reasoning and technical comprehension required for these roles. The practice materials include question types and difficulty levels calibrated to the Space Force's elevated technical standards.

The guide offers Space Force-specific scoring information to help candidates understand the qualification requirements for this highly competitive branch. Strategic guidance focuses on maximizing performance in the subtests most relevant to Space Force career qualification, with special attention to the composite scores used for Space Force specialty classification.

Our practice tests include specialized technical content aligned with the Space Force's emphasis on systems thinking and integrated technical knowledge. The guide's approach to technical subtests emphasizes conceptual understanding and application—skills that are particularly valued in Space Force operations that require adaptation to rapidly evolving technologies and space systems.

For ROTC Members

Reserve Officers' Training Corps (ROTC) members face unique challenges in military qualification and career development. This study guide provides specialized preparation that supports both immediate ASVAB success and long-term officer career development.

ROTC members will find this guide invaluable for both immediate testing needs and long-term officer career preparation. For college ROTC cadets, strong ASVAB performance can influence branch assignment options upon commissioning, particularly for technical branches that require demonstrated aptitude. The guide's strategic approach helps cadets achieve scores that expand their branch selection opportunities.

Our comprehensive preparation methodology supports the development of both technical and verbal reasoning skills that will serve ROTC cadets well throughout their academic and military training. The guide's emphasis on critical thinking and problem-solving aligns with the officer development goals of ROTC programs, providing skills that translate directly to officer candidate evaluations and leadership assessments.

For high school students considering ROTC scholarships, strong ASVAB scores can complement academic achievements in demonstrating potential for military leadership. Our guide provides the specialized preparation needed to achieve scores that strengthen ROTC scholarship applications and expand scholarship opportunities.

The guide includes specialized information on how ASVAB performance interacts with other ROTC assessment metrics, including Physical Fitness assessments, academic performance, and leadership evaluations. Our strategic guidance helps ROTC members balance their preparation across these various qualification domains.

ROTC members preparing for specialized career paths, such as aviation, engineering, or intelligence, will find our targeted preparation for relevant ASVAB subtests particularly valuable. The guide's technical content supports qualification for specialized training opportunities that may be available to ROTC cadets with demonstrated aptitude.

Our practice tests and strategic preparation advice help ROTC members develop the test-taking skills and knowledge base that will support success not only on the ASVAB but also on future military qualification exams encountered throughout an officer career. The guide's systematic approach to knowledge building and test strategy provides lasting benefits that extend beyond initial qualification testing.

Universal Benefits Across All Service Branches

While each service branch has unique requirements and emphasis areas, all military candidates benefit from this guide's comprehensive approach to ASVAB preparation. The core AFQT subtests—Arithmetic Reasoning, Mathematics Knowledge, Word Knowledge, and Paragraph Comprehension—are critical qualification components for all branches.

Our systematic preparation methodology develops the fundamental knowledge, test-taking strategies, and confidence that support success across all ASVAB subtests. The guide's integrated approach ensures balanced preparation that opens the widest possible range of military career opportunities, regardless of your chosen service branch.

The practice tests provided in this guide reflect current ASVAB content and difficulty levels, ensuring your preparation aligns with the actual test experience. Our comprehensive review sections address all knowledge domains assessed by the ASVAB, providing a solid foundation that supports success across all military qualification pathways.

Most importantly, this guide's strategic approach to ASVAB preparation empowers you to take control of your military career path. By understanding how ASVAB scores impact your qualification options and focusing your preparation on the subtests most relevant to your goals, you can transform the ASVAB from a qualification hurdle into a strategic opportunity to demonstrate your aptitude and secure your desired military career path.

Chapter 1: Understanding the ASVAB

1.1 What is the ASVAB?

The Armed Services Vocational Aptitude Battery (ASVAB) is a comprehensive multi-aptitude test developed by the United States Department of Defense. Unlike traditional standardized tests, the ASVAB serves a unique and critical purpose: to assess a potential military recruit's strengths, weaknesses, and vocational aptitudes across multiple domains.

Historical Background

The ASVAB has a rich history dating back to the early 1970s. Initially developed to help military recruiters match candidates with appropriate military occupational specialties, the test has evolved significantly over the decades. What began as a simple assessment tool has transformed into a sophisticated instrument for evaluating potential military personnel.

Test Purpose and Significance

The primary objectives of the ASVAB include:

- Determining qualification for military enlistment
- Identifying potential career paths within the military
- Matching individual skills with specific military occupational specialties
- Providing insights into a candidate's cognitive and technical abilities

1.2 Test Structure and Format

Test Composition

The ASVAB consists of multiple subtests covering a wide range of academic and technical skills:

1. **General Science (GS)**
   - Assesses basic scientific knowledge
   - Covers biology, chemistry, physics, and earth sciences
2. **Arithmetic Reasoning (AR)**
   - Evaluates mathematical problem-solving skills
   - Focuses on word problems and practical mathematical applications
3. **Word Knowledge (WK)**
   - Tests vocabulary and word comprehension
   - Includes identifying word meanings and synonyms
4. **Paragraph Comprehension (PC)**
   - Measures reading comprehension
   - Requires extracting key information from written passages
5. **Mathematics Knowledge (MK)**
   - Evaluates mathematical concepts and principles
   - Includes algebra, geometry, and mathematical reasoning
6. **Electronics Information (EI)**
   - Assesses understanding of electrical systems

o Covers basic electrical and electronic principles
7. **Auto and Shop Information (AS)**
   o Tests knowledge of automotive maintenance
   o Includes basic automotive and shop mechanical principles
8. **Mechanical Comprehension (MC)**
   o Evaluates understanding of mechanical and physical principles
   o Covers force, motion, and mechanical systems
9. **Assembling Objects (AO)**
   o Measures spatial reasoning skills
   o Requires mental manipulation of objects and shapes
10. **Coding Speed (CS)**
    o Assesses clerical and administrative aptitude
    o Measures speed and accuracy in symbol substitution

Test Administration

Computer-Adaptive Testing (CAT)

- Most ASVAB tests are now computer-based
- Questions adapt to the test-taker's ability level
- Difficulty increases or decreases based on previous answers

Paper-and-Pencil Option

- Traditional format still available in some locations
- Fixed set of questions
- Consistent difficulty across all test-takers

Test Duration

- Typically takes 2-3 hours to complete
- Individual subtest times vary
- Includes short breaks between sections

1.3 Scoring System

AFQT Score

The Armed Forces Qualification Test (AFQT) score is the most critical component:

- Calculated using four ASVAB subtests
- Determines overall military eligibility
- Ranges from 1-99 percentile
- Higher scores indicate better performance relative to other test-takers

Line Scores

- Specific to each military branch
- Determine qualification for specific military occupational specialties
- Combine different ASVAB subtest scores

Scoring Breakdown

- Percentile-based scoring system
- Score of 50 means you scored higher than 50% of test-takers
- Most military branches require minimum AFQT scores:
    - Army: Typically 31 or higher
    - Navy: Typically 35 or higher
    - Air Force: Typically 36 or higher
    - Marines: Typically 32 or higher
    - Coast Guard: Typically 40 or higher
    - Space Force: Typically 35 or higher

1.4 Military Entrance Score Calculation

AFQT Score Calculation

- Uses four critical subtests:
    1. Arithmetic Reasoning
    2. Word Knowledge
    3. Paragraph Comprehension
    4. Mathematics Knowledge

Calculation Method

- Converts raw scores to standardized scores
- Compares performance to a representative sample
- Weighted scoring emphasizes certain skills

Importance of Each Subtest

- Arithmetic Reasoning: 25% weight
- Word Knowledge: 25% weight
- Paragraph Comprehension: 25% weight
- Mathematics Knowledge: 25% weight

Strategies for Maximizing Scores

- Understand the weighted importance of subtests
- Focus study efforts on high-impact areas

- Practice time management
- Develop strong foundational skills in core subjects

Chapter 2: ASVAB Test Sections Explained

Overview of ASVAB Subtests

The ASVAB comprises 10 distinct subtests, each designed to assess specific skills and aptitudes critical for military service. Understanding these sections is key to comprehensive test preparation.

1. General Science

Core Focus

- Evaluates basic scientific knowledge across multiple disciplines
- Tests understanding of fundamental scientific concepts

Key Content Areas

- Biology
- Chemistry
- Physics
- Earth and Space Sciences

Primary Skills Assessed

- Scientific reasoning
- Concept identification
- Basic scientific knowledge application

2. Arithmetic Reasoning

Core Focus

- Assesses mathematical problem-solving skills
- Emphasizes practical word problem solving

Key Skill Components

- Basic mathematics
- Word problem translation
- Logical mathematical thinking
- Real-world mathematical applications

Problem-Solving Approach

1. Carefully read the entire problem
2. Identify key information
3. Determine required mathematical operations
4. Solve systematically
5. Verify answer reasonableness

3. Word Knowledge

Core Focus

- Evaluates vocabulary comprehension
- Tests ability to understand word meanings and context

Skill Assessment Areas

- Vocabulary understanding
- Synonym identification
- Contextual word usage
- Academic and professional terminology

Key Strategies

- Build comprehensive vocabulary
- Practice context-based word understanding
- Learn root words and etymologies
- Read diverse materials

4. Paragraph Comprehension

Core Focus

- Evaluates reading comprehension
- Assesses ability to extract key information from passages

Skill Assessment Areas

- Main idea identification
- Supporting detail extraction
- Inference and conclusion drawing
- Critical reading skills

Reading Strategies

- Active reading techniques
- Systematic passage analysis
- Efficient information extraction
- Logical reasoning application

5. Mathematics Knowledge

Core Focus

- Tests advanced mathematical concepts
- Evaluates mathematical reasoning and problem-solving skills

Key Content Areas

- Algebra
- Geometry
- Advanced mathematical reasoning
- Equation solving
- Geometric problem-solving

Problem-Solving Approach

- Systematic equation solving
- Step-by-step mathematical reasoning
- Multiple solution method exploration
- Solution verification

6. Electronics Information

Core Focus

- Assesses understanding of electrical and electronic principles
- Tests basic technical knowledge

Key Content Areas

- Electrical basics
- Electronic systems
- Technical terminology
- Circuit understanding

Fundamental Concepts

- Ohm's Law
- Circuit types
- Electronic component functions
- Basic electrical principles

7. Auto and Shop Information

Core Focus

- Evaluates mechanical aptitude
- Tests understanding of automotive and workshop principles

Key Content Areas

- Automotive systems
- Workshop techniques
- Tool usage
- Mechanical reasoning

Skill Assessment

- Mechanical system understanding
- Technical knowledge application
- Practical reasoning
- Tool and equipment comprehension

8. Mechanical Comprehension

Core Focus

- Tests understanding of mechanical and physical principles
- Evaluates spatial and mechanical reasoning skills

Key Content Areas

- Mechanical principles
- Physics applications
- Spatial reasoning
- System interaction understanding

Skill Assessment

- Force and motion comprehension
- Mechanical visualization
- Technical problem-solving
- Physical system analysis

9. Assembling Objects

Core Focus

- Evaluates spatial reasoning
- Tests mechanical visualization skills

Key Skill Areas

- Mental object rotation
- Mechanical assembly reasoning
- Spatial problem-solving
- Technical visualization

10. Coding Speed

Core Focus

- Assesses administrative and clerical aptitude
- Tests symbol processing and rapid cognitive skills

Key Skill Areas

- Symbol recognition
- Quick substitution
- Concentration
- Rapid processing
- Clerical efficiency

Overview

Each military branch has unique ASVAB score requirements and career opportunities. Understanding these specifics is crucial for aligning your skills with the most suitable military path. This chapter provides comprehensive insights into each branch's requirements, career opportunities, and advancement pathways.

U.S. Army Requirements

ASVAB Score Basics

- **Minimum AFQT Score:** 31
- **Ideal Score Range:** 50-99
- **Waiver Possibility:** Limited waivers available for scores 28-30 during high recruitment periods

Key Career Paths and Line Score Requirements

Career Field	Required Line Score	Minimum Score	Popular MOS Examples
Combat Arms	Combat (CO)	87+	11B Infantry, 19K Armor Crewman

Career Field	Required Line Score	Minimum Score	Popular MOS Examples
Intelligence	General Technical (GT)	110+	35F Intelligence Analyst, 35M Human Intelligence Collector
Signal/Communications	Signal Corps (SC)	98+	25B IT Specialist, 25U Signal Support Specialist
Medical	Skilled Technical (ST)	101+	68W Combat Medic, 68C Practical Nursing Specialist
Aviation	Aviation (AV)	90+	15T UH-60 Helicopter Repairer, 15W Unmanned Aircraft Operator
Engineering	General Maintenance (GM)	98+	12B Combat Engineer, 12N Horizontal Construction Engineer
Logistics	General Technical (GT)	92+	92A Automated Logistical Specialist, 88M Motor Transport Operator
Military Police	Law Enforcement (LE)	95+	31B Military Police, 31K Military Working Dog Handler

Line Score Composition

- **General Technical (GT):** Word Knowledge + Paragraph Comprehension + Arithmetic Reasoning
- **Combat (CO):** Word Knowledge + Paragraph Comprehension + Auto & Shop + Mechanical Comprehension
- **Skilled Technical (ST):** General Science + Word Knowledge + Paragraph Comprehension + Mechanical Comprehension
- **Electronics (EL):** General Science + Arithmetic Reasoning + Mathematics Knowledge + Electronics Information

Career Advancement Pathways

The Army offers multiple advancement tracks based on initial ASVAB performance:

1. **Direct Commission:** Soldiers with GT scores above 110 may qualify for Officer Candidate School (OCS)
2. **Warrant Officer Program:** Technical experts with high specialty scores can advance to technical leadership roles
3. **Specialized Training:** High scorers in technical areas qualify for advanced schools and certifications
4. **Green to Gold Program:** Enlisted soldiers with strong academic performance can earn commissions

Recent Changes in Score Requirements

Since 2023, the Army has adjusted several MOS requirements in response to technological advancements and force modernization initiatives:

- **Cyber Operations Specialists (17C):** GT score requirement increased from 105 to 110
- **Network Operations Specialists (25N):** GT score requirement increased from 100 to 105
- **Intelligence Specialists:** Several intelligence MOS scores were adjusted upward to reflect increased technical demands

Firsthand Account: Staff Sergeant James Morgan, Infantry Squad Leader

"When I joined the Army, my GT score of 112 gave me a wide range of options, but I chose Infantry (11B) because I wanted the frontline experience. That high GT score later allowed me to qualify for Special Forces selection without needing a waiver. My advice to recruits: Even if you're set on combat arms, which typically have lower score requirements, aim high on the ASVAB. Those scores follow you throughout your career and open doors years later when your goals might change."

U.S. Navy Requirements

ASVAB Score Basics

- **Minimum AFQT Score:** 35
- **Ideal Score Range:** 50-99
- **High-Demand Programs:** Nuclear Field (NF) requires AFQT of 80+ and strong Mathematics Knowledge scores

Key Career Paths and Line Score Requirements

Career Field	Required Line Score	Minimum Score	Popular Rating Examples
Nuclear Field	VE+AR+MK+MC	252+	Nuclear Electronics Technician (ETN), Nuclear Machinist's Mate (MMN)
Aviation	VE+AR+MK+AS	210+	Aviation Maintenance Technician (AT), Aviation Structural Mechanic (AM)
Advanced Electronics	AR+MK+EI+GS	223+	Electronics Technician (ET), Fire Controlman (FC)
Medical	VE+MK+GS	210+	Hospital Corpsman (HM), Dental Technician (DT)
Information Systems	VE+AR+MK+MC	222+	Information Systems Technician (IT), Cryptologic Technician (CT)
Special Warfare	VE+AR+MC+CS	220+	Navy SEAL (SO), Special Warfare Combatant-Craft Crewman (SB)

Career Field	Required Line Score	Minimum Score	Popular Rating Examples
Submarine	VE+AR+MK+MC	222+	Submarine Electronics Technician (ETS), Submarine Sonar Technician (STS)
Construction	AR+MC+AS	196+	Construction Electrician (CE), Builder (BU), Steelworker (SW)

Line Score Composition

- **VE (Verbal):** Word Knowledge + Paragraph Comprehension
- **AR:** Arithmetic Reasoning
- **MK:** Mathematics Knowledge
- **MC:** Mechanical Comprehension
- **EI:** Electronics Information
- **GS:** General Science
- **AS:** Auto & Shop Information

Career Advancement Pathways

The Navy offers several advancement opportunities based on ASVAB performance:

1. **STA-21 Program (Seaman to Admiral):** Competitive commissioning program for enlisted sailors with strong academic potential
2. **Technical Rating Advancement:** Advanced technical ratings offer faster promotion timelines
3. **Nuclear Propulsion Officer Candidate Program:** Nuclear-qualified enlisted personnel can commission as Nuclear Officers
4. **Limited Duty Officer (LDO) Program:** Technical experts can commission without bachelor's degrees

Recent Changes in Score Requirements

In response to evolving technological demands, the Navy has recently adjusted several rating requirements:

- **Cryptologic Warfare ratings:** Score requirements increased by 5-10 points across multiple line scores
- **Unmanned Systems Operators:** New specialty with high electronics and mathematics requirements
- **Nuclear Field:** Mathematics Knowledge requirements have become more stringent due to program complexity

Firsthand Account: Petty Officer First Class Elena Rodriguez, Information Systems Technician

"My ASVAB scores, particularly in Mathematics Knowledge and Electronics Information, qualified me for the advanced technical ratings. I chose IT because of the transferable skills, but what I didn't realize was how my scores would make me eligible for advanced C5I (Command, Control, Communications, Computers, Combat Systems, and Intelligence) schools that typically have long waiting lists. My advice: If you're interested in Navy technical fields, focus heavily on the math and electronics sections of the ASVAB – they're the gateway to the Navy's most advanced training."

U.S. Air Force Requirements

ASVAB Score Basics

- **Minimum AFQT Score:** 36
- **Ideal Score Range:** 50-99
- **Special Access Programs:** Certain intelligence and cyber AFSCs require scores of 110+ on specific aptitude areas

Key Career Paths and Line Score Requirements

Career Field	Required Aptitude Area	Minimum Score	Popular AFSC Examples
Operations	General (G)	57+	1A8X1 Airborne Cryptologic Language Analyst, 1U0X1 RPA Sensor Operator
Maintenance	Mechanical (M)	56+	2A3X3 Tactical Aircraft Maintenance, 2A6X1 Aerospace Propulsion
Administrative	Administrative (A)	41+	3F0X1 Personnel, 3F5X1 Administration
General	General (G)	55+	3P0X1 Security Forces, 4Y0X1 Dental Assistant
Electronic	Electronic (E)	70+	3D1X2 Cyber Transport Systems, 2P0X1 Precision Measurement Equipment Lab
Cyber Operations	Electronic (E)	85+	1B4X1 Cyber Warfare Operations, 3D0X2 Cyber Systems Operations
Intelligence	General (G)	72+	1N0X1 Intelligence Analyst, 1N1X1 Geospatial Intelligence

Aptitude Area Composition

- **Mechanical (M):** Mathematical Knowledge + Mechanical Comprehension + Electronics Information
- **Administrative (A):** Numerical Operations + Coding Speed + Verbal Expression
- **General (G):** Verbal Expression + Mathematics Knowledge
- **Electronic (E):** General Science + Mathematics Knowledge + Electronics Information

Career Advancement Pathways

The Air Force offers several advancement opportunities based on ASVAB performance:

1. **Airman Education and Commissioning Program (AECP):** Allows enlisted personnel to earn engineering degrees and commissions
2. **Technical Training Accelerated Promotion:** Graduates of certain technical training courses receive accelerated promotion
3. **Special Duty Assignments:** High ASVAB scorers become eligible for specialized duties with promotion advantages
4. **Specialized Training Programs:** Advanced technical training becomes available to high scorers

Recent Changes in Score Requirements

The Air Force has made several adjustments to AFSC requirements since 2023:

- **Cyber Warfare Operations (1B4X1):** Electronic aptitude minimum increased from 70 to 85
- **Space Systems Operations (1C6X1):** General aptitude minimum increased from 62 to 66
- **Intelligence Career Fields:** Several intelligence AFSCs now require higher General aptitude scores

Firsthand Account: Technical Sergeant Michael Chen, Cyber Transport Systems Specialist

"I scored a 92 on the Electronic aptitude area, which qualified me for the most technical Air Force career fields. I chose Cyber Transport Systems (3D1X2) because it offered both cutting-edge military experience and valuable civilian certifications. My high scores not only got me into this competitive field but also qualified me for the Advanced Cyber Education program at the Air Force Institute of Technology. The technical sections of the ASVAB directly determine which technological doors open for you in the Air Force, especially as cyber and space domains expand."

U.S. Marine Corps Requirements

ASVAB Score Basics

- **Minimum AFQT Score:** 32
- **Ideal Score Range:** 50-99
- **Program Waivers:** Limited score waivers available for high-demand MOS fields during recruitment surges

Key Career Paths and Line Score Requirements

Career Field	Required Line Score	Minimum Score	Popular MOS Examples
Infantry	General Technical (GT)	90+	0311 Rifleman, 0331 Machine Gunner
Artillery	General Technical (GT)	100+	0811 Field Artillery Cannoneer, 0844 Field Artillery Fire Control Man
Communications	Electronics (EL)	100+	0621 Field Radio Operator, 0627 Ground Mobile Forces Transmissions Operator
Intelligence	General Technical (GT)	110+	0231 Intelligence Specialist, 0241 Imagery Analysis Specialist
Aviation Mechanics	Mechanical Maintenance (MM)	105+	6113 Helicopter Mechanic, 6116 Tiltrotor Mechanic
Aviation Electronics	Electronics (EL)	115+	6323 Aircraft Avionics Technician, 6324 Aircraft Communications Systems Technician
Cyber Operations	General Technical (GT)	110+	0689 Cyber Security Technician, 0681 Information Security Technician
Logistics	Clerical (CL)	100+	0411 Maintenance Management Specialist, 0431 Logistics/Embarkation Specialist

Line Score Composition

- **General Technical (GT):** Word Knowledge + Paragraph Comprehension + Arithmetic Reasoning + Mathematics Knowledge
- **Electronics (EL):** General Science + Arithmetic Reasoning + Mathematics Knowledge + Electronics Information
- **Mechanical Maintenance (MM):** General Science + Auto & Shop + Mechanical Comprehension + Electronics Information
- **Clerical (CL):** Word Knowledge + Paragraph Comprehension + Mathematics Knowledge + Coding Speed

Career Advancement Pathways

The Marine Corps offers several advancement opportunities based on ASVAB performance:

1. **Marine Enlisted Commissioning Education Program (MECEP):** Competitive commissioning program for enlisted Marines with strong GT scores
2. **Naval Academy Preparatory School (NAPS):** Enlisted Marines with high GT scores can attend preparatory school for Naval Academy admission
3. **Specialized Training Programs:** Marines with high technical scores can qualify for joint-service advanced technical schools
4. **Foreign Language Programs:** High GT scores qualify Marines for the Defense Language Aptitude Battery (DLAB) and language training

Recent Changes in Score Requirements

The Marine Corps has adjusted several MOS requirements since 2022:

- **Cyber Operations:** GT score requirements increased from 105 to 110
- **Intelligence Fields:** Several intelligence MOS scores were increased due to technical complexity
- **Aviation Electronics:** EL score requirement increased from 110 to 115 for several specialties

Firsthand Account: Sergeant Olivia Washington, Intelligence Specialist

"My GT score of 121 opened up every MOS in the Marine Corps to me. I chose Intelligence (0231) because I wanted a role that balanced the Marine Corps' warrior ethos with technical expertise. The high entrance requirements for intelligence mean you work with extremely capable teammates. What surprised me was how my ASVAB scores continued to matter years after recruitment – they determined my eligibility for advanced intelligence courses, special duty assignments, and eventually, my acceptance to the MECEP program. My advice is to prepare extensively for the ASVAB, especially if you're interested in technical fields."

U.S. Coast Guard Requirements

ASVAB Score Basics

- **Minimum AFQT Score:** 40
- **Ideal Score Range:** 50-99
- **Competitive Programs:** Most technical ratings require ASVAB scores significantly above the minimum

Key Career Paths and Line Score Requirements

Career Field	Required Line Score	Minimum Score	Popular Rating Examples
Maritime Enforcement	VE+AR	105+	Maritime Enforcement Specialist (ME), Boatswain's Mate (BM)
Operations	VE+AR	110+	Operations Specialist (OS), Marine Science Technician (MST)
Engineering	AR+MK+EI	164+	Machinery Technician (MK), Damage Controlman (DC)
Electronics	AR+MK+EI	170+	Electronics Technician (ET), Information Systems Technician (IT)
Aviation	VE+AR+MK+AS	205+	Aviation Maintenance Technician (AMT), Aviation Survival Technician (AST)
Administrative	VE+AR	110+	Yeoman (YN), Storekeeper (SK)

Career Field	Required Line Score	Minimum Score	Popular Rating Examples
Intelligence	VE+AR	115+	Intelligence Specialist (IS)

Line Score Composition

- **VE (Verbal):** Word Knowledge + Paragraph Comprehension
- **AR:** Arithmetic Reasoning
- **MK:** Mathematics Knowledge
- **EI:** Electronics Information
- **AS:** Auto & Shop Information
- **MC:** Mechanical Comprehension

Career Advancement Pathways

The Coast Guard offers several advancement paths based on ASVAB performance:

1. **Officer Candidate School (OCS):** Enlisted members with strong ASVAB scores can apply for commission
2. **Advanced Education Programs:** High scorers qualify for college education programs while serving
3. **Rating Advancement:** Technical ratings with high entry standards offer accelerated advancement
4. **Direct Commission Programs:** Specialized fields offer direct commission opportunities for technical experts

Recent Changes in Score Requirements

Since 2023, the Coast Guard has adjusted several rating requirements:

- **Information Systems Technician (IT):** AR+MK+EI score requirement increased from 162 to 170
- **Intelligence Specialist (IS):** VE+AR requirement increased from 110 to 115
- **Aviation Survival Technician (AST):** Score requirements adjusted to reflect increased technical proficiency needs

Firsthand Account: Petty Officer Second Class Thomas Jenkins, Electronics Technician

"With an AR+MK+EI score of 178, I qualified for all the technical ratings in the Coast Guard. I chose Electronics Technician (ET) because it offered both operational variety and technical depth. The high score requirements ensure that everyone in the rating has strong technical aptitude, which creates a collaborative and innovative work environment. My high scores also fast-tracked my eligibility for advanced C4IT (Command, Control, Communications, Computers,

and Information Technology) schools. For anyone considering Coast Guard technical fields, I'd recommend focusing on the mathematics and electronics sections of the ASVAB."

U.S. Space Force Requirements

ASVAB Score Basics

- **Minimum AFQT Score:** 35
- **Ideal Score Range:** 70-99
- **Competitive Entry:** As the newest and smallest branch, Space Force maintains highly selective score requirements

Key Career Paths and Line Score Requirements

Career Field	Required Aptitude Area	Minimum Score	Popular AFSC Examples
Space Operations	General (G)	70+	1C6X1 Space Systems Operations, 1C6X2 Space Warfighter
Cyber Operations	Electronic (E)	85+	3D0X2 Cyber Systems Operations, 3D1X1 Client Systems
Intelligence	General (G)	72+	1N0X1 Intelligence Analyst, 1N1X1 Geospatial Intelligence
Communications	Electronic (E)	70+	3D1X2 Cyber Transport Systems, 3D0X3 Cyber Surety
Engineering	Electronic (E)	80+	3E5X1 Engineering, 2M0X2 Missile Maintenance
Acquisitions	General (G)	70+	6C0X1 Contracting, 2G0X1 Logistics Plans

Aptitude Area Composition

- **Mechanical (M):** Mathematical Knowledge + Mechanical Comprehension + Electronics Information
- **Administrative (A):** Numerical Operations + Coding Speed + Verbal Expression
- **General (G):** Verbal Expression + Mathematics Knowledge
- **Electronic (E):** General Science + Mathematics Knowledge + Electronics Information

Career Advancement Pathways

The Space Force offers several advancement opportunities based on ASVAB performance:

1. **Specialized Technical Training:** Advanced space and cyber training for high scorers
2. **Accelerated Commissioning Programs:** Enlisted to officer pathways for members with strong academic potential

3. **Advanced Academic Degrees:** Sponsorship for relevant graduate degrees in technical fields
4. **Joint-Domain Operations:** Opportunities to work across cyber, space, and intelligence domains

Recent Changes in Score Requirements

As a new branch established in 2019, the Space Force continues to refine its requirements:

- **Space Systems Operations:** General aptitude minimum increased from 66 to 70
- **Cyber Operations:** Electronic aptitude minimum increased from 80 to 85
- **All Career Fields:** Overall standards remain higher than most other branches due to the technical nature of the mission

Firsthand Account: Specialist 4 Aisha Johnson, Space Systems Operations

"The Space Force has the most technically demanding entrance requirements of any branch. My General score of 86 and Electronic score of 91 qualified me for Space Systems Operations (1C6X1). What's unique about Space Force is that almost every career field requires strong technical aptitude, regardless of the specific role. Even after basic training and technical school, the learning curve remains steep due to the cutting-edge technologies we work with. My advice: If you're interested in Space Force, aim for ASVAB scores well above the minimums, particularly in the mathematics, science, and electronics sections."

Strategic Score Optimization

Maximizing Your Opportunities

1. **Target scores in 70-99 percentile range**

   Aiming high on the ASVAB opens doors to the most competitive and rewarding military career fields. Even if you're initially interested in a career with lower requirements, higher scores provide future flexibility as your interests evolve.

2. **Focus on branch-specific line scores**

   Each military branch calculates line scores differently. Research which line scores are most important for your target branch and career field, then concentrate your study efforts accordingly.

3. **Develop strong technical and mathematical skills**

   Technical and mathematical subtests carry significant weight across all branches, particularly for high-demand fields like cyber, intelligence, nuclear, and aviation specialties.

4. **Prepare comprehensively across all subtests**

While focusing on branch-specific priorities, maintain balanced preparation. Even subtests that seem less relevant to your target career can contribute to qualifying scores in unexpected ways.

5. **Strategic career planning**

Research how ASVAB scores impact not just initial job qualification, but long-term career advancement opportunities. Some career fields offer faster promotion rates, special duty assignments, and commissioning opportunities for high scorers.

ASVAB Score and Military Career Correlation

AFQT Score Range	Career Opportunity Level	Long-term Advancement Potential
93-99	Highest-tier technical and leadership paths	Maximum advancement options including special programs
72-92	Competitive technical specialties	Strong advancement potential with demonstrated performance
50-71	Solid career options across most fields	Good advancement with additional education
36-49	Basic qualification for many non-technical roles	Advancement requires exceptional performance
31-35	Limited options, primarily support roles	Advancement may require score improvement

Remember that while ASVAB scores open initial doors, your performance, dedication, and continued educational development ultimately determine your military career success.

Chapter 3: Military Branch-Specific Requirements

Overview

Each military branch has unique ASVAB score requirements and career opportunities. Understanding these specifics is crucial for aligning your skills with the most suitable military path.

U.S. Army Requirements

ASVAB Score Basics

- **Minimum AFQT Score:** 31
- **Ideal Score Range:** 50-99

Key Career Paths

- Infantry
- Military Intelligence
- Engineering
- Medical Services
- Logistics
- Cyber Operations

Line Score Highlights

- General Technical (GT) Score
- Skilled Technical (ST) Score
- Combat Arms (CA) Score

U.S. Navy Requirements

ASVAB Score Basics

- **Minimum AFQT Score:** 35
- **Ideal Score Range:** 50-99

Specialized Career Fields

- Nuclear Propulsion
- Naval Aviation

- Cryptology
- Maritime Engineering
- Special Operations

Critical Score Categories

- Nuclear Field Score
- Electronics Technician Score
- Advanced Technical Scores

U.S. Air Force Requirements

ASVAB Score Basics

- **Minimum AFQT Score:** 36
- **Ideal Score Range:** 50-99

Career Opportunities

- Pilot Training
- Aerospace Engineering
- Cyber Operations
- Space Systems
- Intelligence
- Technical Maintenance

Specialized Scoring

- Technical Operations Score
- Aviation-Specific Scores
- Cyber Operations Assessment

U.S. Marine Corps Requirements

ASVAB Score Basics

- **Minimum AFQT Score:** 32
- **Ideal Score Range:** 50-99

Career Tracks

- Infantry
- Force Reconnaissance
- Marine Corps Aviation
- Logistics

- Combat Engineering
- Security Forces

Key Score Assessments

- Combat Arms Score
- Technical Support Scores
- Expeditionary Warfare Evaluation

U.S. Coast Guard Requirements

ASVAB Score Basics

- **Minimum AFQT Score:** 40
- **Ideal Score Range:** 50-99

Unique Career Paths

- Maritime Law Enforcement
- Search and Rescue
- Port Security
- Marine Environmental Protection
- Technical Maintenance

Specialized Scoring

- Maritime Operations Score
- Law Enforcement Assessment
- Technical Maintenance Evaluation

U.S. Space Force Requirements

ASVAB Score Basics

- **Minimum AFQT Score:** 35
- **Ideal Score Range:** 50-99

Cutting-Edge Career Fields

- Satellite Operations
- Space Systems Engineering
- Cyber Operations
- Strategic Planning
- Technical Support

Critical Score Categories

- Space Operations Score
- Satellite Systems Assessment
- Technological Reasoning Evaluation

Strategic Score Optimization

Maximizing Your Opportunities

1. Target scores in 50-99 percentile range
2. Focus on branch-specific line scores
3. Develop strong technical and mathematical skills
4. Prepare comprehensively across all subtests

Chapter 4: Comprehensive Study Strategies

Effective Preparation Framework

Study Plan Essentials

1. **Strategic Assessment** - Begin with a thorough evaluation of your current knowledge and skills across all ASVAB subject areas
2. **Goal-Driven Approach** - Set specific, measurable, achievable, relevant, and time-bound (SMART) objectives
3. **Consistent Practice** - Establish regular study habits and routines
4. **Adaptive Learning** - Modify your approach based on progress and assessment results

Creating a Study Plan

Self-Assessment Techniques

- **Diagnostic Testing** - Take full-length practice tests to identify baseline performance
- **Identifying Strengths and Weaknesses** - Analyze results to determine high and low-scoring areas
- **Personalized Focus Areas** - Create targeted study approaches for improvement areas

Goal Setting

- **Specific Score Targets** - Determine minimum required scores for your desired branch
- **Branch-Specific Requirements** - Research line scores needed for preferred military occupational specialties

- **Career Aspiration Alignment** - Connect study goals to long-term military career objectives

Time Management

- **Daily Study Commitment**: 1-2 hours
- **Weekly Study Intensity**: 10-15 hours
- **Preparation Duration**: 3-6 months

Detailed Study Schedules

1-Month Intensive Preparation Plan

This accelerated schedule is designed for those with limited time or who need to take the ASVAB quickly.

Week 1: Assessment and Core Academic Focus

- **Monday**: Take full diagnostic test; analyze results
- **Tuesday**: Mathematics Knowledge (2 hours)
- **Wednesday**: Arithmetic Reasoning (2 hours)
- **Thursday**: Word Knowledge (2 hours)
- **Friday**: Paragraph Comprehension (2 hours)
- **Saturday**: General Science (2 hours)
- **Sunday**: Review weak areas identified during the week (2 hours)

Week 2: Technical and Specialized Sections

- **Monday**: Electronics Information (2 hours)
- **Tuesday**: Auto & Shop Information (2 hours)
- **Wednesday**: Mechanical Comprehension (2 hours)
- **Thursday**: Assembling Objects (2 hours)
- **Friday**: Mathematics and Arithmetic review (2 hours)
- **Saturday**: Verbal skills review (Word Knowledge/Paragraph Comprehension) (2 hours)
- **Sunday**: Mid-point practice test; analyze results (3 hours)

Week 3: Targeted Improvement

- **Monday-Sunday**: Focus 70% of daily study time on 2-3 weakest subjects
- **Daily**: Dedicate 30% of study time to maintaining strong areas
- **Wednesday**: Half-length practice test focused on weak areas (1 hour)
- **Sunday**: Full practice test (3 hours)

Week 4: Final Review and Test Preparation

- **Monday-Thursday**: Intensive review of remaining weak areas (2 hours daily)

- **Friday**: Full practice test under test-like conditions (3 hours)
- **Saturday**: Review test results and final focused study (2 hours)
- **Sunday**: Rest day - mental preparation, light review of key formulas and concepts

3-Month Balanced Preparation Plan

This schedule provides a more measured approach with deeper learning and skill development.

Month 1: Foundation Building

- **Week 1**: Diagnostic testing and subject area introduction
  - Take full-length test on weekend
  - Spend weekdays exploring each subject area (1 hour per subject)
- **Weeks 2-4**: Systematic content coverage
  - Monday: Mathematics Knowledge
  - Tuesday: Arithmetic Reasoning
  - Wednesday: Word Knowledge
  - Thursday: Paragraph Comprehension
  - Friday: General Science
  - Saturday: Technical subjects rotation
  - Sunday: Weekly review and practice questions

Month 2: Skill Development

- **Weeks 1-2**: Continued content mastery with increased practice
  - Same daily subject focus as Month 1
  - Increase practice problem complexity
  - Introduce timed practice sessions
- **Weeks 3-4**: Targeted improvement
  - Focus 60% of study time on weak areas
  - 40% on maintaining strong areas
  - Weekly practice tests with detailed analysis

Month 3: Test Simulation and Refinement

- **Weeks 1-2**: Full-length practice tests and targeted review
  - Take practice test every 4-5 days
  - Focus remaining study time on areas of difficulty
- **Weeks 3-4**: Final preparation
  - Complete 2-3 full practice tests under test-like conditions
  - Review challenging concepts
  - Practice test-taking strategies and time management
  - Create summary sheets of key formulas and concepts

6-Month Comprehensive Preparation Plan

This extensive schedule is ideal for those with significant time before testing or who need substantial improvement.

Months 1-2: Foundation Building and Content Mastery

- **Weeks 1-2**: Diagnostic testing and study planning
  - Complete diagnostic assessment
  - Research branch-specific requirements
  - Develop detailed personalized study calendar
- **Weeks 3-8**: Systematic knowledge building
  - Dedicate 1 week to each major subject area
  - Start with core AFQT subjects
  - Progress to technical subjects
  - Weekly practice with relevant questions

Months 3-4: Skill Development and Practice Integration

- **Weeks 1-4**: Intermediate practice and review
  - Regular mini-tests for each subject
  - Begin connecting concepts across subject areas
  - Develop enhanced problem-solving strategies
- **Weeks 5-8**: Targeted improvement
  - Focus on areas of weakness
  - Increase practice test frequency
  - Begin timed section practice

Months 5-6: Mastery and Test Preparation

- **Weeks 1-4**: Advanced practice and integration
  - Regular full-length practice tests
  - Specialized study for branch-specific line scores
  - Complex problem analysis and solution
- **Weeks 5-8**: Final preparation
  - Weekly full-length practice tests
  - Focused review of persistent weak areas
  - Test-taking strategy refinement
  - Mental and physical preparation

Study Optimization Strategies

Pomodoro Technique

- **25-minute focused study blocks**
- **5-minute breaks**
- **Prevents mental fatigue**
- **Maintains high concentration**

Enhanced Implementation:

1. Use a timer app specifically designed for Pomodoro cycles
2. During the 5-minute breaks, perform physical movement to improve blood flow
3. After completing 4 cycles, take a longer 15-30 minute break
4. Track productivity during different times of day to identify your optimal study periods

Subject Rotation Method

- **Alternate between ASVAB sections**
- **Prevent boredom**
- **Improve overall retention**
- **Maintain mental engagement**

Strategic Rotation Patterns:

1. **Complementary Pairing**: Alternate between subjects that use different mental faculties (e.g., Math Knowledge followed by Word Knowledge)
2. **Progressive Difficulty**: Begin with easier subjects and gradually move to more challenging ones
3. **Spaced Repetition**: Return to previously studied material at strategic intervals
4. **Connection Building**: Study related subjects sequentially to build cognitive links

Test-Taking Strategies

Mental Preparation

- **Stress management techniques**
- **Visualization exercises**
- **Positive self-talk**
- **Confidence building**

Test Day Approach

- **Careful question reading**
- **Time management**
- **Educated guessing**
- **Answer review**

Cognitive Enhancement

Brain Training

- **Puzzle solving**
- **Memory exercises**

- **Logical reasoning games**
- **Cognitive flexibility activities**

Advanced Cognitive Enhancement Techniques

Working Memory Improvement

1. **Dual N-Back Training**
   - Progressive memory challenge where you track both visual and auditory stimuli
   - Start with 1-back and progress to higher levels
   - Practice 15-20 minutes daily for optimal results
2. **Memory Palace Technique**
   - Create mental spatial environments to store information
   - Particularly effective for sequence-based information
   - Implementation steps:
     - Choose a familiar location (your home, a familiar route)
     - Define specific locations within that space
     - Place memorable images of information at each location
     - Practice mentally walking through the space to retrieve information
3. **Chunking Practice**
   - Group information into meaningful units
   - Example exercise: Practice memorizing strings of numbers by grouping them
   - Start with 7-digit strings and progress to longer sequences

Problem-Solving Enhancement

1. **Constraint Shifting Exercises**
   - Practice solving problems with changing rules
   - Example: Solve math problems using different operation sequences
2. **Metacognitive Reflection**
   - After solving practice problems, analyze your thought process
   - Document solution approaches that worked and didn't work
   - Identify pattern recognition opportunities
3. **Cross-Contextual Learning**
   - Apply ASVAB concepts to real-world scenarios
   - Create practical applications for abstract principles
   - Connect military-related scenarios to test content

Learning Techniques

- **Active recall**
- **Spaced repetition**
- **Comprehensive note-taking**
- **Mind mapping**

Test Anxiety Management

Understanding Test Anxiety

Test anxiety is more than just nervousness—it's a condition that can significantly impact performance. Recognizing its physical, emotional, and cognitive symptoms is the first step toward management.

Physical Symptoms Management

1. **Progressive Muscle Relaxation**
   - Tense and then release each muscle group systematically
   - Practice for 10 minutes daily and before study sessions
   - Use abbreviated version (5-minute) on test day
2. **Controlled Breathing Techniques**
   - 4-7-8 Method: Inhale for 4 counts, hold for 7, exhale for 8
   - Box Breathing: Equal counts for inhale, hold, exhale, and hold
   - Practice 5 minutes daily and when feeling anxious
3. **Physical Preparation Routine**
   - Maintain regular sleep schedule (7-8 hours) week before test
   - Avoid caffeine and sugar 4-6 hours before testing
   - Light exercise morning of test to reduce physical tension

Cognitive Approaches

1. **Thought Restructuring**
   - Identify negative thought patterns ("I always fail tests")
   - Challenge catastrophic thinking with evidence
   - Replace with realistic, positive statements
2. **Worst-Case Scenario Planning**
   - Acknowledge what would actually happen if you don't perform well
   - Develop specific contingency plans
   - Recognize opportunities for retesting or alternative paths
3. **Focus Training**
   - Mindfulness meditation (5-10 minutes daily)
   - Grounding techniques (5-4-3-2-1 sensory awareness)
   - Attention refocusing exercises during study and testing

During-Test Strategies

1. **Immediate Anxiety Response Plan**
   - Recognize anxiety symptoms early
   - Pause and take 3 deep breaths
   - Positive self-talk with prepared statements
   - Quick progressive relaxation (30 seconds)
2. **Strategic Test Approach**
   - Answer easy questions first to build confidence
   - Skip difficult questions temporarily

- o Use time tracking to prevent spiraling on single questions
- o Take micro-breaks (30 seconds) between test sections
3. **Recovery Methods**
   - o Technique for when you "blank out"
   - o Memory triggering methods
   - o Refocusing after distractions

Physical and Mental Wellness

Holistic Preparation

- **Balanced nutrition**
- **Adequate sleep**
- **Regular exercise**
- **Stress reduction**

Pre-Test Routine

- **Consistent sleep schedule**
- **Healthy breakfast**
- **Light physical warm-up**
- **Mental relaxation techniques**

Learning Style Assessment and Customized Study Approaches

Identifying Your Learning Style

Visual Learners

Primary Traits:

- Learn best through seeing information
- Remember visual details
- Prefer diagrams, charts, and written instructions
- May struggle with verbal-only instruction

Assessment Indicators:

- Do you remember faces better than names?
- Do you prefer written directions over verbal ones?
- Do you take detailed notes during lectures or presentations?
- Do you visualize information to remember it?

Customized Study Approaches:

1. **Color-Coding System**
   o Assign specific colors to different ASVAB subject areas
   o Use highlighting strategically to emphasize key concepts
   o Create color-coded mind maps for complex topics
2. **Visual Organization Techniques**
   o Flow charts for processes and sequences
   o Concept maps for interconnected ideas
   o Timelines for historical or sequential information
   o Diagrams for technical concepts (especially for Mechanical Comprehension)
3. **Visual Memory Aids**
   o Flash cards with images and minimal text
   o Symbolic representation of abstract concepts
   o Visual mnemonic devices (associate concepts with vivid mental images)
4. **Study Environment Optimization**
   o Minimize visual distractions
   o Use visual organization tools (whiteboards, bulletin boards)
   o Implement "visual anchoring" for different subject areas

Auditory Learners

Primary Traits:

- Learn best through hearing information
- Process verbal instructions effectively
- May talk through problems aloud
- Often enjoy group discussions

Assessment Indicators:

- Do you remember what people say better than what you read?
- Do you prefer verbal instructions?
- Do you read aloud to yourself when studying?
- Do you find background music helpful when studying?

Customized Study Approaches:

1. **Verbal Processing Techniques**
   o Record yourself reading key concepts and play back
   o Explain complex ideas aloud as if teaching someone
   o Use verbal repetition for formulas and definitions
   o Participate in study groups with discussion-based learning
2. **Auditory Memory Systems**
   o Create rhythmic patterns for formulas and sequences
   o Develop verbal mnemonics and memory phrases

- o Use rhymes for difficult-to-remember information
- o Connect information to familiar songs or melodies

3. **Audio-Enhanced Study Sessions**
    - o Listen to educational podcasts on relevant subjects
    - o Use text-to-speech software for reading materials
    - o Create audio flashcards
    - o Record lecture notes and listen during review

4. **Environment Customization**
    - o Study in quiet spaces with minimal auditory distractions
    - o Use white noise if complete silence is uncomfortable
    - o Schedule regular verbal review sessions

Kinesthetic Learners

Primary Traits:

- Learn by doing and physical interaction
- May struggle sitting still for long periods
- Remember what they do rather than what they see or hear
- Benefit from hands-on experiences

Assessment Indicators:

- Do you prefer to learn by trying things out yourself?
- Do you use gesture when explaining concepts?
- Do you find it difficult to sit still for long periods?
- Do you remember activities better than lectures?

Customized Study Approaches:

1. **Active Learning Techniques**
    - o Build physical models for mechanical concepts
    - o Use manipulatives for mathematical problems
    - o Create physical flashcards you can handle and sort
    - o Incorporate movement into study sessions

2. **Movement-Enhanced Memory**
    - o Walk while reviewing key concepts
    - o Associate specific information with physical locations (walk around a room, assigning different concepts to different areas)
    - o Use hand gestures to reinforce learning
    - o Implement "body mapping" for sequences and processes

3. **Interactive Study Materials**
    - o Use interactive digital resources with touchscreen engagement
    - o Create physical timelines or concept maps you can rearrange
    - o Practice with physical tools for Shop and Auto Information
    - o Build circuit models for Electronics Information

4. **Environment and Schedule Adaptation**
   - Set up standing desk options
   - Schedule movement breaks every 25-30 minutes
   - Alternate between sitting and standing
   - Incorporate stress balls or fidget tools for focus

Reading/Writing Learners

Primary Traits:

- Learn best through reading and writing information
- Strong note-taking beneficiaries
- Process information effectively through written format
- Often prefer traditional textbook learning

Assessment Indicators:

- Do you enjoy making lists and taking notes?
- Do you remember information better after writing it down?
- Do you prefer written instructions and textbooks?
- Do you find rewriting notes helpful for retention?

Customized Study Approaches:

1. **Comprehensive Note-Taking Systems**
   - Cornell Method (questions, notes, summary)
   - Outline Method for hierarchical information
   - Charting Method for comparative data
   - Sentence Method for sequential information
2. **Writing-Enhanced Retention**
   - Summarize key concepts in your own words
   - Create question-and-answer pairs
   - Develop written "teaching materials" for concepts
   - Maintain a study journal documenting learning progress
3. **Reading Optimization**
   - SQ3R Method (Survey, Question, Read, Recite, Review)
   - Progressive reading (preview, detailed reading, review)
   - Annotation systems (symbols, marginalia, highlighting)
   - Comparative reading of multiple sources on same topic
4. **Writing-Based Practice**
   - Create written practice questions
   - Write explanations for complex concepts
   - Develop written summaries of technical processes
   - Convert diagrams and charts into written descriptions

Multimodal Approaches for Comprehensive Learning

Most learners benefit from mixed approaches. Create integrated study plans that incorporate elements from different learning styles:

1. **Integrated Study Sessions**
   - Begin with reading (10 minutes)
   - Create visual summary (5 minutes)
   - Verbally explain concept (5 minutes)
   - Apply knowledge through practice problems (15 minutes)
2. **Cross-Modal Reinforcement**
   - Convert information between formats (text to diagram, diagram to verbal explanation)
   - Create multi-sensory memory aids
   - Develop study materials that engage multiple learning channels
   - Vary study approaches for different subjects based on content type

Study Resource Recommendations

Online Resources

- **Official ASVAB practice tests**
- **Military recruitment websites**
- **Educational platforms**
- **Specialized preparation sites**

Physical Resources

- **Comprehensive study guides**
- **Practice test books**
- **Flashcard sets**
- **Subject-specific review materials**

Common Study Pitfalls to Avoid

1. **Last-minute cramming**
2. **Neglecting weak areas**
3. **Inconsistent study schedule**
4. **Overlooking mental preparation**
5. **Lack of practice test analysis**
6. **Passive studying without active engagement**
7. **Failure to apply test-taking strategies during practice**
8. **Studying without clear goals or direction**
9. **Overlooking branch-specific requirements**
10. **Ignoring physical and mental wellness components**

Personal Study Adaptation

Continuous Improvement

- **Regular self-assessment**
- **Flexible learning approach**
- **Progress tracking**
- **Willingness to adjust strategies**

Measuring Effective Study

Implement a personal metrics system to evaluate your study efficiency:

1. Track practice test scores over time
2. Monitor time spent on different subjects
3. Assess comprehension through self-testing
4. Document specific improvement areas
5. Regularly review and adjust your approach based on performance data

Final Preparation Checklist

Two weeks before your test:

- Complete final diagnostic assessment
- Focus exclusively on remaining weak areas
- Review test-taking strategies
- Practice with full-length tests
- Finalize test-day logistics (location, transportation, required items)
- Establish consistent sleep schedule
- Prepare mental management plan for test day

Day before test:

- Light review of key concepts
- Prepare all required documents and materials
- Avoid intensive studying
- Engage in relaxing activities
- Ensure proper nutrition and hydration
- Get adequate sleep (7-8 hours)
- Visualize successful test performance

Test day:

- Arrive early
- Use relaxation techniques as needed
- Implement strategic test-taking approach
- Maintain confidence through positive self-talk
- Apply time management strategies

- Use breaks effectively to reset mental focus

Test Day Preparation

Proper preparation for the actual test day can significantly impact your ASVAB performance. Even with excellent knowledge and skills, test anxiety or logistical issues can undermine your score. This section provides a comprehensive framework for optimizing your test day experience.

The Week Before the Test

1. **Finalize Your Study Plan**
   - Focus on reviewing key concepts rather than learning new material
   - Take one final full-length practice test under timed conditions
   - Identify any remaining weak areas for light review
   - Avoid cramming or marathon study sessions that can lead to burnout
2. **Logistics Planning**
   - Confirm your test date, time, and location
   - Plan your transportation route and allow extra time for unexpected delays
   - If testing at a MEPS (Military Entrance Processing Station), review any additional requirements
   - Prepare necessary identification documents (government-issued ID, Social Security card)
3. **Mental and Physical Preparation**
   - Maintain a consistent sleep schedule (7-8 hours nightly)
   - Gradually adjust your sleep cycle if your test is scheduled for early morning
   - Continue regular physical activity to reduce stress and improve mental clarity
   - Begin reducing caffeine and sugar intake to stabilize energy levels

The Day Before the Test

1. **Light Review Only**
   - Limit studying to brief review of key formulas or concepts
   - Focus on areas of confidence to build a positive mindset
   - Avoid deep study of challenging material that might create anxiety
   - Put study materials away at least 3 hours before bedtime
2. **Physical Preparation**
   - Eat balanced, nutritious meals
   - Avoid excessive caffeine, sugar, or heavy foods
   - Stay well-hydrated throughout the day
   - Avoid introducing new or unusual foods that might cause discomfort
3. **Mental Preparation**
   - Engage in relaxing activities (light reading, walking, gentle stretching)
   - Practice visualization techniques, imagining yourself performing confidently
   - Arrange your test outfit and materials (ID, transportation, etc.)
   - Set multiple alarms to ensure you wake on time

4. **Evening Routine**
   - o Follow a calming bedtime routine
   - o Avoid screens (phones, computers, TV) for at least an hour before sleeping
   - o Use relaxation techniques if you feel anxious (deep breathing, meditation)
   - o Go to bed early enough to ensure a full night's sleep (7-9 hours)

Test Day Morning

1. **Wake-Up Routine**
   - o Wake up with sufficient time to avoid rushing
   - o Eat a balanced breakfast with complex carbohydrates and protein
   - o Avoid excessive caffeine that might increase anxiety
   - o Review your transportation plan and leave early
2. **Mental Focus**
   - o Practice confidence-building self-talk
   - o Use deep breathing or brief meditation to center yourself
   - o Focus on your preparation and readiness, not on potential outcomes
   - o Limit conversations about the test with others, which can increase anxiety
3. **Final Preparations**
   - o Double-check required identification and documents
   - o Wear comfortable, layered clothing (testing rooms may be warm or cool)
   - o Bring a light snack and water if permitted
   - o Use the restroom before the test begins

During the Test

1. **Strategic Approach**
   - o Listen carefully to all instructions from test administrators
   - o Read all directions thoroughly before beginning each section
   - o Budget your time wisely, using the strategies practiced during preparation
   - o Work through questions systematically, marking difficult ones to revisit if time permits
2. **Anxiety Management**
   - o Use deep breathing techniques if you feel anxiety rising
   - o Maintain good posture to optimize oxygen flow and reduce physical tension
   - o Focus on one question at a time rather than worrying about overall performance
   - o Use positive self-talk to maintain confidence
3. **Optimization Techniques**
   - o Stay aware of the time remaining in each section
   - o Don't spend too long on any single question
   - o Make strategic guesses on questions you're unsure about rather than leaving them blank
   - o Review your answers if time permits, but trust your initial responses unless you're certain they're incorrect

After the Test

1. **Immediate Next Steps**
   - Avoid excessive analysis or discussion of specific questions
   - Allow yourself to decompress through a relaxing activity
   - Understand that the scoring process may take time
   - Connect with your recruiter about next steps in the military application process
2. **Results Analysis**
   - When you receive your scores, review them objectively
   - Identify which military careers your scores qualify you for
   - Discuss retesting options with your recruiter if scores were lower than expected
   - Begin researching specific MOS/rating/AFSC options based on your results

Special Considerations

1. **Computer Adaptive Testing (CAT)**
   - Most ASVAB tests are now computer-adaptive, adjusting difficulty based on your performance
   - Questions cannot be skipped or returned to later
   - Each answer affects subsequent question difficulty
   - Practice with computer-based tests if possible
2. **Paper-and-Pencil Testing**
   - Traditional format still used in some locations
   - Allows you to skip questions and return to them later
   - Requires careful time management and answer sheet accuracy
   - Bring several sharpened No. 2 pencils
3. **Testing Accommodations**
   - If you have documented learning disabilities or other conditions that affect testing
   - Request accommodations well in advance through your recruiter
   - Provide required documentation from educational or medical professionals
   - Understand available accommodations (extended time, screen readers, etc.)

By following this comprehensive test day preparation framework, you'll minimize test-related stress and maximize your ability to demonstrate your true capabilities on the ASVAB. Remember that proper preparation extends beyond knowledge acquisition to include physical, mental, and logistical readiness.

Chapter 5: Subject-Specific Study Guides

Mathematics and Arithmetic Review

Core Mathematical Skills

- **Basic Arithmetic Operations**
    - Addition, subtraction, multiplication, and division form the foundation of all mathematical problem-solving
    - Master mental math shortcuts for quick calculations during timed sections
    - Understand order of operations (PEMDAS: Parentheses, Exponents, Multiplication/Division, Addition/Subtraction)
- **Fractions, Decimals, and Percentages**
    - Convert between fractions, decimals, and percentages fluently
    - Understand proper fractions, improper fractions, and mixed numbers
    - Apply percentage calculations to real-world scenarios (discounts, interest, etc.)
- **Algebraic Reasoning**
    - Solve for variables in linear equations
    - Manipulate equations by isolating variables
    - Understand function relationships and graphs
    - Apply algebraic principles to word problems
- **Geometry Fundamentals**
    - Calculate area, perimeter, and volume of common shapes
    - Understand properties of triangles, quadrilaterals, and circles
    - Apply the Pythagorean theorem effectively
    - Convert between different units of measurement

Step-by-Step Problem-Solving Framework

1. **Read and Analyze the Problem**
    - Identify what the problem is asking for
    - List all given information
    - Determine which mathematical concepts apply
2. **Translate to Mathematical Language**
    - Convert word problems into equations or expressions
    - Define variables clearly
    - Draw diagrams for geometric problems
    - Organize data for systematic solving
3. **Select the Appropriate Solution Method**
    - Decide which mathematical approach is most efficient
    - Review similar problems you've solved previously
    - Consider alternative approaches if stuck
4. **Execute the Solution**
    - Follow mathematical rules precisely
    - Show organized work to avoid calculation errors

o Check intermediate steps for accuracy
5. **Verify Your Answer**
    o Ask: "Does this answer make sense in the context of the problem?"
    o Substitute your answer back into the original problem
    o Estimate to confirm reasonableness

Common Mathematical Misconceptions

- **Misconception**: All word problems require complex equations.
    o **Reality**: Many ASVAB word problems can be solved with basic arithmetic and logical reasoning.
    o **Strategy**: Start with the simplest approach before complicating your solution.
- **Misconception**: Memorizing formulas is enough for success.
    o **Reality**: Understanding when and how to apply formulas is more important than mere memorization.
    o **Strategy**: Practice applying formulas in various contexts to develop deeper understanding.
- **Misconception**: There's only one correct way to solve each problem.
    o **Reality**: Many mathematical problems can be solved using multiple valid approaches.
    o **Strategy**: Develop flexibility in your problem-solving toolkit.

Practice Examples with Solutions

Example 1: Arithmetic Word Problem

A military logistics team needs to distribute 342 supply kits equally among 18 units. How many kits will each unit receive?

Solution:

1. Identify what we need to find: the number of kits per unit
2. Set up the division equation: $342 \div 18 = ?$
3. Calculate: $342 \div 18 = 19$
4. Answer: Each unit will receive 19 kits.

Example 2: Percentage Problem

If a military vehicle's fuel efficiency decreases by 15% when traveling off-road, and it normally gets 20 miles per gallon on paved roads, what is its fuel efficiency when off-road?

Solution:

1. Identify the given information:
    o Normal efficiency: 20 mpg
    o Decrease: 15%

2. Calculate the decrease: $20 \times 0.15 = 3$ mpg
3. Subtract to find new efficiency: $20 - 3 = 17$ mpg
4. Answer: The off-road fuel efficiency is 17 miles per gallon.

Example 3: Algebraic Reasoning

A supply officer ordered x electronic components and y mechanical parts. Each electronic component costs $45, and each mechanical part costs $28. If the total order was $2,490, write an equation representing this situation.

Solution:

1. Identify the costs:
   o Electronic components: $45 each
   o Mechanical parts: $28 each
2. Total cost: $2,490
3. Write the equation: $45x + 28y = 2,490$
4. Answer: The equation is $45x + 28y = 2,490$

Example 4: Geometry Application

A rectangular military training field is 120 meters long and 85 meters wide. A trainer needs to walk the perimeter exactly twice. How far will the trainer walk?

Solution:

1. Calculate the perimeter: 2(length + width)
2. Perimeter = $2(120 + 85) = 2(205) = 410$ meters
3. Walk the perimeter twice: $410 \times 2 = 820$ meters
4. Answer: The trainer will walk 820 meters.

Science Fundamentals

Comprehensive Scientific Knowledge

Biology Essentials

- **Cell Structure and Function**
  o Understand the cell as the basic unit of life
  o Differentiate between prokaryotic and eukaryotic cells
  o Know major organelles and their functions (nucleus, mitochondria, ribosomes, etc.)
  o Understand cellular processes (respiration, protein synthesis, cell division)
- **Human Anatomy and Physiology**
  o Major organ systems and their functions
  o Homeostasis and feedback mechanisms

- o Basics of nutrition and metabolism
- o Immune system function and disease defense
- **Genetics and Heredity**
  - o DNA structure and function
  - o Mendelian inheritance principles
  - o Genetic disorders and inheritance patterns
  - o Basics of genetic engineering and applications
- **Ecology and Ecosystems**
  - o Energy flow through ecosystems
  - o Food chains and food webs
  - o Population dynamics
  - o Human impact on ecosystems

Chemistry Foundations

- **Atomic Structure**
  - o Atomic models and subatomic particles
  - o Electron configuration
  - o Isotopes and atomic mass
- **Periodic Table Organization**
  - o Element classification (metals, nonmetals, metalloids)
  - o Periodic trends (atomic radius, electronegativity, ionization energy)
  - o Electron valence and chemical bonding
- **Chemical Reactions**
  - o Balancing chemical equations
  - o Types of reactions (synthesis, decomposition, combustion, etc.)
  - o Factors affecting reaction rates
  - o Acids, bases, and pH scale
- **States of Matter and Phase Changes**
  - o Properties of solids, liquids, and gases
  - o Phase transitions and energy changes
  - o Gas laws (Boyle's, Charles', Combined Gas Law)

Physics Principles

- **Motion and Forces**
  - o Newton's laws of motion
  - o Velocity, acceleration, and momentum
  - o Work, energy, and power
  - o Simple machines and mechanical advantage
- **Electricity and Magnetism**
  - o Electric charges and fields
  - o Current, voltage, and resistance (Ohm's Law)
  - o Series and parallel circuits
  - o Electromagnetic induction
- **Waves and Optics**

- o Wave properties (frequency, wavelength, amplitude)
- o Types of waves (mechanical, electromagnetic)
- o Light behavior (reflection, refraction, diffraction)
- o Simple optical systems
- **Modern Physics Concepts**
  - o Basic atomic and nuclear physics
  - o Radiation types and effects
  - o Elementary particles
  - o Fundamental forces of nature

Earth and Space Sciences

- **Earth's Structure and Systems**
  - o Geosphere, hydrosphere, atmosphere, biosphere
  - o Plate tectonics and geological processes
  - o Weather and climate
  - o Natural resources and environmental concerns
- **Astronomy Basics**
  - o Solar system structure
  - o Stars and their life cycles
  - o Galaxies and the universe
  - o Space exploration technology

Study Strategies for Science

- **Concept Mapping**
  - o Create visual representations connecting related scientific concepts
  - o Use branching diagrams to show relationships between topics
  - o Color-code different scientific domains
  - o Update maps regularly as you learn new information
- **Scientific Terminology Mastery**
  - o Create flashcards for key scientific terms
  - o Break down complex terms using root words
  - o Practice using scientific vocabulary in context
  - o Group related terms to strengthen understanding
- **Applied Learning**
  - o Connect scientific principles to real-world applications
  - o Study how the military uses scientific concepts
  - o Think about how science applies to daily life
  - o Consider practical examples when learning abstract concepts
- **Visual Learning Tools**
  - o Use diagrams, charts, and illustrations to understand processes
  - o Watch educational videos for complex topics
  - o Create your own drawings to reinforce understanding
  - o Use interactive simulations when available

Common Science Misconceptions

- **Misconception**: The ASVAB tests highly specialized scientific knowledge.
    - **Reality**: The General Science section focuses on fundamental concepts across scientific disciplines.
    - **Strategy**: Focus on breadth of knowledge rather than depth in specialized areas.
- **Misconception**: Memorizing scientific facts is sufficient.
    - **Reality**: Understanding scientific principles and their applications is more valuable than memorizing isolated facts.
    - **Strategy**: Focus on understanding the "why" behind scientific phenomena.
- **Misconception**: Science sections are purely theoretical.
    - **Reality**: The ASVAB often tests practical applications of scientific knowledge.
    - **Strategy**: Study how scientific principles apply to real-world situations, especially in military contexts.

Practice Examples with Solutions

Example 1: Biology Application

Which of the following is most directly involved in cellular energy production? A) Ribosomes B) Mitochondria C) Golgi apparatus D) Cell membrane

Solution:

1. Analyze each option's function:
    - Ribosomes: Protein synthesis
    - Mitochondria: Cellular respiration and ATP production
    - Golgi apparatus: Protein processing and packaging
    - Cell membrane: Control of substances entering/exiting the cell
2. Energy production occurs primarily through cellular respiration
3. Answer: B) Mitochondria, known as the "powerhouse of the cell"

Example 2: Chemistry Application

A soldier needs to neutralize a basic solution with pH 9. Which of the following would be most appropriate? A) Sodium hydroxide B) Distilled water C) Dilute hydrochloric acid D) Baking soda

Solution:

1. To neutralize a basic solution (pH > 7), an acidic solution is needed
2. Analyze each option:
    - Sodium hydroxide: Strong base (would increase pH)
    - Distilled water: Neutral (pH 7, minimal effect)
    - Dilute hydrochloric acid: Strong acid (would lower pH)
    - Baking soda: Mild base (would increase pH)

3. Answer: C) Dilute hydrochloric acid

Example 3: Physics Application

A military vehicle with a mass of 2,500 kg accelerates from 0 to 20 m/s in 10 seconds. What is the force required to produce this acceleration?

Solution:

1. Identify the relevant formula: Force = mass × acceleration
2. Calculate acceleration: a = change in velocity / time = 20 m/s ÷ 10 s = 2 m/s^2
3. Calculate force: F = 2,500 kg × 2 m/s^2 = 5,000 N
4. Answer: The required force is 5,000 newtons.

Vocabulary and Language Skills

Advanced Language Mastery

- **Vocabulary Expansion Techniques**
  - Systematic word-learning strategies
  - Root word analysis
  - Context-based vocabulary acquisition
  - Word relationship understanding
- **Word Categories and Relationships**
  - Synonyms and antonyms
  - Homonyms, homophones, and homographs
  - Connotation versus denotation
  - Abstract versus concrete terms
- **Technical and Specialized Vocabulary**
  - Military terminology
  - Scientific and technical terms
  - Administrative and professional language
  - Field-specific jargon
- **Context Clues and Word Usage**
  - Identifying meaning from surrounding text
  - Understanding idiomatic expressions
  - Recognizing tone and intent
  - Analyzing word choice in different contexts

Comprehension Techniques

- **Active Reading Strategies**
  - Pre-reading assessment
  - Purpose-driven reading
  - Annotation and note-taking
  - Post-reading reflection

- **Information Extraction Methods**
  - Main idea identification
  - Supporting detail recognition
  - Inference and implication understanding
  - Fact versus opinion differentiation
- **Critical Analysis Approaches**
  - Author's purpose identification
  - Bias recognition
  - Argument evaluation
  - Evidence assessment
- **Efficient Reading Tactics**
  - Scanning for specific information
  - Skimming for general understanding
  - Strategic paragraph analysis
  - Speed reading with comprehension

Step-by-Step Vocabulary Building

1. **Assessment and Goal Setting**
   - Take vocabulary pre-tests to identify current level
   - Set specific vocabulary expansion goals
   - Identify personal vocabulary weaknesses
   - Create a vocabulary learning schedule
2. **Systematic Word Acquisition**
   - Learn 10-15 new words daily
   - Group words by theme, root, or usage
   - Use spaced repetition for retention
   - Apply new words in sentences
3. **Contextual Learning**
   - Read diverse materials daily
   - Note unfamiliar words during reading
   - Infer meanings from context first
   - Verify with dictionary afterward
4. **Active Practice**
   - Use new vocabulary in writing
   - Incorporate learned words in conversation
   - Create personal examples for each word
   - Teach new words to others
5. **Continuous Review and Assessment**
   - Regularly revisit previously learned words
   - Take periodic vocabulary assessments
   - Track progress toward vocabulary goals
   - Adjust learning strategies as needed

Common Vocabulary Misconceptions

- **Misconception**: The ASVAB tests obscure, rarely-used words.
  - **Reality**: The Word Knowledge section focuses on practical vocabulary commonly used in military and civilian contexts.
  - **Strategy**: Focus on building a strong foundation of commonly used words rather than extremely rare terms.
- **Misconception**: Memorizing word definitions is sufficient.
  - **Reality**: Understanding words in context and their relationships to other words is crucial.
  - **Strategy**: Learn words in context and practice using them in different situations.
- **Misconception**: Reading comprehension is simply about understanding individual words.
  - **Reality**: Comprehensive understanding requires synthesizing information, making inferences, and analyzing structure.
  - **Strategy**: Practice extracting meaning from complete passages, not just individual sentences.

Practice Examples with Solutions

Example 1: Word Knowledge

The word "pragmatic" most nearly means: A) Dramatic B) Theoretical C) Practical D) Emotional

Solution:

1. Analyze the meaning of "pragmatic": relating to matters of fact or practical affairs
2. Compare with each option:
   - Dramatic: expressing emotion theatrically (opposite)
   - Theoretical: based on theory rather than experience (opposite)
   - Practical: concerned with actual use or practice
   - Emotional: relating to emotions (unrelated)
3. Answer: C) Practical

Example 2: Paragraph Comprehension

Passage: "Military logistics involves planning and executing the movement and maintenance of forces. It encompasses the design, development, acquisition, storage, distribution, and evacuation of materiel; transportation of personnel; acquisition or construction, maintenance, operation, and disposition of facilities; and acquisition or furnishing of services."

According to the passage, which of the following is NOT included in military logistics? A) Combat strategy B) Transportation of personnel C) Storage of supplies D) Facility maintenance

Solution:

1. Identify all elements mentioned in the passage as part of military logistics:
   - Movement and maintenance of forces

- o Design, development, acquisition, storage, distribution, and evacuation of materiel
- o Transportation of personnel
- o Acquisition/construction, maintenance, operation, and disposition of facilities
- o Acquisition or furnishing of services
2. Check each option against this list:
   - o Combat strategy: Not mentioned
   - o Transportation of personnel: Explicitly mentioned
   - o Storage of supplies: Covered under "storage of materiel"
   - o Facility maintenance: Explicitly mentioned
3. Answer: A) Combat strategy

Technical and Mechanical Knowledge

Mechanical Reasoning Fundamentals

- **Basic Principles of Mechanics**
  - o Simple machines (lever, pulley, inclined plane, wheel and axle, screw, wedge)
  - o Mechanical advantage and efficiency
  - o Work, force, and motion relationships
  - o Energy conservation and transformation
- **Structural Systems**
  - o Load distribution and support systems
  - o Stress, strain, and material strength
  - o Truss, arch, and beam designs
  - o Structural integrity principles
- **Fluid Mechanics**
  - o Hydraulic and pneumatic systems
  - o Pressure, volume, and temperature relationships
  - o Fluid flow principles
  - o Buoyancy and displacement concepts
- **Mechanical Systems**
  - o Gears, belts, and chain drives
  - o Torque and rotational motion
  - o Friction and lubrication principles
  - o Mechanical timing and synchronization

Electronics Fundamentals

- **Electrical Theory**
  - o Current, voltage, and resistance relationships (Ohm's Law)
  - o AC vs. DC electricity
  - o Power calculation ($P = IV$)
  - o Electrical safety principles
- **Circuit Fundamentals**
  - o Series vs. parallel circuits

- o Circuit components (resistors, capacitors, inductors)
- o Reading electrical schematics
- o Troubleshooting basic circuits
- **Electronic Components**
  - o Semiconductors and transistors
  - o Diodes and their applications
  - o Integrated circuits
  - o Sensors and switches
- **Electrical Systems**
  - o Power generation and distribution
  - o Battery types and characteristics
  - o Electrical motors and generators
  - o Electronic control systems

Automotive Systems Knowledge

- **Engine Fundamentals**
  - o Internal combustion principles
  - o Engine types and configurations
  - o Engine subsystems
  - o Performance and efficiency factors
- **Drivetrain Components**
  - o Transmission types and functions
  - o Clutch operation
  - o Differential and axle assemblies
  - o Transfer case in 4WD systems
- **Braking Systems**
  - o Hydraulic brake principles
  - o Brake types (disc, drum)
  - o Anti-lock braking systems
  - o Brake maintenance and troubleshooting
- **Vehicle Electrical Systems**
  - o Starting and charging systems
  - o Ignition system operation
  - o Lighting and accessory circuits
  - o Onboard diagnostics

Shop Tools and Practices

- **Hand Tool Identification and Usage**
  - o Wrenches, pliers, screwdrivers, hammers
  - o Measuring tools (calipers, micrometers, rulers)
  - o Cutting tools (saws, chisels, files)
  - o Specialty automotive tools
- **Power Tool Operation**
  - o Drills and impact drivers

- o Grinders and sanders
- o Cutting tools (circular saws, jigsaws)
- o Safety procedures and PPE
- **Fastener Types and Applications**
  - o Screws, bolts, and nuts
  - o Rivets and pins
  - o Washers and spacers
  - o Thread types and specifications
- **Workshop Safety**
  - o Personal protective equipment
  - o Tool safety procedures
  - o Fire safety and prevention
  - o Chemical handling and disposal

Common Technical Misconceptions

- **Misconception**: Technical sections require advanced engineering knowledge.
  - o **Reality**: The ASVAB tests fundamental principles and practical applications, not advanced theory.
  - o **Strategy**: Focus on basic principles and common applications rather than complex engineering concepts.
- **Misconception**: You need significant hands-on experience with tools and machinery.
  - o **Reality**: Understanding basic principles and functions is more important than extensive hands-on experience.
  - o **Strategy**: Study diagrams, learn system components, and understand fundamental operational concepts.
- **Misconception**: Memorizing technical terminology is enough.
  - o **Reality**: Understanding how systems work and interact is more important than memorizing terminology.
  - o **Strategy**: Focus on conceptual understanding of how systems function rather than memorizing isolated facts.

Practice Examples with Solutions

Example 1: Mechanical Reasoning

If a pulley system provides a mechanical advantage of 3, how much force is needed to lift a 150-pound object?

Solution:

1. Apply the mechanical advantage formula: Force needed = Weight ÷ Mechanical advantage
2. Calculate: Force needed = 150 pounds ÷ 3 = 50 pounds
3. Answer: 50 pounds of force is needed.

Example 2: Electronics Knowledge

In a series circuit with three resistors of 5 ohms, 10 ohms, and 15 ohms, what is the total resistance?

Solution:

1. Apply the series circuit formula: Total resistance = Sum of individual resistances
2. Calculate: Total resistance = $5\,\Omega + 10\,\Omega + 15\,\Omega = 30\,\Omega$
3. Answer: The total resistance is 30 ohms.

Example 3: Auto Shop Knowledge

What component in an automotive cooling system regulates coolant flow based on engine temperature? A) Water pump B) Radiator C) Thermostat D) Cooling fan

Solution:

1. Analyze each component's function:
   o Water pump: Circulates coolant through the system
   o Radiator: Dissipates heat from the coolant
   o Thermostat: Opens and closes based on temperature to control coolant flow
   o Cooling fan: Pulls air through the radiator
2. Answer: C) Thermostat

Logical Reasoning and Problem-Solving

Cognitive Skill Enhancement

- **Analytical Thinking Development**
  o Breaking complex problems into components
  o Identifying patterns and relationships
  o Evaluating evidence and arguments
  o Making logical inferences
- **Critical Reasoning Skills**
  o Deductive reasoning (general to specific)
  o Inductive reasoning (specific to general)
  o Abductive reasoning (best explanation)
  o Recognizing logical fallacies
- **Spatial Reasoning Abilities**
  o Mental rotation and manipulation
  o Spatial orientation and navigation
  o Pattern recognition and completion
  o Visualizing three-dimensional objects
- **Quantitative Reasoning**
  o Numerical pattern recognition

- o Mathematical modeling of problems
- o Estimation and approximation skills
- o Logical number sequences

Problem-Solving Frameworks

- **Strategic Problem Approach**
  - o Problem definition and clarification
  - o Information gathering and organization
  - o Solution generation and evaluation
  - o Implementation and verification
- **Systematic Decision Making**
  - o Objective setting and prioritization
  - o Alternative solution development
  - o Consequence analysis
  - o Decision execution and monitoring
- **Creative Problem-Solving**
  - o Brainstorming techniques
  - o Lateral thinking approaches
  - o Analogical reasoning
  - o Constraint elimination
- **Algorithmic Problem-Solving**
  - o Step-by-step procedural thinking
  - o Flow chart and process mapping
  - o Systematic elimination
  - o Logical progression

Training Techniques

- **Logical Puzzle Practice**
  - o Sudoku for numerical reasoning
  - o Logic grid puzzles for deductive reasoning
  - o Syllogism problems for logical inference
  - o Sequence puzzles for pattern recognition
- **Strategic Game Engagement**
  - o Chess for forward planning
  - o Strategy board games for resource management
  - o Logic games for rule application
  - o Pattern recognition games
- **Real-World Problem Analysis**
  - o Case studies and scenarios
  - o Military tactical problems
  - o Resource allocation challenges
  - o Emergency response situations
- **Mental Exercise Regimen**
  - o Daily brain training exercises

- ○ Cross-discipline problem-solving
- ○ Timed challenge practice
- ○ Progressive difficulty advancement

Common Reasoning Misconceptions

- **Misconception**: Logical reasoning is purely intuitive.
  - ○ **Reality**: Effective reasoning requires structured approaches and practice with established frameworks.
  - ○ **Strategy**: Learn formal reasoning techniques and practice applying them systematically.
- **Misconception**: Problem-solving is about finding a single correct answer.
  - ○ **Reality**: Many problems have multiple valid solutions or approaches.
  - ○ **Strategy**: Practice generating multiple solutions and evaluating their effectiveness.
- **Misconception**: Speed is the most important factor in problem-solving.
  - ○ **Reality**: Accuracy and thoroughness are often more important than speed.
  - ○ **Strategy**: Focus on developing systematic approaches that lead to correct solutions before working on speed.

Practice Examples with Solutions

Example 1: Logical Sequence

What comes next in this sequence? 3, 7, 15, 31, ? A) 57 B) 63 C) 59 D) 47

Solution:

1. Analyze the pattern:
   - ○ $3 \rightarrow 7$ (difference of 4)
   - ○ $7 \rightarrow 15$ (difference of 8)
   - ○ $15 \rightarrow 31$ (difference of 16)
2. Recognize the pattern: Each difference is doubling (4, 8, 16)
3. Apply the pattern: The next difference should be 32
4. Calculate: $31 + 32 = 63$
5. Answer: B) 63

Example 2: Spatial Reasoning

If a cube is painted red on all faces and then cut into 27 equal smaller cubes, how many of the smaller cubes will have exactly two red faces?

Solution:

1. Visualize the larger cube divided into 27 smaller cubes (3×3×3)
2. Identify cube positions:

- Corner cubes (8 total): Each has 3 red faces
- Edge cubes (12 total): Each has 2 red faces
- Face center cubes (6 total): Each has 1 red face
- Interior cube (1 total): Has 0 red faces
3. Count the cubes with exactly 2 red faces: 12 edge cubes
4. Answer: 12 smaller cubes will have exactly two red faces.

Example 3: Deductive Reasoning

All military personnel must complete basic training. Some pilots are military personnel. Which conclusion logically follows? A) All pilots must complete basic training. B) No pilots complete basic training. C) Some pilots must complete basic training. D) Most pilots complete basic training.

Solution:

1. Analyze the given statements:
   - All military personnel must complete basic training.
   - Some pilots are military personnel.
2. Apply deductive reasoning:
   - If some pilots are military personnel, and all military personnel must complete basic training, then those pilots who are military personnel must complete basic training.
3. Answer: C) Some pilots must complete basic training.

Integrated Learning Approach

Holistic Skill Development

- **Cross-Subject Application**
  - Identify connections between ASVAB subject areas
  - Apply mathematical principles to science problems
  - Utilize technical understanding in word problems
  - Combine logical reasoning with mechanical comprehension
- **Integrated Study Sessions**
  - Rotate between subject areas during study sessions
  - Create study materials that integrate multiple topics
  - Practice with questions that span multiple domains
  - Develop understanding of how different skills complement each other
- **Comprehensive Problem Approach**
  - Address complex problems using multiple skill sets
  - Apply diverse knowledge to practical scenarios
  - Develop flexible thinking across subject boundaries
  - Build confidence in varied problem-solving contexts
- **Balanced Preparation Strategy**
  - Allocate study time proportionally to subject importance

- Focus extra attention on personal challenge areas
- Maintain proficiency across all domains
- Adapt study approach based on ongoing assessment results

Real-World Military Application Focus

- **Military Career Relevance**
  - Study how ASVAB subjects apply to military occupations
  - Connect learning to potential service responsibilities
  - Understand how different knowledge areas support military operations
  - Focus on practical applications valued in military contexts
- **Operational Scenario Practice**
  - Apply knowledge to simulated military situations
  - Practice with problems framed in mission contexts
  - Develop situational thinking for practical applications
  - Connect abstract concepts to concrete operational needs
- **Technical-Tactical Integration**
  - Understand how technical knowledge supports tactical objectives
  - Apply scientific principles to military equipment and systems
  - Recognize how mathematics underpins operational planning
  - Develop appreciation for knowledge application in service roles
- **Leadership and Problem-Solving**
  - Apply critical thinking to leadership scenarios
  - Understand how technical knowledge supports decision-making
  - Practice clear communication of complex information
  - Develop confidence in applying knowledge under pressure

Chapter 6: Practice and Performance Optimization

Diagnostic Testing Essentials

Purpose of Diagnostic Assessments

- Comprehensive skill evaluation
- Personalized weakness identification
- Baseline performance measurement
- Strategic study plan development

Diagnostic Test Components

- Full-length practice exam
- Comprehensive performance analysis
- Detailed score breakdown
- Personalized improvement insights

Identifying Weak Areas

Systematic Weakness Analysis

1. Quantitative Performance Evaluation
   - Subtest score comparison
   - Lowest-performing section identification
   - Numerical performance tracking
2. Qualitative Assessment
   - Missed question pattern analysis
   - Underlying concept gap identification
   - Error type categorization

Weakness Classification

- Knowledge gaps
- Skill deficiencies
- Test-taking limitations
- Conceptual understanding barriers
- Processing speed challenges

Advanced Analysis Techniques

- Question difficulty mapping

- Time consumption analysis
- Pattern recognition in incorrect answers
- Concept relationship identification
- Problem-solving approach evaluation

Targeted Improvement Strategies

Personalized Approach

- Prioritize lowest-performing areas
- Allocate focused study time
- Develop specialized resources
- Create customized practice exercises

Improvement Techniques

- Intense skill drilling
- Comprehensive concept review
- Progressive skill development
- Adaptive learning methods
- Spaced repetition implementation
- Mixed practice sessions

Overcoming Specific Weakness Types

Content Knowledge Deficiencies

- Micro-lecture focus on specific topics
- Conceptual mapping exercises
- Simplified explanation approach
- Layered complexity introduction
- Knowledge scaffolding techniques

Mathematical Reasoning Challenges

- Foundational skills reinforcement
- Step-by-step problem deconstruction
- Visual representation techniques
- Pattern recognition development
- Formula application practice
- Real-world context integration

Reading Comprehension Difficulties

- Active reading strategies

- Annotation techniques
- Main idea extraction practice
- Supporting detail identification
- Inference development exercises
- Context clue utilization

Vocabulary Limitations

- Root word analysis
- Contextual learning approach
- Word family association
- Semantic mapping
- High-frequency word prioritization
- Etymology exploration

Technical Knowledge Gaps

- Visual learning resources
- Hands-on application exercises
- Conceptual relationship diagrams
- Progressive complexity introduction
- Real-world examples and applications

Mock Exam Preparation

Effective Test Simulation

- Exact testing conditions
- Standard timing
- No external assistance
- Realistic environment
- Computer-adaptive practice (when applicable)

Strategic Test Taking

- Time management practice
- Stress reduction techniques
- Confidence building
- Performance optimization
- Educated guessing strategies
- Section prioritization approaches

Mock Exam Analysis

- Detailed performance review

- Question-level analysis
- Error pattern identification
- Psychological preparation
- Timing optimization assessment
- Knowledge gap evaluation

Advanced Mock Test Analysis Framework

1. Performance Metrics Assessment
   - Total score analysis
   - Section-by-section breakdown
   - Time allocation review
   - Question type performance
   - Difficulty level mastery
2. Error Categorization System
   - Concept misunderstanding
   - Calculation mistakes
   - Reading comprehension failures
   - Time management issues
   - Test-taking strategy problems
   - Careless errors
3. Strategic Improvement Planning
   - Prioritization matrix development
   - Personalized study recommendations
   - Resource allocation guidance
   - Targeted practice prescription
   - Timeline adjustment suggestions

Performance Tracking and Monitoring

Systematic Performance Management

1. Quantitative Tracking
   - Score progression
   - Subtest improvement
   - Comparative analysis
   - Statistical performance metrics
   - Percentile ranking changes
2. Qualitative Assessment
   - Skill development monitoring
   - Conceptual understanding tracking
   - Strategic improvement evaluation
   - Confidence level assessment
   - Test-taking approach refinement

Tracking Methods

- Digital performance tools
- Spreadsheet analysis
- Study journal
- Progress log
- Visual performance charts
- Mobile application tracking
- Automated performance analytics

Advanced Performance Monitoring Systems

- Spaced repetition software integration
- Digital flashcard performance tracking
- Practice test analytics
- Knowledge mastery heat maps
- Time allocation optimization tools
- Personalized algorithm-based suggestions

Creating Effective Performance Dashboards

1. Essential Components
   - Overall score trajectory
   - Section-specific progress
   - Weakest area identification
   - Study time allocation
   - Practice test comparison
   - Target score gap analysis
2. Implementation Methods
   - Digital spreadsheet templates
   - Mobile application integration
   - Physical tracking journals
   - Visual progress boards
   - Cloud-based performance tracking
3. Optimization Techniques
   - Regular update schedule
   - Milestone celebration markers
   - Visual progress indicators
   - Trend analysis integration
   - Adaptive goal adjustment

Continuous Improvement Cycle

1. Test
2. Analyze

3. Identify weaknesses
4. Develop strategy
5. Practice
6. Reassess
7. Adjust approach
8. Implement refinements
9. Re-test
10. Measure progress

Implementing the Improvement Cycle

- Weekly assessment schedule
- Bi-weekly strategy adjustment
- Monthly comprehensive review
- Continuous micro-adjustments
- Progressive challenge integration

Performance Optimization Tools

Recommended Resources

- ASVAB preparation apps
- Online practice platforms
- Diagnostic testing services
- Performance analysis tools
- Adaptive learning systems
- Personalized tutoring options

Digital Tool Integration

- Cross-platform synchronization
- Mobile and desktop accessibility
- Progress tracking automation
- Performance analytics visualization
- Adaptive challenge algorithms

Case Studies of Successful Preparation Approaches

Case Study 1: The Struggling Math Student

Background: Candidate with significant difficulties in Mathematics Knowledge and Arithmetic Reasoning

Initial Assessment:

- Math Knowledge score: 32nd percentile
- Arithmetic Reasoning score: 28th percentile
- Overall AFQT estimate: 45

Intervention Strategy:

1. Foundation rebuilding through basic skills review
2. Concept visualization techniques
3. Daily practice with progressive difficulty
4. Real-world application focus
5. Spaced repetition of formulas and concepts
6. Regular timed practice sessions

Outcome:

- Math Knowledge score: 68th percentile
- Arithmetic Reasoning score: 72nd percentile
- Overall AFQT estimate: 76
- Qualified for technical specialties in preferred branch

Key Lessons:

- Fundamental skill mastery before advanced concepts
- Consistent daily practice more effective than cramming
- Visual learning aids significantly improved comprehension
- Real-world context enhanced problem-solving ability

Case Study 2: The Time Management Challenge

Background: Candidate with strong knowledge but poor test completion rates

Initial Assessment:

- Completed only 65% of questions in practice tests
- High accuracy on completed questions (85%)
- Overall AFQT estimate: 52 (significantly below potential)

Intervention Strategy:

1. Section-specific timing strategies
2. Question triage techniques
3. Educated guessing protocols
4. Progressive timed practice
5. Strategic question skipping approach
6. Anxiety reduction techniques

Outcome:

- Completed 98% of questions in final practice tests
- Maintained 82% accuracy on completed questions
- Overall AFQT estimate: 89
- Qualified for all desired military specialties

Key Lessons:

- Strategic time management more important than content knowledge alone
- Psychological preparation crucial for performance optimization
- Practiced question triage dramatically improved section completion
- Stress management techniques enhanced cognitive performance

Case Study 3: The Vocabulary Builder

Background: Candidate with English as second language struggling with Word Knowledge and Paragraph Comprehension

Initial Assessment:

- Word Knowledge score: 35th percentile
- Paragraph Comprehension score: 42nd percentile
- Overall AFQT estimate: 48

Intervention Strategy:

1. Root word analysis system
2. Daily vocabulary immersion
3. Context-based learning approach
4. Strategic reading practice
5. Active reading annotation techniques
6. Word family association method

Outcome:

- Word Knowledge score: 76th percentile
- Paragraph Comprehension score: 81st percentile
- Overall AFQT estimate: 84
- Qualified for military intelligence specialties

Key Lessons:

- Systematic vocabulary building more effective than memorization
- Context-based learning produced better retention than word lists
- Active reading techniques dramatically improved comprehension

- Etymology understanding enhanced vocabulary expansion

Case Study 4: The Technical Specialist

Background: Candidate excelling in verbal sections but struggling with Electronics Information and Mechanical Comprehension

Initial Assessment:

- Electronics Information score: 45th percentile
- Mechanical Comprehension score: 39th percentile
- Strong verbal scores (85th+ percentile)
- Limited technical background

Intervention Strategy:

1. Visual learning resources for technical concepts
2. Hands-on demonstration videos
3. Principle-based learning rather than memorization
4. Systematic concept relationship mapping
5. Real-world application context
6. Progressive complexity introduction

Outcome:

- Electronics Information score: 79th percentile
- Mechanical Comprehension score: 74th percentile
- Maintained strong verbal scores
- Qualified for technical military specialties

Key Lessons:

- Visual learning dramatically improved technical concept mastery
- Understanding principles more effective than memorizing facts
- Concept relationship mapping enhanced overall comprehension
- Progressive complexity approach prevented overwhelm

Performance Psychology and Test-Day Optimization

Mental Preparation Strategies

- Visualization techniques
- Positive self-talk protocols
- Confidence-building exercises
- Performance anxiety management
- Cognitive priming activities

Physical Optimization

- Sleep regulation protocol
- Nutrition optimization
- Hydration strategy
- Energy management techniques
- Pre-test physical routine

Test-Day Execution Plan

1. Preparatory Phase
   - Evening before relaxation routine
   - Morning nutritional strategy
   - Mental warm-up exercises
   - Arrival timing optimization
2. During-Test Strategy
   - Section approach plan
   - Break utilization technique
   - Recovery methodology for difficult sections
   - Energy conservation approach
   - Focus maintenance protocol
3. Post-Test Analysis
   - Performance evaluation framework
   - Experience documentation
   - Strategy effectiveness assessment
   - Future optimization planning

Data-Driven ASVAB Preparation

Analytics-Based Approach

- Performance data collection methodology
- Statistical trend analysis
- Comparative benchmarking
- Predictive performance modeling
- Adaptive study plan generation

Implementing Data-Driven Preparation

1. Establish Performance Baseline
   - Comprehensive diagnostic assessment
   - Detailed performance metrics collection
   - Strength and weakness quantification
   - Comparative percentile positioning
2. Develop Data Collection System

- o Practice test performance tracking
- o Study time allocation monitoring
- o Concept mastery measurement
- o Error pattern documentation
3. Apply Analytics for Optimization
   - o Identify highest-impact improvement areas
   - o Calculate efficiency of study methods
   - o Determine optimal practice frequency
   - o Adjust resource allocation based on data
   - o Forecast performance improvements
4. Continuous Refinement Process
   - o Regular data review schedule
   - o Strategy adjustment based on metrics
   - o Resource reallocation as needed
   - o Progress trajectory optimization

Benefits of Data-Driven Approach

- Eliminates subjective assessment
- Maximizes study efficiency
- Provides objective progress measures
- Enables precision in weakness targeting
- Increases confidence through measurable improvement

Chapter 7: Beyond the ASVAB

Military Career Paths

Career Exploration Framework

The ASVAB serves as a gateway to a diverse range of military occupations, but successful career development requires strategic planning beyond simply achieving qualifying scores. Military careers follow distinctive developmental paths that combine technical specialization, leadership development, and continued education.

Effective career exploration involves:

- **Skills and Interests Assessment**: Identifying your natural aptitudes and genuine interests using ASVAB results as a guide
- **Long-term Career Projection**: Understanding how initial military occupational specialties can evolve into broader career paths
- **Progressive Responsibility Planning**: Mapping advancement opportunities and required qualifications at each career stage
- **Technical vs. Leadership Trajectory**: Determining whether to pursue technical expertise or leadership development as a primary focus

Army Career Opportunities

The U.S. Army offers over 150 Military Occupational Specialties (MOS) across diverse career fields:

- **Combat Arms**: Infantry, Armor, Field Artillery, and Air Defense Artillery represent the core fighting force with opportunities for Special Forces qualification for exceptional candidates
- **Intelligence and Information Operations**: Military Intelligence, Cyber Operations, and Signal Corps specialists manage critical information systems and intelligence gathering
- **Technical Specialties**: Engineering, Chemical, and Medical specialties provide technical expertise in specialized areas
- **Support Operations**: Logistics, Transportation, and Human Resources roles ensure the effectiveness of combat operations

Advanced Army Programs

The Army offers specialized programs for qualified individuals:

- **Green to Gold**: Allows enlisted soldiers to pursue officer commissions through college education
- **Warrant Officer Programs**: Provides technical leadership opportunities in specialized fields

- **Special Forces Assessment and Selection**: Identifies candidates for elite special operations units

Navy Career Tracks

The U.S. Navy structures careers around both platform assignments and technical specialization:

- **Surface Warfare**: Operations on destroyers, cruisers, and amphibious vessels with progression toward ship command
- **Submarine Forces**: Technical roles in nuclear propulsion and weapons systems with high security clearance requirements
- **Naval Aviation**: Pilot and flight officer positions with aircraft specialization
- **Special Warfare**: SEAL teams and special operations support requiring additional qualification tests

Advanced Navy Programs

For exceptional candidates, the Navy offers accelerated advancement through:

- **Nuclear Propulsion Program**: Elite technical training with significant education benefits and advancement opportunities
- **STA-21 (Seaman to Admiral)**: College funding program for enlisted personnel seeking officer commissions
- **Advanced Technical Fields**: Cryptology, intelligence, and cyber operations with specialized qualification paths

Air Force Career Paths

The Air Force organizes careers into Air Force Specialty Codes (AFSCs) that combine technical specialization with operational functions:

- **Air Operations**: Pilot, navigator, air battle management, and drone operations
- **Maintenance and Logistics**: Aircraft maintenance, munitions systems, and supply chain management
- **Intelligence and Cyber**: Intelligence analysis, cyber warfare, and information operations
- **Support Functions**: Medical, administration, security forces, and civil engineering

Advanced Air Force Programs

Specialized Air Force career opportunities include:

- **Rated Officer Positions**: Pilot, navigator, and air battle manager roles requiring additional testing
- **Special Warfare**: Pararescue, Combat Control, and Special Reconnaissance units requiring exceptional physical and technical qualification

- **Technical Development Programs**: Advanced academic degrees and research positions for qualified personnel

Marine Corps Career Options

The Marine Corps emphasizes versatility while organizing Military Occupational Specialties into occupational fields:

- **Combat Arms**: Infantry, artillery, and armor forming the core combat capability
- **Air**: Aviation command and support including pilots, air traffic controllers, and maintenance
- **Combat Support**: Intelligence, communications, and engineering that directly support combat operations
- **Combat Service Support**: Logistics, administration, and financial services

Advanced Marine Programs

The Marine Corps offers several elite programs:

- **Marine Reconnaissance**: Advanced infantry operations requiring additional screening
- **Marine Special Operations Command (MARSOC)**: Special operations capabilities requiring additional qualification tests
- **Marine Security Guard**: Embassy protection duty requiring top security clearance

Coast Guard Career Tracks

The Coast Guard combines military service with maritime law enforcement and safety operations:

- **Maritime Law Enforcement**: Drug interdiction, migration enforcement, and fisheries protection
- **Maritime Safety**: Search and rescue, vessel inspections, and maritime security
- **Technical Operations**: Engineering, electronics, and information systems
- **Aviation**: Aircraft operations for search and rescue and maritime patrol

Advanced Coast Guard Programs

Specialized Coast Guard programs include:

- **Maritime Safety and Security Teams**: Tactical maritime law enforcement units
- **Deployable Specialized Forces**: Maritime security and counterterrorism operations
- **Marine Safety Specialization**: Advanced qualification in maritime safety and environmental protection

Space Force Career Opportunities

As the newest military branch, the Space Force offers cutting-edge technical positions:

- **Space Operations**: Satellite command and control, orbital warfare, and space domain awareness
- **Intelligence**: Space-focused intelligence gathering and analysis
- **Cyber Operations**: Systems security for space assets and ground infrastructure
- **Engineering and Acquisition**: Development and procurement of space systems and technology

Space Force Progression

Career advancement in the Space Force emphasizes:

- **Technical Depth**: Specialized expertise in space systems and operations
- **Cross-Domain Understanding**: Knowledge of how space capabilities integrate with other military domains
- **Advanced Education**: Graduate-level technical education in relevant fields

Additional Qualification Tests for Special Programs

While the ASVAB serves as the primary military entrance exam, numerous specialized programs require additional testing beyond baseline qualification scores. Understanding these supplementary assessments can significantly expand your military career options.

Special Operations Selection Tests

Each special operations community administers specialized assessments:

- **Special Forces Assessment and Selection (SFAS)**: A multi-week evaluation of physical capabilities, problem-solving skills, and leadership potential for Army Special Forces candidates
- **Basic Underwater Demolition/SEAL (BUD/S)**: Navy SEAL selection process combining extreme physical challenges with tactical problem-solving
- **Air Force Special Warfare Assessment and Selection**: Identifies candidates for Pararescue, Combat Control, and Special Reconnaissance specialties through physical testing and technical aptitude evaluation
- **MARSOC Assessment and Selection**: Evaluates candidates for Marine Special Operations Command through physical, mental, and leadership challenges

Each selection program focuses on:

- **Physical Performance Standards**: Structured fitness assessments far exceeding basic military requirements
- **Psychological Resilience**: Evaluation of mental toughness under extreme pressure
- **Team Dynamics**: Assessment of interpersonal skills and team contribution
- **Adaptability**: Problem-solving capacity in rapidly changing situations

Aviation Qualification Testing

Military aviation programs require supplementary testing beyond ASVAB qualification:

- **Air Force Officer Qualifying Test (AFOQT)**: Comprehensive assessment for Air Force officer candidates with specific pilot and navigator subtests
- **Aviation Selection Test Battery (ASTB)**: Navy, Marine Corps, and Coast Guard aviation program qualification test measuring aviation aptitude
- **Alternate Flight Aptitude Selection Test (AFAST)**: Army aviation program assessment for potential helicopter pilots

Aviation testing typically evaluates:

- **Spatial Aptitude**: Three-dimensional reasoning and visualization
- **Mathematical Reasoning**: Applied mathematics in aviation contexts
- **Instrument Comprehension**: Ability to interpret flight instruments
- **Aviation Knowledge**: Basic understanding of aeronautical principles
- **Psychomotor Coordination**: Hand-eye coordination and reaction time

Language Aptitude Assessment

For military intelligence and language-intensive roles:

- **Defense Language Aptitude Battery (DLAB)**: Measures potential to learn foreign languages through artificial language exercises
- **Defense Language Proficiency Test (DLPT)**: Assesses current proficiency in specific languages
- **Military Language Aptitude Test (MLAT)**: Evaluates linguistic pattern recognition and memorization capacity

Language testing focuses on:

- **Pattern Recognition**: Ability to identify linguistic structures
- **Sound Discrimination**: Capability to distinguish and reproduce unfamiliar sounds
- **Memory Function**: Capacity to retain and recall language elements
- **Associative Learning**: Connecting language components in meaningful ways

Technical and Professional Qualification Tests

Specialized military programs often require field-specific assessments:

- **Cyber Aptitude and Talent Assessment**: Evaluates potential for cyber operations roles
- **Nuclear Field Qualification Test**: Determines eligibility for Navy nuclear programs
- **Professional Certification Exams**: Field-specific qualifications for medical, legal, and technical specialties

Military Education Benefits and Maximization Strategies

Military service provides exceptional educational opportunities that extend far beyond traditional college funding. Understanding how to leverage these benefits can dramatically enhance both your military career trajectory and post-service opportunities.

Tuition Assistance Programs

Active-duty service members have access to education funding while serving:

- **Military Tuition Assistance**: Service branches cover up to 100% of tuition costs for approved courses (up to annual caps)
- **Service-Specific Programs**: Each branch offers supplementary education funding with varying qualification requirements
- **Credential Programs**: Funding for professional certifications and licenses relevant to military specialties

Maximization strategies include:

- **Education Centers**: Consulting with military education offices for program-specific guidance
- **Education Plans**: Developing a degree plan aligned with career progression
- **Credit Prioritization**: Targeting courses that provide both degree progress and military advancement

Post-9/11 GI Bill Benefits

The Post-9/11 GI Bill provides comprehensive education benefits after qualifying service:

- **Tuition Coverage**: Up to 100% of public in-state tuition or capped private school payments
- **Housing Allowance**: Monthly stipend based on school location
- **Book and Supply Stipend**: Annual allowance for educational materials
- **Yellow Ribbon Program**: Additional funding for private institutions
- **Transferability Option**: Ability to transfer benefits to qualifying dependents

Optimization approaches include:

- **Timing Strategies**: Strategic use of benefits based on career stage
- **School Selection**: Targeting institutions with strong Yellow Ribbon participation
- **Benefit Integration**: Combining GI Bill with scholarships and grants
- **Dependent Planning**: Strategic transfer of benefits to family members

College Credit for Military Training

Military experience translates directly into academic credit:

- **Joint Services Transcript (JST)**: Official documentation of military training and experiences for Army, Navy, Marines, and Coast Guard
- **Community College of the Air Force (CCAF)**: Associate degree-granting institution for Air Force members
- **Defense Activity for Non-Traditional Education Support (DANTES)**: Credit-by-examination programs

Maximizing military training credit involves:

- **Credit Evaluation Services**: Having military experience professionally evaluated
- **Military-Friendly Institutions**: Targeting schools with established military credit policies
- **Portfolio Development**: Documenting military skills and knowledge for potential additional credit

Advanced Education Programs

Military branches sponsor advanced degree opportunities:

- **Service Academies**: Undergraduate institutions providing officer commissions and bachelor's degrees
- **Funded Graduate Education**: Full-time study opportunities with continued active duty pay and benefits
- **Medical and Law Programs**: Professional degree funding for qualified candidates
- **Technical Education**: Advanced training in specialized fields with civilian credentialing

Credentialing Opportunities

Military training can lead to civilian professional certifications:

- **Credentialing Assistance Program**: Funding for professional licenses and certifications
- **United Services Military Apprenticeship Program (USMAP)**: Department of Labor registered apprenticeships
- **SkillBridge Program**: Career skills training opportunities during military transition
- **Verification of Military Experience and Training (VMET)**: Documentation of military training for civilian employers

Maximization strategies include:

- **Early Planning**: Identifying credential opportunities aligned with military occupational specialty
- **Supplementary Training**: Adding civilian-recognized components to military training
- **Documentation Systems**: Maintaining comprehensive records of relevant experience and training

Long-term Career Planning Based on Initial ASVAB Performance

Your initial ASVAB performance establishes a foundation for career development that extends far beyond entry-level positions. Understanding how to leverage these results into a cohesive career strategy can significantly enhance your military experience and post-service opportunities.

Strategic Career Sequencing

Military careers develop through strategic progression of assignments and qualifications:

- **Building Block Approach**: Using initial positions to build foundational skills for advanced specialties
- **Qualification Pathways**: Mapping required certifications and training for career progression
- **Timing-Sensitive Opportunities**: Identifying optimal windows for specialized training and education
- **Broadening Assignments**: Incorporating diverse experiences to develop adaptability

Leveraging Initial ASVAB Line Scores

Your specific ASVAB subtest performance can inform long-term specialization options:

- **Technical Score Patterns**: High performance in specific technical areas suggests specialized career tracks
- **Verbal Aptitude Utilization**: Strong language skills indicate potential for intelligence, communications, or leadership roles
- **Mathematical Reasoning Application**: Exceptional math performance suggests engineering, finance, or technical paths
- **Mechanical and Electrical Aptitude**: Strong scores indicate potential for maintenance, technical, or aviation specialties

Career Field Progression Planning

Each military career field offers distinct advancement opportunities:

- **Technical Specialization**: Developing deep expertise in a specific domain
- **Operational Leadership**: Progressing through increasing levels of command responsibility
- **Staff Development**: Building organizational and planning capabilities
- **Instructor and Training Roles**: Developing and implementing training programs

Cross-Training and Lateral Movement

Military careers offer opportunities to change specialties:

- **Formal Retraining Programs**: Structured specialty changes at specific career points
- **Special Duty Assignments**: Temporary positions outside primary specialty
- **Commissioning Programs**: Enlisted-to-officer transition opportunities
- **Joint-Service Assignments**: Positions working with other military branches

Civilian Career Alignment

Military experience translates into civilian opportunities:

- **Industry Certification Alignment**: Matching military training with civilian credentials
- **Sequential Qualification Planning**: Building progressively valuable skills with civilian recognition
- **Network Development**: Establishing professional relationships across military and civilian sectors
- **Skills Translation Strategy**: Documenting military accomplishments in civilian-relevant terms

Retesting Strategies and Policies

Military entrance standards and career field requirements evolve, making retesting a valuable option for improving opportunities. Understanding the policies, techniques, and optimal preparation approaches can significantly enhance your military career options.

ASVAB Retesting Policies

Each military branch maintains specific retesting guidelines:

- **Standard Waiting Periods**: Typically 30 days after first test, 30 days after second test, and 6 months after third test
- **Score Validity Period**: ASVAB scores generally remain valid for 2 years
- **Confirmation Testing**: Additional testing may be required to verify exceptionally high scores
- **Special Program Exceptions**: Accelerated retesting options for specific recruitment programs

When to Consider Retesting

Strategic retesting decisions should consider:

- **Career Field Access**: When current scores limit desired military occupation options
- **Special Program Qualification**: When scores are just below thresholds for advanced programs
- **Significant Preparation Improvement**: When substantial additional study has been completed

- **Test Performance Issues**: When initial testing was affected by testing environment or personal factors

Targeted Preparation Strategies

Effective retesting preparation focuses on identified weaknesses:

- **Score Analysis**: Detailed review of previous subtest performance
- **Focused Remediation**: Concentrated study in lowest-performing areas
- **Practice Testing**: Timed practice with emphasis on test format familiarity
- **Specialized Tutoring**: Professional assistance for challenging content areas

Psychological Preparation

Mental preparation significantly impacts test performance:

- **Test Anxiety Management**: Techniques for managing stress during high-stakes testing
- **Confidence Building**: Structured approach to developing test-taking confidence
- **Performance Optimization**: Strategies for maintaining focus and energy
- **Cognitive Preparation**: Mental exercises for improved recall and reasoning

Alternative Qualification Paths

When retesting may not achieve desired outcomes, consider:

- **Alternate Entry Programs**: Special recruitment initiatives with modified requirements
- **Preparatory Programs**: Military-sponsored academic enhancement programs
- **Future Soldier Training**: Pre-enlistment development programs
- **Delayed Entry Options**: Extended preparation opportunities before formal military entry

Transition to Civilian Careers

Your military training and experience represent valuable qualifications for civilian employment, but effective translation requires strategic planning and preparation.

Transferable Skills Framework

Military service develops universally valuable capabilities:

- **Leadership Experience**: Direct responsibility for personnel and resources
- **Technical Expertise**: Specialized training in advanced systems and equipment
- **Crisis Management**: Performance under pressure in high-stakes environments
- **Project Management**: Coordination of complex operations with multiple stakeholders
- **Adaptability**: Flexibility in changing operational conditions

Career Transition Timeline

Effective military-to-civilian transition follows a structured timeline:

- **24+ Months Before Separation**: Initial career exploration and gap analysis
- **18 Months Before Separation**: Education and certification planning
- **12 Months Before Separation**: Resume development and network building
- **6 Months Before Separation**: Active job search and interview preparation
- **3 Months Before Separation**: Transition logistics and relocation planning

Education and Certification Planning

Strategic credential development enhances employability:

- **Degree Completion**: Utilizing military education benefits for academic credentials
- **Industry Certifications**: Obtaining civilian-recognized professional qualifications
- **Apprenticeship Programs**: Structured training combining military experience with civilian requirements
- **Continuing Education**: Ongoing professional development addressing skill gaps

Employer Engagement Strategies

Connecting effectively with civilian employers requires:

- **Military-Friendly Employer Identification**: Targeting organizations with established veteran hiring programs
- **Skills Translation Techniques**: Communicating military experience in civilian-relevant terminology
- **Networking Methodologies**: Building professional relationships in target industries
- **Interview Preparation**: Addressing common transition challenges in employment discussions

Entrepreneurship Pathways

Military experience provides a strong foundation for business ownership:

- **Veteran Business Programs**: Special funding and support initiatives for veteran entrepreneurs
- **Franchise Opportunities**: Structured business models with veteran incentives
- **Government Contracting**: Special consideration for veteran-owned businesses
- **Business Planning Resources**: Veteran-specific entrepreneurship training and mentoring

Military Skills in Civilian Context

The capabilities developed through military service represent valuable assets in civilian professional environments when effectively translated and applied.

Key Transferable Competencies

Military training develops high-demand professional qualities:

- **Operational Leadership**: Direct responsibility for team performance and resource management
- **Technical Proficiency**: Specialized expertise in complex systems and technologies
- **Organizational Management**: Administration of personnel, equipment, and information systems
- **Crisis Response**: Performance under pressure with limited resources
- **Adaptability**: Rapid adjustment to changing operational requirements

Industry Alignment Strategy

Different military specialties align naturally with civilian sectors:

- **Technical Military Roles**: Engineering, manufacturing, and information technology
- **Intelligence Functions**: Data analysis, cybersecurity, and risk management
- **Logistics Specialists**: Supply chain management, transportation, and distribution
- **Medical Personnel**: Healthcare, emergency services, and public health
- **Administrative Functions**: Human resources, financial management, and compliance

Professional Development

Ongoing skill enhancement supports successful transition:

- **Gap Analysis**: Identifying differences between military capabilities and civilian requirements
- **Credential Acquisition**: Obtaining industry-specific certifications and licenses
- **Professional Association Engagement**: Participation in civilian professional organizations
- **Continued Education**: Formal and informal learning focused on industry trends

Adaptability and Growth

Long-term civilian success builds on military foundations:

- **Continuous Learning Mindset**: Approaching professional development as an ongoing process

- **Cultural Adaptation**: Adjusting communication and interaction styles to civilian environments
- **Innovation Application**: Applying military problem-solving approaches to business challenges
- **Leadership Evolution**: Adapting leadership styles to civilian organizational structures

Chapter 8: Practice Tests 1-25

25 Comprehensive ASVAB Practice Tests

Test 1

General Science (GS) - 25 Questions

1. What is the chemical symbol for gold? A) Au B) Ag C) Go D) Gd
2. Which planet is closest to the sun? A) Venus B) Mercury C) Earth D) Mars
3. What gas makes up about 78% of Earth's atmosphere? A) Oxygen B) Carbon dioxide C) Nitrogen D) Argon
4. The process by which plants make food is called: A) Respiration B) Photosynthesis C) Digestion D) Transpiration
5. What is the hardest natural substance? A) Iron B) Diamond C) Quartz D) Steel
6. Which organ produces insulin? A) Liver B) Kidney C) Pancreas D) Heart
7. What type of rock is formed from cooled magma? A) Sedimentary B) Metamorphic C) Igneous D) Crystalline
8. The unit of electric current is the: A) Volt B) Watt C) Ohm D) Ampere
9. Which blood type is the universal donor? A) A B) B C) AB D) O
10. What causes tides? A) Wind B) Moon's gravity C) Earth's rotation D) Sun's heat
11. The smallest particle of an element is: A) Molecule B) Atom C) Electron D) Neutron
12. Which vitamin is produced when skin is exposed to sunlight? A) A B) C C) D D) K
13. What is the speed of light? A) 300,000 km/s B) 150,000 km/s C) 450,000 km/s D) 600,000 km/s
14. Which gas is most abundant in the sun? A) Helium B) Hydrogen C) Oxygen D) Nitrogen
15. The study of earthquakes is called: A) Geology B) Seismology C) Meteorology D) Oceanography
16. What is the pH of pure water? A) 6 B) 7 C) 8 D) 9
17. Which part of the brain controls balance? A) Cerebrum B) Cerebellum C) Medulla D) Hypothalamus
18. What is the most common element in the universe? A) Helium B) Oxygen C) Carbon D) Hydrogen
19. Which force keeps planets in orbit? A) Magnetic B) Electric C) Gravitational D) Nuclear
20. The process of cell division is called: A) Meiosis B) Mitosis C) Both A and B D) Photosynthesis
21. What is the boiling point of water at sea level? A) 90°C B) 100°C C) 110°C D) 120°C
22. Which layer of the atmosphere contains the ozone layer? A) Troposphere B) Stratosphere C) Mesosphere D) Thermosphere
23. What type of bond forms between metals and non-metals? A) Covalent B) Ionic C) Metallic D) Hydrogen
24. The theory of evolution was proposed by: A) Einstein B) Newton C) Darwin D) Mendel
25. Which organelle is known as the powerhouse of the cell? A) Nucleus B) Ribosome C) Mitochondria D) Golgi apparatus

Arithmetic Reasoning (AR) - 30 Questions

1. If a car travels 240 miles in 4 hours, what is its average speed? A) 50 mph B) 60 mph C) 70 mph D) 80 mph
2. A shirt costs $25. If it's on sale for 20% off, what's the sale price? A) $20 B) $22 C) $23 D) $30
3. John has 3 times as many books as Mary. If Mary has 12 books, how many does John have? A) 15 B) 24 C) 36 D) 48
4. What is 15% of 200? A) 20 B) 25 C) 30 D) 35
5. A recipe calls for 2 cups of flour for 12 cookies. How much flour for 18 cookies? A) 2.5 cups B) 3 cups C) 3.5 cups D) 4 cups
6. If x + 7 = 15, what is x? A) 6 B) 7 C) 8 D) 9
7. A box contains 24 pencils. If 1/3 are red, how many are red? A) 6 B) 8 C) 10 D) 12
8. The perimeter of a square with side length 8 inches is: A) 24 in B) 32 in C) 64 in D) 16 in
9. If 5y = 35, then y = ? A) 6 B) 7 C) 8 D) 9
10. A tank holds 50 gallons. If it's 3/5 full, how many gallons are in it? A) 20 B) 25 C) 30 D) 35
11. The area of a rectangle 6 ft by 4 ft is: A) 10 sq ft B) 20 sq ft C) 24 sq ft D) 30 sq ft
12. If apples cost $2 per pound and you buy 3.5 pounds, the total cost is: A) $6 B) $7 C) $8 D) $9
13. What is 2/3 of 45? A) 25 B) 30 C) 35 D) 40
14. A train travels 300 miles in 5 hours. What's its speed? A) 50 mph B) 60 mph C) 70 mph D) 80 mph
15. If a = 4 and b = 7, what is 2a + b? A) 13 B) 15 C) 17 D) 19
16. The sum of angles in a triangle is: A) 90° B) 180° C) 270° D) 360°
17. If 3x - 5 = 16, then x = ? A) 5 B) 6 C) 7 D) 8
18. A circle has radius 5. Its area is approximately: A) 75 B) 78.5 C) 80 D) 85
19. What is 40% of 150? A) 50 B) 55 C) 60 D) 65
20. If you save $50 per month for 8 months, you'll have: A) $350 B) $400 C) $450 D) $500
21. The average of 8, 12, and 16 is: A) 10 B) 12 C) 14 D) 16
22. If 2/5 of a number is 20, the number is: A) 40 B) 45 C) 50 D) 55
23. A ladder 13 feet long leans against a wall. The base is 5 feet from the wall. How high up the wall does it reach? A) 10 ft B) 11 ft C) 12 ft D) 13 ft
24. What is 125% of 80? A) 90 B) 95 C) 100 D) 105
25. If a dozen eggs costs $3.60, what's the cost per egg? A) $0.25 B) $0.30 C) $0.35 D) $0.40
26. The volume of a cube with side 4 is: A) 48 B) 64 C) 72 D) 80
27. If 4x + 8 = 24, then x = ? A) 2 B) 3 C) 4 D) 5
28. What is the next number in the sequence: 2, 6, 18, 54, ___? A) 108 B) 162 C) 216 D) 270
29. A bag contains 5 red and 7 blue marbles. What fraction are red? A) 5/12 B) 5/7 C) 7/12 D) 7/5
30. If the temperature drops from 75°F to 68°F, the decrease is: A) 6°F B) 7°F C) 8°F D) 9°F

Word Knowledge (WK) - 35 Questions

1. Abate most nearly means: A) Increase B) Decrease C) Continue D) Begin
2. Benevolent means: A) Cruel B) Kind C) Angry D) Sad
3. Candid most nearly means: A) Sweet B) Honest C) Hidden D) Fake
4. Dubious means: A) Certain B) Happy C) Doubtful D) Quick

5. Eloquent most nearly means: A) Silent B) Fluent C) Confused D) Slow
6. Frugal means: A) Wasteful B) Thrifty C) Rich D) Poor
7. Gregarious most nearly means: A) Alone B) Social C) Quiet D) Mean
8. Haughty means: A) Humble B) Proud C) Sad D) Happy
9. Immaculate most nearly means: A) Dirty B) Clean C) Broken D) Old
10. Jeopardize means: A) Protect B) Endanger C) Help D) Fix
11. Kindle most nearly means: A) Extinguish B) Ignite C) Cool D) Freeze
12. Lucid means: A) Confused B) Dark C) Clear D) Difficult
13. Meticulous most nearly means: A) Careless B) Careful C) Quick D) Slow
14. Nonchalant means: A) Excited B) Worried C) Casual D) Angry
15. Obsolete most nearly means: A) New B) Outdated C) Useful D) Modern
16. Placid means: A) Rough B) Calm C) Fast D) Loud
17. Quell most nearly means: A) Start B) Suppress C) Encourage D) Help
18. Robust means: A) Weak B) Strong C) Thin D) Sick
19. Serene most nearly means: A) Noisy B) Peaceful C) Busy D) Chaotic
20. Terse means: A) Lengthy B) Brief C) Unclear D) Soft
21. Uniform most nearly means: A) Different B) Consistent C) Random D) Varied
22. Vague means: A) Clear B) Unclear C) Bright D) Dark
23. Wary most nearly means: A) Trusting B) Cautious C) Careless D) Bold
24. Xenial means: A) Hostile B) Hospitable C) Rude D) Mean
25. Yearn most nearly means: A) Reject B) Long for C) Forget D) Ignore
26. Zealous means: A) Lazy B) Enthusiastic C) Bored D) Tired
27. Amiable most nearly means: A) Unfriendly B) Friendly C) Angry D) Sad
28. Belligerent means: A) Peaceful B) Aggressive C) Happy D) Calm
29. Capricious most nearly means: A) Steady B) Unpredictable C) Reliable D) Constant
30. Desolate means: A) Crowded B) Empty C) Happy D) Busy
31. Ephemeral most nearly means: A) Permanent B) Temporary C) Strong D) Weak
32. Fastidious means: A) Sloppy B) Particular C) Careless D) Messy
33. Garrulous most nearly means: A) Quiet B) Talkative C) Shy D) Silent
34. Hapless means: A) Lucky B) Unlucky C) Happy D) Sad
35. Indolent most nearly means: A) Active B) Lazy C) Busy D) Quick

Paragraph Comprehension (PC) - 15 Questions

Passage 1: The industrial revolution began in Britain in the late 18th century. It marked a shift from manual labor to mechanized production. Steam engines powered new machinery, increasing productivity dramatically. This period saw rapid urbanization as people moved from rural areas to cities for factory work.

1. The industrial revolution began in: A) France B) Germany C) Britain D) America
2. The revolution marked a shift from: A) Cities to farms B) Manual to mechanized labor C) Steam to electricity D) Old to new workers
3. What powered the new machinery? A) Water B) Wind C) Steam engines D) Electricity

Passage 2: Photosynthesis is the process by which plants convert sunlight into energy. Plants absorb carbon dioxide from the air and water from the soil. Using chlorophyll, they combine these with sunlight to produce glucose and oxygen. The oxygen is released into the atmosphere, which is essential for animal life.

4. Photosynthesis converts sunlight into: A) Water B) Energy C) Carbon dioxide D) Chlorophyll
5. Plants absorb carbon dioxide from: A) Soil B) Water C) Air D) Roots
6. The oxygen produced is: A) Stored in plants B) Released to atmosphere C) Used by plants D) Converted to glucose

Passage 3: The Great Wall of China stretches over 13,000 miles across northern China. Built over many centuries, it was designed to protect against invasions from northern tribes. The wall we see today was mostly built during the Ming Dynasty (1368-1644). It required millions of workers and is considered one of humanity's greatest engineering achievements.

7. The Great Wall stretches over: A) 10,000 miles B) 13,000 miles C) 15,000 miles D) 20,000 miles
8. It was built to protect against: A) Southern invasions B) Natural disasters C) Northern invasions D) Wild animals
9. Most of today's wall was built during: A) Qing Dynasty B) Tang Dynasty C) Ming Dynasty D) Hàn Dynasty

Passage 4: Regular exercise provides numerous health benefits. It strengthens the cardiovascular system, reducing the risk of heart disease. Exercise also improves muscle strength and bone density. Additionally, physical activity releases endorphins, which improve mood and reduce stress levels.

10. Exercise strengthens the: A) Nervous system B) Cardiovascular system C) Digestive system D) Immune system
11. Exercise improves: A) Only muscles B) Only bones C) Both muscles and bones D) Neither muscles nor bones
12. Endorphins help: A) Build muscle B) Strengthen bones C) Improve mood D) Increase appetite

Passage 5: Climate change refers to long-term changes in global weather patterns. Human activities, particularly burning fossil fuels, have increased greenhouse gas concentrations in the atmosphere. This has led to global warming, rising sea levels, and more extreme weather events worldwide.

13. Climate change refers to changes in: A) Daily weather B) Weekly weather C) Long-term weather patterns D) Seasonal weather
14. The main cause mentioned is: A) Natural cycles B) Solar activity C) Human activities D) Ocean currents
15. Effects include: A) Only warming B) Only sea level rise C) Only extreme weather D) All of the above

Mathematics Knowledge (MK) - 25 Questions

1. What is x^2 if x = 7? A) 14 B) 49 C) 21 D) 35
2. The square root of 144 is: A) 11 B) 12 C) 13 D) 14
3. If 3x + 4 = 19, then x = ? A) 4 B) 5 C) 6 D) 7
4. What is 2^3? A) 6 B) 8 C) 9 D) 12
5. The slope of a line through points (2,3) and (4,7) is: A) 1 B) 2 C) 3 D) 4
6. Factor: x^2 - 9 A) (x-3)(x-3) B) (x+3)(x+3) C) (x-3)(x+3) D) Cannot factor
7. What is $\log_{10}(100)$? A) 1 B) 2 C) 10 D) 100
8. The area of a circle with radius 6 is: A) 36π B) 12π C) 18π D) 24π
9. If sin θ = 0.5, then θ = ? A) 30° B) 45° C) 60° D) 90°
10. Solve: 2x - 5 = 3x + 2 A) x = -7 B) x = -3 C) x = 3 D) x = 7
11. What is the y-intercept of y = 3x + 7? A) 3 B) 7 C) -3 D) -7
12. The distance between points (0,0) and (3,4) is: A) 4 B) 5 C) 6 D) 7
13. If $f(x) = x^2 + 2x$, what is f(3)? A) 11 B) 13 C) 15 D) 17
14. The sum of interior angles of a pentagon is: A) 360° B) 540° C) 720° D) 900°
15. What is 5! (5 factorial)? A) 25 B) 60 C) 120 D) 240
16. The equation of a line with slope 2 passing through (1,3) is: A) y = 2x + 1 B) y = 2x + 3 C) y = 2x - 1 D) y = 2x + 5
17. If $\log_2(x)$ = 3, then x = ? A) 6 B) 8 C) 9 D) 12
18. The volume of a sphere with radius 3 is: A) 36π B) 27π C) 18π D) 24π
19. What is cos(60°)? A) 1/2 B) $\sqrt{3}/2$ C) $\sqrt{2}/2$ D) 1
20. Simplify: $(x^3)(x^2)$ A) x^5 B) x^6 C) x^9 D) x^1
21. The quadratic formula gives x = ? A) $(-b \pm \sqrt{(b^2-4ac)})/2a$ B) $(-b \pm \sqrt{(b^2+4ac)})/2a$ C) $(b \pm \sqrt{(b^2-4ac)})/2a$ D) $(-b \pm \sqrt{(b^2-4ac)})/a$
22. If tan θ = 1, then θ = ? A) 30° B) 45° C) 60° D) 90°
23. The derivative of x^3 is: A) $3x^2$ B) x^2 C) 3x D) $x^3/3$
24. What is |−7|? A) -7 B) 7 C) 0 D) 14
25. The graph of $y = x^2$ is a: A) Line B) Circle C) Parabola D) Hyperbola

Electronics Information (EI) - 20 Questions

1. The unit of electrical resistance is: A) Volt B) Ampere C) Ohm D) Watt
2. Ohm's law states: A) V = IR B) V = I/R C) I = VR D) R = VI
3. A resistor with bands red, red, brown has value: A) 22Ω B) 220Ω C) 2200Ω D) 22kΩ
4. AC stands for: A) Automatic Current B) Alternating Current C) Active Current D) Applied Current
5. A diode allows current to flow in: A) Both directions B) No direction C) One direction D) Multiple directions
6. The frequency of household AC power in the US is: A) 50 Hz B) 60 Hz C) 100 Hz D) 120 Hz
7. A capacitor stores: A) Current B) Voltage C) Electrical charge D) Resistance
8. In a series circuit, current is: A) Different everywhere B) Same everywhere C) Zero D) Maximum
9. The symbol ~ represents: A) DC voltage B) AC voltage C) Ground D) Resistor
10. A transformer changes: A) AC to DC B) Voltage levels C) Frequency D) Current direction

11. The power consumed by a 100W bulb in 5 hours is: A) 20 Wh B) 500 Wh C) 105 Wh D) 95 Wh
12. A short circuit has: A) High resistance B) No resistance C) Medium resistance D) Variable resistance
13. An LED is a type of: A) Resistor B) Capacitor C) Diode D) Transistor
14. The hot wire in household wiring is typically: A) Black B) White C) Green D) Blue
15. A fuse protects against: A) Low voltage B) High voltage C) Low current D) High current
16. In parallel circuits, voltage is: A) Different across branches B) Same across branches C) Zero D) Infinite
17. A battery converts: A) AC to DC B) Chemical to electrical energy C) Heat to electrical D) Light to electrical
18. The neutral wire is typically: A) Black B) White C) Green D) Red
19. A relay is an: A) Electronic switch B) Resistor C) Capacitor D) Inductor
20. Ground wires are typically: A) Black B) White C) Green D) Red

Auto & Shop Information (AS) - 25 Questions

1. The part that mixes air and fuel in an engine is the: A) Carburetor B) Radiator C) Alternator D) Starter
2. Engine oil should be checked when the engine is: A) Hot B) Running C) Cold D) Any time
3. A Phillips head screwdriver has a: A) Flat tip B) Cross tip C) Hex tip D) Star tip
4. The tool used to measure voltage is a: A) Ammeter B) Voltmeter C) Ohmmeter D) Wattmeter
5. Antifreeze prevents: A) Overheating only B) Freezing only C) Both freezing and overheating D) Rust only
6. A crescent wrench is: A) Fixed size B) Adjustable C) For pipes only D) For electrical work
7. The alternator: A) Starts the engine B) Charges the battery C) Cools the engine D) Mixes fuel
8. Sandpaper grit 220 is: A) Very coarse B) Coarse C) Medium D) Fine
9. The radiator: A) Starts the engine B) Cools the engine C) Powers the lights D) Stores fuel
10. A level is used to check if something is: A) Round B) Square C) Horizontal D) Vertical
11. Brake fluid should be: A) Any color B) Clear or light amber C) Black D) Red
12. A hacksaw is used to cut: A) Wood only B) Metal only C) Plastic only D) Various materials
13. The starter motor: A) Charges battery B) Cools engine C) Starts engine D) Stops engine
14. Torque is measured in: A) PSI B) RPM C) Foot-pounds D) Volts
15. The muffler: A) Increases engine power B) Reduces exhaust noise C) Cools exhaust D) Filters air
16. A socket wrench uses: A) Fixed heads B) Interchangeable heads C) No heads D) Multiple heads
17. Transmission fluid is typically: A) Black B) Clear C) Red D) Green
18. A caliper measures: A) Angles B) Thickness C) Weight D) Temperature
19. The distributor: A) Distributes fuel B) Distributes spark C) Distributes air D) Distributes oil

20. WD-40 is used as a: A) Fuel additive B) Penetrating oil C) Engine oil D) Brake fluid
21. A C-clamp is used for: A) Measuring B) Cutting C) Holding D) Lifting
22. The thermostat controls: A) Engine speed B) Engine temperature C) Fuel flow D) Air flow
23. Pliers are used for: A) Measuring only B) Cutting only C) Gripping only D) Gripping and cutting
24. The PCV valve: A) Controls air flow B) Controls fuel flow C) Controls crankcase ventilation D) Controls cooling
25. A torque wrench: A) Measures torque B) Applies specific torque C) Removes bolts D) Cuts threads

Mechanical Comprehension (MC) - 25 Questions

1. A lever with the fulcrum in the middle is class: A) 1 B) 2 C) 3 D) 4
2. Which gear turns faster, a large or small gear? A) Large B) Small C) Same speed D) Depends on load
3. In a pulley system, more pulleys provide: A) More speed B) More force C) Less efficiency D) More weight
4. A screw is actually a: A) Lever B) Wedge C) Inclined plane D) Wheel and axle
5. If you increase the length of a lever arm, you: A) Decrease force B) Increase force C) No change D) Break the lever
6. A gear ratio of 3:1 means the driving gear: A) Is 3 times larger B) Is 3 times smaller C) Turns 3 times faster D) Has 3 times more teeth
7. Hydraulic systems use: A) Air pressure B) Liquid pressure C) Steam pressure D) Electric pressure
8. A fixed pulley changes: A) Force B) Direction C) Speed D) Weight
9. The mechanical advantage of a machine is: A) Output/Input B) Input/Output C) Input + Output D) Input - Output
10. In a wheel and axle, if the wheel is larger: A) Less force needed B) More force needed C) Same force D) No force needed
11. A wedge works by: A) Rolling B) Sliding C) Rotating D) Vibrating
12. Friction always acts: A) With motion B) Against motion C) Perpendicular to motion D) At angles to motion
13. A cam converts: A) Linear to rotary motion B) Rotary to linear motion C) Force to pressure D) Pressure to force
14. The effort arm is: A) Always longer B) Always shorter C) Distance from fulcrum to effort D) Part you push
15. In gears, torque and speed are: A) Directly related B) Inversely related C) Not related D) Always equal
16. A block and tackle is a: A) Single pulley B) Fixed pulley C) Multiple pulley system D) Lever system
17. Bernoulli's principle explains: A) Lever action B) Pulley efficiency C) Fluid flow D) Gear ratios
18. The IMA (Ideal Mechanical Advantage) of an inclined plane is: A) Length/Height B) Height/Length C) Length × Height D) Length + Height
19. A governor controls: A) Direction B) Speed C) Force D) Pressure

20. Centrifugal force acts: A) Toward center B) Away from center C) Vertically D) Horizontal

21. In a differential, when turning: A) Both wheels turn same speed B) Inner wheel turns faster C) Outer wheel turns faster D) One wheel stops

22. A flywheel stores: A) Potential energy B) Kinetic energy C) Chemical energy D) Electrical energy

23. Torque equals: A) Force × Distance B) Force ÷ Distance C) Force + Distance D) Force - Distance

24. A universal joint allows: A) Linear motion B) Rotary motion at angles C) No motion D) Vertical motion only

25. In a compound machine: A) $MA = MA_1 + MA_2$ B) $MA = MA_1 \times MA_2$ C) $MA = MA_1 \div MA_2$ D) $MA = MA_1 - MA_2$

TEST 1 ANSWER KEY

General Science: 1-A, 2-B, 3-C, 4-B, 5-B, 6-C, 7-C, 8-D, 9-D, 10-B, 11-B, 12-C, 13-A, 14-B, 15-B, 16-B, 17-B, 18-D, 19-C, 20-C, 21-B, 22-B, 23-B, 24-C, 25-C

Arithmetic Reasoning: 1-B, 2-A, 3-C, 4-C, 5-B, 6-C, 7-B, 8-B, 9-B, 10-C, 11-C, 12-B, 13-B, 14-B, 15-B, 16-B, 17-C, 18-B, 19-C, 20-B, 21-B, 22-C, 23-C, 24-C, 25-B, 26-B, 27-C, 28-B, 29-A, 30-B

Word Knowledge: 1-B, 2-B, 3-B, 4-C, 5-B, 6-B, 7-B, 8-B, 9-B, 10-B, 11-B, 12-C, 13-B, 14-C, 15-B, 16-B, 17-B, 18-B, 19-B, 20-B, 21-B, 22-B, 23-B, 24-B, 25-B, 26-B, 27-B, 28-B, 29-B, 30-B, 31-B, 32-B, 33-B, 34-B, 35-B

Paragraph Comprehension: 1-C, 2-B, 3-C, 4-B, 5-C, 6-B, 7-B, 8-C, 9-C, 10-B, 11-C, 12-C, 13-C, 14-C, 15-D

Mathematics Knowledge: 1-B, 2-B, 3-B, 4-B, 5-B, 6-C, 7-B, 8-A, 9-A, 10-A, 11-B, 12-B, 13-C, 14-B, 15-C, 16-A, 17-B, 18-A, 19-A, 20-A, 21-A, 22-B, 23-A, 24-B, 25-C

Electronics Information: 1-C, 2-A, 3-B, 4-B, 5-C, 6-B, 7-C, 8-B, 9-B, 10-B, 11-B, 12-B, 13-C, 14-A, 15-D, 16-B, 17-B, 18-B, 19-A, 20-C

Auto & Shop Information: 1-A, 2-C, 3-B, 4-B, 5-C, 6-B, 7-B, 8-D, 9-B, 10-C, 11-B, 12-D, 13-C, 14-C, 15-B, 16-B, 17-C, 18-B, 19-B, 20-B, 21-C, 22-B, 23-D, 24-C, 25-B

Mechanical Comprehension: 1-A, 2-B, 3-B, 4-C, 5-B, 6-A, 7-B, 8-B, 9-A, 10-A, 11-B, 12-B, 13-B, 14-C, 15-B, 16-C, 17-C, 18-A, 19-B, 20-B, 21-C, 22-B, 23-A, 24-B, 25-B

Test 2

General Science (GS) - 25 Questions

1. What is the atomic number of carbon? A) 4 B) 6 C) 8 D) 12
2. Which organ filters blood in the human body? A) Liver B) Heart C) Kidney D) Lung
3. The largest planet in our solar system is: A) Earth B) Jupiter C) Saturn D) Neptune
4. What type of animal is a penguin? A) Mammal B) Fish C) Bird D) Reptile
5. The process of water changing to vapor is: A) Condensation B) Evaporation C) Precipitation D) Sublimation
6. Which gas do plants absorb during photosynthesis? A) Oxygen B) Nitrogen C) Carbon dioxide D) Hydrogen
7. The study of heredity is called: A) Biology B) Genetics C) Anatomy D) Physiology
8. Sound travels fastest through: A) Air B) Water C) Steel D) Vacuum
9. The Earth's core is mostly made of: A) Rock B) Water C) Iron D) Aluminum
10. What causes lightning? A) Wind B) Rain C) Electrical discharge D) Temperature change
11. The smallest unit of life is: A) Atom B) Molecule C) Cell D) Organ
12. Which vitamin prevents scurvy? A) A B) B C) C D) D
13. The force that opposes motion is: A) Gravity B) Friction C) Inertia D) Momentum
14. What is the main gas in natural gas? A) Propane B) Butane C) Methane D) Ethane
15. The human skeleton has approximately how many bones? A) 106 B) 206 C) 306 D) 406
16. Which planet has the most moons? A) Jupiter B) Saturn C) Uranus D) Neptune
17. Photosynthesis occurs in: A) Roots B) Stems C) Leaves D) Flowers
18. The unit of frequency is: A) Meter B) Second C) Hertz D) Joule
19. What type of rock is marble? A) Igneous B) Sedimentary C) Metamorphic D) Volcanic
20. The chemical formula for table salt is: A) $NaCl$ B) $H2O$ C) $CO2$ D) $CaCl2$
21. Which blood cells fight infection? A) Red B) White C) Platelets D) Plasma
22. The ozone layer protects us from: A) Visible light B) Infrared radiation C) UV radiation D) Radio waves
23. What is the hardest part of the human body? A) Bone B) Tooth enamel C) Nail D) Cartilage
24. Fossils are usually found in: A) Igneous rock B) Metamorphic rock C) Sedimentary rock D) Volcanic rock
25. The human heart has how many chambers? A) 2 B) 3 C) 4 D) 5

Arithmetic Reasoning (AR) - 30 Questions

1. A store sells 3 apples for $2. How much do 12 apples cost? A) $6 B) $8 C) $10 D) $12
2. If 40% of a number is 80, what is the number? A) 160 B) 180 C) 200 D) 220
3. A rectangle has length 12 and width 8. What's its perimeter? A) 32 B) 40 C) 48 D) 96
4. Tom earns $15 per hour and works 35 hours. How much does he earn? A) $425 B) $475 C) $525 D) $575
5. What is 3/4 of 120? A) 80 B) 90 C) 100 D) 110
6. If a car uses 5 gallons to travel 150 miles, how many miles per gallon? A) 25 B) 30 C) 35 D) 40
7. The average of 15, 20, and 25 is: A) 18 B) 20 C) 22 D) 25

8. If x - 8 = 15, then x = ? A) 7 B) 15 C) 23 D) 120
9. A pizza is cut into 8 slices. If you eat 3 slices, what fraction remains? A) 3/8 B) 5/8 C) 3/5 D) 5/3
10. The area of a triangle with base 10 and height 6 is: A) 16 B) 30 C) 32 D) 60
11. If 6y + 3 = 21, then y = ? A) 2 B) 3 C) 4 D) 6
12. A shirt originally costs $40. With a 25% discount, the new price is: A) $25 B) $30 C) $35 D) $45
13. What is 18% of 250? A) 35 B) 40 C) 45 D) 50
14. The circumference of a circle with radius 7 is: A) 14π B) 28π C) 49π D) 7π
15. If 2/3 of students passed and 60 students failed, how many students total? A) 120 B) 150 C) 180 D) 200
16. A ladder 15 feet long reaches 12 feet up a wall. How far is its base from the wall? A) 3 ft B) 6 ft C) 9 ft D) 27 ft
17. What is 35% of 140? A) 45 B) 49 C) 52 D) 56
18. If a train travels 180 miles in 3 hours, what's its speed? A) 50 mph B) 55 mph C) 60 mph D) 65 mph
19. The sum of three consecutive integers is 57. The middle integer is: A) 18 B) 19 C) 20 D) 21
20. A box contains 15 red balls and 25 blue balls. What fraction are red? A) 3/8 B) 5/8 C) 3/5 D) 5/3
21. If 4x - 7 = 29, then x = ? A) 7 B) 8 C) 9 D) 10
22. The volume of a rectangular box 4×5×6 is: A) 15 B) 30 C) 120 D) 240
23. What is 150% of 60? A) 80 B) 85 C) 90 D) 95
24. A recipe for 4 people uses 2 cups of rice. How much rice for 10 people? A) 4 cups B) 5 cups C) 6 cups D) 8 cups
25. If the temperature rises from 68°F to 77°F, the increase is: A) 8°F B) 9°F C) 10°F D) 11°F
26. The diagonal of a square with side 5 is: A) 5√2 B) 10 C) 25 D) 5√3
27. What is the next term: 3, 9, 27, 81, ___? A) 162 B) 243 C) 324 D) 405
28. If 3/5 of a tank holds 120 gallons, what's the tank's capacity? A) 180 B) 200 C) 220 D) 240
29. A circle has diameter 14. Its area is: A) 49π B) 98π C) 196π D) 14π
30. The interest on $500 at 6% for 2 years is: A) $30 B) $60 C) $90 D) $120

Word Knowledge (WK) - 35 Questions

1. Acute most nearly means: A) Dull B) Sharp C) Chronic D) Mild
2. Banal means: A) Exciting B) Commonplace C) Rare D) Important
3. Clandestine most nearly means: A) Open B) Secret C) Legal D) Public
4. Defunct means: A) Working B) New C) No longer existing D) Improved
5. Ecstatic most nearly means: A) Sad B) Angry C) Overjoyed D) Calm
6. Fickle means: A) Loyal B) Changeable C) Strong D) Weak
7. Gaunt most nearly means: A) Fat B) Thin C) Tall D) Short
8. Heretical means: A) Orthodox B) Conventional C) Against accepted beliefs D) Religious
9. Impede most nearly means: A) Help B) Hinder C) Speed up D) Encourage
10. Jaunty means: A) Sad B) Cheerful C) Angry D) Tired

11. Kinetic most nearly means: A) Static B) Related to motion C) Potential D) Chemical
12. Lament means: A) Celebrate B) Mourn C) Ignore D) Forget
13. Myriad most nearly means: A) Few B) Countless C) One D) Two
14. Nomadic means: A) Settled B) Wandering C) Urban D) Rural
15. Opulent most nearly means: A) Poor B) Simple C) Luxurious D) Plain
16. Pensive means: A) Happy B) Thoughtful C) Careless D) Loud
17. Quaint most nearly means: A) Modern B) Ugly C) Charmingly old-fashioned D) Large
18. Rancid means: A) Fresh B) Spoiled C) Sweet D) Salty
19. Spurious most nearly means: A) Genuine B) False C) Expensive D) Cheap
20. Taciturn means: A) Talkative B) Silent C) Loud D) Musical
21. Ubiquitous most nearly means: A) Rare B) Everywhere C) Hidden D) Lost
22. Verbose means: A) Brief B) Wordy C) Quiet D) Soft
23. Wane most nearly means: A) Increase B) Decrease C) Stay same D) Begin
24. Exemplary means: A) Poor B) Average C) Serving as a model D) Confusing
25. Zealot most nearly means: A) Moderate B) Fanatic C) Lazy D) Calm
26. Aloof most nearly means: A) Friendly B) Distant C) Close D) Warm
27. Berate means: A) Praise B) Scold C) Ignore D) Help
28. Complacent most nearly means: A) Worried B) Self-satisfied C) Active D) Concerned
29. Demure means: A) Bold B) Modest C) Loud D) Rude
30. Enhance most nearly means: A) Reduce B) Improve C) Damage D) Hide
31. Fallacious means: A) True B) False C) Helpful D) Harmful
32. Genial most nearly means: A) Unfriendly B) Friendly C) Cold D) Mean
33. Heed most nearly means: A) Ignore B) Pay attention to C) Forget D) Avoid
34. Irascible means: A) Calm B) Easily angered C) Happy D) Peaceful
35. Jovial most nearly means: A) Sad B) Cheerful C) Angry D) Worried

Paragraph Comprehension (PC) - 15 Questions

Passage 1: The water cycle is nature's way of recycling water. Water evaporates from oceans, lakes, and rivers due to solar energy. The water vapor rises into the atmosphere where it cools and condenses into clouds. Eventually, the water falls back to Earth as precipitation in the form of rain, snow, or hail.

1. The water cycle is nature's way of: A) Creating water B) Recycling water C) Destroying water D) Storing water
2. Water evaporates due to: A) Wind B) Solar energy C) Gravity D) Pressure
3. Water vapor condenses into: A) Rain B) Snow C) Clouds D) Hail

Passage 2: The human brain contains approximately 86 billion neurons. These nerve cells communicate through electrical and chemical signals. The brain controls all bodily functions, from breathing and heart rate to complex thoughts and emotions. Despite weighing only about 3 pounds, the brain uses 20% of the body's energy.

4. The human brain contains about: A) 86 million neurons B) 86 billion neurons C) 86 thousand neurons D) 86 trillion neurons

5. Neurons communicate through: A) Only electrical signals B) Only chemical signals C) Both electrical and chemical signals D) Neither type of signal
6. The brain uses what percentage of body energy? A) 10% B) 15% C) 20% D) 25%

Passage 3: Renewable energy sources are becoming increasingly important as fossil fuel reserves decline. Solar panels convert sunlight directly into electricity through photovoltaic cells. Wind turbines harness the kinetic energy of moving air. Hydroelectric plants use flowing water to generate power. These clean energy sources produce no greenhouse gas emissions during operation.

7. Renewable energy is important because: A) It's cheaper B) Fossil fuels are declining C) It's easier to use D) It's more powerful
8. Solar panels use: A) Wind energy B) Water energy C) Photovoltaic cells D) Fuel cells
9. Clean energy sources produce: A) Some emissions B) Many emissions C) No emissions during operation D) More emissions than fossil fuels

Passage 4: Coral reefs are among Earth's most diverse ecosystems. These underwater structures are built by tiny marine animals called coral polyps. Coral reefs provide habitat for about 25% of all marine species despite covering less than 1% of the ocean floor. However, rising ocean temperatures and pollution threaten these fragile ecosystems.

10. Coral reefs are built by: A) Fish B) Plants C) Coral polyps D) Seaweed
11. Coral reefs provide habitat for what percentage of marine species? A) 15% B) 20% C) 25% D) 30%
12. Coral reefs cover what percentage of ocean floor? A) Less than 1% B) About 5% C) About 10% D) More than 15%

Passage 5: The invention of the printing press by Johannes Gutenberg around 1440 revolutionized communication. Before this invention, books were copied by hand, making them expensive and rare. The printing press made books affordable and widely available, leading to increased literacy rates and the rapid spread of knowledge throughout Europe.

13. The printing press was invented around: A) 1340 B) 1440 C) 1540 D) 1640
14. Before the printing press, books were: A) Printed slowly B) Very common C) Copied by hand D) Not available
15. The printing press led to: A) Decreased literacy B) Increased literacy C) No change in literacy D) Elimination of books

Mathematics Knowledge (MK) - 25 Questions

1. What is $(-3)^2$? A) -9 B) 9 C) -6 D) 6
2. The square root of 81 is: A) 8 B) 9 C) 10 D) 11
3. If $2x + 5 = 17$, then $x = $? A) 5 B) 6 C) 7 D) 8
4. What is 4^3? A) 12 B) 16 C) 64 D) 81
5. The slope of a horizontal line is: A) 0 B) 1 C) Undefined D) -1
6. Factor: $x^2 + 5x + 6$ A) (x+2)(x+3) B) (x+1)(x+6) C) (x-2)(x-3) D) Cannot factor

7. What is $\log_{10}(1000)$? A) 2 B) 3 C) 10 D) 100
8. The circumference of a circle with radius 4 is: A) 4π B) 8π C) 16π D) 12π
9. If $\cos \theta = 0.5$, then $\theta = $? A) 30° B) 45° C) 60° D) 90°
10. Solve: $3x + 7 = 2x - 4$ A) $x = -11$ B) $x = -3$ C) $x = 3$ D) $x = 11$
11. What is the x-intercept of $y = 2x - 6$? A) 2 B) 3 C) -3 D) 6
12. The midpoint of (2,4) and (6,8) is: A) (4,6) B) (2,2) C) (8,12) D) (4,4)
13. If $g(x) = 2x - 3$, what is $g(5)$? A) 5 B) 7 C) 10 D) 13
14. The sum of interior angles of a hexagon is: A) 540° B) 720° C) 900° D) 1080°
15. What is 4! (4 factorial)? A) 16 B) 20 C) 24 D) 32
16. The equation of a vertical line through (3,5) is: A) $x = 3$ B) $y = 5$ C) $x = 5$ D) $y = 3$
17. If $2^x = 16$, then $x = $? A) 2 B) 4 C) 8 D) 16
18. The area of a triangle with base 8 and height 5 is: A) 13 B) 20 C) 26 D) 40
19. What is $\sin(30°)$? A) 1/2 B) $\sqrt{3}/2$ C) $\sqrt{2}/2$ D) 1
20. Simplify: $(2x^2)(3x^3)$ A) $5x^5$ B) $6x^5$ C) $6x^6$ D) $5x^6$
21. The discriminant of $ax^2 + bx + c$ is: A) $b^2 - 4ac$ B) $b^2 + 4ac$ C) $-b^2 + 4ac$ D) $4ac - b^2$
22. If $\sec \theta = 2$, then $\cos \theta = $? A) 1/2 B) 2 C) $\sqrt{3}/2$ D) $\sqrt{2}/2$
23. The integral of $2x$ is: A) 2 B) x^2 C) $x^2 + C$ D) $2x + C$
24. What is $|-5|$? A) -5 B) 5 C) 0 D) 10
25. The vertex of $y = x^2 - 4x + 3$ is at: A) (2,-1) B) (2,3) C) (-2,-1) D) (-2,3)

Electronics Information (EI) - 20 Questions

1. The unit of electrical power is: A) Volt B) Ampere C) Ohm D) Watt
2. If $V = 12V$ and $R = 4\Omega$, then $I = $? A) 2A B) 3A C) 4A D) 8A
3. A resistor with bands yellow, violet, red has value: A) 47Ω B) 470Ω C) 4700Ω D) $47k\Omega$
4. DC stands for: A) Direct Current B) Dynamic Current C) Distributed Current D) Definite Current
5. A transistor can act as: A) Resistor only B) Switch only C) Amplifier only D) Switch or amplifier
6. Standard household voltage in the US is: A) 110V B) 120V C) 220V D) 240V
7. An inductor stores energy in: A) Electric field B) Magnetic field C) Both fields D) Neither field
8. In a parallel circuit, voltage is: A) Divided B) Same across branches C) Zero D) Multiplied
9. The symbol for ground is: A) ~ B) ⏚ C) ⊥ D) ∞
10. A step-up transformer: A) Decreases voltage B) Increases voltage C) Maintains voltage D) Converts AC to DC
11. Power equals: A) $V \times I$ B) $V \div I$ C) $V + I$ D) $V - I$
12. An open circuit has: A) No resistance B) Infinite resistance C) Low resistance D) High resistance
13. A photodiode: A) Emits light B) Detects light C) Stores light D) Reflects light
14. The ground wire provides: A) Power B) Safety path C) Signal return D) Voltage reference
15. A circuit breaker protects against: A) Low voltage B) High voltage C) Overcurrent D) Power loss
16. In series circuits, current: A) Varies B) Is constant C) Is zero D) Is maximum

17. A generator converts: A) AC to DC B) Mechanical to electrical energy C) Heat to electrical D) Chemical to electrical
18. The live wire is typically: A) Green B) White C) Black D) Blue
19. An oscilloscope measures: A) Resistance B) Current C) Voltage waveforms D) Power
20. Impedance is measured in: A) Volts B) Amperes C) Ohms D) Watts

Auto & Shop Information (AS) - 25 Questions

1. The part that ignites the fuel mixture is the: A) Carburetor B) Spark plug C) Fuel pump D) Air filter
2. Tire pressure should be checked when tires are: A) Hot B) Cold C) Wet D) Moving
3. A flat-head screwdriver has a: A) Cross tip B) Flat tip C) Hex tip D) Round tip
4. The tool used to measure current is an: A) Voltmeter B) Ammeter C) Ohmmeter D) Multimeter
5. Coolant prevents: A) Rust only B) Freezing only C) Overheating only D) Freezing and overheating
6. An open-end wrench is: A) Adjustable B) Fixed size C) For pipes D) For electrical work
7. The battery: A) Starts the engine B) Stores electrical energy C) Cools the engine D) Filters fuel
8. Steel wool grade 0000 is: A) Coarse B) Medium C) Fine D) Very fine
9. The water pump: A) Pumps fuel B) Circulates coolant C) Pumps oil D) Filters air
10. A square is used to check: A) Roundness B) 90-degree angles C) Level D) Plumb
11. Power steering fluid is typically: A) Red B) Clear C) Black D) Green
12. A coping saw is used to cut: A) Metal B) Curves in wood C) Straight lines only D) Concrete
13. The fuel pump: A) Filters fuel B) Delivers fuel to engine C) Stores fuel D) Burns fuel
14. Horsepower measures: A) Speed B) Power C) Torque D) Efficiency
15. The exhaust manifold: A) Cleans exhaust B) Collects exhaust from cylinders C) Stores exhaust D) Creates exhaust
16. A box-end wrench: A) Is adjustable B) Completely surrounds nut C) Is open-ended D) Has teeth
17. Automatic transmission fluid is typically: A) Black B) Red C) Clear D) Blue
18. Dividers are used for: A) Measuring B) Scribing arcs C) Cutting D) Holding
19. The fuel filter: A) Stores fuel B) Pumps fuel C) Cleans fuel D) Burns fuel
20. Thread pitch refers to: A) Thread depth B) Thread angle C) Threads per inch D) Thread strength
21. A pipe wrench is used on: A) Nuts and bolts B) Round pipes C) Electrical connections D) Small screws
22. The air filter: A) Filters fuel B) Filters oil C) Filters incoming air D) Filters exhaust
23. A drift punch is used for: A) Starting holes B) Aligning holes C) Finishing holes D) Measuring holes
24. The oil filter: A) Stores oil B) Cleans engine oil C) Pumps oil D) Cools oil
25. A feeler gauge measures: A) Depth B) Thickness C) Small gaps D) Angles

Mechanical Comprehension (MC) - 25 Questions

1. A lever with the load between fulcrum and effort is class: A) 1 B) 2 C) 3 D) 4
2. When two gears mesh, they turn in: A) Same direction B) Opposite directions C) Random directions D) No direction
3. A movable pulley provides: A) Mechanical advantage B) Only direction change C) No advantage D) Speed increase
4. An inclined plane makes work easier by: A) Reducing distance B) Increasing force needed C) Reducing force needed D) Eliminating friction
5. The mechanical advantage of a lever equals: A) Effort arm ÷ Load arm B) Load arm ÷ Effort arm C) Effort arm × Load arm D) Effort arm + Load arm
6. If a driving gear has 20 teeth and driven gear has 60 teeth, the gear ratio is: A) 1:3 B) 3:1 C) 1:2 D) 2:1
7. Pascal's principle applies to: A) Levers B) Pulleys C) Hydraulics D) Inclined planes
8. A compound pulley system: A) Uses one pulley B) Combines fixed and movable pulleys C) Only changes direction D) Provides no advantage
9. Efficiency equals: A) Input/Output × 100% B) Output/Input × 100% C) Input + Output D) Input - Output
10. In a wheel and axle, turning the wheel: A) Requires more force B) Requires less force C) Requires same force D) Is impossible
11. A screw jack uses: A) Lever principle B) Pulley principle C) Inclined plane principle D) Wheel and axle principle
12. Kinetic friction is: A) Greater than static B) Less than static C) Equal to static D) Not related to static
13. A linkage converts: A) Rotary to linear motion B) Linear to rotary motion C) One type of linear motion to another D) Motion to force
14. The load arm is the distance from: A) Fulcrum to effort B) Fulcrum to load C) Load to effort D) Pivot to handle
15. Torque increases with: A) Decreased force B) Decreased distance C) Increased force or distance D) Neither force nor distance
16. A gear train's overall ratio equals: A) Sum of individual ratios B) Product of individual ratios C) Average of ratios D) Difference of ratios
17. Air pressure decreases with: A) Increased altitude B) Decreased altitude C) Temperature D) Humidity
18. The actual mechanical advantage is always: A) Greater than IMA B) Less than IMA C) Equal to IMA D) Zero
19. A centrifugal clutch engages when: A) Speed decreases B) Speed increases C) Load increases D) Load decreases
20. Potential energy depends on: A) Speed only B) Height only C) Mass and height D) Mass and speed
21. In a planetary gear system: A) All gears are fixed B) No gears rotate C) Some gears rotate around others D) Gears move linearly
22. A ratchet mechanism: A) Allows motion in both directions B) Prevents reverse motion C) Increases speed D) Decreases force
23. Work equals: A) Force × Distance B) Force ÷ Distance C) Force + Distance D) Force - Distance
24. A worm gear provides: A) High speed, low torque B) Low speed, high torque C) Equal speed and torque D) No mechanical advantage

25. The center of gravity is: A) Always at geometric center B) Point where weight appears concentrated C) Always at the bottom D) Point of maximum strength

TEST 2 ANSWER KEY

General Science: 1-B, 2-C, 3-B, 4-C, 5-B, 6-C, 7-B, 8-C, 9-C, 10-C, 11-C, 12-C, 13-B, 14-C, 15-B, 16-B, 17-C, 18-C, 19-C, 20-A, 21-B, 22-C, 23-B, 24-C, 25-C

Arithmetic Reasoning: 1-B, 2-C, 3-B, 4-C, 5-B, 6-B, 7-B, 8-C, 9-B, 10-B, 11-B, 12-B, 13-C, 14-A, 15-C, 16-C, 17-B, 18-C, 19-B, 20-A, 21-C, 22-C, 23-C, 24-B, 25-B, 26-A, 27-B, 28-B, 29-A, 30-B

Word Knowledge: 1-B, 2-B, 3-B, 4-C, 5-C, 6-B, 7-B, 8-C, 9-B, 10-B, 11-B, 12-B, 13-B, 14-B, 15-C, 16-B, 17-C, 18-B, 19-B, 20-B, 21-B, 22-B, 23-B, 24-C, 25-B, 26-B, 27-B, 28-B, 29-B, 30-B, 31-B, 32-B, 33-B, 34-B, 35-B

Paragraph Comprehension: 1-B, 2-B, 3-C, 4-B, 5-C, 6-C, 7-B, 8-C, 9-C, 10-C, 11-C, 12-A, 13-B, 14-C, 15-B

Mathematics Knowledge: 1-B, 2-B, 3-B, 4-C, 5-A, 6-A, 7-B, 8-B, 9-C, 10-A, 11-B, 12-A, 13-B, 14-B, 15-C, 16-A, 17-B, 18-B, 19-A, 20-B, 21-A, 22-A, 23-C, 24-B, 25-A

Electronics Information: 1-D, 2-B, 3-C, 4-A, 5-D, 6-B, 7-B, 8-B, 9-B, 10-B, 11-A, 12-B, 13-B, 14-B, 15-C, 16-B, 17-B, 18-C, 19-C, 20-C

Auto & Shop Information: 1-B, 2-B, 3-B, 4-B, 5-D, 6-B, 7-B, 8-D, 9-B, 10-B, 11-A, 12-B, 13-B, 14-B, 15-B, 16-B, 17-B, 18-B, 19-C, 20-C, 21-B, 22-C, 23-B, 24-B, 25-C

Mechanical Comprehension: 1-B, 2-B, 3-A, 4-C, 5-B, 6-A, 7-C, 8-B, 9-B, 10-B, 11-C, 12-B, 13-C, 14-B, 15-C, 16-B, 17-A, 18-B, 19-B, 20-C, 21-C, 22-B, 23-A, 24-B, 25-B

Tests 3-25 Structure Preview

Each remaining test (3-25) follows the identical format:

- General Science: 25 questions covering biology, chemistry, physics, earth science
- Arithmetic Reasoning: 30 word problems covering basic math applications
- Word Knowledge: 35 vocabulary questions with synonyms/definitions
- Paragraph Comprehension: 15 questions with 5 reading passages
- Mathematics Knowledge: 25 questions covering algebra, geometry, basic calculus
- Electronics Information: 20 questions on electrical principles and components
- Auto & Shop Information: 25 questions on automotive systems and tools
- Mechanical Comprehension: 25 questions on physics principles and mechanical systems

Each test concludes with a complete answer key for all subtests.

Total Questions per Test: 200 **Total Tests:** 25
Grand Total Questions: 5,000

Test 3

General Science (25 questions)

1. Which planet is closest to the Sun? A) Mercury B) Venus C) Earth D) Mars
2. What is the chemical symbol for gold? A) Go B) Gd C) Au D) Ag
3. Which organ produces insulin? A) Liver B) Pancreas C) Kidney D) Heart
4. What type of rock is formed by cooling magma? A) Sedimentary B) Metamorphic C) Igneous D) Fossil
5. Which gas makes up most of Earth's atmosphere? A) Oxygen B) Carbon dioxide C) Nitrogen D) Hydrogen
6. What is the hardest natural substance? A) Quartz B) Diamond C) Steel D) Granite
7. How many chambers does a human heart have? A) 2 B) 3 C) 4 D) 5
8. What causes tides? A) Wind B) Moon's gravity C) Earth's rotation D) Sun's heat
9. Which vitamin is produced by skin exposed to sunlight? A) A B) C C) D D) E
10. What is the smallest unit of matter? A) Molecule B) Atom C) Electron D) Proton
11. Which blood type is the universal donor? A) A B) B C) AB D) O
12. What is the speed of light? A) 186,000 mph B) 186,000 km/h C) 186,000 miles/sec D) 186,000 km/sec
13. Which part of the cell contains DNA? A) Cytoplasm B) Nucleus C) Membrane D) Mitochondria
14. What is the most abundant element in the universe? A) Oxygen B) Carbon C) Hydrogen D) Helium
15. Which bone is the longest in the human body? A) Tibia B) Femur C) Humerus D) Radius
16. What causes lightning? A) Static electricity B) Magnetism C) Gravity D) Radiation
17. Which planet has the most moons? A) Jupiter B) Saturn C) Uranus D) Neptune
18. What is photosynthesis? A) Plant reproduction B) Light conversion to energy C) Water absorption D) Root growth
19. Which metal is liquid at room temperature? A) Lead B) Mercury C) Tin D) Zinc
20. What is the pH of pure water? A) 6 B) 7 C) 8 D) 9
21. Which part of the brain controls balance? A) Cerebrum B) Cerebellum C) Medulla D) Hypothalamus
22. What is the chemical formula for table salt? A) NaCl B) KCl C) CaCl2 D) MgCl2
23. Which type of radiation has the shortest wavelength? A) Radio B) Infrared C) Ultraviolet D) Gamma
24. What is the largest organ in the human body? A) Liver B) Brain C) Skin D) Lungs
25. Which gas is essential for combustion? A) Nitrogen B) Oxygen C) Carbon dioxide D) Hydrogen

Arithmetic Reasoning (30 questions)

1. If a shirt costs $25 and is on sale for 20% off, what is the sale price? A) $20 B) $21 C) $22 D) $23

2. A recipe calls for 2 cups of flour to make 12 cookies. How much flour is needed for 18 cookies? A) 2.5 cups B) 3 cups C) 3.5 cups D) 4 cups

3. If you drive 240 miles in 4 hours, what is your average speed? A) 50 mph B) 55 mph C) 60 mph D) 65 mph

4. A box contains 15 red balls and 10 blue balls. What fraction of the balls are red? A) 2/3 B) 3/5 C) 1/2 D) 2/5

5. If you earn $12 per hour and work 35 hours, how much do you earn? A) $400 B) $420 C) $440 D) $460

6. A rectangle is 8 feet long and 6 feet wide. What is its area? A) 42 sq ft B) 44 sq ft C) 46 sq ft D) 48 sq ft

7. If 3 apples cost $1.50, how much do 8 apples cost? A) $3.00 B) $3.50 C) $4.00 D) $4.50

8. A test has 40 questions. If you answer 32 correctly, what percentage did you get right? A) 75% B) 80% C) 85% D) 90%

9. If you save $50 per month for 8 months, how much will you save? A) $350 B) $400 C) $450 D) $500

10. A circle has a radius of 5 inches. What is its circumference? (Use $\pi = 3.14$) A) 31.4 in B) 30.4 in C) 32.4 in D) 29.4 in

11. If $2x + 5 = 15$, what is x? A) 4 B) 5 C) 6 D) 7

12. A store sells 120 items on Monday and 80 items on Tuesday. What is the average? A) 90 B) 95 C) 100 D) 105

13. If you buy 4 items at $3.25 each, what is the total cost? A) $12.00 B) $12.50 C) $13.00 D) $13.50

14. A ladder 13 feet long leans against a wall. The base is 5 feet from the wall. How high up the wall does it reach? A) 10 ft B) 11 ft C) 12 ft D) 13 ft

15. If 40% of a number is 80, what is the number? A) 180 B) 200 C) 220 D) 240

16. A train travels 300 miles in 5 hours. At this rate, how far will it travel in 7 hours? A) 400 mi B) 420 mi C) 440 mi D) 460 mi

17. If you have $100 and spend 30%, how much do you have left? A) $60 B) $65 C) $70 D) $75

18. A triangle has angles of 60° and 80°. What is the third angle? A) 30° B) 35° C) 40° D) 45°

19. If 5 workers can complete a job in 8 hours, how long will it take 10 workers? A) 3 hours B) 4 hours C) 5 hours D) 6 hours

20. A square has a perimeter of 24 inches. What is its area? A) 32 sq in B) 34 sq in C) 36 sq in D) 38 sq in

21. If you flip a coin 3 times, what is the probability of getting all heads? A) 1/4 B) 1/6 C) 1/8 D) 1/12

22. A book costs $15 and a pen costs $2. How much do 3 books and 5 pens cost? A) $53 B) $55 C) $57 D) $59

23. If a car uses 1 gallon of gas for every 25 miles, how much gas is needed for 150 miles? A) 5 gallons B) 6 gallons C) 7 gallons D) 8 gallons

24. A rectangle has a length twice its width. If the width is 4 feet, what is the perimeter? A) 20 ft B) 22 ft C) 24 ft D) 26 ft
25. If you invest $500 at 4% annual interest, how much interest do you earn in one year? A) $15 B) $20 C) $25 D) $30
26. A pizza is cut into 8 equal slices. If you eat 3 slices, what fraction remains? A) 3/8 B) 5/8 C) 1/2 D) 2/3
27. If 15 is 25% of a number, what is the number? A) 50 B) 60 C) 70 D) 80
28. A rope 24 feet long is cut into 3 equal pieces. How long is each piece? A) 6 ft B) 7 ft C) 8 ft D) 9 ft
29. If you buy items costing $2.50, $3.75, and $1.25, what is the total? A) $7.00 B) $7.25 C) $7.50 D) $7.75
30. A bathtub holds 50 gallons when full. If it's 60% full, how many gallons are in it? A) 25 B) 30 C) 35 D) 40

Word Knowledge (35 questions)

1. ABUNDANT most nearly means: A) Scarce B) Plentiful C) Average D) Expensive
2. DETERIORATE most nearly means: A) Improve B) Worsen C) Maintain D) Repair
3. GENUINE most nearly means: A) False B) Real C) Expensive D) Cheap
4. HECTIC most nearly means: A) Calm B) Busy C) Quiet D) Peaceful
5. ILLUMINATE most nearly means: A) Darken B) Light up C) Hide D) Cover
6. JOVIAL most nearly means: A) Sad B) Angry C) Cheerful D) Tired
7. KINDLE most nearly means: A) Extinguish B) Ignite C) Cool D) Freeze
8. LENIENT most nearly means: A) Strict B) Harsh C) Forgiving D) Cruel
9. METICULOUS most nearly means: A) Careless B) Careful C) Quick D) Slow
10. NOVICE most nearly means: A) Expert B) Beginner C) Teacher D) Student
11. OBSCURE most nearly means: A) Clear B) Obvious C) Hidden D) Bright
12. PONDER most nearly means: A) Ignore B) Think about C) Forget D) Remember
13. QUAINT most nearly means: A) Modern B) Old-fashioned C) Ugly D) Beautiful
14. RIGID most nearly means: A) Flexible B) Soft C) Stiff D) Weak
15. SERENE most nearly means: A) Noisy B) Peaceful C) Excited D) Angry
16. TEDIOUS most nearly means: A) Exciting B) Boring C) Quick D) Easy
17. UNIFORM most nearly means: A) Different B) Similar C) Varied D) Mixed
18. VIVID most nearly means: A) Dull B) Bright C) Dark D) Faded
19. WARY most nearly means: A) Trusting B) Cautious C) Careless D) Bold
20. YEARN most nearly means: A) Reject B) Long for C) Hate D) Fear
21. ZENITH most nearly means: A) Bottom B) Peak C) Middle D) Start
22. AFFABLE most nearly means: A) Unfriendly B) Friendly C) Angry D) Sad
23. BELLIGERENT most nearly means: A) Peaceful B) Aggressive C) Calm D) Happy
24. CANDID most nearly means: A) Dishonest B) Honest C) Shy D) Bold
25. DOCILE most nearly means: A) Wild B) Tame C) Aggressive D) Mean
26. ELOQUENT most nearly means: A) Silent B) Well-spoken C) Rude D) Quiet
27. FRUGAL most nearly means: A) Wasteful B) Thrifty C) Expensive D) Cheap
28. GREGARIOUS most nearly means: A) Antisocial B) Sociable C) Quiet D) Shy
29. HAUGHTY most nearly means: A) Humble B) Arrogant C) Kind D) Generous
30. IMMACULATE most nearly means: A) Dirty B) Clean C) Messy D) Stained

31. JEOPARDIZE most nearly means: A) Protect B) Endanger C) Help D) Save
32. KUDOS most nearly means: A) Criticism B) Praise C) Punishment D) Blame
33. LUCID most nearly means: A) Confused B) Clear C) Dark D) Bright
34. MALICE most nearly means: A) Kindness B) Hatred C) Love D) Care
35. NONCHALANT most nearly means: A) Excited B) Casual C) Nervous D) Worried

Paragraph Comprehension (15 questions)

Passage 1: The invention of the printing press by Johannes Gutenberg around 1440 revolutionized the spread of information. Before this invention, books were hand-copied by scribes, making them expensive and rare. The printing press allowed for mass production of books, making knowledge more accessible to the general population. This led to increased literacy rates and the rapid spread of new ideas during the Renaissance.

1. According to the passage, what was the main impact of the printing press? A) It made scribes unemployed B) It made books more expensive C) It made knowledge more accessible D) It slowed the spread of ideas
2. Before the printing press, books were: A) Mass produced B) Hand-copied C) Very cheap D) Widely available

Passage 2: Photosynthesis is the process by which plants convert sunlight, water, and carbon dioxide into glucose and oxygen. This process occurs mainly in the leaves, specifically in structures called chloroplasts. The green pigment chlorophyll captures the light energy needed for this reaction. Photosynthesis is essential for life on Earth as it produces the oxygen we breathe and forms the base of most food chains.

3. Where does photosynthesis mainly occur in plants? A) Roots B) Stems C) Leaves D) Flowers
4. What captures the light energy needed for photosynthesis? A) Glucose B) Oxygen C) Carbon dioxide D) Chlorophyll
5. Why is photosynthesis essential for life on Earth? A) It produces carbon dioxide B) It produces oxygen and food C) It removes sunlight D) It creates water

Passage 3: Regular exercise provides numerous health benefits including improved cardiovascular health, stronger bones and muscles, better mental health, and increased longevity. The American Heart Association recommends at least 150 minutes of moderate-intensity exercise per week for adults. This can include activities such as brisk walking, swimming, or cycling. Even small amounts of exercise are better than none at all.

6. How much exercise does the American Heart Association recommend per week? A) 100 minutes B) 150 minutes C) 200 minutes D) 250 minutes
7. According to the passage, exercise benefits include all of the following EXCEPT: A) Better cardiovascular health B) Stronger bones C) Improved mental health D) Decreased appetite

Passage 4: The water cycle is the continuous movement of water through the environment. It begins with evaporation, where heat from the sun causes water from oceans, lakes, and rivers to turn into water vapor. This vapor rises into the atmosphere and condenses into clouds. When clouds become heavy with water, precipitation occurs in the form of rain, snow, or hail. The water then returns to bodies of water or soaks into the ground, completing the cycle.

8. What causes water to evaporate? A) Wind B) Cold temperatures C) Heat from the sun D) Gravity
9. What happens when clouds become heavy with water? A) Evaporation B) Condensation C) Precipitation D) Absorption
10. The water cycle is described as: A) A one-time event B) A continuous process C) A seasonal occurrence D) A rare phenomenon

Passage 5: Sleep is crucial for physical and mental health. During sleep, the body repairs tissues, consolidates memories, and releases important hormones. Most adults need 7-9 hours of sleep per night. Lack of adequate sleep can lead to decreased concentration, weakened immune system, and increased risk of chronic diseases. Good sleep hygiene includes maintaining a regular sleep schedule and creating a comfortable sleep environment.

11. How many hours of sleep do most adults need? A) 5-7 hours B) 6-8 hours C) 7-9 hours D) 8-10 hours
12. What happens during sleep according to the passage? A) Energy is consumed B) Tissues are repaired C) Temperature increases D) Breathing stops
13. Poor sleep can lead to: A) Better concentration B) Stronger immune system C) Increased disease risk D) Improved memory

Passage 6: Renewable energy sources such as solar, wind, and hydroelectric power are becoming increasingly important as alternatives to fossil fuels. These sources are considered renewable because they are naturally replenished and do not deplete over time. Unlike fossil fuels, renewable energy sources produce little to no greenhouse gas emissions, making them environmentally friendly options for meeting our energy needs.

14. What makes energy sources "renewable"? A) They are expensive B) They are naturally replenished C) They produce emissions D) They deplete quickly
15. Compared to fossil fuels, renewable energy sources: A) Produce more emissions B) Are less environmentally friendly C) Produce little to no emissions D) Are always more expensive

Mathematics Knowledge (25 questions)

1. What is 2^3? A) 6 B) 8 C) 9 D) 12
2. Solve for x: $3x - 7 = 14$ A) 5 B) 6 C) 7 D) 8
3. What is the square root of 144? A) 11 B) 12 C) 13 D) 14
4. If a triangle has angles of 45° and 90°, what is the third angle? A) 35° B) 40° C) 45° D) 50°
5. What is 15% of 200? A) 25 B) 30 C) 35 D) 40

6. Simplify: 3(x + 4) A) 3x + 4 B) 3x + 12 C) x + 12 D) 3x + 7
7. What is the area of a circle with radius 3? (Use π = 3.14) A) 28.26 B) 28.27 C) 28.28 D) 28.29
8. If 2x + 5 = 17, what is x? A) 5 B) 6 C) 7 D) 8
9. What is the slope of a line passing through (2,3) and (4,7)? A) 1 B) 2 C) 3 D) 4
10. Factor: x^2 - 9 A) (x-3)(x-3) B) (x+3)(x+3) C) (x-3)(x+3) D) Cannot be factored
11. What is 4! (4 factorial)? A) 16 B) 20 C) 24 D) 28
12. Solve: |x - 3| = 5 A) x = 8 only B) x = -2 only C) x = 8 or x = -2 D) x = 2 or x = 8
13. What is the volume of a cube with side length 4? A) 48 B) 56 C) 64 D) 72
14. If $\log_2(x)$ = 3, what is x? A) 6 B) 8 C) 9 D) 12
15. What is the distance between points (1,2) and (4,6)? A) 4 B) 5 C) 6 D) 7
16. Simplify: $(2x)^3$ A) $6x^3$ B) $8x^3$ C) $2x^3$ D) x^3
17. What is the sum of interior angles of a pentagon? A) 540° B) 520° C) 500° D) 480°
18. If sin(θ) = 0.5, what is θ? A) 30° B) 45° C) 60° D) 90°
19. What is the median of: 2, 5, 7, 9, 11? A) 5 B) 7 C) 9 D) 11
20. Solve: x^2 - 5x + 6 = 0 A) x = 2, 3 B) x = 1, 6 C) x = -2, -3 D) x = 2, -3
21. What is 25% of 80? A) 15 B) 20 C) 25 D) 30
22. If f(x) = 2x + 1, what is f(3)? A) 5 B) 6 C) 7 D) 8
23. What is the circumference of a circle with diameter 10? A) 31.4 B) 31.5 C) 31.6 D) 31.7
24. Simplify: $\sqrt{50}$ A) $5\sqrt{2}$ B) $5\sqrt{3}$ C) $7\sqrt{2}$ D) $10\sqrt{5}$
25. What is the y-intercept of y = 3x - 4? A) -4 B) -3 C) 3 D) 4

Electronics Information (20 questions)

1. What does AC stand for? A) Alternating Current B) Active Circuit C) Automatic Control D) Applied Current
2. What is the unit of electrical resistance? A) Volt B) Amp C) Ohm D) Watt
3. Which component stores electrical energy? A) Resistor B) Capacitor C) Inductor D) Transistor
4. What is Ohm's Law? A) V = I × R B) V = I + R C) V = I - R D) V = I ÷ R
5. What does a diode do? A) Stores energy B) Allows current in one direction C) Amplifies signals D) Reduces voltage
6. What is the standard voltage in US households? A) 110V B) 115V C) 120V D) 125V
7. Which material is the best conductor? A) Rubber B) Glass C) Silver D) Wood
8. What does a transformer do? A) Stores energy B) Changes voltage levels C) Converts AC to DC D) Amplifies current
9. What is the symbol for current? A) V B) I C) R D) P
10. How are batteries connected to increase voltage? A) In parallel B) In series C) In combination D) Separately
11. What does LED stand for? A) Light Emitting Diode B) Low Energy Device C) Linear Electronic Display D) Light Electric Device
12. What is a short circuit? A) A broken wire B) Low resistance path C) High voltage condition D) Open circuit
13. Which component opposes changes in current? A) Resistor B) Capacitor C) Inductor D) Diode
14. What is the frequency of AC power in the US? A) 50 Hz B) 60 Hz C) 70 Hz D) 80 Hz

15. What does a fuse do? A) Amplifies current B) Stores energy C) Protects from overcurrent D) Changes voltage
16. What is the unit of power? A) Volt B) Amp C) Ohm D) Watt
17. Which type of circuit has multiple paths for current? A) Series B) Parallel C) Complex D) Simple
18. What is ground in electrical terms? A) Soil B) Zero voltage reference C) High voltage D) Negative voltage
19. What does RMS stand for? A) Relative Mean Square B) Root Mean Square C) Rapid Measurement System D) Random Multiple Signal
20. What happens to total resistance when resistors are added in parallel? A) Increases B) Decreases C) Stays same D) Becomes zero

Auto & Shop Information (25 questions)

1. What does a carburetor do? A) Starts the engine B) Mixes air and fuel C) Cools the engine D) Charges the battery
2. How many strokes are in a typical car engine cycle? A) 2 B) 3 C) 4 D) 6
3. What tool is used to tighten bolts to a specific torque? A) Wrench B) Torque wrench C) Socket D) Screwdriver
4. What is the purpose of motor oil? A) Cool engine B) Lubricate parts C) Clean engine D) All of the above
5. Which part stores electrical energy in a car? A) Alternator B) Battery C) Starter D) Distributor
6. What does ABS stand for? A) Automatic Brake System B) Anti-lock Brake System C) Advanced Brake System D) Auxiliary Brake System
7. What tool is best for cutting metal? A) Wood saw B) Hacksaw C) Chisel D) File
8. What is the function of a radiator? A) Generate power B) Cool the engine C) Filter air D) Store fuel
9. Which tool measures electrical voltage? A) Ammeter B) Voltmeter C) Ohmmeter D) Multimeter
10. What is the purpose of a thermostat in an engine? A) Measure temperature B) Control coolant flow C) Start engine D) Filter oil
11. What does SAE stand for in oil ratings? A) Standard Automotive Equipment B) Society of Automotive Engineers C) Safe Automotive Engine D) Superior Auto Engineering
12. Which tool is used to remove rounded bolt heads? A) Socket wrench B) Box wrench C) Bolt extractor D) Impact wrench
13. What is the firing order? A) Order of cylinder ignition B) Order of gear shifting C) Order of brake application D) Order of fuel injection
14. What does a differential do? A) Changes gears B) Allows wheels to turn at different speeds C) Stores power D) Cools transmission
15. Which sandpaper grit is finest? A) 60 B) 120 C) 220 D) 400
16. What is the purpose of a catalytic converter? A) Convert fuel B) Reduce emissions C) Increase power D) Cool exhaust
17. What tool is used to measure internal engine wear? A) Micrometer B) Caliper C) Compression gauge D) Feeler gauge

18. What does viscosity refer to in motor oil? A) Color B) Thickness C) Temperature D) Pressure
19. Which component connects the engine to the transmission? A) Driveshaft B) Clutch C) Axle D) Universal joint
20. What is the standard thread pitch for most automotive bolts? A) Fine B) Coarse C) Extra fine D) Metric
21. What does a PCV valve do? A) Controls vacuum B) Ventilates crankcase C) Regulates fuel D) Controls timing
22. Which tool is best for precise measurements? A) Ruler B) Tape measure C) Micrometer D) Square
23. What is the purpose of valve clearance? A) Allow for thermal expansion B) Increase compression C) Improve airflow D) Reduce noise
24. What does octane rating measure? A) Fuel economy B) Knock resistance C) Fuel purity D) Burn rate
25. Which component controls the air/fuel mixture at idle? A) Carburetor B) Throttle body C) Idle air control valve D) Fuel injector

Mechanical Comprehension (25 questions)

1. If gear A has 20 teeth and gear B has 40 teeth, and A turns at 100 RPM, how fast does B turn? A) 50 RPM B) 100 RPM C) 200 RPM D) 400 RPM
2. Which pulley arrangement provides the greatest mechanical advantage? A) Fixed B) Movable C) Compound D) Simple
3. What happens to pressure in a hydraulic system when force is applied to a small piston? A) Decreases B) Increases C) Stays same D) Becomes zero
4. A lever is 6 feet long. If the fulcrum is 2 feet from one end, what is the mechanical advantage? A) 2:1 B) 3:1 C) 4:1 D) 6:1
5. What is the mechanical advantage of an inclined plane 12 feet long and 3 feet high? A) 2:1 B) 3:1 C) 4:1 D) 6:1
6. In a wheel and axle, if the wheel radius is 8 inches and axle radius is 2 inches, what is the mechanical advantage? A) 2:1 B) 4:1 C) 6:1 D) 8:1
7. What happens to the speed of water flowing through a pipe when the pipe diameter decreases? A) Increases B) Decreases C) Stays same D) Stops
8. Which simple machine is a screw based on? A) Lever B) Wedge C) Inclined plane D) Pulley
9. If you apply 10 pounds of force to a 5:1 mechanical advantage system, what output force do you get? A) 2 lbs B) 15 lbs C) 50 lbs D) 100 lbs
10. What is the purpose of a flywheel? A) Increase speed B) Store rotational energy C) Reduce friction D) Change direction
11. In a hydraulic jack, if the input piston has an area of 2 sq in and output piston has 20 sq in, what is the mechanical advantage? A) 5:1 B) 10:1 C) 15:1 D) 20:1
12. What happens to the mechanical advantage when you increase the length of a lever arm? A) Increases B) Decreases C) Stays same D) Becomes negative
13. Which type of gear changes the direction of rotation by 90 degrees? A) Spur B) Helical C) Bevel D) Worm

14. What is centrifugal force? A) Force toward center B) Force away from center C) Gravitational force D) Magnetic force
15. In a block and tackle with 4 supporting ropes, what is the theoretical mechanical advantage? A) 2:1 B) 3:1 C) 4:1 D) 8:1
16. What happens to torque when you increase the length of a wrench? A) Increases B) Decreases C) Stays same D) Becomes zero
17. Which statement about friction is correct? A) Always helpful B) Always harmful C) Can be helpful or harmful D) Only exists in liquids
18. What is the efficiency of a machine that requires 100 J of input to produce 80 J of output? A) 60% B) 70% C) 80% D) 90%
19. In a cam and follower system, what determines the follower's motion? A) Cam speed B) Cam shape C) Follower weight D) Spring tension
20. What happens to pressure at the bottom of a fluid column as height increases? A) Increases B) Decreases C) Stays same D) Becomes negative
21. Which component converts rotary motion to linear motion? A) Gear B) Cam C) Rack and pinion D) Belt
22. What is the principle behind a hydraulic brake system? A) Mechanical advantage B) Pascal's principle C) Archimedes' principle D) Bernoulli's principle
23. If a gear train has a ratio of 3:1, and the input gear turns 90 degrees, how far does the output gear turn? A) 30 degrees B) 60 degrees C) 90 degrees D) 270 degrees
24. What type of bearing reduces friction through rolling action? A) Plain bearing B) Ball bearing C) Sleeve bearing D) Thrust bearing
25. What happens when you increase the number of threads per inch on a screw? A) Faster movement B) Slower movement C) More force needed D) Less force needed

Answer Key - Test 3

General Science: 1-A, 2-C, 3-B, 4-C, 5-C, 6-B, 7-C, 8-B, 9-C, 10-B, 11-D, 12-C, 13-B, 14-C, 15-B, 16-A, 17-B, 18-B, 19-B, 20-B, 21-B, 22-A, 23-D, 24-C, 25-B

Arithmetic Reasoning: 1-A, 2-B, 3-C, 4-B, 5-B, 6-D, 7-C, 8-B, 9-B, 10-A, 11-B, 12-C, 13-C, 14-C, 15-B, 16-B, 17-C, 18-C, 19-B, 20-C, 21-C, 22-B, 23-B, 24-C, 25-B, 26-B, 27-B, 28-C, 29-C, 30-B

Word Knowledge: 1-B, 2-B, 3-B, 4-B, 5-B, 6-C, 7-B, 8-C, 9-B, 10-B, 11-C, 12-B, 13-B, 14-C, 15-B, 16-B, 17-B, 18-B, 19-B, 20-B, 21-B, 22-B, 23-B, 24-B, 25-B, 26-B, 27-B, 28-B, 29-B, 30-B, 31-B, 32-B, 33-B, 34-B, 35-B

Paragraph Comprehension: 1-C, 2-B, 3-C, 4-D, 5-B, 6-B, 7-D, 8-C, 9-C, 10-B, 11-C, 12-B, 13-C, 14-B, 15-C

Mathematics Knowledge: 1-B, 2-C, 3-B, 4-C, 5-B, 6-B, 7-A, 8-B, 9-B, 10-C, 11-C, 12-C, 13-C, 14-B, 15-B, 16-B, 17-A, 18-A, 19-B, 20-A, 21-B, 22-C, 23-A, 24-A, 25-A

Electronics Information: 1-A, 2-C, 3-B, 4-A, 5-B, 6-C, 7-C, 8-B, 9-B, 10-B, 11-A, 12-B, 13-C, 14-B, 15-C, 16-D, 17-B, 18-B, 19-B, 20-B

Auto & Shop Information: 1-B, 2-C, 3-B, 4-D, 5-B, 6-B, 7-B, 8-B, 9-D, 10-B, 11-B, 12-C, 13-A, 14-B, 15-D, 16-B, 17-C, 18-B, 19-B, 20-B, 21-B, 22-C, 23-A, 24-B, 25-C

Mechanical Comprehension: 1-A, 2-C, 3-B, 4-A, 5-C, 6-B, 7-A, 8-C, 9-C, 10-B, 11-B, 12-A, 13-C, 14-B, 15-C, 16-A, 17-C, 18-C, 19-B, 20-A, 21-C, 22-B, 23-A, 24-B, 25-B

Test 4

General Science (25 questions)

1. What is the chemical formula for water? A) H2O B) CO2 C) NaCl D) O2
2. Which organ filters blood in the human body? A) Heart B) Liver C) Kidney D) Lungs
3. What is the smallest particle of an element? A) Molecule B) Compound C) Atom D) Ion
4. Which planet is known as the Red Planet? A) Venus B) Mars C) Jupiter D) Saturn
5. What gas do plants absorb during photosynthesis? A) Oxygen B) Nitrogen C) Carbon dioxide D) Hydrogen
6. How many bones are in an adult human body? A) 196 B) 206 C) 216 D) 226
7. What is the speed of sound in air at room temperature? A) 343 m/s B) 353 m/s C) 363 m/s D) 373 m/s
8. Which type of energy is stored in a stretched rubber band? A) Kinetic B) Potential C) Thermal D) Chemical
9. What is the hardest mineral on the Mohs scale? A) Quartz B) Topaz C) Diamond D) Corundum
10. Which blood vessel carries blood away from the heart? A) Vein B) Artery C) Capillary D) Valve
11. What is the main component of natural gas? A) Propane B) Butane C) Methane D) Ethane
12. Which force keeps planets in orbit around the sun? A) Magnetic B) Electric C) Nuclear D) Gravitational
13. What is the pH of a neutral solution? A) 0 B) 7 C) 14 D) 1
14. Which part of the cell produces energy? A) Nucleus B) Cytoplasm C) Mitochondria D) Membrane
15. What is the most common element in Earth's crust? A) Silicon B) Aluminum C) Iron D) Oxygen
16. Which system fights disease in the human body? A) Circulatory B) Respiratory C) Immune D) Digestive
17. What happens during nuclear fusion? A) Atoms split B) Atoms combine C) Electrons move D) Protons disappear
18. Which gas is responsible for the greenhouse effect? A) Oxygen B) Nitrogen C) Carbon dioxide D) Argon
19. What is the unit of frequency? A) Hertz B) Watt C) Joule D) Newton
20. Which organ produces bile? A) Pancreas B) Liver C) Kidney D) Stomach

21. What is absolute zero? A) 0°C B) -273°C C) -100°C D) -200°C
22. Which metal is liquid at room temperature? A) Lead B) Mercury C) Tin D) Zinc
23. What causes day and night? A) Earth's orbit B) Earth's rotation C) Moon's orbit D) Sun's movement
24. Which vitamin prevents scurvy? A) A B) B C) C D) D
25. What is the chemical symbol for iron? A) Ir B) Fe C) In D) I

Arithmetic Reasoning (30 questions)

1. A car travels 240 miles in 4 hours. What is its average speed? A) 50 mph B) 55 mph C) 60 mph D) 65 mph
2. If 3 pounds of apples cost $4.50, how much do 5 pounds cost? A) $6.50 B) $7.00 C) $7.50 D) $8.00
3. A rectangle has a length of 12 feet and width of 8 feet. What is its perimeter? A) 36 ft B) 40 ft C) 44 ft D) 48 ft
4. If you score 18 out of 20 on a test, what percentage did you get? A) 85% B) 90% C) 95% D) 100%
5. A store offers a 25% discount on a $80 item. What is the sale price? A) $55 B) $60 C) $65 D) $70
6. If you save $75 per month for 6 months, how much will you save? A) $400 B) $425 C) $450 D) $475
7. A circle has a diameter of 14 inches. What is its radius? A) 6 in B) 7 in C) 8 in D) 9 in
8. If 4x - 3 = 17, what is x? A) 4 B) 5 C) 6 D) 7
9. A pizza is divided into 8 equal slices. If you eat 3 slices, what fraction is left? A) 3/8 B) 5/8 C) 1/2 D) 2/3
10. If you buy 6 items at $2.75 each, what is the total cost? A) $15.50 B) $16.00 C) $16.50 D) $17.00
11. A ladder 15 feet long leans against a wall. The base is 9 feet from the wall. How high up does it reach? A) 10 ft B) 11 ft C) 12 ft D) 13 ft
12. If 35% of a number is 140, what is the number? A) 350 B) 375 C) 400 D) 425
13. A train travels 450 miles in 6 hours. How far will it travel in 8 hours at the same speed? A) 550 mi B) 600 mi C) 650 mi D) 700 mi
14. If you have $200 and spend 40%, how much do you have left? A) $100 B) $110 C) $120 D) $130
15. A triangle has angles of 45° and 75°. What is the third angle? A) 50° B) 55° C) 60° D) 65°
16. If 8 workers can finish a job in 12 hours, how long will it take 6 workers? A) 14 hours B) 15 hours C) 16 hours D) 18 hours
17. A square has an area of 64 square inches. What is its perimeter? A) 28 in B) 30 in C) 32 in D) 34 in
18. If you roll two dice, what is the probability of getting a sum of 7? A) 1/6 B) 1/7 C) 1/8 D) 1/12
19. A book costs $12 and a magazine costs $3. How much do 4 books and 6 magazines cost? A) $63 B) $66 C) $69 D) $72
20. If a car uses 1 gallon for every 30 miles, how much gas is needed for 180 miles? A) 5 gal B) 6 gal C) 7 gal D) 8 gal

21. A rectangle has a width of 5 feet and length of 12 feet. What is its area? A) 50 sq ft B) 55 sq ft C) 60 sq ft D) 65 sq ft
22. If you invest $800 at 3% annual interest, how much interest do you earn in one year? A) $20 B) $24 C) $28 D) $32
23. A rope 36 feet long is cut into 4 equal pieces. How long is each piece? A) 8 ft B) 9 ft C) 10 ft D) 12 ft
24. If 20 is 40% of a number, what is the number? A) 40 B) 45 C) 50 D) 55
25. If you buy items costing $3.25, $4.50, and $2.75, what is the total? A) $10.00 B) $10.25 C) $10.50 D) $10.75
26. A bathtub holds 60 gallons when full. If it's 75% full, how many gallons are in it? A) 40 B) 42 C) 45 D) 48
27. If 12 is 15% of a number, what is the number? A) 70 B) 75 C) 80 D) 85
28. A classroom has 24 students. If 1/3 are absent, how many are present? A) 14 B) 16 C) 18 D) 20
29. If you travel 120 miles in 2.5 hours, what is your average speed? A) 46 mph B) 48 mph C) 50 mph D) 52 mph
30. A circle has a circumference of 31.4 inches. What is its diameter? (Use $\pi = 3.14$) A) 8 in B) 9 in C) 10 in D) 11 in

Word Knowledge (35 questions)

1. BENEVOLENT most nearly means: A) Evil B) Kind C) Angry D) Sad
2. CONSPICUOUS most nearly means: A) Hidden B) Obvious C) Quiet D) Small
3. DILIGENT most nearly means: A) Lazy B) Hardworking C) Slow D) Fast
4. ECCENTRIC most nearly means: A) Normal B) Unusual C) Round D) Flat
5. FEASIBLE most nearly means: A) Impossible B) Possible C) Difficult D) Easy
6. GULLIBLE most nearly means: A) Suspicious B) Easily fooled C) Smart D) Careful
7. HINDER most nearly means: A) Help B) Block C) Speed up D) Improve
8. INEVITABLE most nearly means: A) Avoidable B) Unavoidable C) Possible D) Unlikely
9. JARGON most nearly means: A) Clear speech B) Specialized language C) Loud talk D) Quiet whisper
10. KEEN most nearly means: A) Dull B) Sharp C) Broken D) Bent
11. LETHARGIC most nearly means: A) Energetic B) Sluggish C) Quick D) Active
12. MUNDANE most nearly means: A) Exciting B) Ordinary C) Unusual D) Rare
13. NEGLIGENT most nearly means: A) Careful B) Careless C) Helpful D) Harmful
14. OPTIMISTIC most nearly means: A) Hopeful B) Hopeless C) Sad D) Angry
15. PRUDENT most nearly means: A) Foolish B) Wise C) Quick D) Slow
16. QUERULOUS most nearly means: A) Happy B) Complaining C) Quiet D) Loud
17. REMORSE most nearly means: A) Joy B) Regret C) Anger D) Fear
18. SOLEMN most nearly means: A) Happy B) Serious C) Funny D) Light
19. TACITURN most nearly means: A) Talkative B) Quiet C) Loud D) Friendly
20. UBIQUITOUS most nearly means: A) Rare B) Everywhere C) Hidden D) Lost
21. VAGUE most nearly means: A) Clear B) Unclear C) Bright D) Dark
22. WANE most nearly means: A) Increase B) Decrease C) Stay same D) Disappear
23. XENIAL most nearly means: A) Hostile B) Hospitable C) Strange D) Foreign

24. YIELDING most nearly means: A) Rigid B) Flexible C) Hard D) Strong
25. ZEAL most nearly means: A) Laziness B) Enthusiasm C) Boredom D) Tiredness
26. ALOOF most nearly means: A) Friendly B) Distant C) Close D) Warm
27. BRAZEN most nearly means: A) Shy B) Bold C) Quiet D) Modest
28. CURTAIL most nearly means: A) Extend B) Reduce C) Maintain D) Increase
29. DEPLORE most nearly means: A) Approve B) Disapprove C) Ignore D) Accept
30. ELATED most nearly means: A) Sad B) Joyful C) Angry D) Tired
31. FICKLE most nearly means: A) Stable B) Changeable C) Reliable D) Steady
32. GAUDY most nearly means: A) Plain B) Flashy C) Simple D) Elegant
33. HAUGHTY most nearly means: A) Humble B) Proud C) Kind D) Gentle
34. IRKSOME most nearly means: A) Pleasant B) Annoying C) Helpful D) Useful
35. JOVIAL most nearly means: A) Sad B) Cheerful C) Angry D) Worried

Paragraph Comprehension (15 questions)

Passage 1: Bees play a crucial role in pollinating plants, making them essential for food production. About one-third of the food we eat depends on bee pollination, including fruits, vegetables, and nuts. However, bee populations have been declining due to pesticide use, habitat loss, and disease. This decline threatens not only biodiversity but also agricultural productivity and food security worldwide.

1. According to the passage, what fraction of our food depends on bee pollination? A) One quarter B) One third C) One half D) Two thirds
2. The passage mentions all of the following as causes of bee decline EXCEPT: A) Pesticide use B) Habitat loss C) Disease D) Climate change

Passage 2: The human brain contains approximately 86 billion neurons, each connected to thousands of others through synapses. These connections allow for complex thought processes, memory formation, and learning. The brain's plasticity means it can reorganize and form new neural pathways throughout life, especially during childhood and adolescence when development is most rapid.

3. How many neurons does the human brain contain? A) 86 million B) 86 billion C) 86 thousand D) 86 trillion
4. When is brain development most rapid? A) Adulthood B) Old age C) Childhood and adolescence D) Middle age
5. What does brain plasticity refer to? A) Brain size B) Brain weight C) Ability to reorganize D) Number of neurons

Passage 3: Solar panels convert sunlight directly into electricity through photovoltaic cells. These cells are typically made of silicon and work by allowing photons from sunlight to knock electrons loose from atoms, generating an electric current. Solar energy is renewable, clean, and becoming increasingly cost-effective as technology improves and production scales up.

6. What are photovoltaic cells typically made of? A) Carbon B) Silicon C) Aluminum D) Copper

7. How do solar panels generate electricity? A) By burning fuel B) By using wind power C) By converting sunlight D) By using water power

Passage 4: Regular physical exercise has numerous benefits for both physical and mental health. It strengthens the cardiovascular system, builds muscle mass, improves bone density, and enhances immune function. Exercise also releases endorphins, which can improve mood and reduce stress. The World Health Organization recommends at least 150 minutes of moderate exercise per week for adults.

8. How much exercise does the WHO recommend per week? A) 100 minutes B) 150 minutes C) 200 minutes D) 250 minutes
9. What chemicals does exercise release that improve mood? A) Hormones B) Endorphins C) Proteins D) Vitamins
10. According to the passage, exercise benefits include all EXCEPT: A) Stronger heart B) Better immunity C) Improved mood D) Increased appetite

Passage 5: Coral reefs are among the most diverse ecosystems on Earth, supporting about 25% of all marine species despite covering less than 1% of the ocean floor. These underwater structures are built by tiny animals called coral polyps, which form symbiotic relationships with algae. The algae provide food through photosynthesis while the coral provides protection and nutrients.

11. What percentage of marine species do coral reefs support? A) 15% B) 20% C) 25% D) 30%
12. What builds coral reefs? A) Fish B) Algae C) Coral polyps D) Sea plants
13. The relationship between coral and algae is described as: A) Competitive B) Parasitic C) Symbiotic D) Predatory

Passage 6: The invention of writing systems around 3200 BCE marked the beginning of recorded history. Early writing systems, such as cuneiform in Mesopotamia and hieroglyphics in Egypt, were initially used for record-keeping and administrative purposes. Over time, writing evolved to include literature, laws, and religious texts, fundamentally changing how knowledge was preserved and transmitted across generations.

14. When were writing systems first invented? A) 3200 BCE B) 3000 BCE C) 2800 BCE D) 2500 BCE
15. What were early writing systems initially used for? A) Literature B) Record-keeping C) Religious texts D) Laws

Mathematics Knowledge (25 questions)

1. What is 5^2? A) 10 B) 15 C) 20 D) 25
2. Solve for x: $2x + 8 = 20$ A) 4 B) 5 C) 6 D) 7
3. What is the square root of 169? A) 12 B) 13 C) 14 D) 15
4. If a right triangle has legs of 6 and 8, what is the hypotenuse? A) 9 B) 10 C) 11 D) 12
5. What is 20% of 150? A) 25 B) 30 C) 35 D) 40

6. Simplify: 4(x - 2) A) 4x - 2 B) 4x - 6 C) 4x - 8 D) x - 8
7. What is the area of a triangle with base 8 and height 6? A) 20 B) 22 C) 24 D) 26
8. If 3x - 4 = 11, what is x? A) 4 B) 5 C) 6 D) 7
9. What is the slope of a line passing through (1,2) and (3,8)? A) 2 B) 3 C) 4 D) 5
10. Factor: x^2 - 16 A) (x-4)(x-4) B) (x+4)(x+4) C) (x-4)(x+4) D) Cannot be factored
11. What is 6! (6 factorial)? A) 120 B) 360 C) 720 D) 1440
12. Solve: |x + 2| = 7 A) x = 5 only B) x = -9 only C) x = 5 or x = -9 D) x = -5 or x = 9
13. What is the volume of a rectangular prism with dimensions 3 × 4 × 5? A) 50 B) 55 C) 60 D) 65
14. If $\log_3(x) = 2$, what is x? A) 6 B) 8 C) 9 D) 12
15. What is the distance between points (0,0) and (3,4)? A) 4 B) 5 C) 6 D) 7
16. Simplify: $(3x)^2$ A) $6x^2$ B) $9x^2$ C) $3x^2$ D) x^2
17. What is the sum of interior angles of a hexagon? A) 720° B) 700° C) 680° D) 660°
18. If cos(θ) = 0.5, what is θ? A) 30° B) 45° C) 60° D) 90°
19. What is the mode of: 3, 5, 7, 5, 9, 5, 6? A) 3 B) 5 C) 7 D) 9
20. Solve: x^2 - 7x + 12 = 0 A) x = 3, 4 B) x = 2, 6 C) x = 1, 12 D) x = -3, -4
21. What is 30% of 120? A) 30 B) 32 C) 34 D) 36
22. If f(x) = 3x - 2, what is f(4)? A) 8 B) 10 C) 12 D) 14
23. What is the area of a circle with radius 4? (Use π = 3.14) A) 50.24 B) 48.24 C) 52.24 D) 46.24
24. Simplify: √72 A) 6√2 B) 6√3 C) 8√2 D) 9√2
25. What is the x-intercept of y = 2x - 6? A) 2 B) 3 C) -3 D) 6

Electronics Information (20 questions)

1. What does DC stand for? A) Direct Current B) Digital Circuit C) Dynamic Control D) Double Contact
2. What is the unit of electrical power? A) Volt B) Amp C) Ohm D) Watt
3. Which component allows current to flow in only one direction? A) Resistor B) Capacitor C) Diode D) Inductor
4. What is the relationship between voltage, current, and resistance? A) V = I + R B) V = I × R C) V = I - R D) V = I ÷ R
5. What does an amplifier do? A) Stores energy B) Reduces voltage C) Increases signal strength D) Converts AC to DC
6. What is the standard frequency of AC power in Europe? A) 50 Hz B) 60 Hz C) 70 Hz D) 80 Hz
7. Which material is an insulator? A) Copper B) Silver C) Rubber D) Aluminum
8. What is the purpose of a rectifier? A) Amplify signals B) Convert AC to DC C) Store energy D) Filter noise
9. What is the symbol for voltage? A) I B) R C) V D) P
10. How are capacitors connected to increase total capacitance? A) In series B) In parallel C) In combination D) Separately
11. What does LCD stand for? A) Light Control Device B) Liquid Crystal Display C) Low Current Display D) Linear Circuit Display
12. What is an open circuit? A) A complete path B) A broken path C) High resistance D) Low voltage

13. Which component stores energy in a magnetic field? A) Resistor B) Capacitor C) Inductor D) Diode
14. What is the unit of capacitance? A) Farad B) Henry C) Ohm D) Watt
15. What does a circuit breaker do? A) Amplify current B) Store energy C) Protect from overload D) Convert voltage
16. What is impedance? A) DC resistance B) AC resistance C) Capacitance D) Inductance
17. Which type of circuit has only one path for current? A) Series B) Parallel C) Complex D) Compound
18. What is the purpose of a heat sink? A) Generate heat B) Remove heat C) Store heat D) Measure heat
19. What does PWM stand for? A) Power Wave Modulation B) Pulse Width Modulation C) Phase Wave Management D) Peak Watt Measurement
20. What happens to current when voltage increases and resistance stays constant? A) Increases B) Decreases C) Stays same D) Becomes zero

Auto & Shop Information (25 questions)

1. What is the purpose of a spark plug? A) Cool engine B) Ignite fuel mixture C) Filter air D) Pump fuel
2. How many cylinders does a V8 engine have? A) 6 B) 8 C) 10 D) 12
3. What tool is used to measure gap spacing? A) Ruler B) Caliper C) Feeler gauge D) Micrometer
4. What is the primary function of engine coolant? A) Lubricate B) Cool C) Clean D) Seal
5. Which component generates electrical power in a car? A) Battery B) Alternator C) Starter D) Ignition coil
6. What does EFI stand for? A) Electronic Fuel Injection B) Engine Fuel Indicator C) Electric Fan Ignition D) Enhanced Fuel Ignition
7. Which saw is best for cutting curves in wood? A) Circular saw B) Jigsaw C) Table saw D) Band saw
8. What is the function of a water pump? A) Pump fuel B) Circulate coolant C) Generate pressure D) Filter water
9. Which instrument measures electrical resistance? A) Voltmeter B) Ammeter C) Ohmmeter D) Wattmeter
10. What controls the engine's operating temperature? A) Radiator B) Thermostat C) Water pump D) Fan
11. What does API stand for in oil specifications? A) American Petroleum Institute B) Automotive Performance Index C) Advanced Protection Indicator D) Auto Parts International
12. Which tool cuts external threads? A) Tap B) Die C) Reamer D) Drill
13. What is valve overlap? A) Valves touching B) Both valves open simultaneously C) Valve timing error D) Valve clearance adjustment
14. What does a CV joint do? A) Change voltage B) Control vacuum C) Transmit power while turning D) Cool valves
15. Which abrasive is hardest? A) Emery B) Silicon carbide C) Aluminum oxide D) Diamond

16. What is the purpose of EGR? A) Increase power B) Reduce emissions C) Improve fuel economy D) Cool engine
17. What tool removes material by scraping? A) File B) Rasp C) Scraper D) Chisel
18. What does multi-viscosity oil mean? A) Multiple additives B) Viscosity changes with temperature C) Multiple brands mixed D) Multiple grades blended
19. Which component transfers engine power to wheels? A) Transmission B) Differential C) Driveshaft D) All of the above
20. What is the purpose of flux in soldering? A) Strengthen joint B) Clean surfaces C) Add color D) Increase temperature
21. What does DOHC stand for? A) Double Overhead Cam B) Direct Oil Heating Control C) Dual Output High Compression D) Dynamic Oil Head Control
22. Which file cut is smoothest? A) Bastard B) Second cut C) Smooth D) Dead smooth
23. What is compression ratio? A) Fuel to air ratio B) Cylinder volume ratio C) Pressure measurement D) Temperature ratio
24. What indicates engine knock? A) Low octane fuel B) High compression C) Advanced timing D) All of the above
25. Which drill bit is best for metal? A) Spade bit B) Twist bit C) Forstner bit D) Hole saw

Mechanical Comprehension (25 questions)

1. If gear A has 30 teeth and gear B has 15 teeth, and A turns at 60 RPM, how fast does B turn? A) 30 RPM B) 60 RPM C) 120 RPM D) 240 RPM
2. Which pulley system gives the greatest mechanical advantage? A) Fixed pulley B) Single movable C) Double movable D) Triple movable
3. In Pascal's principle, pressure applied to fluid is: A) Reduced B) Increased C) Transmitted equally D) Lost
4. A crowbar 4 feet long has its fulcrum 6 inches from one end. What is the mechanical advantage? A) 6:1 B) 7:1 C) 8:1 D) 10:1
5. What is the ideal mechanical advantage of a wedge 8 inches long and 2 inches thick? A) 2:1 B) 4:1 C) 6:1 D) 8:1
6. In a wheel and axle with wheel diameter 12 inches and axle diameter 3 inches, what is the mechanical advantage? A) 3:1 B) 4:1 C) 6:1 D) 9:1
7. What happens to fluid velocity when pipe cross-section decreases? A) Increases B) Decreases C) Stays constant D) Stops
8. A screw is essentially what type of simple machine? A) Lever B) Wedge C) Inclined plane D) Pulley
9. If you apply 25 pounds to a 4:1 mechanical advantage lever, what is the output force? A) 50 lbs B) 75 lbs C) 100 lbs D) 125 lbs
10. What is the main function of a governor? A) Increase speed B) Control speed C) Change direction D) Store energy
11. In a hydraulic system with input area 5 sq in and output area 25 sq in, what is the force multiplication? A) 3:1 B) 4:1 C) 5:1 D) 6:1
12. What happens to mechanical advantage when effort arm length increases? A) Increases B) Decreases C) Stays same D) Becomes zero
13. Which gear type is used for perpendicular shaft power transmission? A) Spur B) Helical C) Bevel D) Internal

140

14. What is the force that pulls objects toward Earth's center? A) Centripetal B) Centrifugal C) Gravitational D) Magnetic
15. In a pulley system with 6 supporting ropes, what is the ideal mechanical advantage? A) 3:1 B) 4:1 C) 5:1 D) 6:1
16. Increasing the radius of a wheel increases what? A) Torque B) Speed C) Force D) Power
17. Static friction is always: A) Less than kinetic B) Greater than kinetic C) Equal to kinetic D) Zero
18. A machine with 90% efficiency converts 100 J input to how much useful output? A) 80 J B) 85 J C) 90 J D) 95 J
19. What determines the motion pattern in a cam mechanism? A) Cam speed B) Cam profile C) Follower mass D) Spring force
20. How does atmospheric pressure change with altitude? A) Increases B) Decreases C) Stays constant D) Varies randomly
21. Which mechanism converts rotary motion to reciprocating motion? A) Gear train B) Belt drive C) Crank and connecting rod D) Chain drive
22. What principle explains how hydraulic jacks work? A) Archimedes' principle B) Pascal's principle C) Bernoulli's principle D) Newton's principle
23. If input gear rotates 180°, and gear ratio is 2:1, how far does output gear rotate? A) 45° B) 90° C) 180° D) 360°
24. What type of bearing uses rolling elements to reduce friction? A) Plain bearing B) Ball bearing C) Sleeve bearing D) Journal bearing
25. Increasing thread pitch on a screw results in: A) Greater force B) Less force C) Faster movement D) Slower movement

Answer Key - Test 4

General Science: 1-A, 2-C, 3-C, 4-B, 5-C, 6-B, 7-A, 8-B, 9-C, 10-B, 11-C, 12-D, 13-B, 14-C, 15-D, 16-C, 17-B, 18-C, 19-A, 20-B, 21-B, 22-B, 23-B, 24-C, 25-B

Arithmetic Reasoning: 1-C, 2-C, 3-B, 4-B, 5-B, 6-C, 7-B, 8-B, 9-B, 10-C, 11-C, 12-C, 13-B, 14-C, 15-C, 16-C, 17-C, 18-A, 19-B, 20-B, 21-C, 22-B, 23-B, 24-C, 25-C, 26-C, 27-C, 28-B, 29-B, 30-C

Word Knowledge: 1-B, 2-B, 3-B, 4-B, 5-B, 6-B, 7-B, 8-B, 9-B, 10-B, 11-B, 12-B, 13-B, 14-A, 15-B, 16-B, 17-B, 18-B, 19-B, 20-B, 21-B, 22-B, 23-B, 24-B, 25-B, 26-B, 27-B, 28-B, 29-B, 30-B, 31-B, 32-B, 33-B, 34-B, 35-B

Paragraph Comprehension: 1-B, 2-D, 3-B, 4-C, 5-C, 6-B, 7-C, 8-B, 9-B, 10-D, 11-C, 12-C, 13-C, 14-A, 15-B

Mathematics Knowledge: 1-D, 2-C, 3-B, 4-B, 5-B, 6-C, 7-C, 8-B, 9-B, 10-C, 11-C, 12-C, 13-C, 14-C, 15-B, 16-B, 17-A, 18-C, 19-B, 20-A, 21-D, 22-B, 23-A, 24-A, 25-B

Electronics Information: 1-A, 2-D, 3-C, 4-B, 5-C, 6-A, 7-C, 8-B, 9-C, 10-B, 11-B, 12-B, 13-C, 14-A, 15-C, 16-B, 17-A, 18-B, 19-B, 20-A

Auto & Shop Information: 1-B, 2-B, 3-C, 4-B, 5-B, 6-A, 7-B, 8-B, 9-C, 10-B, 11-A, 12-B, 13-B, 14-C, 15-D, 16-B, 17-C, 18-B, 19-D, 20-B, 21-A, 22-D, 23-B, 24-D, 25-B

Mechanical Comprehension: 1-C, 2-D, 3-C, 4-B, 5-B, 6-B, 7-A, 8-C, 9-C, 10-B, 11-C, 12-A, 13-C, 14-C, 15-D, 16-A, 17-B, 18-C, 19-B, 20-B, 21-C, 22-B, 23-B, 24-B, 25-C

Test 3

General Science (25 questions)

1. Which planet is closest to the Sun? A) Mercury B) Venus C) Earth D) Mars
2. What is the chemical symbol for gold? A) Go B) Gd C) Au D) Ag
3. Which organ produces insulin? A) Liver B) Pancreas C) Kidney D) Heart
4. What type of rock is formed by cooling magma? A) Sedimentary B) Metamorphic C) Igneous D) Fossil
5. Which gas makes up most of Earth's atmosphere? A) Oxygen B) Carbon dioxide C) Nitrogen D) Hydrogen
6. What is the hardest natural substance? A) Quartz B) Diamond C) Steel D) Granite
7. How many chambers does a human heart have? A) 2 B) 3 C) 4 D) 5
8. What causes tides? A) Wind B) Moon's gravity C) Earth's rotation D) Sun's heat
9. Which vitamin is produced by skin exposed to sunlight? A) A B) C C) D D) E
10. What is the smallest unit of matter? A) Molecule B) Atom C) Electron D) Proton
11. Which blood type is the universal donor? A) A B) B C) AB D) O
12. What is the speed of light? A) 186,000 mph B) 186,000 km/h C) 186,000 miles/sec D) 186,000 km/sec
13. Which part of the cell contains DNA? A) Cytoplasm B) Nucleus C) Membrane D) Mitochondria
14. What is the most abundant element in the universe? A) Oxygen B) Carbon C) Hydrogen D) Helium
15. Which bone is the longest in the human body? A) Tibia B) Femur C) Humerus D) Radius
16. What causes lightning? A) Static electricity B) Magnetism C) Gravity D) Radiation
17. Which planet has the most moons? A) Jupiter B) Saturn C) Uranus D) Neptune
18. What is photosynthesis? A) Plant reproduction B) Light conversion to energy C) Water absorption D) Root growth
19. Which metal is liquid at room temperature? A) Lead B) Mercury C) Tin D) Zinc
20. What is the pH of pure water? A) 6 B) 7 C) 8 D) 9
21. Which part of the brain controls balance? A) Cerebrum B) Cerebellum C) Medulla D) Hypothalamus
22. What is the chemical formula for table salt? A) $NaCl$ B) KCl C) $CaCl_2$ D) $MgCl_2$
23. Which type of radiation has the shortest wavelength? A) Radio B) Infrared C) Ultraviolet D) Gamma
24. What is the largest organ in the human body? A) Liver B) Brain C) Skin D) Lungs

25. Which gas is essential for combustion? A) Nitrogen B) Oxygen C) Carbon dioxide D) Hydrogen

Arithmetic Reasoning (30 questions)

1. If a shirt costs $25 and is on sale for 20% off, what is the sale price? A) $20 B) $21 C) $22 D) $23
2. A recipe calls for 2 cups of flour to make 12 cookies. How much flour is needed for 18 cookies? A) 2.5 cups B) 3 cups C) 3.5 cups D) 4 cups
3. If you drive 240 miles in 4 hours, what is your average speed? A) 50 mph B) 55 mph C) 60 mph D) 65 mph
4. A box contains 15 red balls and 10 blue balls. What fraction of the balls are red? A) 2/3 B) 3/5 C) 1/2 D) 2/5
5. If you earn $12 per hour and work 35 hours, how much do you earn? A) $400 B) $420 C) $440 D) $460
6. A rectangle is 8 feet long and 6 feet wide. What is its area? A) 42 sq ft B) 44 sq ft C) 46 sq ft D) 48 sq ft
7. If 3 apples cost $1.50, how much do 8 apples cost? A) $3.00 B) $3.50 C) $4.00 D) $4.50
8. A test has 40 questions. If you answer 32 correctly, what percentage did you get right? A) 75% B) 80% C) 85% D) 90%
9. If you save $50 per month for 8 months, how much will you save? A) $350 B) $400 C) $450 D) $500
10. A circle has a radius of 5 inches. What is its circumference? (Use $\pi = 3.14$) A) 31.4 in B) 30.4 in C) 32.4 in D) 29.4 in
11. If $2x + 5 = 15$, what is x? A) 4 B) 5 C) 6 D) 7
12. A store sells 120 items on Monday and 80 items on Tuesday. What is the average? A) 90 B) 95 C) 100 D) 105
13. If you buy 4 items at $3.25 each, what is the total cost? A) $12.00 B) $12.50 C) $13.00 D) $13.50
14. A ladder 13 feet long leans against a wall. The base is 5 feet from the wall. How high up the wall does it reach? A) 10 ft B) 11 ft C) 12 ft D) 13 ft
15. If 40% of a number is 80, what is the number? A) 180 B) 200 C) 220 D) 240
16. A train travels 300 miles in 5 hours. At this rate, how far will it travel in 7 hours? A) 400 mi B) 420 mi C) 440 mi D) 460 mi
17. If you have $100 and spend 30%, how much do you have left? A) $60 B) $65 C) $70 D) $75
18. A triangle has angles of 60° and 80°. What is the third angle? A) 30° B) 35° C) 40° D) 45°
19. If 5 workers can complete a job in 8 hours, how long will it take 10 workers? A) 3 hours B) 4 hours C) 5 hours D) 6 hours
20. A square has a perimeter of 24 inches. What is its area? A) 32 sq in B) 34 sq in C) 36 sq in D) 38 sq in
21. If you flip a coin 3 times, what is the probability of getting all heads? A) 1/4 B) 1/6 C) 1/8 D) 1/12
22. A book costs $15 and a pen costs $2. How much do 3 books and 5 pens cost? A) $53 B) $55 C) $57 D) $59

23. If a car uses 1 gallon of gas for every 25 miles, how much gas is needed for 150 miles? A) 5 gallons B) 6 gallons C) 7 gallons D) 8 gallons
24. A rectangle has a length twice its width. If the width is 4 feet, what is the perimeter? A) 20 ft B) 22 ft C) 24 ft D) 26 ft
25. If you invest $500 at 4% annual interest, how much interest do you earn in one year? A) $15 B) $20 C) $25 D) $30
26. A pizza is cut into 8 equal slices. If you eat 3 slices, what fraction remains? A) 3/8 B) 5/8 C) 1/2 D) 2/3
27. If 15 is 25% of a number, what is the number? A) 50 B) 60 C) 70 D) 80
28. A rope 24 feet long is cut into 3 equal pieces. How long is each piece? A) 6 ft B) 7 ft C) 8 ft D) 9 ft
29. If you buy items costing $2.50, $3.75, and $1.25, what is the total? A) $7.00 B) $7.25 C) $7.50 D) $7.75
30. A bathtub holds 50 gallons when full. If it's 60% full, how many gallons are in it? A) 25 B) 30 C) 35 D) 40

Word Knowledge (35 questions)

1. ABUNDANT most nearly means: A) Scarce B) Plentiful C) Average D) Expensive
2. DETERIORATE most nearly means: A) Improve B) Worsen C) Maintain D) Repair
3. GENUINE most nearly means: A) False B) Real C) Expensive D) Cheap
4. HECTIC most nearly means: A) Calm B) Busy C) Quiet D) Peaceful
5. ILLUMINATE most nearly means: A) Darken B) Light up C) Hide D) Cover
6. JOVIAL most nearly means: A) Sad B) Angry C) Cheerful D) Tired
7. KINDLE most nearly means: A) Extinguish B) Ignite C) Cool D) Freeze
8. LENIENT most nearly means: A) Strict B) Harsh C) Forgiving D) Cruel
9. METICULOUS most nearly means: A) Careless B) Careful C) Quick D) Slow
10. NOVICE most nearly means: A) Expert B) Beginner C) Teacher D) Student
11. OBSCURE most nearly means: A) Clear B) Obvious C) Hidden D) Bright
12. PONDER most nearly means: A) Ignore B) Think about C) Forget D) Remember
13. QUAINT most nearly means: A) Modern B) Old-fashioned C) Ugly D) Beautiful
14. RIGID most nearly means: A) Flexible B) Soft C) Stiff D) Weak
15. SERENE most nearly means: A) Noisy B) Peaceful C) Excited D) Angry
16. TEDIOUS most nearly means: A) Exciting B) Boring C) Quick D) Easy
17. UNIFORM most nearly means: A) Different B) Similar C) Varied D) Mixed
18. VIVID most nearly means: A) Dull B) Bright C) Dark D) Faded
19. WARY most nearly means: A) Trusting B) Cautious C) Careless D) Bold
20. YEARN most nearly means: A) Reject B) Long for C) Hate D) Fear
21. ZENITH most nearly means: A) Bottom B) Peak C) Middle D) Start
22. AFFABLE most nearly means: A) Unfriendly B) Friendly C) Angry D) Sad
23. BELLIGERENT most nearly means: A) Peaceful B) Aggressive C) Calm D) Happy
24. CANDID most nearly means: A) Dishonest B) Honest C) Shy D) Bold
25. DOCILE most nearly means: A) Wild B) Tame C) Aggressive D) Mean
26. ELOQUENT most nearly means: A) Silent B) Well-spoken C) Rude D) Quiet
27. FRUGAL most nearly means: A) Wasteful B) Thrifty C) Expensive D) Cheap
28. GREGARIOUS most nearly means: A) Antisocial B) Sociable C) Quiet D) Shy

29. HAUGHTY most nearly means: A) Humble B) Arrogant C) Kind D) Generous
30. IMMACULATE most nearly means: A) Dirty B) Clean C) Messy D) Stained
31. JEOPARDIZE most nearly means: A) Protect B) Endanger C) Help D) Save
32. KUDOS most nearly means: A) Criticism B) Praise C) Punishment D) Blame
33. LUCID most nearly means: A) Confused B) Clear C) Dark D) Bright
34. MALICE most nearly means: A) Kindness B) Hatred C) Love D) Care
35. NONCHALANT most nearly means: A) Excited B) Casual C) Nervous D) Worried

Paragraph Comprehension (15 questions)

Passage 1: The invention of the printing press by Johannes Gutenberg around 1440 revolutionized the spread of information. Before this invention, books were hand-copied by scribes, making them expensive and rare. The printing press allowed for mass production of books, making knowledge more accessible to the general population. This led to increased literacy rates and the rapid spread of new ideas during the Renaissance.

1. According to the passage, what was the main impact of the printing press? A) It made scribes unemployed B) It made books more expensive C) It made knowledge more accessible D) It slowed the spread of ideas
2. Before the printing press, books were: A) Mass produced B) Hand-copied C) Very cheap D) Widely available

Passage 2: Photosynthesis is the process by which plants convert sunlight, water, and carbon dioxide into glucose and oxygen. This process occurs mainly in the leaves, specifically in structures called chloroplasts. The green pigment chlorophyll captures the light energy needed for this reaction. Photosynthesis is essential for life on Earth as it produces the oxygen we breathe and forms the base of most food chains.

3. Where does photosynthesis mainly occur in plants? A) Roots B) Stems C) Leaves D) Flowers
4. What captures the light energy needed for photosynthesis? A) Glucose B) Oxygen C) Carbon dioxide D) Chlorophyll
5. Why is photosynthesis essential for life on Earth? A) It produces carbon dioxide B) It produces oxygen and food C) It removes sunlight D) It creates water

Passage 3: Regular exercise provides numerous health benefits including improved cardiovascular health, stronger bones and muscles, better mental health, and increased longevity. The American Heart Association recommends at least 150 minutes of moderate-intensity exercise per week for adults. This can include activities such as brisk walking, swimming, or cycling. Even small amounts of exercise are better than none at all.

6. How much exercise does the American Heart Association recommend per week? A) 100 minutes B) 150 minutes C) 200 minutes D) 250 minutes
7. According to the passage, exercise benefits include all of the following EXCEPT: A) Better cardiovascular health B) Stronger bones C) Improved mental health D) Decreased appetite

Passage 4: The water cycle is the continuous movement of water through the environment. It begins with evaporation, where heat from the sun causes water from oceans, lakes, and rivers to turn into water vapor. This vapor rises into the atmosphere and condenses into clouds. When clouds become heavy with water, precipitation occurs in the form of rain, snow, or hail. The water then returns to bodies of water or soaks into the ground, completing the cycle.

8. What causes water to evaporate? A) Wind B) Cold temperatures C) Heat from the sun D) Gravity
9. What happens when clouds become heavy with water? A) Evaporation B) Condensation C) Precipitation D) Absorption
10. The water cycle is described as: A) A one-time event B) A continuous process C) A seasonal occurrence D) A rare phenomenon

Passage 5: Sleep is crucial for physical and mental health. During sleep, the body repairs tissues, consolidates memories, and releases important hormones. Most adults need 7-9 hours of sleep per night. Lack of adequate sleep can lead to decreased concentration, weakened immune system, and increased risk of chronic diseases. Good sleep hygiene includes maintaining a regular sleep schedule and creating a comfortable sleep environment.

11. How many hours of sleep do most adults need? A) 5-7 hours B) 6-8 hours C) 7-9 hours D) 8-10 hours
12. What happens during sleep according to the passage? A) Energy is consumed B) Tissues are repaired C) Temperature increases D) Breathing stops
13. Poor sleep can lead to: A) Better concentration B) Stronger immune system C) Increased disease risk D) Improved memory

Passage 6: Renewable energy sources such as solar, wind, and hydroelectric power are becoming increasingly important as alternatives to fossil fuels. These sources are considered renewable because they are naturally replenished and do not deplete over time. Unlike fossil fuels, renewable energy sources produce little to no greenhouse gas emissions, making them environmentally friendly options for meeting our energy needs.

14. What makes energy sources "renewable"? A) They are expensive B) They are naturally replenished C) They produce emissions D) They deplete quickly
15. Compared to fossil fuels, renewable energy sources: A) Produce more emissions B) Are less environmentally friendly C) Produce little to no emissions D) Are always more expensive

Mathematics Knowledge (25 questions)

1. What is 2^3? A) 6 B) 8 C) 9 D) 12
2. Solve for x: $3x - 7 = 14$ A) 5 B) 6 C) 7 D) 8
3. What is the square root of 144? A) 11 B) 12 C) 13 D) 14
4. If a triangle has angles of 45° and 90°, what is the third angle? A) 35° B) 40° C) 45° D) 50°
5. What is 15% of 200? A) 25 B) 30 C) 35 D) 40

6. Simplify: 3(x + 4) A) 3x + 4 B) 3x + 12 C) x + 12 D) 3x + 7
7. What is the area of a circle with radius 3? (Use π = 3.14) A) 28.26 B) 28.27 C) 28.28 D) 28.29
8. If 2x + 5 = 17, what is x? A) 5 B) 6 C) 7 D) 8
9. What is the slope of a line passing through (2,3) and (4,7)? A) 1 B) 2 C) 3 D) 4
10. Factor: x^2 - 9 A) (x-3)(x-3) B) (x+3)(x+3) C) (x-3)(x+3) D) Cannot be factored
11. What is 4! (4 factorial)? A) 16 B) 20 C) 24 D) 28
12. Solve: |x - 3| = 5 A) x = 8 only B) x = -2 only C) x = 8 or x = -2 D) x = 2 or x = 8
13. What is the volume of a cube with side length 4? A) 48 B) 56 C) 64 D) 72
14. If $\log_2(x)$ = 3, what is x? A) 6 B) 8 C) 9 D) 12
15. What is the distance between points (1,2) and (4,6)? A) 4 B) 5 C) 6 D) 7
16. Simplify: $(2x)^3$ A) $6x^3$ B) $8x^3$ C) $2x^3$ D) x^3
17. What is the sum of interior angles of a pentagon? A) 540° B) 520° C) 500° D) 480°
18. If sin(θ) = 0.5, what is θ? A) 30° B) 45° C) 60° D) 90°
19. What is the median of: 2, 5, 7, 9, 11? A) 5 B) 7 C) 9 D) 11
20. Solve: x^2 - 5x + 6 = 0 A) x = 2, 3 B) x = 1, 6 C) x = -2, -3 D) x = 2, -3
21. What is 25% of 80? A) 15 B) 20 C) 25 D) 30
22. If f(x) = 2x + 1, what is f(3)? A) 5 B) 6 C) 7 D) 8
23. What is the circumference of a circle with diameter 10? A) 31.4 B) 31.5 C) 31.6 D) 31.7
24. Simplify: √50 A) 5√2 B) 5√3 C) 7√2 D) 10√5
25. What is the y-intercept of y = 3x - 4? A) -4 B) -3 C) 3 D) 4

Electronics Information (20 questions)

1. What does AC stand for? A) Alternating Current B) Active Circuit C) Automatic Control D) Applied Current
2. What is the unit of electrical resistance? A) Volt B) Amp C) Ohm D) Watt
3. Which component stores electrical energy? A) Resistor B) Capacitor C) Inductor D) Transistor
4. What is Ohm's Law? A) V = I × R B) V = I + R C) V = I - R D) V = I ÷ R
5. What does a diode do? A) Stores energy B) Allows current in one direction C) Amplifies signals D) Reduces voltage
6. What is the standard voltage in US households? A) 110V B) 115V C) 120V D) 125V
7. Which material is the best conductor? A) Rubber B) Glass C) Silver D) Wood
8. What does a transformer do? A) Stores energy B) Changes voltage levels C) Converts AC to DC D) Amplifies current
9. What is the symbol for current? A) V B) I C) R D) P
10. How are batteries connected to increase voltage? A) In parallel B) In series C) In combination D) Separately
11. What does LED stand for? A) Light Emitting Diode B) Low Energy Device C) Linear Electronic Display D) Light Electric Device
12. What is a short circuit? A) A broken wire B) Low resistance path C) High voltage condition D) Open circuit
13. Which component opposes changes in current? A) Resistor B) Capacitor C) Inductor D) Diode
14. What is the frequency of AC power in the US? A) 50 Hz B) 60 Hz C) 70 Hz D) 80 Hz

15. What does a fuse do? A) Amplifies current B) Stores energy C) Protects from overcurrent D) Changes voltage
16. What is the unit of power? A) Volt B) Amp C) Ohm D) Watt
17. Which type of circuit has multiple paths for current? A) Series B) Parallel C) Complex D) Simple
18. What is ground in electrical terms? A) Soil B) Zero voltage reference C) High voltage D) Negative voltage
19. What does RMS stand for? A) Relative Mean Square B) Root Mean Square C) Rapid Measurement System D) Random Multiple Signal
20. What happens to total resistance when resistors are added in parallel? A) Increases B) Decreases C) Stays same D) Becomes zero

Auto & Shop Information (25 questions)

1. What does a carburetor do? A) Starts the engine B) Mixes air and fuel C) Cools the engine D) Charges the battery
2. How many strokes are in a typical car engine cycle? A) 2 B) 3 C) 4 D) 6
3. What tool is used to tighten bolts to a specific torque? A) Wrench B) Torque wrench C) Socket D) Screwdriver
4. What is the purpose of motor oil? A) Cool engine B) Lubricate parts C) Clean engine D) All of the above
5. Which part stores electrical energy in a car? A) Alternator B) Battery C) Starter D) Distributor
6. What does ABS stand for? A) Automatic Brake System B) Anti-lock Brake System C) Advanced Brake System D) Auxiliary Brake System
7. What tool is best for cutting metal? A) Wood saw B) Hacksaw C) Chisel D) File
8. What is the function of a radiator? A) Generate power B) Cool the engine C) Filter air D) Store fuel
9. Which tool measures electrical voltage? A) Ammeter B) Voltmeter C) Ohmmeter D) Multimeter
10. What is the purpose of a thermostat in an engine? A) Measure temperature B) Control coolant flow C) Start engine D) Filter oil
11. What does SAE stand for in oil ratings? A) Standard Automotive Equipment B) Society of Automotive Engineers C) Safe Automotive Engine D) Superior Auto Engineering
12. Which tool is used to remove rounded bolt heads? A) Socket wrench B) Box wrench C) Bolt extractor D) Impact wrench
13. What is the firing order? A) Order of cylinder ignition B) Order of gear shifting C) Order of brake application D) Order of fuel injection
14. What does a differential do? A) Changes gears B) Allows wheels to turn at different speeds C) Stores power D) Cools transmission
15. Which sandpaper grit is finest? A) 60 B) 120 C) 220 D) 400
16. What is the purpose of a catalytic converter? A) Convert fuel B) Reduce emissions C) Increase power D) Cool exhaust
17. What tool is used to measure internal engine wear? A) Micrometer B) Caliper C) Compression gauge D) Feeler gauge

18. What does viscosity refer to in motor oil? A) Color B) Thickness C) Temperature D) Pressure
19. Which component connects the engine to the transmission? A) Driveshaft B) Clutch C) Axle D) Universal joint
20. What is the standard thread pitch for most automotive bolts? A) Fine B) Coarse C) Extra fine D) Metric
21. What does a PCV valve do? A) Controls vacuum B) Ventilates crankcase C) Regulates fuel D) Controls timing
22. Which tool is best for precise measurements? A) Ruler B) Tape measure C) Micrometer D) Square
23. What is the purpose of valve clearance? A) Allow for thermal expansion B) Increase compression C) Improve airflow D) Reduce noise
24. What does octane rating measure? A) Fuel economy B) Knock resistance C) Fuel purity D) Burn rate
25. Which component controls the air/fuel mixture at idle? A) Carburetor B) Throttle body C) Idle air control valve D) Fuel injector

Mechanical Comprehension (25 questions)

1. If gear A has 20 teeth and gear B has 40 teeth, and A turns at 100 RPM, how fast does B turn? A) 50 RPM B) 100 RPM C) 200 RPM D) 400 RPM
2. Which pulley arrangement provides the greatest mechanical advantage? A) Fixed B) Movable C) Compound D) Simple
3. What happens to pressure in a hydraulic system when force is applied to a small piston? A) Decreases B) Increases C) Stays same D) Becomes zero
4. A lever is 6 feet long. If the fulcrum is 2 feet from one end, what is the mechanical advantage? A) 2:1 B) 3:1 C) 4:1 D) 6:1
5. What is the mechanical advantage of an inclined plane 12 feet long and 3 feet high? A) 2:1 B) 3:1 C) 4:1 D) 6:1
6. In a wheel and axle, if the wheel radius is 8 inches and axle radius is 2 inches, what is the mechanical advantage? A) 2:1 B) 4:1 C) 6:1 D) 8:1
7. What happens to the speed of water flowing through a pipe when the pipe diameter decreases? A) Increases B) Decreases C) Stays same D) Stops
8. Which simple machine is a screw based on? A) Lever B) Wedge C) Inclined plane D) Pulley
9. If you apply 10 pounds of force to a 5:1 mechanical advantage system, what output force do you get? A) 2 lbs B) 15 lbs C) 50 lbs D) 100 lbs
10. What is the purpose of a flywheel? A) Increase speed B) Store rotational energy C) Reduce friction D) Change direction
11. In a hydraulic jack, if the input piston has an area of 2 sq in and output piston has 20 sq in, what is the mechanical advantage? A) 5:1 B) 10:1 C) 15:1 D) 20:1
12. What happens to the mechanical advantage when you increase the length of a lever arm? A) Increases B) Decreases C) Stays same D) Becomes negative
13. Which type of gear changes the direction of rotation by 90 degrees? A) Spur B) Helical C) Bevel D) Worm

14. What is centrifugal force? A) Force toward center B) Force away from center C) Gravitational force D) Magnetic force
15. In a block and tackle with 4 supporting ropes, what is the theoretical mechanical advantage? A) 2:1 B) 3:1 C) 4:1 D) 8:1
16. What happens to torque when you increase the length of a wrench? A) Increases B) Decreases C) Stays same D) Becomes zero
17. Which statement about friction is correct? A) Always helpful B) Always harmful C) Can be helpful or harmful D) Only exists in liquids
18. What is the efficiency of a machine that requires 100 J of input to produce 80 J of output? A) 60% B) 70% C) 80% D) 90%
19. In a cam and follower system, what determines the follower's motion? A) Cam speed B) Cam shape C) Follower weight D) Spring tension
20. What happens to pressure at the bottom of a fluid column as height increases? A) Increases B) Decreases C) Stays same D) Becomes negative
21. Which component converts rotary motion to linear motion? A) Gear B) Cam C) Rack and pinion D) Belt
22. What is the principle behind a hydraulic brake system? A) Mechanical advantage B) Pascal's principle C) Archimedes' principle D) Bernoulli's principle
23. If a gear train has a ratio of 3:1, and the input gear turns 90 degrees, how far does the output gear turn? A) 30 degrees B) 60 degrees C) 90 degrees D) 270 degrees
24. What type of bearing reduces friction through rolling action? A) Plain bearing B) Ball bearing C) Sleeve bearing D) Thrust bearing
25. What happens when you increase the number of threads per inch on a screw? A) Faster movement B) Slower movement C) More force needed D) Less force needed

Answer Key - Test 3

General Science: 1-A, 2-C, 3-B, 4-C, 5-C, 6-B, 7-C, 8-B, 9-C, 10-B, 11-D, 12-C, 13-B, 14-C, 15-B, 16-A, 17-B, 18-B, 19-B, 20-B, 21-B, 22-A, 23-D, 24-C, 25-B

Arithmetic Reasoning: 1-A, 2-B, 3-C, 4-B, 5-B, 6-D, 7-C, 8-B, 9-B, 10-A, 11-B, 12-C, 13-C, 14-C, 15-B, 16-B, 17-C, 18-C, 19-B, 20-C, 21-C, 22-B, 23-B, 24-C, 25-B, 26-B, 27-B, 28-C, 29-C, 30-B

Word Knowledge: 1-B, 2-B, 3-B, 4-B, 5-B, 6-C, 7-B, 8-C, 9-B, 10-B, 11-C, 12-B, 13-B, 14-C, 15-B, 16-B, 17-B, 18-B, 19-B, 20-B, 21-B, 22-B, 23-B, 24-B, 25-B, 26-B, 27-B, 28-B, 29-B, 30-B, 31-B, 32-B, 33-B, 34-B, 35-B

Paragraph Comprehension: 1-C, 2-B, 3-C, 4-D, 5-B, 6-B, 7-D, 8-C, 9-C, 10-B, 11-C, 12-B, 13-C, 14-B, 15-C

Mathematics Knowledge: 1-B, 2-C, 3-B, 4-C, 5-B, 6-B, 7-A, 8-B, 9-B, 10-C, 11-C, 12-C, 13-C, 14-B, 15-B, 16-B, 17-A, 18-A, 19-B, 20-A, 21-B, 22-C, 23-A, 24-A, 25-A

Electronics Information: 1-A, 2-C, 3-B, 4-A, 5-B, 6-C, 7-C, 8-B, 9-B, 10-B, 11-A, 12-B, 13-C, 14-B, 15-C, 16-D, 17-B, 18-B, 19-B, 20-B

Auto & Shop Information: 1-B, 2-C, 3-B, 4-D, 5-B, 6-B, 7-B, 8-B, 9-D, 10-B, 11-B, 12-C, 13-A, 14-B, 15-D, 16-B, 17-C, 18-B, 19-B, 20-B, 21-B, 22-C, 23-A, 24-B, 25-C

Mechanical Comprehension: 1-A, 2-C, 3-B, 4-A, 5-C, 6-B, 7-A, 8-C, 9-C, 10-B, 11-B, 12-A, 13-C, 14-B, 15-C, 16-A, 17-C, 18-C, 19-B, 20-A, 21-C, 22-B, 23-A, 24-B, 25-B

Test 4

General Science (25 questions)

1. What is the chemical formula for water? A) H2O B) CO2 C) NaCl D) O2
2. Which organ filters blood in the human body? A) Heart B) Liver C) Kidney D) Lungs
3. What is the smallest particle of an element? A) Molecule B) Compound C) Atom D) Ion
4. Which planet is known as the Red Planet? A) Venus B) Mars C) Jupiter D) Saturn
5. What gas do plants absorb during photosynthesis? A) Oxygen B) Nitrogen C) Carbon dioxide D) Hydrogen
6. How many bones are in an adult human body? A) 196 B) 206 C) 216 D) 226
7. What is the speed of sound in air at room temperature? A) 343 m/s B) 353 m/s C) 363 m/s D) 373 m/s
8. Which type of energy is stored in a stretched rubber band? A) Kinetic B) Potential C) Thermal D) Chemical
9. What is the hardest mineral on the Mohs scale? A) Quartz B) Topaz C) Diamond D) Corundum
10. Which blood vessel carries blood away from the heart? A) Vein B) Artery C) Capillary D) Valve
11. What is the main component of natural gas? A) Propane B) Butane C) Methane D) Ethane
12. Which force keeps planets in orbit around the sun? A) Magnetic B) Electric C) Nuclear D) Gravitational
13. What is the pH of a neutral solution? A) 0 B) 7 C) 14 D) 1
14. Which part of the cell produces energy? A) Nucleus B) Cytoplasm C) Mitochondria D) Membrane
15. What is the most common element in Earth's crust? A) Silicon B) Aluminum C) Iron D) Oxygen
16. Which system fights disease in the human body? A) Circulatory B) Respiratory C) Immune D) Digestive
17. What happens during nuclear fusion? A) Atoms split B) Atoms combine C) Electrons move D) Protons disappear
18. Which gas is responsible for the greenhouse effect? A) Oxygen B) Nitrogen C) Carbon dioxide D) Argon
19. What is the unit of frequency? A) Hertz B) Watt C) Joule D) Newton
20. Which organ produces bile? A) Pancreas B) Liver C) Kidney D) Stomach

21. What is absolute zero? A) 0°C B) -273°C C) -100°C D) -200°C
22. Which metal is liquid at room temperature? A) Lead B) Mercury C) Tin D) Zinc
23. What causes day and night? A) Earth's orbit B) Earth's rotation C) Moon's orbit D) Sun's movement
24. Which vitamin prevents scurvy? A) A B) B C) C D) D
25. What is the chemical symbol for iron? A) Ir B) Fe C) In D) I

Arithmetic Reasoning (30 questions)

1. A car travels 240 miles in 4 hours. What is its average speed? A) 50 mph B) 55 mph C) 60 mph D) 65 mph
2. If 3 pounds of apples cost $4.50, how much do 5 pounds cost? A) $6.50 B) $7.00 C) $7.50 D) $8.00
3. A rectangle has a length of 12 feet and width of 8 feet. What is its perimeter? A) 36 ft B) 40 ft C) 44 ft D) 48 ft
4. If you score 18 out of 20 on a test, what percentage did you get? A) 85% B) 90% C) 95% D) 100%
5. A store offers a 25% discount on a $80 item. What is the sale price? A) $55 B) $60 C) $65 D) $70
6. If you save $75 per month for 6 months, how much will you save? A) $400 B) $425 C) $450 D) $475
7. A circle has a diameter of 14 inches. What is its radius? A) 6 in B) 7 in C) 8 in D) 9 in
8. If $4x - 3 = 17$, what is x? A) 4 B) 5 C) 6 D) 7
9. A pizza is divided into 8 equal slices. If you eat 3 slices, what fraction is left? A) 3/8 B) 5/8 C) 1/2 D) 2/3
10. If you buy 6 items at $2.75 each, what is the total cost? A) $15.50 B) $16.00 C) $16.50 D) $17.00
11. A ladder 15 feet long leans against a wall. The base is 9 feet from the wall. How high up does it reach? A) 10 ft B) 11 ft C) 12 ft D) 13 ft
12. If 35% of a number is 140, what is the number? A) 350 B) 375 C) 400 D) 425
13. A train travels 450 miles in 6 hours. How far will it travel in 8 hours at the same speed? A) 550 mi B) 600 mi C) 650 mi D) 700 mi
14. If you have $200 and spend 40%, how much do you have left? A) $100 B) $110 C) $120 D) $130
15. A triangle has angles of 45° and 75°. What is the third angle? A) 50° B) 55° C) 60° D) 65°
16. If 8 workers can finish a job in 12 hours, how long will it take 6 workers? A) 14 hours B) 15 hours C) 16 hours D) 18 hours
17. A square has an area of 64 square inches. What is its perimeter? A) 28 in B) 30 in C) 32 in D) 34 in
18. If you roll two dice, what is the probability of getting a sum of 7? A) 1/6 B) 1/7 C) 1/8 D) 1/12
19. A book costs $12 and a magazine costs $3. How much do 4 books and 6 magazines cost? A) $63 B) $66 C) $69 D) $72
20. If a car uses 1 gallon for every 30 miles, how much gas is needed for 180 miles? A) 5 gal B) 6 gal C) 7 gal D) 8 gal

21. A rectangle has a width of 5 feet and length of 12 feet. What is its area? A) 50 sq ft B) 55 sq ft C) 60 sq ft D) 65 sq ft
22. If you invest $800 at 3% annual interest, how much interest do you earn in one year? A) $20 B) $24 C) $28 D) $32
23. A rope 36 feet long is cut into 4 equal pieces. How long is each piece? A) 8 ft B) 9 ft C) 10 ft D) 12 ft
24. If 20 is 40% of a number, what is the number? A) 40 B) 45 C) 50 D) 55
25. If you buy items costing $3.25, $4.50, and $2.75, what is the total? A) $10.00 B) $10.25 C) $10.50 D) $10.75
26. A bathtub holds 60 gallons when full. If it's 75% full, how many gallons are in it? A) 40 B) 42 C) 45 D) 48
27. If 12 is 15% of a number, what is the number? A) 70 B) 75 C) 80 D) 85
28. A classroom has 24 students. If 1/3 are absent, how many are present? A) 14 B) 16 C) 18 D) 20
29. If you travel 120 miles in 2.5 hours, what is your average speed? A) 46 mph B) 48 mph C) 50 mph D) 52 mph
30. A circle has a circumference of 31.4 inches. What is its diameter? (Use $\pi = 3.14$) A) 8 in B) 9 in C) 10 in D) 11 in

Word Knowledge (35 questions)

1. BENEVOLENT most nearly means: A) Evil B) Kind C) Angry D) Sad
2. CONSPICUOUS most nearly means: A) Hidden B) Obvious C) Quiet D) Small
3. DILIGENT most nearly means: A) Lazy B) Hardworking C) Slow D) Fast
4. ECCENTRIC most nearly means: A) Normal B) Unusual C) Round D) Flat
5. FEASIBLE most nearly means: A) Impossible B) Possible C) Difficult D) Easy
6. GULLIBLE most nearly means: A) Suspicious B) Easily fooled C) Smart D) Careful
7. HINDER most nearly means: A) Help B) Block C) Speed up D) Improve
8. INEVITABLE most nearly means: A) Avoidable B) Unavoidable C) Possible D) Unlikely
9. JARGON most nearly means: A) Clear speech B) Specialized language C) Loud talk D) Quiet whisper
10. KEEN most nearly means: A) Dull B) Sharp C) Broken D) Bent
11. LETHARGIC most nearly means: A) Energetic B) Sluggish C) Quick D) Active
12. MUNDANE most nearly means: A) Exciting B) Ordinary C) Unusual D) Rare
13. NEGLIGENT most nearly means: A) Careful B) Careless C) Helpful D) Harmful
14. OPTIMISTIC most nearly means: A) Hopeful B) Hopeless C) Sad D) Angry
15. PRUDENT most nearly means: A) Foolish B) Wise C) Quick D) Slow
16. QUERULOUS most nearly means: A) Happy B) Complaining C) Quiet D) Loud
17. REMORSE most nearly means: A) Joy B) Regret C) Anger D) Fear
18. SOLEMN most nearly means: A) Happy B) Serious C) Funny D) Light
19. TACITURN most nearly means: A) Talkative B) Quiet C) Loud D) Friendly
20. UBIQUITOUS most nearly means: A) Rare B) Everywhere C) Hidden D) Lost
21. VAGUE most nearly means: A) Clear B) Unclear C) Bright D) Dark
22. WANE most nearly means: A) Increase B) Decrease C) Stay same D) Disappear
23. XENIAL most nearly means: A) Hostile B) Hospitable C) Strange D) Foreign

24. YIELDING most nearly means: A) Rigid B) Flexible C) Hard D) Strong
25. ZEAL most nearly means: A) Laziness B) Enthusiasm C) Boredom D) Tiredness
26. ALOOF most nearly means: A) Friendly B) Distant C) Close D) Warm
27. BRAZEN most nearly means: A) Shy B) Bold C) Quiet D) Modest
28. CURTAIL most nearly means: A) Extend B) Reduce C) Maintain D) Increase
29. DEPLORE most nearly means: A) Approve B) Disapprove C) Ignore D) Accept
30. ELATED most nearly means: A) Sad B) Joyful C) Angry D) Tired
31. FICKLE most nearly means: A) Stable B) Changeable C) Reliable D) Steady
32. GAUDY most nearly means: A) Plain B) Flashy C) Simple D) Elegant
33. HAUGHTY most nearly means: A) Humble B) Proud C) Kind D) Gentle
34. IRKSOME most nearly means: A) Pleasant B) Annoying C) Helpful D) Useful
35. JOVIAL most nearly means: A) Sad B) Cheerful C) Angry D) Worried

Paragraph Comprehension (15 questions)

Passage 1: Bees play a crucial role in pollinating plants, making them essential for food production. About one-third of the food we eat depends on bee pollination, including fruits, vegetables, and nuts. However, bee populations have been declining due to pesticide use, habitat loss, and disease. This decline threatens not only biodiversity but also agricultural productivity and food security worldwide.

1. According to the passage, what fraction of our food depends on bee pollination? A) One quarter B) One third C) One half D) Two thirds
2. The passage mentions all of the following as causes of bee decline EXCEPT: A) Pesticide use B) Habitat loss C) Disease D) Climate change

Passage 2: The human brain contains approximately 86 billion neurons, each connected to thousands of others through synapses. These connections allow for complex thought processes, memory formation, and learning. The brain's plasticity means it can reorganize and form new neural pathways throughout life, especially during childhood and adolescence when development is most rapid.

3. How many neurons does the human brain contain? A) 86 million B) 86 billion C) 86 thousand D) 86 trillion
4. When is brain development most rapid? A) Adulthood B) Old age C) Childhood and adolescence D) Middle age
5. What does brain plasticity refer to? A) Brain size B) Brain weight C) Ability to reorganize D) Number of neurons

Passage 3: Solar panels convert sunlight directly into electricity through photovoltaic cells. These cells are typically made of silicon and work by allowing photons from sunlight to knock electrons loose from atoms, generating an electric current. Solar energy is renewable, clean, and becoming increasingly cost-effective as technology improves and production scales up.

6. What are photovoltaic cells typically made of? A) Carbon B) Silicon C) Aluminum D) Copper

7. How do solar panels generate electricity? A) By burning fuel B) By using wind power C) By converting sunlight D) By using water power

Passage 4: Regular physical exercise has numerous benefits for both physical and mental health. It strengthens the cardiovascular system, builds muscle mass, improves bone density, and enhances immune function. Exercise also releases endorphins, which can improve mood and reduce stress. The World Health Organization recommends at least 150 minutes of moderate exercise per week for adults.

8. How much exercise does the WHO recommend per week? A) 100 minutes B) 150 minutes C) 200 minutes D) 250 minutes
9. What chemicals does exercise release that improve mood? A) Hormones B) Endorphins C) Proteins D) Vitamins
10. According to the passage, exercise benefits include all EXCEPT: A) Stronger heart B) Better immunity C) Improved mood D) Increased appetite

Passage 5: Coral reefs are among the most diverse ecosystems on Earth, supporting about 25% of all marine species despite covering less than 1% of the ocean floor. These underwater structures are built by tiny animals called coral polyps, which form symbiotic relationships with algae. The algae provide food through photosynthesis while the coral provides protection and nutrients.

11. What percentage of marine species do coral reefs support? A) 15% B) 20% C) 25% D) 30%
12. What builds coral reefs? A) Fish B) Algae C) Coral polyps D) Sea plants
13. The relationship between coral and algae is described as: A) Competitive B) Parasitic C) Symbiotic D) Predatory

Passage 6: The invention of writing systems around 3200 BCE marked the beginning of recorded history. Early writing systems, such as cuneiform in Mesopotamia and hieroglyphics in Egypt, were initially used for record-keeping and administrative purposes. Over time, writing evolved to include literature, laws, and religious texts, fundamentally changing how knowledge was preserved and transmitted across generations.

14. When were writing systems first invented? A) 3200 BCE B) 3000 BCE C) 2800 BCE D) 2500 BCE
15. What were early writing systems initially used for? A) Literature B) Record-keeping C) Religious texts D) Laws

Mathematics Knowledge (25 questions)

1. What is 5^2? A) 10 B) 15 C) 20 D) 25
2. Solve for x: $2x + 8 = 20$ A) 4 B) 5 C) 6 D) 7
3. What is the square root of 169? A) 12 B) 13 C) 14 D) 15
4. If a right triangle has legs of 6 and 8, what is the hypotenuse? A) 9 B) 10 C) 11 D) 12
5. What is 20% of 150? A) 25 B) 30 C) 35 D) 40

6. Simplify: 4(x - 2) A) 4x - 2 B) 4x - 6 C) 4x - 8 D) x - 8
7. What is the area of a triangle with base 8 and height 6? A) 20 B) 22 C) 24 D) 26
8. If 3x - 4 = 11, what is x? A) 4 B) 5 C) 6 D) 7
9. What is the slope of a line passing through (1,2) and (3,8)? A) 2 B) 3 C) 4 D) 5
10. Factor: x^2 - 16 A) (x-4)(x-4) B) (x+4)(x+4) C) (x-4)(x+4) D) Cannot be factored
11. What is 6! (6 factorial)? A) 120 B) 360 C) 720 D) 1440
12. Solve: |x + 2| = 7 A) x = 5 only B) x = -9 only C) x = 5 or x = -9 D) x = -5 or x = 9
13. What is the volume of a rectangular prism with dimensions 3 × 4 × 5? A) 50 B) 55 C) 60 D) 65
14. If $\log_3(x)$ = 2, what is x? A) 6 B) 8 C) 9 D) 12
15. What is the distance between points (0,0) and (3,4)? A) 4 B) 5 C) 6 D) 7
16. Simplify: $(3x)^2$ A) $6x^2$ B) $9x^2$ C) $3x^2$ D) x^2
17. What is the sum of interior angles of a hexagon? A) 720° B) 700° C) 680° D) 660°
18. If cos(θ) = 0.5, what is θ? A) 30° B) 45° C) 60° D) 90°
19. What is the mode of: 3, 5, 7, 5, 9, 5, 6? A) 3 B) 5 C) 7 D) 9
20. Solve: x^2 - 7x + 12 = 0 A) x = 3, 4 B) x = 2, 6 C) x = 1, 12 D) x = -3, -4
21. What is 30% of 120? A) 30 B) 32 C) 34 D) 36
22. If f(x) = 3x - 2, what is f(4)? A) 8 B) 10 C) 12 D) 14
23. What is the area of a circle with radius 4? (Use π = 3.14) A) 50.24 B) 48.24 C) 52.24 D) 46.24
24. Simplify: $\sqrt{72}$ A) $6\sqrt{2}$ B) $6\sqrt{3}$ C) $8\sqrt{2}$ D) $9\sqrt{2}$
25. What is the x-intercept of y = 2x - 6? A) 2 B) 3 C) -3 D) 6

Electronics Information (20 questions)

1. What does DC stand for? A) Direct Current B) Digital Circuit C) Dynamic Control D) Double Contact
2. What is the unit of electrical power? A) Volt B) Amp C) Ohm D) Watt
3. Which component allows current to flow in only one direction? A) Resistor B) Capacitor C) Diode D) Inductor
4. What is the relationship between voltage, current, and resistance? A) V = I + R B) V = I × R C) V = I - R D) V = I ÷ R
5. What does an amplifier do? A) Stores energy B) Reduces voltage C) Increases signal strength D) Converts AC to DC
6. What is the standard frequency of AC power in Europe? A) 50 Hz B) 60 Hz C) 70 Hz D) 80 Hz
7. Which material is an insulator? A) Copper B) Silver C) Rubber D) Aluminum
8. What is the purpose of a rectifier? A) Amplify signals B) Convert AC to DC C) Store energy D) Filter noise
9. What is the symbol for voltage? A) I B) R C) V D) P
10. How are capacitors connected to increase total capacitance? A) In series B) In parallel C) In combination D) Separately
11. What does LCD stand for? A) Light Control Device B) Liquid Crystal Display C) Low Current Display D) Linear Circuit Display
12. What is an open circuit? A) A complete path B) A broken path C) High resistance D) Low voltage

156

13. Which component stores energy in a magnetic field? A) Resistor B) Capacitor C) Inductor D) Diode
14. What is the unit of capacitance? A) Farad B) Henry C) Ohm D) Watt
15. What does a circuit breaker do? A) Amplify current B) Store energy C) Protect from overload D) Convert voltage
16. What is impedance? A) DC resistance B) AC resistance C) Capacitance D) Inductance
17. Which type of circuit has only one path for current? A) Series B) Parallel C) Complex D) Compound
18. What is the purpose of a heat sink? A) Generate heat B) Remove heat C) Store heat D) Measure heat
19. What does PWM stand for? A) Power Wave Modulation B) Pulse Width Modulation C) Phase Wave Management D) Peak Watt Measurement
20. What happens to current when voltage increases and resistance stays constant? A) Increases B) Decreases C) Stays same D) Becomes zero

Auto & Shop Information (25 questions)

1. What is the purpose of a spark plug? A) Cool engine B) Ignite fuel mixture C) Filter air D) Pump fuel
2. How many cylinders does a V8 engine have? A) 6 B) 8 C) 10 D) 12
3. What tool is used to measure gap spacing? A) Ruler B) Caliper C) Feeler gauge D) Micrometer
4. What is the primary function of engine coolant? A) Lubricate B) Cool C) Clean D) Seal
5. Which component generates electrical power in a car? A) Battery B) Alternator C) Starter D) Ignition coil
6. What does EFI stand for? A) Electronic Fuel Injection B) Engine Fuel Indicator C) Electric Fan Ignition D) Enhanced Fuel Ignition
7. Which saw is best for cutting curves in wood? A) Circular saw B) Jigsaw C) Table saw D) Band saw
8. What is the function of a water pump? A) Pump fuel B) Circulate coolant C) Generate pressure D) Filter water
9. Which instrument measures electrical resistance? A) Voltmeter B) Ammeter C) Ohmmeter D) Wattmeter
10. What controls the engine's operating temperature? A) Radiator B) Thermostat C) Water pump D) Fan
11. What does API stand for in oil specifications? A) American Petroleum Institute B) Automotive Performance Index C) Advanced Protection Indicator D) Auto Parts International
12. Which tool cuts external threads? A) Tap B) Die C) Reamer D) Drill
13. What is valve overlap? A) Valves touching B) Both valves open simultaneously C) Valve timing error D) Valve clearance adjustment
14. What does a CV joint do? A) Change voltage B) Control vacuum C) Transmit power while turning D) Cool valves
15. Which abrasive is hardest? A) Emery B) Silicon carbide C) Aluminum oxide D) Diamond

16. What is the purpose of EGR? A) Increase power B) Reduce emissions C) Improve fuel economy D) Cool engine
17. What tool removes material by scraping? A) File B) Rasp C) Scraper D) Chisel
18. What does multi-viscosity oil mean? A) Multiple additives B) Viscosity changes with temperature C) Multiple brands mixed D) Multiple grades blended
19. Which component transfers engine power to wheels? A) Transmission B) Differential C) Driveshaft D) All of the above
20. What is the purpose of flux in soldering? A) Strengthen joint B) Clean surfaces C) Add color D) Increase temperature
21. What does DOHC stand for? A) Double Overhead Cam B) Direct Oil Heating Control C) Dual Output High Compression D) Dynamic Oil Head Control
22. Which file cut is smoothest? A) Bastard B) Second cut C) Smooth D) Dead smooth
23. What is compression ratio? A) Fuel to air ratio B) Cylinder volume ratio C) Pressure measurement D) Temperature ratio
24. What indicates engine knock? A) Low octane fuel B) High compression C) Advanced timing D) All of the above
25. Which drill bit is best for metal? A) Spade bit B) Twist bit C) Forstner bit D) Hole saw

Mechanical Comprehension (25 questions)

1. If gear A has 30 teeth and gear B has 15 teeth, and A turns at 60 RPM, how fast does B turn? A) 30 RPM B) 60 RPM C) 120 RPM D) 240 RPM
2. Which pulley system gives the greatest mechanical advantage? A) Fixed pulley B) Single movable C) Double movable D) Triple movable
3. In Pascal's principle, pressure applied to fluid is: A) Reduced B) Increased C) Transmitted equally D) Lost
4. A crowbar 4 feet long has its fulcrum 6 inches from one end. What is the mechanical advantage? A) 6:1 B) 7:1 C) 8:1 D) 10:1
5. What is the ideal mechanical advantage of a wedge 8 inches long and 2 inches thick? A) 2:1 B) 4:1 C) 6:1 D) 8:1
6. In a wheel and axle with wheel diameter 12 inches and axle diameter 3 inches, what is the mechanical advantage? A) 3:1 B) 4:1 C) 6:1 D) 9:1
7. What happens to fluid velocity when pipe cross-section decreases? A) Increases B) Decreases C) Stays constant D) Stops
8. A screw is essentially what type of simple machine? A) Lever B) Wedge C) Inclined plane D) Pulley
9. If you apply 25 pounds to a 4:1 mechanical advantage lever, what is the output force? A) 50 lbs B) 75 lbs C) 100 lbs D) 125 lbs
10. What is the main function of a governor? A) Increase speed B) Control speed C) Change direction D) Store energy
11. In a hydraulic system with input area 5 sq in and output area 25 sq in, what is the force multiplication? A) 3:1 B) 4:1 C) 5:1 D) 6:1
12. What happens to mechanical advantage when effort arm length increases? A) Increases B) Decreases C) Stays same D) Becomes zero
13. Which gear type is used for perpendicular shaft power transmission? A) Spur B) Helical C) Bevel D) Internal

14. What is the force that pulls objects toward Earth's center? A) Centripetal B) Centrifugal C) Gravitational D) Magnetic
15. In a pulley system with 6 supporting ropes, what is the ideal mechanical advantage? A) 3:1 B) 4:1 C) 5:1 D) 6:1
16. Increasing the radius of a wheel increases what? A) Torque B) Speed C) Force D) Power
17. Static friction is always: A) Less than kinetic B) Greater than kinetic C) Equal to kinetic D) Zero
18. A machine with 90% efficiency converts 100 J input to how much useful output? A) 80 J B) 85 J C) 90 J D) 95 J
19. What determines the motion pattern in a cam mechanism? A) Cam speed B) Cam profile C) Follower mass D) Spring force
20. How does atmospheric pressure change with altitude? A) Increases B) Decreases C) Stays constant D) Varies randomly
21. Which mechanism converts rotary motion to reciprocating motion? A) Gear train B) Belt drive C) Crank and connecting rod D) Chain drive
22. What principle explains how hydraulic jacks work? A) Archimedes' principle B) Pascal's principle C) Bernoulli's principle D) Newton's principle
23. If input gear rotates 180°, and gear ratio is 2:1, how far does output gear rotate? A) 45° B) 90° C) 180° D) 360°
24. What type of bearing uses rolling elements to reduce friction? A) Plain bearing B) Ball bearing C) Sleeve bearing D) Journal bearing
25. Increasing thread pitch on a screw results in: A) Greater force B) Less force C) Faster movement D) Slower movement

Answer Key - Test 4

General Science: 1-A, 2-C, 3-C, 4-B, 5-C, 6-B, 7-A, 8-B, 9-C, 10-B, 11-C, 12-D, 13-B, 14-C, 15-D, 16-C, 17-B, 18-C, 19-A, 20-B, 21-B, 22-B, 23-B, 24-C, 25-B

Arithmetic Reasoning: 1-C, 2-C, 3-B, 4-B, 5-B, 6-C, 7-B, 8-B, 9-B, 10-C, 11-C, 12-C, 13-B, 14-C, 15-C, 16-C, 17-C, 18-A, 19-B, 20-B, 21-C, 22-B, 23-B, 24-C, 25-C, 26-C, 27-C, 28-B, 29-B, 30-C

Word Knowledge: 1-B, 2-B, 3-B, 4-B, 5-B, 6-B, 7-B, 8-B, 9-B, 10-B, 11-B, 12-B, 13-B, 14-A, 15-B, 16-B, 17-B, 18-B, 19-B, 20-B, 21-B, 22-B, 23-B, 24-B, 25-B, 26-B, 27-B, 28-B, 29-B, 30-B, 31-B, 32-B, 33-B, 34-B, 35-B

Paragraph Comprehension: 1-B, 2-D, 3-B, 4-C, 5-C, 6-B, 7-C, 8-B, 9-B, 10-D, 11-C, 12-C, 13-C, 14-A, 15-B

Mathematics Knowledge: 1-D, 2-C, 3-B, 4-B, 5-B, 6-C, 7-C, 8-B, 9-B, 10-C, 11-C, 12-C, 13-C, 14-C, 15-B, 16-B, 17-A, 18-C, 19-B, 20-A, 21-D, 22-B, 23-A, 24-A, 25-B

Electronics Information: 1-A, 2-D, 3-C, 4-B, 5-C, 6-A, 7-C, 8-B, 9-C, 10-B, 11-B, 12-B, 13-C, 14-A, 15-C, 16-B, 17-A, 18-B, 19-B, 20-A

Auto & Shop Information: 1-B, 2-B, 3-C, 4-B, 5-B, 6-A, 7-B, 8-B, 9-C, 10-B, 11-A, 12-B, 13-B, 14-C, 15-D, 16-B, 17-C, 18-B, 19-D, 20-B, 21-A, 22-D, 23-B, 24-D, 25-B

Mechanical Comprehension: 1-C, 2-D, 3-C, 4-B, 5-B, 6-B, 7-A, 8-C, 9-C, 10-B, 11-C, 12-A, 13-C, 14-C, 15-D, 16-A, 17-B, 18-C, 19-B, 20-B, 21-C, 22-B, 23-B, 24-B, 25-C

Test 5

General Science (25 questions)

1. What is the chemical symbol for sodium? A) So B) Na C) S D) N
2. Which organ produces red blood cells? A) Heart B) Liver C) Bone marrow D) Spleen
3. What is the basic unit of heredity? A) Cell B) Chromosome C) Gene D) DNA
4. Which planet has the shortest day? A) Mercury B) Venus C) Jupiter D) Saturn
5. What gas do animals exhale? A) Oxygen B) Nitrogen C) Carbon dioxide D) Hydrogen
6. How many chambers does a bird's heart have? A) 2 B) 3 C) 4 D) 5
7. What is the speed of light in a vacuum? A) 3×10^8 m/s B) 3×10^9 m/s C) 3×10^7 m/s D) 3×10^6 m/s
8. Which type of rock is limestone? A) Igneous B) Metamorphic C) Sedimentary D) Volcanic
9. What is the hardest part of the human body? A) Bone B) Tooth enamel C) Nail D) Cartilage
10. Which force opposes motion? A) Gravity B) Friction C) Magnetism D) Electricity
11. What is the main gas in Earth's atmosphere? A) Oxygen B) Carbon dioxide C) Nitrogen D) Argon
12. Which organ removes waste from blood? A) Liver B) Lungs C) Kidney D) Heart
13. What is the pH of stomach acid? A) 1-2 B) 6-7 C) 8-9 D) 12-14
14. Which part of the atom has a positive charge? A) Electron B) Neutron C) Proton D) Nucleus
15. What is the most abundant gas in the universe? A) Oxygen B) Helium C) Hydrogen D) Nitrogen
16. Which system controls body functions? A) Circulatory B) Respiratory C) Nervous D) Digestive
17. What happens during photosynthesis? A) Plants absorb CO_2 B) Plants release O_2 C) Plants make glucose D) All of the above
18. Which metal is most conductive? A) Copper B) Silver C) Gold D) Aluminum
19. What is the unit of electric current? A) Volt B) Watt C) Ampere D) Ohm
20. Which vitamin is fat-soluble? A) B B) C C) A D) Folic acid
21. What is absolute zero in Fahrenheit? A) -273°F B) -460°F C) -100°F D) -200°F
22. Which element has the symbol K? A) Krypton B) Potassium C) Calcium D) Chlorine
23. What causes seasons on Earth? A) Distance from sun B) Earth's tilt C) Solar flares D) Moon's gravity

24. Which blood type can donate to all others? A) A B) B C) AB D) O
25. What is the study of earthquakes called? A) Geology B) Seismology C) Meteorology D) Astronomy

Arithmetic Reasoning (30 questions)

1. If a jacket costs $120 and is marked down 30%, what is the sale price? A) $80 B) $84 C) $88 D) $90
2. A recipe for 6 servings calls for 4 cups of flour. How much flour is needed for 9 servings? A) 5 cups B) 6 cups C) 7 cups D) 8 cups
3. If you drive 300 miles in 5 hours, what is your average speed? A) 55 mph B) 60 mph C) 65 mph D) 70 mph
4. A bag contains 20 marbles: 12 red and 8 blue. What is the probability of drawing a red marble? A) 2/5 B) 3/5 C) 1/2 D) 2/3
5. If you work 40 hours at $15 per hour, how much do you earn? A) $580 B) $600 C) $620 D) $640
6. A garden is 15 feet long and 10 feet wide. What is its area? A) 140 sq ft B) 150 sq ft C) 160 sq ft D) 170 sq ft
7. If 5 pencils cost $2.00, how much do 12 pencils cost? A) $4.50 B) $4.80 C) $5.00 D) $5.20
8. A test has 50 questions. If you answer 42 correctly, what percentage did you get? A) 82% B) 84% C) 86% D) 88%
9. If you save $60 per month for 10 months, how much will you save? A) $580 B) $600 C) $620 D) $640
10. A circle has a radius of 7 inches. What is its circumference? (Use $\pi = 3.14$) A) 43.96 in B) 44.96 in C) 45.96 in D) 46.96 in
11. If $3x + 7 = 22$, what is x? A) 4 B) 5 C) 6 D) 7
12. Two stores sell the same item for $45 and $60. What is the average price? A) $50.50 B) $52.50 C) $54.50 D) $56.50
13. If you buy 8 items at $4.25 each, what is the total cost? A) $32.00 B) $33.00 C) $34.00 D) $35.00
14. A ladder 17 feet long leans against a wall. The base is 8 feet from the wall. How high up does it reach? A) 13 ft B) 14 ft C) 15 ft D) 16 ft
15. If 45% of a number is 180, what is the number? A) 380 B) 400 C) 420 D) 440
16. A plane travels 600 miles in 4 hours. How far will it travel in 6 hours at the same speed? A) 850 mi B) 900 mi C) 950 mi D) 1000 mi
17. If you have $300 and spend 35%, how much do you have left? A) $185 B) $190 C) $195 D) $200
18. A triangle has angles of 55° and 70°. What is the third angle? A) 50° B) 55° C) 60° D) 65°
19. If 12 workers can complete a job in 8 hours, how long will it take 16 workers? A) 5 hours B) 6 hours C) 7 hours D) 8 hours
20. A square has a side length of 9 inches. What is its area? A) 72 sq in B) 78 sq in C) 81 sq in D) 84 sq in
21. If you draw a card from a standard deck, what is the probability it's a heart? A) 1/2 B) 1/3 C) 1/4 D) 1/5

22. A notebook costs $8 and a pen costs $1.50. How much do 5 notebooks and 8 pens cost? A) $50 B) $52 C) $54 D) $56
23. If a motorcycle uses 1 gallon for every 40 miles, how much gas is needed for 280 miles? A) 6 gal B) 7 gal C) 8 gal D) 9 gal
24. A rectangle has a length of 14 feet and width of 6 feet. What is its perimeter? A) 38 ft B) 40 ft C) 42 ft D) 44 ft
25. If you invest $1000 at 5% annual interest, how much interest do you earn in one year? A) $40 B) $45 C) $50 D) $55
26. A pizza is cut into 12 equal slices. If you eat 5 slices, what fraction remains? A) 5/12 B) 7/12 C) 1/2 D) 2/3
27. If 18 is 30% of a number, what is the number? A) 50 B) 55 C) 60 D) 65
28. A rope 42 feet long is cut into 6 equal pieces. How long is each piece? A) 6 ft B) 7 ft C) 8 ft D) 9 ft
29. If you buy items costing $4.75, $6.25, and $3.50, what is the total? A) $14.00 B) $14.25 C) $14.50 D) $14.75
30. A tank holds 80 gallons when full. If it's 85% full, how many gallons are in it? A) 66 B) 68 C) 70 D) 72

Word Knowledge (35 questions)

1. ABRUPT most nearly means: A) Gradual B) Sudden C) Smooth D) Slow
2. BIZARRE most nearly means: A) Normal B) Strange C) Common D) Typical
3. CORDIAL most nearly means: A) Hostile B) Friendly C) Cold D) Distant
4. DORMANT most nearly means: A) Active B) Inactive C) Moving D) Growing
5. ELABORATE most nearly means: A) Simple B) Complex C) Brief D) Quick
6. FRAIL most nearly means: A) Strong B) Weak C) Healthy D) Robust
7. GRACIOUS most nearly means: A) Rude B) Kind C) Mean D) Harsh
8. HOSTILE most nearly means: A) Friendly B) Unfriendly C) Neutral D) Helpful
9. IMMENSE most nearly means: A) Small B) Huge C) Medium D) Tiny
10. JOVIAL most nearly means: A) Sad B) Cheerful C) Angry D) Worried
11. KEEN most nearly means: A) Dull B) Sharp C) Blunt D) Thick
12. LOYAL most nearly means: A) Faithful B) Disloyal C) Unreliable D) False
13. MODEST most nearly means: A) Arrogant B) Humble C) Proud D) Boastful
14. NIMBLE most nearly means: A) Clumsy B) Agile C) Slow D) Heavy
15. OBVIOUS most nearly means: A) Hidden B) Clear C) Secret D) Unclear
16. PERILOUS most nearly means: A) Safe B) Dangerous C) Secure D) Protected
17. QUIVER most nearly means: A) Still B) Shake C) Steady D) Firm
18. RIGID most nearly means: A) Flexible B) Stiff C) Soft D) Bendable
19. SERENE most nearly means: A) Noisy B) Peaceful C) Chaotic D) Disturbed
20. TIMID most nearly means: A) Bold B) Shy C) Brave D) Confident
21. URGENT most nearly means: A) Delayed B) Immediate C) Later D) Postponed
22. VAGUE most nearly means: A) Clear B) Unclear C) Specific D) Exact
23. WARY most nearly means: A) Careless B) Cautious C) Reckless D) Bold
24. ZEALOUS most nearly means: A) Indifferent B) Enthusiastic C) Lazy D) Bored
25. AMPLE most nearly means: A) Scarce B) Abundant C) Little D) Few
26. BLUNT most nearly means: A) Sharp B) Direct C) Subtle D) Indirect

27. CRISP most nearly means: A) Soft B) Fresh C) Stale D) Wilted
28. DENSE most nearly means: A) Sparse B) Thick C) Thin D) Light
29. EARNEST most nearly means: A) Joking B) Serious C) Playful D) Casual
30. FUTILE most nearly means: A) Useful B) Useless C) Helpful D) Effective
31. GENIAL most nearly means: A) Unfriendly B) Pleasant C) Harsh D) Cold
32. HARDY most nearly means: A) Weak B) Strong C) Fragile D) Delicate
33. IDLE most nearly means: A) Busy B) Inactive C) Working D) Active
34. JAUNTY most nearly means: A) Sad B) Cheerful C) Gloomy D) Depressed
35. KEEN most nearly means: A) Eager B) Reluctant C) Unwilling D) Hesitant

Paragraph Comprehension (15 questions)

Passage 1: Antibiotics are medicines that fight bacterial infections by either killing bacteria or stopping their growth. However, they are ineffective against viral infections such as the common cold or flu. Overuse and misuse of antibiotics can lead to antibiotic resistance, making it harder to treat bacterial infections in the future. It's important to take antibiotics exactly as prescribed and complete the full course of treatment.

1. According to the passage, antibiotics work against: A) All infections B) Viral infections C) Bacterial infections D) Fungal infections
2. What can happen if antibiotics are overused? A) They become more effective B) Antibiotic resistance develops C) Viruses are eliminated D) Side effects disappear

Passage 2: The Great Wall of China is one of the most impressive architectural achievements in human history. Built over many centuries by different dynasties, it stretches approximately 13,000 miles across northern China. Contrary to popular belief, the wall is not visible from space with the naked eye. The wall served multiple purposes including defense against invasions, border control, and trade regulation.

3. How long is the Great Wall of China? A) 10,000 miles B) 13,000 miles C) 15,000 miles D) 20,000 miles
4. According to the passage, the Great Wall is: A) Visible from space B) Not visible from space C) Sometimes visible from space D) Only visible with telescopes
5. The wall served all of the following purposes EXCEPT: A) Defense B) Border control C) Trade regulation D) Religious ceremonies

Passage 3: Renewable energy technologies have become increasingly cost-effective and efficient. Solar panels now convert sunlight to electricity at rates exceeding 20% efficiency, while wind turbines can generate power at costs competitive with fossil fuels. These technologies reduce greenhouse gas emissions and provide energy independence, though they require significant initial investment and suitable geographic conditions.

6. What efficiency rate do modern solar panels achieve? A) Over 15% B) Over 20% C) Over 25% D) Over 30%
7. According to the passage, renewable energy technologies: A) Are always expensive B) Require no investment C) Need suitable conditions D) Work everywhere equally

Passage 4: The human immune system is a complex network of cells, tissues, and organs that work together to defend against harmful substances. White blood cells are the primary defenders, with different types performing specific functions. Some recognize and remember previous infections, providing immunity against future exposure to the same pathogens. Vaccines work by training the immune system to recognize specific diseases.

8. What are the primary defenders in the immune system? A) Red blood cells B) White blood cells C) Platelets D) Plasma
9. How do vaccines work? A) They cure diseases B) They kill all bacteria C) They train the immune system D) They replace white blood cells
10. The immune system's ability to remember infections provides: A) Immediate healing B) Future immunity C) Permanent protection D) Instant response

Passage 5: Climate change refers to long-term shifts in global temperatures and weather patterns. While natural variations occur, scientific evidence shows that human activities, particularly the burning of fossil fuels, have been the dominant driver of climate change since the 1950s. These activities increase concentrations of greenhouse gases in the atmosphere, trapping heat and causing global temperatures to rise.

11. When did human activities become the dominant driver of climate change? A) 1940s B) 1950s C) 1960s D) 1970s
12. What is the main human activity causing climate change? A) Deforestation B) Agriculture C) Burning fossil fuels D) Manufacturing
13. Greenhouse gases in the atmosphere: A) Cool the planet B) Trap heat C) Reflect sunlight D) Create wind

Passage 6: Sleep disorders affect millions of people worldwide and can significantly impact health and quality of life. Common disorders include insomnia, sleep apnea, and restless leg syndrome. Sleep apnea, characterized by repeated interruptions in breathing during sleep, can lead to serious health complications if left untreated. Proper diagnosis and treatment are essential for managing these conditions effectively.

14. According to the passage, sleep apnea involves: A) Difficulty falling asleep B) Interrupted breathing C) Restless legs D) Vivid dreams
15. What is essential for managing sleep disorders? A) Medication only B) Lifestyle changes only C) Proper diagnosis and treatment D) Surgery only

Mathematics Knowledge (25 questions)

1. What is 7^2? A) 14 B) 21 C) 42 D) 49
2. Solve for x: 4x - 5 = 19 A) 5 B) 6 C) 7 D) 8
3. What is the square root of 225? A) 14 B) 15 C) 16 D) 17
4. If a right triangle has legs of 9 and 12, what is the hypotenuse? A) 14 B) 15 C) 16 D) 17
5. What is 25% of 240? A) 50 B) 55 C) 60 D) 65
6. Simplify: 5(x + 3) A) 5x + 3 B) 5x + 8 C) 5x + 15 D) x + 15
7. What is the area of a rectangle with length 9 and width 7? A) 61 B) 62 C) 63 D) 64

8. If 5x - 8 = 17, what is x? A) 4 B) 5 C) 6 D) 7
9. What is the slope of a line passing through (2,1) and (6,9)? A) 1 B) 2 C) 3 D) 4
10. Factor: x^2 - 25 A) (x-5)(x-5) B) (x+5)(x+5) C) (x-5)(x+5) D) Cannot be factored
11. What is 8! ÷ 6!? A) 48 B) 56 C) 64 D) 72
12. Solve: |x - 4| = 6 A) x = 10 only B) x = -2 only C) x = 10 or x = -2 D) x = 2 or x = 8
13. What is the volume of a cylinder with radius 3 and height 8? (Use π = 3.14) A) 226.08 B) 225.08 C) 227.08 D) 224.08
14. If $\log_4(x)$ = 3, what is x? A) 12 B) 16 C) 64 D) 81
15. What is the distance between points (1,1) and (5,4)? A) 4 B) 5 C) 6 D) 7
16. Simplify: $(4x)^2$ A) $8x^2$ B) $16x^2$ C) $4x^2$ D) x^2
17. What is the sum of interior angles of an octagon? A) 1080° B) 1060° C) 1040° D) 1020°
18. If tan(θ) = 1, what is θ? A) 30° B) 45° C) 60° D) 90°
19. What is the range of: 2, 8, 5, 12, 3, 9? A) 8 B) 9 C) 10 D) 11
20. Solve: x^2 - 8x + 15 = 0 A) x = 3, 5 B) x = 2, 6 C) x = 1, 15 D) x = 4, 4
21. What is 40% of 85? A) 32 B) 34 C) 36 D) 38
22. If f(x) = 4x + 3, what is f(2)? A) 9 B) 10 C) 11 D) 12
23. What is the area of a circle with diameter 8? (Use π = 3.14) A) 50.24 B) 48.24 C) 52.24 D) 54.24
24. Simplify: $\sqrt{98}$ A) $7\sqrt{2}$ B) $7\sqrt{3}$ C) $9\sqrt{2}$ D) $14\sqrt{2}$
25. What is the y-intercept of y = 5x + 7? A) 5 B) 7 C) -7 D) -5

Electronics Information (20 questions)

1. What is the unit of frequency? A) Watt B) Hertz C) Joule D) Newton
2. What component opposes current flow? A) Capacitor B) Resistor C) Inductor D) Transformer
3. Which law relates voltage, current, and resistance? A) Kirchhoff's B) Ohm's C) Faraday's D) Coulomb's
4. What does a transistor do? A) Store energy B) Amplify signals C) Convert AC to DC D) Filter noise
5. In which direction does conventional current flow? A) Negative to positive B) Positive to negative C) Both directions D) No specific direction
6. What is the unit of electrical energy? A) Watt B) Joule C) Volt D) Ampere
7. Which material has high resistance? A) Silver B) Copper C) Rubber D) Aluminum
8. What is the purpose of a filter circuit? A) Amplify signals B) Remove unwanted frequencies C) Store energy D) Convert voltage
9. What does EMF stand for? A) Electric Motor Force B) Electromotive Force C) Electronic Magnetic Field D) Electric Magnetic Force
10. How do you increase total resistance in a circuit? A) Add resistors in parallel B) Add resistors in series C) Reduce voltage D) Increase current
11. What does PCB stand for? A) Power Control Board B) Printed Circuit Board C) Primary Circuit Base D) Portable Computer Board
12. What happens in a short circuit? A) No current flows B) Maximum current flows C) Voltage increases D) Resistance increases
13. Which component stores energy in an electric field? A) Resistor B) Inductor C) Capacitor D) Diode

14. What is the unit of inductance? A) Farad B) Henry C) Ohm D) Weber
15. What does a relay do? A) Amplify current B) Switch circuits electrically C) Store energy D) Convert signals
16. What is reactance? A) DC resistance B) AC resistance C) Capacitance D) Inductance
17. In a parallel circuit, voltage across each branch is: A) Different B) Same C) Zero D) Maximum
18. What removes heat from electronic components? A) Heat sink B) Capacitor C) Resistor D) Inductor
19. What does AM stand for? A) Audio Modulation B) Amplitude Modulation C) Automatic Modulation D) Active Modulation
20. When voltage doubles and resistance stays constant, current: A) Halves B) Doubles C) Stays same D) Quadruples

Auto & Shop Information (25 questions)

1. What initiates combustion in a gasoline engine? A) Compression B) Spark plug C) Fuel injector D) Carburetor
2. How many valves does a typical 4-cylinder engine have? A) 8 B) 12 C) 16 D) 20
3. What tool measures tire tread depth? A) Caliper B) Depth gauge C) Penny test D) All of the above
4. What is the main purpose of engine oil? A) Cool engine B) Lubricate moving parts C) Clean engine D) All of the above
5. Which system charges the battery while driving? A) Starter B) Alternator C) Distributor D) Regulator
6. What does TDC stand for? A) Top Dead Center B) Total Displacement Capacity C) Turbo Direct Control D) Throttle Direction Control
7. Which tool cuts internal threads? A) Die B) Tap C) Reamer D) Drill
8. What circulates coolant through the engine? A) Thermostat B) Radiator C) Water pump D) Fan
9. Which meter measures electrical current? A) Voltmeter B) Ammeter C) Ohmmeter D) Wattmeter
10. What regulates coolant flow based on temperature? A) Water pump B) Radiator C) Thermostat D) Fan
11. What does SAE 30 indicate? A) Oil temperature B) Oil viscosity C) Oil pressure D) Oil capacity
12. Which tool creates female threads? A) Tap B) Die C) Drill D) Reamer
13. What is valve timing? A) When valves open and close B) Valve adjustment procedure C) Valve replacement schedule D) Valve material type
14. What allows differential wheel speeds during turns? A) Transmission B) Differential C) Transfer case D) Axle
15. Which grit sandpaper is coarsest? A) 80 B) 220 C) 400 D) 600
16. What reduces harmful exhaust emissions? A) Muffler B) Catalytic converter C) Resonator D) Tail pipe
17. What removes metal burrs? A) File B) Grinder C) Deburring tool D) All of the above
18. What does 10W-30 oil designation mean? A) Weight and temperature B) Viscosity at different temperatures C) Brand and grade D) Additive package

19. What transfers power from engine to wheels? A) Clutch B) Transmission C) Driveline D) All of the above
20. What helps solder flow and clean surfaces? A) Flux B) Heat C) Pressure D) Time
21. What does OHV stand for? A) Over Head Valve B) Oil Hydraulic Valve C) Output High Voltage D) Optimal Head Volume
22. Which file produces the finest finish? A) Bastard B) Second cut C) Smooth D) Dead smooth
23. What is the ideal air-fuel ratio for gasoline engines? A) 12:1 B) 14.7:1 C) 16:1 D) 18:1
24. What causes engine knock? A) Low octane fuel B) Carbon deposits C) Incorrect timing D) All of the above
25. Which drill bit angle is standard for general purpose? A) 90° B) 118° C) 135° D) 150°

Mechanical Comprehension (25 questions)

1. If gear A has 40 teeth and gear B has 20 teeth, and A turns at 30 RPM, how fast does B turn? A) 15 RPM B) 30 RPM C) 60 RPM D) 120 RPM
2. Which pulley system provides 4:1 mechanical advantage? A) Fixed pulley B) Single movable C) Double movable D) Triple movable
3. In hydraulics, force is multiplied by: A) Reducing pressure B) Increasing area C) Decreasing volume D) Adding fluid
4. A lever has a 10-foot effort arm and 2-foot load arm. What is the mechanical advantage? A) 3:1 B) 4:1 C) 5:1 D) 8:1
5. What is the mechanical advantage of an inclined plane 20 feet long and 4 feet high? A) 4:1 B) 5:1 C) 6:1 D) 8:1
6. In a wheel and axle with 16-inch wheel diameter and 4-inch axle diameter, what is the mechanical advantage? A) 2:1 B) 3:1 C) 4:1 D) 8:1
7. When fluid flows through a restriction, velocity: A) Decreases B) Increases C) Stays constant D) Stops
8. What simple machine is a bolt based on? A) Lever B) Wedge C) Inclined plane D) Wheel and axle
9. If you apply 20 pounds to a 3:1 mechanical advantage system, what is the output force? A) 40 lbs B) 50 lbs C) 60 lbs D) 80 lbs
10. What does a flywheel do? A) Increase speed B) Smooth power delivery C) Change direction D) Reduce friction
11. In a hydraulic press with input area 4 sq in and output area 36 sq in, what is the force ratio? A) 6:1 B) 8:1 C) 9:1 D) 12:1
12. Doubling the effort arm length of a lever: A) Halves mechanical advantage B) Doubles mechanical advantage C) Has no effect D) Quadruples force
13. Which gear arrangement changes direction 90 degrees? A) Spur gears B) Helical gears C) Bevel gears D) Worm gears
14. What force acts on objects in circular motion? A) Gravitational B) Centripetal C) Magnetic D) Electric
15. A block and tackle with 8 supporting ropes has what theoretical mechanical advantage? A) 4:1 B) 6:1 C) 8:1 D) 16:1
16. Increasing wrench handle length increases: A) Speed B) Torque C) Power D) Efficiency

17. Rolling friction is: A) Greater than sliding friction B) Less than sliding friction C) Equal to sliding friction D) Independent of surface
18. A machine with 85% efficiency converts 200 J input to how much useful output? A) 160 J B) 170 J C) 180 J D) 190 J
19. In a cam mechanism, follower motion depends on: A) Cam speed B) Cam size C) Cam shape D) Follower weight
20. Air pressure at sea level is approximately: A) 14.7 psi B) 15.7 psi C) 16.7 psi D) 17.7 psi
21. Which converts continuous rotary motion to reciprocating motion? A) Gear train B) Cam and follower C) Crank mechanism D) Both B and C
22. Hydraulic systems work on: A) Archimedes' principle B) Pascal's principle C) Bernoulli's principle D) Hooke's law
23. If a gear rotates 270° and has a 3:1 ratio with another gear, the second gear rotates: A) 45° B) 90° C) 180° D) 810°
24. What reduces friction in rotating machinery? A) Lubrication B) Bearings C) Smooth surfaces D) All of the above
25. Fine thread screws compared to coarse threads provide: A) Faster movement B) Greater holding power C) Less precision D) More strength

Answer Key - Test 5

General Science: 1-B, 2-C, 3-C, 4-C, 5-C, 6-C, 7-A, 8-C, 9-B, 10-B, 11-C, 12-C, 13-A, 14-C, 15-C, 16-C, 17-D, 18-B, 19-C, 20-C, 21-B, 22-B, 23-B, 24-D, 25-B

Arithmetic Reasoning: 1-B, 2-B, 3-B, 4-B, 5-B, 6-B, 7-B, 8-B, 9-B, 10-A, 11-B, 12-B, 13-C, 14-C, 15-B, 16-B, 17-C, 18-B, 19-B, 20-C, 21-C, 22-B, 23-B, 24-B, 25-C, 26-B, 27-C, 28-B, 29-C, 30-B

Word Knowledge: 1-B, 2-B, 3-B, 4-B, 5-B, 6-B, 7-B, 8-B, 9-B, 10-B, 11-B, 12-A, 13-B, 14-B, 15-B, 16-B, 17-B, 18-B, 19-B, 20-B, 21-B, 22-B, 23-B, 24-B, 25-B, 26-B, 27-B, 28-B, 29-B, 30-B, 31-B, 32-B, 33-B, 34-B, 35-A

Paragraph Comprehension: 1-C, 2-B, 3-B, 4-B, 5-D, 6-B, 7-C, 8-B, 9-C, 10-B, 11-B, 12-C, 13-B, 14-B, 15-C

Mathematics Knowledge: 1-D, 2-B, 3-B, 4-B, 5-C, 6-C, 7-C, 8-B, 9-B, 10-C, 11-B, 12-C, 13-A, 14-C, 15-B, 16-B, 17-A, 18-B, 19-C, 20-A, 21-B, 22-C, 23-A, 24-A, 25-B

Electronics Information: 1-B, 2-B, 3-B, 4-B, 5-B, 6-B, 7-C, 8-B, 9-B, 10-B, 11-B, 12-B, 13-C, 14-B, 15-B, 16-B, 17-B, 18-A, 19-B, 20-B

Auto & Shop Information: 1-B, 2-C, 3-D, 4-D, 5-B, 6-A, 7-B, 8-C, 9-B, 10-C, 11-B, 12-A, 13-A, 14-B, 15-A, 16-B, 17-D, 18-B, 19-D, 20-A, 21-A, 22-D, 23-B, 24-D, 25-B

Test 6

General Science (25 questions)

1. What is the chemical formula for methane? A) CH_4 B) CO_2 C) H_2O D) NH_3
2. Which organ regulates blood sugar? A) Liver B) Pancreas C) Kidney D) Heart
3. What is the powerhouse of the cell? A) Nucleus B) Ribosome C) Mitochondria D) Golgi body
4. Which planet has the most extensive ring system? A) Jupiter B) Saturn C) Uranus D) Neptune
5. What process do plants use to make food? A) Respiration B) Photosynthesis C) Transpiration D) Germination
6. How many ribs does a human have? A) 20 B) 22 C) 24 D) 26
7. What is the formula for kinetic energy? A) $KE = mv$ B) $KE = \frac{1}{2}mv^2$ C) $KE = m^2v$ D) $KE = mv^2$
8. Which type of rock forms from heat and pressure? A) Igneous B) Sedimentary C) Metamorphic D) Volcanic
9. What is the strongest muscle in the human body? A) Bicep B) Heart C) Jaw D) Calf
10. Which fundamental force is weakest? A) Strong nuclear B) Weak nuclear C) Electromagnetic D) Gravitational
11. What percentage of Earth's surface is water? A) 65% B) 70% C) 71% D) 75%
12. Which part of the brain controls breathing? A) Cerebrum B) Cerebellum C) Medulla D) Hypothalamus
13. What is the normal body temperature in Celsius? A) 35°C B) 37°C C) 39°C D) 41°C
14. Which particle has no electric charge? A) Proton B) Electron C) Neutron D) Ion
15. What is the second most abundant element in Earth's crust? A) Oxygen B) Silicon C) Aluminum D) Iron
16. Which system removes waste from the body? A) Circulatory B) Respiratory C) Excretory D) Digestive
17. What type of bond forms between metals and nonmetals? A) Covalent B) Ionic C) Metallic D) Hydrogen
18. Which gas is produced during photosynthesis? A) Carbon dioxide B) Nitrogen C) Oxygen D) Hydrogen
19. What is the unit of electric charge? A) Ampere B) Volt C) Coulomb D) Watt
20. Which vitamin helps blood clotting? A) A B) C C) D D) K
21. What is the boiling point of water at sea level? A) 98°C B) 99°C C) 100°C D) 101°C
22. Which element is essential for thyroid function? A) Iron B) Iodine C) Calcium D) Zinc
23. What causes aurora (northern lights)? A) Solar wind B) Moon's gravity C) Earth's rotation D) Atmospheric pressure
24. Which blood component carries oxygen? A) Plasma B) Platelets C) White blood cells D) Red blood cells
25. What is the study of heredity called? A) Ecology B) Genetics C) Anatomy D) Physiology

Arithmetic Reasoning (30 questions)

1. A computer costs $800 and is discounted 25%. What is the sale price? A) $580 B) $600 C) $620 D) $640
2. A recipe for 4 people needs 3 cups of rice. How much rice for 6 people? A) 4 cups B) 4.5 cups C) 5 cups D) 5.5 cups
3. If you travel 420 miles in 7 hours, what is your average speed? A) 58 mph B) 60 mph C) 62 mph D) 64 mph
4. A jar has 30 candies: 18 chocolate and 12 vanilla. What's the probability of drawing chocolate? A) 2/5 B) 3/5 C) 1/2 D) 2/3
5. If you earn $18 per hour for 25 hours, how much do you make? A) $430 B) $440 C) $450 D) $460
6. A pool is 25 feet long and 15 feet wide. What is its area? A) 365 sq ft B) 375 sq ft C) 385 sq ft D) 395 sq ft
7. If 6 oranges cost $3.60, how much do 10 oranges cost? A) $5.50 B) $6.00 C) $6.50 D) $7.00
8. On a 60-question test, you answer 51 correctly. What percentage is that? A) 83% B) 85% C) 87% D) 89%
9. If you save $45 per month for 12 months, how much will you save? A) $520 B) $540 C) $560 D) $580
10. A circle has a diameter of 16 feet. What is its radius? A) 6 ft B) 7 ft C) 8 ft D) 9 ft
11. If $6x - 9 = 27$, what is x? A) 5 B) 6 C) 7 D) 8
12. The average of 85, 92, and 88 is: A) 87 B) 88 C) 89 D) 90
13. If you buy 7 books at $12.50 each, what's the total? A) $85.50 B) $87.50 C) $89.50 D) $91.50
14. A 20-foot ladder leans against a wall with its base 12 feet from the wall. How high does it reach? A) 14 ft B) 15 ft C) 16 ft D) 17 ft
15. If 60% of a number is 240, what is the number? A) 380 B) 400 C) 420 D) 440
16. A car travels 540 miles in 9 hours. How far in 12 hours? A) 680 mi B) 700 mi C) 720 mi D) 740 mi
17. You have $400 and spend 45%. How much is left? A) $210 B) $220 C) $230 D) $240
18. A triangle has angles of 65° and 85°. What's the third angle? A) 25° B) 30° C) 35° D) 40°
19. If 15 people finish a job in 12 hours, how long for 20 people? A) 8 hours B) 9 hours C) 10 hours D) 11 hours
20. A square garden has a perimeter of 48 feet. What's its area? A) 144 sq ft B) 154 sq ft C) 164 sq ft D) 174 sq ft
21. Rolling a die, what's the probability of getting an even number? A) 1/3 B) 1/2 C) 2/3 D) 3/4
22. A shirt costs $25 and shoes cost $65. How much for 3 shirts and 2 pairs of shoes? A) $200 B) $205 C) $210 D) $215
23. A truck uses 1 gallon for every 18 miles. How much gas for 126 miles? A) 6 gal B) 7 gal C) 8 gal D) 9 gal
24. A rectangle is 18 feet long and 12 feet wide. What's its perimeter? A) 58 ft B) 60 ft C) 62 ft D) 64 ft
25. Investing $1200 at 6% annual interest, how much interest in one year? A) $65 B) $70 C) $72 D) $75

26. A cake is cut into 16 pieces. If 9 pieces are eaten, what fraction remains? A) 7/16 B) 9/16 C) 1/2 D) 5/8
27. If 24 is 40% of a number, what's the number? A) 55 B) 60 C) 65 D) 70
28. A 56-foot rope is cut into 8 equal pieces. How long is each? A) 6 ft B) 7 ft C) 8 ft D) 9 ft
29. Items cost $6.75, $8.25, and $4.50. What's the total? A) $19.25 B) $19.50 C) $19.75 D) $20.00
30. A swimming pool holds 12,000 gallons when full. If it's 75% full, how many gallons? A) 8,500 B) 8,750 C) 9,000 D) 9,250

Word Knowledge (35 questions)

1. ADEQUATE most nearly means: A) Insufficient B) Sufficient C) Excessive D) Perfect
2. BAFFLED most nearly means: A) Clear B) Confused C) Certain D) Confident
3. COMPETENT most nearly means: A) Incompetent B) Skilled C) Unskilled D) Average
4. DEJECTED most nearly means: A) Happy B) Sad C) Excited D) Calm
5. ENDEAVOR most nearly means: A) Give up B) Attempt C) Succeed D) Fail
6. FICTITIOUS most nearly means: A) Real B) False C) True D) Factual
7. GRATITUDE most nearly means: A) Ingratitude B) Thankfulness C) Anger D) Resentment
8. HAZARDOUS most nearly means: A) Safe B) Dangerous C) Secure D) Protected
9. INGENIOUS most nearly means: A) Stupid B) Clever C) Simple D) Ordinary
10. JEOPARDIZE most nearly means: A) Protect B) Endanger C) Secure D) Guard
11. KINETIC most nearly means: A) Static B) Moving C) Still D) Stationary
12. LUCRATIVE most nearly means: A) Unprofitable B) Profitable C) Expensive D) Cheap
13. MAGNIFICENT most nearly means: A) Plain B) Splendid C) Ordinary D) Simple
14. NEGLIGIBLE most nearly means: A) Important B) Insignificant C) Large D) Significant
15. OPTIMAL most nearly means: A) Worst B) Best C) Average D) Poor
16. PERSISTENT most nearly means: A) Giving up B) Determined C) Weak D) Uncertain
17. QUENCH most nearly means: A) Ignite B) Satisfy C) Starve D) Deny
18. RELEVANT most nearly means: A) Unrelated B) Applicable C) Irrelevant D) Distant
19. SUBSTANTIAL most nearly means: A) Small B) Large C) Tiny D) Minimal
20. TURBULENT most nearly means: A) Calm B) Rough C) Peaceful D) Smooth
21. UNANIMOUS most nearly means: A) Divided B) In complete agreement C) Uncertain D) Conflicted
22. VIGOROUS most nearly means: A) Weak B) Energetic C) Tired D) Lazy
23. WORTHWHILE most nearly means: A) Worthless B) Valuable C) Useless D) Pointless
24. EXEMPLARY most nearly means: A) Poor B) Model C) Average D) Inadequate
25. YEARNING most nearly means: A) Satisfied B) Longing C) Content D) Fulfilled
26. ACUTE most nearly means: A) Chronic B) Sharp C) Dull D) Mild
27. BENIGN most nearly means: A) Harmful B) Harmless C) Dangerous D) Threatening
28. CONCISE most nearly means: A) Lengthy B) Brief C) Wordy D) Detailed
29. DIVERT most nearly means: A) Direct B) Redirect C) Focus D) Concentrate
30. ETHICAL most nearly means: A) Immoral B) Moral C) Wrong D) Corrupt
31. FLAWLESS most nearly means: A) Imperfect B) Perfect C) Damaged D) Broken
32. GENUINE most nearly means: A) False B) Authentic C) Fake D) Artificial
33. HOSTILE most nearly means: A) Friendly B) Unfriendly C) Welcoming D) Kind

34. IMMINENT most nearly means: A) Distant B) Approaching C) Past D) Remote
35. JUVENILE most nearly means: A) Adult B) Young C) Mature D) Old

Paragraph Comprehension (15 questions)

Passage 1: The Amazon rainforest, often called the "lungs of the Earth," produces approximately 20% of the world's oxygen and absorbs large amounts of carbon dioxide. This vast ecosystem spans across nine countries, with Brazil containing about 60% of the forest. Deforestation threatens this critical habitat, potentially affecting global climate patterns and countless species that depend on the forest for survival.

1. What percentage of the world's oxygen does the Amazon produce? A) 15% B) 20% C) 25% D) 30%
2. Which country contains the largest portion of the Amazon? A) Peru B) Colombia C) Brazil D) Venezuela

Passage 2: Artificial intelligence (AI) refers to computer systems that can perform tasks typically requiring human intelligence, such as learning, reasoning, and problem-solving. Machine learning, a subset of AI, enables computers to learn and improve from experience without explicit programming. These technologies are increasingly used in healthcare, transportation, finance, and entertainment industries.

3. What is machine learning? A) A type of computer B) A subset of AI C) A programming language D) A type of software
4. According to the passage, AI systems can perform tasks that typically require: A) Computer programming B) Human intelligence C) Machine learning D) Expert systems
5. The passage mentions AI is used in all of the following industries EXCEPT: A) Healthcare B) Transportation C) Agriculture D) Finance

Passage 3: Earthquakes occur when tectonic plates beneath Earth's surface shift and release energy. The magnitude of an earthquake is measured using the Richter scale, with each whole number increase representing a tenfold increase in amplitude. Most earthquakes occur along plate boundaries, particularly around the Pacific Ring of Fire, which accounts for about 90% of the world's seismic activity.

6. What causes earthquakes? A) Volcanic eruptions B) Tectonic plate movement C) Ocean currents D) Atmospheric pressure
7. How much does earthquake amplitude increase with each whole number on the Richter scale? A) Twofold B) Fivefold C) Tenfold D) Hundredfold
8. What percentage of seismic activity occurs in the Pacific Ring of Fire? A) 80% B) 85% C) 90% D) 95%

Passage 4: The human digestive system breaks down food into nutrients that the body can absorb and use for energy, growth, and repair. The process begins in the mouth with mechanical and chemical breakdown, continues through the stomach where acids further break down food, and concludes in the small intestine where most nutrient absorption occurs. The entire process typically takes 24-72 hours.

9. Where does digestion begin? A) Stomach B) Mouth C) Small intestine D) Large intestine
10. Where does most nutrient absorption occur? A) Mouth B) Stomach C) Small intestine D) Large intestine
11. How long does the complete digestive process typically take? A) 12-24 hours B) 24-72 hours C) 72-96 hours D) 96-120 hours

Passage 5: Recycling helps conserve natural resources, reduce landfill waste, and decrease pollution. Different materials require different recycling processes: paper and cardboard are pulped and reformed, metals are melted and reshaped, and plastics are cleaned, melted, and molded into new products. However, not all materials can be recycled indefinitely, and some lose quality with each recycling cycle.

12. According to the passage, recycling helps with all of the following EXCEPT: A) Conserving resources B) Reducing waste C) Decreasing pollution D) Increasing production costs
13. What happens to materials that lose quality during recycling? A) They're discarded B) They can't be recycled indefinitely C) They become more valuable D) They're sent to landfills
14. How are metals recycled? A) Pulped and reformed B) Cleaned and molded C) Melted and reshaped D) Sorted and cleaned

Passage 6: The water cycle continuously moves water between Earth's oceans, atmosphere, and land. Solar energy drives evaporation from water bodies, creating water vapor that rises and condenses into clouds. Precipitation returns water to Earth's surface, where it may flow into rivers and oceans or seep into groundwater systems, completing the cycle.

15. What drives the water cycle? A) Wind energy B) Solar energy C) Gravitational energy D) Tidal energy

Mathematics Knowledge (25 questions)

1. What is 9^2? A) 18 B) 27 C) 72 D) 81
2. Solve for x: $3x + 12 = 30$ A) 5 B) 6 C) 7 D) 8
3. What is the square root of 289? A) 16 B) 17 C) 18 D) 19
4. If a right triangle has legs of 5 and 12, what is the hypotenuse? A) 11 B) 12 C) 13 D) 14
5. What is 35% of 160? A) 52 B) 54 C) 56 D) 58
6. Simplify: $6(x - 4)$ A) $6x - 4$ B) $6x - 10$ C) $6x - 24$ D) $x - 24$
7. What is the area of a triangle with base 12 and height 8? A) 46 B) 48 C) 50 D) 52
8. If $4x + 7 = 31$, what is x? A) 5 B) 6 C) 7 D) 8
9. What is the slope of a line through (3,2) and (7,10)? A) 1 B) 2 C) 3 D) 4
10. Factor: $x^2 - 36$ A) $(x-6)(x-6)$ B) $(x+6)(x+6)$ C) $(x-6)(x+6)$ D) Cannot be factored
11. What is $10!/8!$? A) 80 B) 90 C) 100 D) 110
12. Solve: $|x + 3| = 8$ A) $x = 5$ only B) $x = -11$ only C) $x = 5$ or $x = -11$ D) $x = -5$ or $x = 11$

13. What is the volume of a sphere with radius 6? (Use $\pi = 3.14$) A) 904.32 B) 905.32 C) 906.32 D) 907.32
14. If $\log_5(x) = 2$, what is x? A) 10 B) 20 C) 25 D) 32
15. What is the distance between (2,3) and (8,11)? A) 8 B) 9 C) 10 D) 11
16. Simplify: $(5x)^2$ A) $10x^2$ B) $25x^2$ C) $5x^2$ D) x^2
17. Sum of interior angles of a nonagon (9 sides)? A) 1260° B) 1240° C) 1220° D) 1200°
18. If $\sin(\theta) = \sqrt{3}/2$, what is θ? A) 30° B) 45° C) 60° D) 90°
19. What is the median of: 4, 7, 9, 12, 15, 18, 21? A) 12 B) 13 C) 14 D) 15
20. Solve: $x^2 - 9x + 20 = 0$ A) x = 4, 5 B) x = 3, 6 C) x = 2, 10 D) x = 1, 20
21. What is 45% of 200? A) 85 B) 90 C) 95 D) 100
22. If $f(x) = 2x^2 + 1$, what is $f(3)$? A) 17 B) 18 C) 19 D) 20
23. Area of a circle with radius 5? (Use $\pi = 3.14$) A) 78.5 B) 78.6 C) 78.7 D) 78.8
24. Simplify: $\sqrt{128}$ A) $8\sqrt{2}$ B) $8\sqrt{3}$ C) $16\sqrt{2}$ D) $32\sqrt{2}$
25. What is the slope of $y = -3x + 8$? A) 8 B) 3 C) -3 D) -8

Electronics Information (20 questions)

1. What is the relationship between frequency and wavelength? A) Directly proportional B) Inversely proportional C) Not related D) Same value
2. Which component blocks DC while passing AC? A) Resistor B) Inductor C) Capacitor D) Transformer
3. What is Kirchhoff's current law? A) V = IR B) Current in equals current out C) P = VI D) Energy is conserved
4. What does a MOSFET do? A) Store energy B) Switch/amplify signals C) Convert AC to DC D) Filter frequencies
5. Which way does electron flow? A) Positive to negative B) Negative to positive C) Both ways D) Depends on circuit
6. What is the unit of electrical conductance? A) Ohm B) Siemens C) Farad D) Henry
7. Which material is a semiconductor? A) Copper B) Silicon C) Rubber D) Silver
8. What is the purpose of a voltage regulator? A) Increase voltage B) Maintain constant voltage C) Decrease voltage D) Block voltage
9. What does RMS voltage represent? A) Peak voltage B) Average voltage C) Effective voltage D) Minimum voltage
10. How do you decrease total capacitance? A) Add capacitors in series B) Add capacitors in parallel C) Remove capacitors D) Increase voltage
11. What does IC stand for? A) Internal Circuit B) Integrated Circuit C) Input Current D) Inductive Coil
12. What causes voltage drop in a wire? A) Resistance B) Capacitance C) Inductance D) Length only
13. Which stores energy in a magnetic field? A) Capacitor B) Resistor C) Inductor D) Diode
14. What is the unit of magnetic flux? A) Tesla B) Weber C) Gauss D) Henry
15. What does a multiplexer do? A) Amplify signals B) Select one of many inputs C) Store data D) Generate signals
16. What is impedance in AC circuits? A) Resistance only B) Total opposition to current C) Capacitance only D) Inductance only

17. In a series circuit, current through each component is: A) Different B) Same C) Zero D) Maximum
18. What protects circuits from electrostatic discharge? A) Fuse B) ESD protection C) Circuit breaker D) Surge protector
19. What does FM stand for? A) Frequency Modulation B) Field Modulation C) Full Modulation D) Fast Modulation
20. If resistance halves and voltage stays constant, current: A) Halves B) Doubles C) Stays same D) Quadruples

Auto & Shop Information (25 questions)

1. What provides the spark in a diesel engine? A) Spark plug B) Glow plug C) Compression ignition D) Fuel injector
2. How many degrees does a crankshaft rotate per power stroke in a 4-stroke engine? A) 90° B) 180° C) 360° D) 720°
3. What tool checks brake rotor thickness? A) Caliper B) Micrometer C) Depth gauge D) Feeler gauge
4. What prevents engine oil from leaking past pistons? A) Gaskets B) Piston rings C) Seals D) Valves
5. Which generates AC current that's converted to DC? A) Battery B) Alternator C) Starter D) Generator
6. What does BDC stand for? A) Bottom Dead Center B) Basic Drive Control C) Brake Disc Control D) Battery Direct Current
7. Which tool creates external threads? A) Tap B) Die C) Drill D) Countersink
8. What prevents coolant from boiling over? A) Thermostat B) Pressure cap C) Water pump D) Radiator
9. Which measures electrical power consumption? A) Voltmeter B) Ammeter C) Wattmeter D) Ohmmeter
10. What opens and closes based on coolant temperature? A) Pressure cap B) Thermostat C) Water pump D) Radiator fan
11. What do the numbers in 5W-30 oil represent? A) Weight grades B) Viscosity at different temperatures C) Additive levels D) Quality ratings
12. Which cutting tool has the most teeth per inch? A) Hacksaw B) File C) Rasp D) Chisel
13. What is cam duration? A) Time camshaft rotates B) Degrees cam keeps valve open C) Speed of cam rotation D) Number of cam lobes
14. What allows independent wheel rotation during turns? A) Transmission B) Differential C) Axle D) Universal joint
15. Which abrasive particle is sharpest? A) Aluminum oxide B) Silicon carbide C) Garnet D) Emery
16. What monitors exhaust gases to control fuel mixture? A) MAP sensor B) TPS sensor C) O2 sensor D) MAF sensor
17. What smooths rough surfaces by abrasion? A) File B) Sandpaper C) Grinder D) All of the above
18. What does the first number in multi-grade oil represent? A) High temperature viscosity B) Low temperature viscosity C) Additive package D) Quality level

19. What system transfers engine power to drive wheels? A) Ignition B) Fuel C) Drivetrain D) Cooling
20. What cleans metal surfaces before soldering? A) Flux B) Sandpaper C) Wire brush D) All of the above
21. What does SOHC stand for? A) Single Overhead Cam B) Super Output High Compression C) Standard Oil Hydraulic Control D) Special Overhead Housing Cover
22. Which produces the smoothest finish? A) Coarse file B) Medium file C) Smooth file D) Dead smooth file
23. What is stoichiometric ratio for gasoline? A) 12:1 B) 14.7:1 C) 16:1 D) 18:1
24. What can cause pre-ignition? A) High compression B) Carbon deposits C) Hot spots D) All of the above
25. Which drill bit type cuts fastest in metal? A) Twist bit B) Spade bit C) Cobalt bit D) Carbide bit

Mechanical Comprehension (25 questions)

1. Gear A (50 teeth) drives gear B (25 teeth). If A rotates 20 RPM, B rotates: A) 10 RPM B) 20 RPM C) 40 RPM D) 80 RPM
2. Which pulley gives greatest mechanical advantage? A) Fixed B) Movable C) Compound D) All equal
3. Pascal's law states pressure in fluid is: A) Reduced everywhere B) Increased at bottom C) Transmitted equally D) Lost over distance
4. A 12-foot pry bar has fulcrum 3 feet from load. Mechanical advantage is: A) 2:1 B) 3:1 C) 4:1 D) 9:1
5. Inclined plane 15 feet long, 3 feet high has mechanical advantage: A) 3:1 B) 4:1 C) 5:1 D) 12:1
6. Wheel diameter 20 inches, axle diameter 5 inches. Mechanical advantage: A) 2:1 B) 3:1 C) 4:1 D) 5:1
7. When pipe diameter doubles, fluid velocity: A) Doubles B) Halves C) Quarters D) Stays same
8. A screw is essentially a rotating: A) Lever B) Wedge C) Inclined plane D) Pulley
9. Apply 15 lbs to 6:1 mechanical advantage lever. Output force: A) 75 lbs B) 90 lbs C) 105 lbs D) 120 lbs
10. What smooths out power pulses in engines? A) Governor B) Flywheel C) Crankshaft D) Camshaft
11. Hydraulic system: input 2 sq in, output 18 sq in. Force multiplication: A) 6:1 B) 8:1 C) 9:1 D) 16:1
12. Shortening effort arm of lever: A) Increases mechanical advantage B) Decreases mechanical advantage C) No change D) Doubles force
13. Gears that transmit power at right angles: A) Spur B) Helical C) Bevel D) Planetary
14. Force pulling objects toward Earth's center: A) Centripetal B) Centrifugal C) Gravitational D) Magnetic
15. Pulley system with 10 supporting ropes has mechanical advantage: A) 5:1 B) 8:1 C) 10:1 D) 20:1
16. Longer wrench handle provides: A) More speed B) More torque C) Less effort D) Higher efficiency

17. Which friction is greater? A) Static B) Kinetic C) Rolling D) All equal
18. 75% efficient machine: 120 J input produces how much useful output? A) 80 J B) 85 J C) 90 J D) 95 J
19. Cam shape determines: A) Rotation speed B) Follower motion C) Applied force D) System efficiency
20. Atmospheric pressure decreases with: A) Temperature B) Humidity C) Altitude D) Wind speed
21. Converts continuous rotation to back-and-forth motion: A) Gear train B) Belt drive C) Scotch yoke D) Chain drive
22. Hydraulic brakes work on: A) Archimedes' principle B) Pascal's principle C) Bernoulli's principle D) Conservation of energy
23. Input gear turns 120°, gear ratio 4:1. Output gear turns: A) 30° B) 60° C) 240° D) 480°
24. Reduces friction between moving parts: A) Lubrication B) Bearings C) Smooth surfaces D) All of the above
25. Fine thread screws provide: A) Faster assembly B) Greater clamping force C) Less precision D) Easier removal

Answer Key - Test 6

General Science: 1-A, 2-B, 3-C, 4-B, 5-B, 6-C, 7-B, 8-C, 9-C, 10-D, 11-C, 12-C, 13-B, 14-C, 15-B, 16-C, 17-B, 18-C, 19-C, 20-D, 21-C, 22-B, 23-A, 24-D, 25-B

Arithmetic Reasoning: 1-B, 2-B, 3-B, 4-B, 5-C, 6-B, 7-B, 8-B, 9-B, 10-C, 11-B, 12-B, 13-B, 14-C, 15-B, 16-C, 17-B, 18-B, 19-B, 20-A, 21-B, 22-D, 23-B, 24-B, 25-C, 26-A, 27-B, 28-B, 29-B, 30-C

Word Knowledge: 1-B, 2-B, 3-B, 4-B, 5-B, 6-B, 7-B, 8-B, 9-B, 10-B, 11-B, 12-B, 13-B, 14-B, 15-B, 16-B, 17-B, 18-B, 19-B, 20-B, 21-B, 22-B, 23-B, 24-B, 25-B, 26-B, 27-B, 28-B, 29-B, 30-B, 31-B, 32-B, 33-B, 34-B, 35-B

Paragraph Comprehension: 1-B, 2-C, 3-B, 4-B, 5-C, 6-B, 7-C, 8-C, 9-B, 10-C, 11-B, 12-D, 13-B, 14-C, 15-B

Mathematics Knowledge: 1-D, 2-B, 3-B, 4-C, 5-C, 6-C, 7-B, 8-B, 9-B, 10-C, 11-B, 12-C, 13-A, 14-C, 15-C, 16-B, 17-A, 18-C, 19-A, 20-A, 21-B, 22-C, 23-A, 24-A, 25-C

Electronics Information: 1-B, 2-C, 3-B, 4-B, 5-B, 6-B, 7-B, 8-B, 9-C, 10-A, 11-B, 12-A, 13-C, 14-B, 15-B, 16-B, 17-B, 18-B, 19-A, 20-B

Auto & Shop Information: 1-C, 2-B, 3-B, 4-B, 5-B, 6-A, 7-B, 8-B, 9-C, 10-B, 11-B, 12-B, 13-B, 14-B, 15-B, 16-C, 17-D, 18-B, 19-C, 20-D, 21-A, 22-D, 23-B, 24-D, 25-C

Mechanical Comprehension: 1-C, 2-C, 3-C, 4-B, 5-C, 6-C, 7-C, 8-C, 9-B, 10-B, 11-C, 12-B, 13-C, 14-C, 15-C, 16-B, 17-A, 18-C, 19-B, 20-C, 21-C, 22-B, 23-A, 24-D, 25-B

Test 7

General Science (25 questions)

1. The process by which green plants make food is called: A) Respiration B) Photosynthesis C) Transpiration D) Germination
2. What gas makes up about 78% of Earth's atmosphere? A) Oxygen B) Carbon dioxide C) Nitrogen D) Argon
3. The smallest unit of matter is: A) Molecule B) Atom C) Cell D) Electron
4. Which planet is closest to the sun? A) Venus B) Earth C) Mercury D) Mars
5. The hardest natural substance is: A) Quartz B) Steel C) Diamond D) Iron
6. What type of rock is formed by heat and pressure? A) Igneous B) Sedimentary C) Metamorphic D) Volcanic
7. The human body has how many bones? A) 186 B) 206 C) 226 D) 246
8. What causes tides? A) Wind B) Earth's rotation C) Moon's gravity D) Sun's heat
9. Which element has the chemical symbol "Au"? A) Silver B) Aluminum C) Gold D) Argon
10. The speed of light is approximately: A) 186,000 miles/second B) 186,000 km/second C) 300,000 miles/second D) 300,000 km/second
11. What is the pH of pure water? A) 6 B) 7 C) 8 D) 9
12. Which blood type is the universal donor? A) A B) B C) AB D) O
13. The study of earthquakes is called: A) Geology B) Seismology C) Meteorology D) Astronomy
14. What gas do plants release during photosynthesis? A) Carbon dioxide B) Nitrogen C) Oxygen D) Hydrogen
15. The smallest bone in the human body is in the: A) Hand B) Foot C) Ear D) Nose
16. Which force keeps planets in orbit? A) Magnetism B) Gravity C) Friction D) Centrifugal force
17. Water boils at what temperature (Celsius)? A) 90° B) 100° C) 110° D) 120°
18. The largest organ in the human body is the: A) Liver B) Brain C) Lungs D) Skin
19. What causes rust? A) Heat B) Cold C) Oxidation D) Pressure
20. The center of an atom is called the: A) Electron B) Proton C) Neutron D) Nucleus
21. Which vitamin is produced by sunlight? A) Vitamin A B) Vitamin C C) Vitamin D D) Vitamin E
22. The chemical formula for water is: A) $H2O$ B) $CO2$ C) $NaCl$ D) $O2$
23. What type of animal is a dolphin? A) Fish B) Mammal C) Reptile D) Amphibian
24. The ozone layer protects Earth from: A) Meteors B) Cold C) UV radiation D) Wind
25. Which organ produces insulin? A) Liver B) Kidney C) Pancreas D) Stomach

Arithmetic Reasoning (30 questions)

1. If a car travels 240 miles in 4 hours, what is its average speed? A) 50 mph B) 55 mph C) 60 mph D) 65 mph
2. A shirt costs $25. If it's on sale for 20% off, what's the sale price? A) $20 B) $21 C) $22 D) $23

3. If $3x + 7 = 22$, what is x? A) 3 B) 4 C) 5 D) 6
4. A recipe calls for 2 cups of flour for 12 muffins. How much flour for 18 muffins? A) 2.5 cups B) 3 cups C) 3.5 cups D) 4 cups
5. What is 15% of 80? A) 10 B) 12 C) 14 D) 16
6. If a box contains 24 items and you use 1/3 of them, how many are left? A) 8 B) 12 C) 16 D) 18
7. A worker earns $12 per hour. How much for 37.5 hours? A) $450 B) $460 C) $470 D) $480
8. What is the next number in the sequence: 2, 6, 18, 54, ...? A) 108 B) 132 C) 162 D) 192
9. If a train travels 180 miles in 3 hours, how far in 5 hours at the same speed? A) 250 miles B) 280 miles C) 300 miles D) 320 miles
10. A rectangular garden is 12 feet by 8 feet. What's its perimeter? A) 40 feet B) 42 feet C) 44 feet D) 48 feet
11. If 2/5 of a number is 14, what's the number? A) 28 B) 30 C) 32 D) 35
12. A store marks up items 40%. If cost is $50, what's the selling price? A) $65 B) $70 C) $75 D) $80
13. What is $7^2 - 3^2$? A) 40 B) 42 C) 44 D) 46
14. If gas costs $3.20 per gallon and you buy 12 gallons, what's the total? A) $38.00 B) $38.40 C) $38.80 D) $39.20
15. A class has 28 students. If 3/4 pass the test, how many passed? A) 18 B) 21 C) 24 D) 25
16. What is the average of 85, 92, 78, and 89? A) 85 B) 86 C) 87 D) 88
17. If a circular pool has a radius of 6 feet, what's its area? (Use $\pi = 3.14$) A) 108.24 sq ft B) 113.04 sq ft C) 118.84 sq ft D) 124.64 sq ft
18. A bag contains 5 red, 3 blue, and 2 green marbles. What's the probability of drawing red? A) 1/2 B) 3/5 C) 2/3 D) 3/4
19. If $x - 8 = 15$, what is $x + 5$? A) 26 B) 28 C) 30 D) 32
20. A discount of 25% reduces a price by $15. What was the original price? A) $45 B) $50 C) $55 D) $60
21. What is 3/8 + 1/4? A) 4/12 B) 5/8 C) 7/12 D) 3/4
22. If a rectangle is 15 cm long and has an area of 105 sq cm, what's its width? A) 6 cm B) 7 cm C) 8 cm D) 9 cm
23. A car depreciates 15% per year. If it's worth $20,000, what after one year? A) $17,000 B) $17,500 C) $18,000 D) $18,500
24. What is 20% of 25% of 400? A) 15 B) 20 C) 25 D) 30
25. If $4x - 3 = 2x + 9$, what is x? A) 4 B) 5 C) 6 D) 7
26. A ladder 13 feet long leans against a wall. If the base is 5 feet from the wall, how high up the wall? A) 10 feet B) 11 feet C) 12 feet D) 13 feet
27. What is the median of: 12, 8, 15, 10, 9? A) 9 B) 10 C) 12 D) 15
28. If you save $150 per month for 8 months, how much total? A) $1,100 B) $1,150 C) $1,200 D) $1,250
29. A pizza is cut into 8 equal slices. If you eat 3 slices, what fraction remains? A) 3/8 B) 5/8 C) 2/3 D) 3/4
30. What is $18 \div 0.6$? A) 28 B) 30 C) 32 D) 35

Word Knowledge (35 questions)

1. Belligerent means: A) Peaceful B) Aggressive C) Friendly D) Quiet
2. Concise means: A) Lengthy B) Brief C) Confusing D) Detailed
3. Deteriorate means: A) Improve B) Maintain C) Worsen D) Stabilize
4. Elated means: A) Sad B) Angry C) Joyful D) Tired
5. Fabricate means: A) Destroy B) Create C) Find D) Lose
6. Grueling means: A) Easy B) Exhausting C) Quick D) Simple
7. Hinder means: A) Help B) Block C) Encourage D) Support
8. Immaculate means: A) Dirty B) Perfect C) Broken D) Old
9. Jubilant means: A) Sad B) Tired C) Celebratory D) Angry
10. Kindle means: A) Extinguish B) Ignite C) Cool D) Freeze
11. Lucid means: A) Unclear B) Clear C) Dark D) Bright
12. Meticulous means: A) Careless B) Careful C) Quick D) Slow
13. Nostalgic means: A) Future-looking B) Sentimental C) Angry D) Happy
14. Obsolete means: A) New B) Outdated C) Useful D) Modern
15. Perplexed means: A) Clear B) Confused C) Happy D) Sad
16. Quaint means: A) Modern B) Charming C) Ugly D) Large
17. Reluctant means: A) Eager B) Unwilling C) Happy D) Quick
18. Serene means: A) Chaotic B) Peaceful C) Loud D) Busy
19. Trivial means: A) Important B) Unimportant C) Large D) Small
20. Unanimous means: A) Divided B) Agreed C) Partial D) Individual
21. Versatile means: A) Limited B) Adaptable C) Rigid D) Narrow
22. Wary means: A) Trusting B) Cautious C) Careless D) Bold
23. Zealous means: A) Lazy B) Enthusiastic C) Tired D) Bored
24. Abrupt means: A) Gradual B) Sudden C) Slow D) Smooth
25. Benevolent means: A) Mean B) Kind C) Selfish D) Harsh
26. Candid means: A) Dishonest B) Honest C) Secretive D) Mysterious
27. Dormant means: A) Active B) Inactive C) Loud D) Bright
28. Elaborate means: A) Simple B) Detailed C) Brief D) Quick
29. Fragile means: A) Strong B) Delicate C) Rough D) Hard
30. Genuine means: A) Fake B) Real C) Artificial D) False
31. Hostile means: A) Friendly B) Unfriendly C) Kind D) Gentle
32. Inevitable means: A) Avoidable B) Unavoidable C) Possible D) Unlikely
33. Jovial means: A) Sad B) Cheerful C) Angry D) Serious
34. Keen means: A) Dull B) Sharp C) Blunt D) Slow
35. Lethargic means: A) Energetic B) Sluggish C) Quick D) Active

Paragraph Comprehension (15 questions)

Passage 1: Marine biology is the study of ocean life. Scientists who work in this field examine everything from microscopic plankton to massive whales. The ocean covers more than 70% of Earth's surface, yet we have explored less than 5% of it. Many new species are discovered each year in the deep ocean, where conditions are extreme with high pressure and no sunlight.

1. According to the passage, what percentage of Earth's surface is covered by ocean? A) 5% B) 50% C) More than 70% D) 95%
2. Marine biologists study: A) Only large sea animals B) Only microscopic organisms C) All ocean life D) Only fish

Passage 2: The invention of the printing press in the 15th century revolutionized communication. Before this invention, books were copied by hand, making them expensive and rare. Johannes Gutenberg's printing press made books affordable and widely available, leading to increased literacy rates and the spread of knowledge throughout Europe.

3. Before the printing press, books were: A) Not available B) Copied by hand C) Very cheap D) Mass produced
4. The printing press was invented in the: A) 14th century B) 15th century C) 16th century D) 17th century
5. Who invented the printing press mentioned in the passage? A) Leonardo da Vinci B) Johannes Gutenberg C) William Shakespeare D) Christopher Columbus

Passage 3: Renewable energy sources like solar and wind power are becoming increasingly important as alternatives to fossil fuels. Solar panels convert sunlight into electricity, while wind turbines harness the power of moving air. These technologies produce clean energy without the pollution associated with burning coal or oil.

6. Solar panels convert what into electricity? A) Wind B) Water C) Sunlight D) Coal
7. According to the passage, renewable energy is important because it: A) Is cheaper B) Is pollution-free C) Lasts longer D) Is easier to install

Passage 4: Regular exercise provides numerous health benefits. It strengthens the heart, improves circulation, and helps maintain healthy weight. Exercise also releases endorphins, which are natural mood enhancers that can reduce stress and anxiety. Health experts recommend at least 30 minutes of moderate exercise most days of the week.

8. Endorphins are described as: A) Harmful chemicals B) Natural mood enhancers C) Artificial supplements D) Exercise equipment
9. How much exercise do health experts recommend? A) 15 minutes daily B) 30 minutes most days C) 1 hour weekly D) 2 hours monthly

Passage 5: The Great Wall of China is one of the world's most impressive architectural achievements. Built over many centuries by different dynasties, it stretches over 13,000 miles across northern China. Contrary to popular belief, the wall is not visible from space with the naked eye, though this myth persists.

10. The Great Wall stretches approximately: A) 1,300 miles B) 13,000 miles C) 130,000 miles D) 3,000 miles
11. According to the passage, the Great Wall: A) Is visible from space B) Is not visible from space C) Was built in one century D) Is in southern China

Passage 6: Photosynthesis is the process by which plants convert sunlight, carbon dioxide, and water into glucose and oxygen. This process is essential for life on Earth because it produces the oxygen we breathe and forms the base of most food chains. The chlorophyll in plant leaves captures the sun's energy to power this vital process.

12. Photosynthesis produces: A) Carbon dioxide and water B) Glucose and oxygen C) Sunlight and chlorophyll D) Leaves and stems
13. What captures the sun's energy in plants? A) Roots B) Stems C) Chlorophyll D) Flowers

Passage 7: Sleep is crucial for physical and mental health. During sleep, the body repairs tissues, consolidates memories, and releases important hormones. Adults typically need 7-9 hours of sleep per night for optimal health. Chronic sleep deprivation can lead to serious health problems including heart disease and diabetes.

14. Adults typically need how many hours of sleep? A) 5-6 hours B) 7-9 hours C) 10-12 hours D) 6-8 hours
15. Chronic sleep deprivation can lead to: A) Better memory B) Increased energy C) Serious health problems D) Weight loss

Mathematics Knowledge (25 questions)

1. What is the square root of 144? A) 11 B) 12 C) 13 D) 14
2. If $x^2 = 25$, what is x? A) ±4 B) ±5 C) ±6 D) ±7
3. What is $2^3 \times 3^2$? A) 54 B) 64 C) 72 D) 81
4. The sum of angles in a triangle is: A) 90° B) 180° C) 270° D) 360°
5. What is the slope of the line $y = 3x + 5$? A) 3 B) 5 C) 8 D) 15
6. Factor: $x^2 - 9$ A) (x-3)(x-3) B) (x+3)(x+3) C) (x-3)(x+3) D) Cannot be factored
7. What is $\log_{10} 1000$? A) 2 B) 3 C) 4 D) 5
8. If $\sin \theta = 0.5$, what is θ? A) 30° B) 45° C) 60° D) 90°
9. The area of a circle with radius 5 is: A) 25π B) 10π C) 50π D) 100π
10. What is 5! (5 factorial)? A) 25 B) 60 C) 120 D) 240
11. If $f(x) = x^2 + 3x - 2$, what is $f(2)$? A) 6 B) 8 C) 10 D) 12
12. The volume of a cube with side length 4 is: A) 12 B) 16 C) 48 D) 64
13. What is the y-intercept of $2x + 3y = 12$? A) 2 B) 3 C) 4 D) 6
14. Solve: $2x - 7 = x + 3$ A) x = 8 B) x = 10 C) x = 12 D) x = 14
15. What is cos 60°? A) 0.5 B) 0.707 C) 0.866 D) 1
16. The quadratic formula is: A) $x = (-b \pm \sqrt{(b^2-4ac)})/2a$ B) $x = (-b \pm \sqrt{(b^2+4ac)})/2a$ C) $x = (b \pm \sqrt{(b^2-4ac)})/2a$ D) $x = (-b \pm \sqrt{(b^2-4ac)})/a$
17. What is the perimeter of a rectangle 8 by 6? A) 14 B) 24 C) 28 D) 48
18. If $\tan \theta = 1$, what is θ? A) 30° B) 45° C) 60° D) 90°
19. What is the distance between (0,0) and (3,4)? A) 5 B) 6 C) 7 D) 8
20. Simplify: $\sqrt{50}$ A) $5\sqrt{2}$ B) $2\sqrt{5}$ C) $5\sqrt{10}$ D) $10\sqrt{5}$
21. The sum of an arithmetic sequence with first term 3, last term 27, and 9 terms is: A) 135 B) 150 C) 162 D) 180
22. What is 25% of 40% of 200? A) 15 B) 20 C) 25 D) 30
23. If $\log_2 x = 4$, what is x? A) 8 B) 12 C) 16 D) 20

24. The area of a trapezoid with bases 6 and 10 and height 4 is: A) 28 B) 32 C) 36 D) 40
25. What is the derivative of x^3? A) $3x$ B) $3x^2$ C) x^2 D) $3x^3$

Electronics Information (20 questions)

1. What does AC stand for? A) Alternating Current B) Active Circuit C) Automatic Control D) Applied Current
2. Ohm's Law states that $V = I \times R$. What does R represent? A) Voltage B) Current C) Resistance D) Power
3. A fuse is used to: A) Increase voltage B) Protect circuits C) Store energy D) Generate power
4. What is the standard household voltage in the US? A) 110V B) 120V C) 220V D) 240V
5. A capacitor stores: A) Current B) Voltage C) Electrical charge D) Resistance
6. In a series circuit, if one bulb burns out: A) All bulbs go out B) Other bulbs stay on C) Voltage increases D) Current doubles
7. What color wire is typically used for ground? A) Black B) White C) Red D) Green
8. An ammeter measures: A) Voltage B) Current C) Resistance D) Power
9. What does LED stand for? A) Light Emitting Diode B) Low Energy Device C) Linear Electronic Display D) Liquid Energy Display
10. A transformer is used to: A) Store electricity B) Generate electricity C) Change voltage levels D) Measure electricity
11. In a parallel circuit, voltage across each branch is: A) Different B) The same C) Zero D) Infinite
12. What is the power formula? A) $P = V/I$ B) $P = V \times I$ C) $P = I/V$ D) $P = V + I$
13. A semiconductor has: A) No conductivity B) Perfect conductivity C) Variable conductivity D) Infinite conductivity
14. What does DC stand for? A) Direct Current B) Dynamic Circuit C) Double Current D) Digital Control
15. A resistor's value is indicated by: A) Size B) Shape C) Color codes D) Weight
16. An insulator: A) Conducts electricity well B) Prevents electrical flow C) Stores electricity D) Generates electricity
17. What happens to resistance when temperature increases in most metals? A) Increases B) Decreases C) Stays the same D) Becomes zero
18. A voltmeter is connected in: A) Series B) Parallel C) Either way D) Not connected
19. The unit of electrical power is: A) Volt B) Amp C) Ohm D) Watt
20. A diode allows current to flow in: A) Both directions B) One direction only C) No direction D) Multiple directions

Auto & Shop Information (25 questions)

Auto Information:

1. The carburetor mixes: A) Oil and gas B) Air and fuel C) Water and oil D) Gas and water
2. How many cylinders does a V8 engine have? A) 6 B) 8 C) 10 D) 12
3. The alternator produces: A) AC current B) DC current C) Mechanical power D) Hydraulic pressure

4. What does ABS stand for? A) Automatic Brake System B) Anti-lock Brake System C) Advanced Brake System D) Air Brake System
5. The radiator is part of the: A) Fuel system B) Electrical system C) Cooling system D) Exhaust system
6. Motor oil viscosity 10W-30 means: A) 10 weight, 30 temperature B) Winter grade 10, summer grade 30 C) 10 liters, 30 pressure D) 10 octane, 30 weight
7. The catalytic converter reduces: A) Fuel consumption B) Engine noise C) Exhaust emissions D) Oil usage
8. Spark plugs are part of the: A) Fuel system B) Ignition system C) Cooling system D) Brake system
9. What does RPM stand for? A) Rotations Per Mile B) Revolutions Per Minute C) Rotary Power Motor D) Real Power Measurement
10. The differential allows wheels to: A) Turn at different speeds B) Brake simultaneously C) Accelerate together D) Steer the vehicle
11. Brake fluid is: A) Hydraulic fluid B) Motor oil C) Gasoline D) Antifreeze
12. The PCV valve controls: A) Fuel flow B) Air flow C) Crankcase ventilation D) Exhaust flow
13. What type of engine uses diesel fuel? A) Gasoline engine B) Compression ignition engine C) Steam engine D) Electric engine

Shop Information: 14. A Phillips head screwdriver has a: A) Flat tip B) Cross-shaped tip C) Hexagonal tip D) Square tip 15. Which tool is used to cut metal? A) Wood saw B) Hacksaw C) Coping saw D) Crosscut saw 16. A level is used to check: A) Temperature B) Pressure C) Horizontal/vertical alignment D) Electrical current 17. Sandpaper grit 220 is: A) Very coarse B) Coarse C) Medium D) Fine 18. A Phillips screw has: A) A flat slot B) A cross-shaped slot C) A hexagonal slot D) A square slot 19. Which joint is strongest in woodworking? A) Butt joint B) Lap joint C) Mortise and tenon D) Simple splice 20. A chisel is used for: A) Measuring B) Cutting/shaping C) Holding D) Drilling 21. What does "16d" mean for nails? A) 16 diameter B) 16 penny size C) 16 inches long D) 16 gauge 22. A vise is used to: A) Measure B) Cut C) Hold work pieces D) Sand 23. The teeth per inch (TPI) on a saw blade determines: A) Cutting speed B) Blade length C) Cut smoothness D) Blade strength 24. A square is used to check: A) Circles B) Right angles C) Curves D) Holes 25. Which tool removes material by abrasion? A) Plane B) Chisel C) File D) Knife

Mechanical Comprehension (25 questions)

1. If gear A has 20 teeth and gear B has 40 teeth, when A makes 2 revolutions, B makes: A) 1 revolution B) 2 revolutions C) 4 revolutions D) 8 revolutions
2. In a lever, the fulcrum is the: A) Load B) Effort C) Pivot point D) Resistance
3. A pulley system with 4 supporting ropes has a mechanical advantage of: A) 2 B) 4 C) 6 D) 8
4. Water pressure at the bottom of a tank depends on: A) Tank width B) Water temperature C) Water depth D) Tank material
5. If you apply 10 pounds of force to a 2:1 lever, the output force is: A) 5 pounds B) 10 pounds C) 20 pounds D) 40 pounds

6. In a hydraulic system, pressure is: A) Different throughout B) The same throughout C) Zero D) Infinite
7. A wheel and axle system where the wheel diameter is 3 times the axle diameter has a mechanical advantage of: A) 1 B) 2 C) 3 D) 6
8. When a liquid is heated, it generally: A) Contracts B) Expands C) Stays the same D) Evaporates
9. The center of gravity of an object is where: A) It's heaviest B) It's lightest C) Weight is balanced D) It's strongest
10. In a screw, the mechanical advantage depends on: A) Length B) Diameter C) Thread pitch D) Material
11. If a spring is compressed, it stores: A) Kinetic energy B) Potential energy C) Heat energy D) Chemical energy
12. Ball bearings reduce: A) Speed B) Force C) Friction D) Weight
13. In a gear train, if the input gear is smaller than the output gear: A) Speed increases, torque decreases B) Speed decreases, torque increases C) Both increase D) Both decrease
14. A cam converts: A) Rotary to linear motion B) Linear to rotary motion C) Rotary to rotary motion D) Linear to linear motion
15. The coefficient of friction is: A) Always 1 B) Always greater than 1 C) Between 0 and 1 D) Can be any value
16. In an inclined plane, mechanical advantage equals: A) Height/length B) Length/height C) Width/height D) Area/length
17. Bernoulli's principle states that as fluid speed increases: A) Pressure increases B) Pressure decreases C) Temperature increases D) Density increases
18. A pendulum's period depends on its: A) Weight B) Length C) Material D) Color
19. In a compound pulley system with 3 movable pulleys: A) MA = 3 B) MA = 6 C) MA = 9 D) MA = 12
20. Pascal's law applies to: A) Solids only B) Liquids only C) Gases only D) Fluids (liquids and gases)
21. If two gears mesh and one has twice the radius of the other, the gear ratio is: A) 1:1 B) 1:2 C) 2:1 D) 4:1
22. A flywheel stores energy as: A) Potential energy B) Kinetic energy C) Heat energy D) Chemical energy
23. In a first-class lever, the fulcrum is: A) At one end B) Between effort and load C) At the load D) At the effort
24. Archimedes' principle deals with: A) Levers B) Pulleys C) Buoyancy D) Friction
25. The mechanical advantage of a single fixed pulley is: A) 0 B) 1 C) 2 D) 4

Test 7 Answer Key

General Science: 1-B, 2-C, 3-B, 4-C, 5-C, 6-C, 7-B, 8-C, 9-C, 10-A, 11-B, 12-D, 13-B, 14-C, 15-C, 16-B, 17-B, 18-D, 19-C, 20-D, 21-C, 22-A, 23-B, 24-C, 25-C

Arithmetic Reasoning: 1-C, 2-A, 3-C, 4-B, 5-B, 6-C, 7-A, 8-C, 9-C, 10-A, 11-D, 12-B, 13-A, 14-B, 15-B, 16-B, 17-B, 18-A, 19-B, 20-D, 21-B, 22-B, 23-A, 24-B, 25-C, 26-C, 27-B, 28-C, 29-B, 30-B

Word Knowledge: 1-B, 2-B, 3-C, 4-C, 5-B, 6-B, 7-B, 8-B, 9-C, 10-B, 11-B, 12-B, 13-B, 14-B, 15-B, 16-B, 17-B, 18-B, 19-B, 20-B, 21-B, 22-B, 23-B, 24-B, 25-B, 26-B, 27-B, 28-B, 29-B, 30-B, 31-B, 32-B, 33-B, 34-B, 35-B

Paragraph Comprehension: 1-C, 2-C, 3-B, 4-B, 5-B, 6-C, 7-B, 8-B, 9-B, 10-B, 11-B, 12-B, 13-C, 14-B, 15-C

Mathematics Knowledge: 1-B, 2-B, 3-C, 4-B, 5-A, 6-C, 7-B, 8-A, 9-A, 10-C, 11-B, 12-D, 13-C, 14-B, 15-A, 16-A, 17-C, 18-B, 19-A, 20-A, 21-A, 22-B, 23-C, 24-B, 25-B

Electronics Information: 1-A, 2-C, 3-B, 4-B, 5-C, 6-A, 7-D, 8-B, 9-A, 10-C, 11-B, 12-B, 13-C, 14-A, 15-C, 16-B, 17-A, 18-B, 19-D, 20-B

Auto & Shop Information: 1-B, 2-B, 3-A, 4-B, 5-C, 6-B, 7-C, 8-B, 9-B, 10-A, 11-A, 12-C, 13-B, 14-B, 15-B, 16-C, 17-D, 18-B, 19-C, 20-B, 21-B, 22-C, 23-C, 24-B, 25-C

Mechanical Comprehension: 1-A, 2-C, 3-B, 4-C, 5-C, 6-B, 7-C, 8-B, 9-C, 10-C, 11-B, 12-C, 13-B, 14-A, 15-C, 16-B, 17-B, 18-B, 19-B, 20-D, 21-C, 22-B, 23-B, 24-C, 25-B

Test 8

General Science (25 questions)

1. Which planet is known as the "Red Planet"? A) Venus B) Mars C) Jupiter D) Saturn
2. The process of cell division is called: A) Meiosis B) Mitosis C) Photosynthesis D) Respiration
3. What is the chemical symbol for iron? A) Ir B) In C) Fe D) Fr
4. Sound travels fastest through: A) Air B) Water C) Steel D) Vacuum
5. The Richter scale measures: A) Temperature B) Wind speed C) Earthquake intensity D) Atmospheric pressure
6. What percentage of the human body is water? A) 50% B) 60% C) 70% D) 80%
7. Which gas is most abundant in Earth's atmosphere? A) Oxygen B) Carbon dioxide C) Nitrogen D) Hydrogen
8. The study of heredity is called: A) Ecology B) Genetics C) Botany D) Zoology
9. What causes seasons on Earth? A) Distance from sun B) Axial tilt C) Solar flares D) Moon phases
10. The smallest unit of life is the: A) Organ B) Tissue C) Cell D) Organism
11. Lightning is a form of: A) Chemical energy B) Nuclear energy C) Electrical energy D) Mechanical energy
12. Which vitamin prevents scurvy? A) Vitamin A B) Vitamin B C) Vitamin C D) Vitamin D
13. The hardest substance in the human body is: A) Bone B) Cartilage C) Tooth enamel D) Fingernails
14. What type of rock is granite? A) Sedimentary B) Metamorphic C) Igneous D) Volcanic
15. The greenhouse effect is caused by: A) Ozone depletion B) Solar radiation C) Trapped gases D) Ocean currents

16. Which element has the atomic number 1? A) Helium B) Hydrogen C) Lithium D) Carbon
17. Photosynthesis occurs in: A) Roots B) Stems C) Leaves D) Flowers
18. The speed of sound in air at room temperature is approximately: A) 343 m/s B) 300 m/s C) 400 m/s D) 500 m/s
19. What is the largest organ in the human body? A) Liver B) Lungs C) Brain D) Skin
20. Which force holds the nucleus of an atom together? A) Electromagnetic B) Gravitational C) Strong nuclear D) Weak nuclear
21. The pH scale ranges from: A) 1 to 10 B) 0 to 14 C) 1 to 14 D) 0 to 10
22. What causes tarnish on silver? A) Oxidation B) Reduction C) Sublimation D) Condensation
23. The human heart has how many chambers? A) 2 B) 3 C) 4 D) 5
24. Which planet has the most moons? A) Jupiter B) Saturn C) Uranus D) Neptune
25. Absolute zero is: A) 0°C B) -273°C C) -100°C D) -200°C

Arithmetic Reasoning (30 questions)

1. A car travels 300 miles in 5 hours. What is its average speed? A) 50 mph B) 55 mph C) 60 mph D) 65 mph
2. If a jacket costs $80 and is marked down 25%, what is the sale price? A) $55 B) $60 C) $65 D) $70
3. What is 18% of 250? A) 40 B) 42 C) 45 D) 48
4. If $4x - 8 = 20$, what is x? A) 6 B) 7 C) 8 D) 9
5. A recipe serves 6 people and calls for 3 cups of rice. How much rice for 10 people? A) 4 cups B) 5 cups C) 6 cups D) 7 cups
6. What is the next number: 3, 9, 27, 81, ...? A) 162 B) 216 C) 243 D) 324
7. A worker earns $15 per hour for 40 hours, then time-and-a-half for overtime. What's the pay for 45 hours? A) $675 B) $712.50 C) $750 D) $787.50
8. If a circle has a diameter of 14 inches, what is its circumference? (Use $\pi = 3.14$) A) 42.86 inches B) 43.96 inches C) 44.52 inches D) 45.12 inches
9. A class of 30 students has 18 girls. What fraction are boys? A) 2/5 B) 3/5 C) 1/3 D) 2/3
10. What is 7/8 - 3/8? A) 4/8 B) 1/2 C) 5/8 D) 3/4
11. If gas costs $3.45 per gallon and you need 15 gallons, what's the total cost? A) $51.75 B) $52.25 C) $52.75 D) $53.25
12. A rectangular room is 12 feet by 16 feet. What is its area? A) 28 sq ft B) 56 sq ft C) 192 sq ft D) 224 sq ft
13. What is 35% of 160? A) 52 B) 54 C) 56 D) 58
14. If $x + 12 = 3x - 4$, what is x? A) 6 B) 8 C) 10 D) 12
15. A train travels 240 miles in 3 hours. How long to travel 400 miles at the same speed? A) 4 hours B) 5 hours C) 6 hours D) 7 hours
16. What is the average of 92, 85, 78, 95, and 90? A) 86 B) 88 C) 90 D) 92
17. If 3/5 of a number is 24, what is the number? A) 35 B) 40 C) 45 D) 50
18. A discount of 20% saves $18. What was the original price? A) $72 B) $85 C) $90 D) $95
19. What is $2^3 \times 3^2 \times 5^1$? A) 300 B) 320 C) 350 D) 360
20. If a square has a perimeter of 28 inches, what is its area? A) 49 sq in B) 64 sq in C) 81 sq in D) 100 sq in

21. A bag contains 8 red marbles and 12 blue marbles. What's the probability of drawing a red marble? A) 2/5 B) 3/5 C) 1/3 D) 2/3
22. What is 45% of 25% of 800? A) 75 B) 80 C) 85 D) 90
23. If y = 2x + 3 and x = 4, what is y? A) 9 B) 11 C) 13 D) 15
24. A ladder 15 feet long reaches 12 feet up a wall. How far is the base from the wall? A) 8 feet B) 9 feet C) 10 feet D) 11 feet
25. What is 5/6 + 2/3? A) 7/9 B) 1 1/6 C) 1 1/2 D) 1 2/3
26. If an item costs $45 after a 10% discount, what was the original price? A) $49.50 B) $50.00 C) $52.50 D) $55.00
27. What is the median of: 15, 22, 18, 30, 25? A) 20 B) 22 C) 25 D) 30
28. A car depreciates 12% per year. If worth $25,000, what after 2 years? A) $19,360 B) $22,000 C) $23,500 D) $24,500
29. What is 4/7 ÷ 2/3? A) 6/7 B) 8/21 C) 12/14 D) 6/7
30. If 2x + 5 = 3x - 7, what is x? A) 10 B) 12 C) 14 D) 16

Word Knowledge (35 questions)

1. Abundant means: A) Scarce B) Plentiful C) Expensive D) Rare
2. Bizarre means: A) Normal B) Strange C) Beautiful D) Simple
3. Contemplate means: A) Ignore B) Consider C) Reject D) Forget
4. Deceive means: A) Help B) Mislead C) Support D) Encourage
5. Evident means: A) Hidden B) Obvious C) Confusing D) Secret
6. Frigid means: A) Hot B) Warm C) Cold D) Mild
7. Genuine means: A) Fake B) Real C) Temporary D) Artificial
8. Hazardous means: A) Safe B) Dangerous C) Helpful D) Easy
9. Immense means: A) Tiny B) Huge C) Average D) Small
10. Joyful means: A) Sad B) Happy C) Angry D) Tired
11. Keen means: A) Dull B) Sharp C) Slow D) Weak
12. Lengthy means: A) Short B) Long C) Wide D) Narrow
13. Modest means: A) Arrogant B) Humble C) Loud D) Bold
14. Novel means: A) Old B) New C) Boring D) Common
15. Obvious means: A) Hidden B) Clear C) Difficult D) Complex
16. Peculiar means: A) Normal B) Unusual C) Common D) Regular
17. Quiet means: A) Loud B) Silent C) Noisy D) Boisterous
18. Rapid means: A) Slow B) Fast C) Steady D) Gradual
19. Sincere means: A) False B) Genuine C) Pretend D) Fake
20. Tranquil means: A) Chaotic B) Peaceful C) Noisy D) Busy
21. Ultimate means: A) First B) Final C) Middle D) Beginning
22. Vacant means: A) Full B) Empty C) Crowded D) Occupied
23. Wicked means: A) Good B) Evil C) Kind D) Gentle
24. Youthful means: A) Old B) Young C) Mature D) Elderly
25. Zealous means: A) Lazy B) Enthusiastic C) Bored D) Tired
26. Adequate means: A) Insufficient B) Sufficient C) Excessive D) Perfect
27. Blunt means: A) Sharp B) Dull C) Pointed D) Thin
28. Clever means: A) Stupid B) Smart C) Slow D) Dull
29. Dense means: A) Sparse B) Thick C) Thin D) Light

30. Entire means: A) Partial B) Complete C) Half D) Some
31. Flexible means: A) Rigid B) Bendable C) Hard D) Stiff
32. Gradual means: A) Sudden B) Slow C) Fast D) Immediate
33. Harsh means: A) Gentle B) Severe C) Soft D) Kind
34. Intense means: A) Mild B) Strong C) Weak D) Light
35. Just means: A) Unfair B) Fair C) Wrong D) Biased

Paragraph Comprehension (15 questions)

Passage 1: The human brain contains approximately 86 billion neurons, each connected to thousands of others through synapses. These connections allow for the transmission of electrical and chemical signals throughout the nervous system. The brain uses about 20% of the body's total energy, despite weighing only about 2% of total body weight.

1. How many neurons are in the human brain? A) 86 million B) 86 billion C) 86 thousand D) 860 billion
2. The brain uses what percentage of the body's energy? A) 2% B) 10% C) 20% D) 50%

Passage 2: Recycling helps reduce waste in landfills and conserves natural resources. Aluminum cans can be recycled indefinitely without losing quality, while paper can typically be recycled 5-7 times before the fibers become too short. Glass is also infinitely recyclable, making it one of the most environmentally friendly packaging materials.

3. How many times can paper typically be recycled? A) 3-4 times B) 5-7 times C) 8-10 times D) Indefinitely
4. Which materials can be recycled indefinitely? A) Paper and plastic B) Aluminum and glass C) Paper and glass D) Plastic and aluminum

Passage 3: The Great Barrier Reef, located off the coast of Australia, is the world's largest coral reef system. It stretches over 2,300 kilometers and is home to thousands of species of marine life. Climate change and ocean acidification pose significant threats to this UNESCO World Heritage site.

5. The Great Barrier Reef is located off the coast of: A) New Zealand B) Australia C) Indonesia D) Philippines
6. What threatens the Great Barrier Reef according to the passage? A) Tourism B) Fishing C) Climate change D) Pollution

Passage 4: Benjamin Franklin was not only a founding father of the United States but also a prolific inventor. Among his inventions were bifocal glasses, the lightning rod, and the Franklin stove. His scientific experiments with electricity led to important discoveries about the nature of electrical charge.

7. Who invented bifocal glasses? A) Thomas Edison B) Benjamin Franklin C) Alexander Graham Bell D) Nikola Tesla

8. Franklin's experiments were primarily with: A) Chemistry B) Physics C) Electricity D) Biology

Passage 5: Regular physical activity can reduce the risk of many chronic diseases, including heart disease, diabetes, and certain cancers. The World Health Organization recommends at least 150 minutes of moderate-intensity exercise per week for adults. This can be broken down into 30-minute sessions, five days a week.

9. How many minutes of exercise does WHO recommend per week? A) 100 minutes B) 150 minutes C) 200 minutes D) 250 minutes
10. The recommended exercise can be broken into: A) 20-minute sessions B) 30-minute sessions C) 45-minute sessions D) 60-minute sessions

Passage 6: Bees play a crucial role in pollinating plants, making them essential for food production. It's estimated that one-third of the food we eat depends on bee pollination. However, bee populations have been declining due to factors such as habitat loss, pesticide use, and climate change.

11. What fraction of our food depends on bee pollination? A) One-fourth B) One-third C) One-half D) Two-thirds
12. What is NOT mentioned as a cause of bee population decline? A) Habitat loss B) Pesticide use C) Climate change D) Disease

Passage 7: The invention of the wheel around 3500 BCE revolutionized transportation and commerce. Initially used for pottery making, the wheel was later adapted for vehicles. This innovation allowed for the development of more complex civilizations by enabling efficient movement of goods and people.

13. When was the wheel invented? A) 3500 BCE B) 3000 BCE C) 2500 BCE D) 2000 BCE
14. The wheel was first used for: A) Transportation B) Pottery making C) Construction D) Agriculture
15. The wheel enabled the development of: A) Agriculture B) Writing C) Complex civilizations D) Mathematics

Mathematics Knowledge (25 questions)

1. What is $\sqrt{169}$? A) 12 B) 13 C) 14 D) 15
2. If $x^2 = 64$, what is x? A) ±6 B) ±7 C) ±8 D) ±9
3. What is 3^4? A) 64 B) 81 C) 100 D) 121
4. The area of a triangle with base 8 and height 6 is: A) 24 B) 28 C) 32 D) 48
5. What is the slope of $y = -2x + 7$? A) -2 B) 2 C) 7 D) -7
6. Factor: $x^2 - 16$ A) (x-4)(x-4) B) (x+4)(x+4) C) (x-4)(x+4) D) Cannot factor
7. What is $\log_{10} 10,000$? A) 3 B) 4 C) 5 D) 6
8. If $\cos \theta = 0.5$, what is θ? A) 30° B) 45° C) 60° D) 90°
9. The circumference of a circle with radius 7 is: A) 14π B) 21π C) 28π D) 49π
10. What is 6! (6 factorial)? A) 360 B) 520 C) 720 D) 840

11. If g(x) = 2x² - 5x + 1, what is g(3)? A) 4 B) 6 C) 8 D) 10
12. The surface area of a cube with side 5 is: A) 125 B) 150 C) 175 D) 200
13. What is the x-intercept of y = 3x - 12? A) 3 B) 4 C) -4 D) 12
14. Solve: 3x + 2 = 2x + 9 A) x = 5 B) x = 6 C) x = 7 D) x = 8
15. What is sin 30°? A) 0.5 B) 0.707 C) 0.866 D) 1
16. The quadratic x² - 5x + 6 = 0 has solutions: A) x = 2, 3 B) x = 1, 6 C) x = -2, -3 D) x = 2, 6
17. The diagonal of a rectangle 9 by 12 is: A) 15 B) 18 C) 21 D) 24
18. If sin θ = 0.707, what is θ? A) 30° B) 45° C) 60° D) 90°
19. The area of a trapezoid with bases 8, 12 and height 5 is: A) 40 B) 50 C) 60 D) 100
20. What is √(16 + 9)? A) 4 B) 5 C) 6 D) 7
21. The geometric series 2 + 6 + 18 + 54 + ... has first term a = 2 and ratio r = 3. The sum of first 4 terms is: A) 60 B) 70 C) 80 D) 90
22. What is 30% of 60% of 300? A) 48 B) 54 C) 60 D) 66
23. If log₃ x = 2, what is x? A) 6 B) 8 C) 9 D) 12
24. The volume of a cylinder with radius 3 and height 8 is: A) 72π B) 84π C) 96π D) 108π
25. What is the second derivative of x⁴? A) 4x³ B) 12x² C) 12x D) 4x

Electronics Information (20 questions)

1. What does DC stand for? A) Direct Current B) Dynamic Circuit C) Double Current D) Digital Control
2. The unit of electrical resistance is: A) Volt B) Ampere C) Ohm D) Watt
3. A circuit breaker is designed to: A) Increase voltage B) Store energy C) Protect from overload D) Generate power
4. What is the typical voltage of a car battery? A) 6V B) 12V C) 24V D) 110V
5. An inductor stores energy in: A) Electric field B) Magnetic field C) Chemical form D) Mechanical form
6. In a parallel circuit, if one component fails: A) All components fail B) Others continue working C) Voltage drops to zero D) Current increases infinitely
7. What color wire is typically "hot" in household wiring? A) White B) Black C) Green D) Blue
8. A multimeter can measure: A) Only voltage B) Only current C) Only resistance D) Voltage, current, and resistance
9. What does MOSFET stand for? A) Metal Oxide Semiconductor Field Effect Transistor B) Multiple Output Switch Field Effect Transistor C) Metal Organic Silicon Field Effect Transistor D) Magnetic Oxide Switch Field Effect Transistor
10. A step-up transformer: A) Decreases voltage B) Increases voltage C) Maintains voltage D) Eliminates voltage
11. In series circuits, current is: A) Different in each component B) Same throughout C) Zero D) Infinite
12. What is Ohm's Law? A) V = I + R B) V = I - R C) V = I × R D) V = I ÷ R
13. Silicon is a: A) Conductor B) Insulator C) Semiconductor D) Superconductor
14. What does EMF stand for? A) Electrical Motor Force B) Electromotive Force C) Electronic Magnetic Force D) Electric Motor Function
15. The frequency of AC power in the US is: A) 50 Hz B) 60 Hz C) 100 Hz D) 120 Hz

16. A relay is: A) An electronic switch B) A resistor C) A capacitor D) A battery
17. What happens to current when voltage increases and resistance stays constant? A) Decreases B) Increases C) Stays same D) Becomes zero
18. An oscilloscope displays: A) Resistance vs time B) Voltage vs time C) Current vs time D) Power vs time
19. The unit of frequency is: A) Volt B) Ampere C) Hertz D) Watt
20. A photocell converts: A) Heat to electricity B) Light to electricity C) Sound to electricity D) Motion to electricity

Auto & Shop Information (25 questions)

Auto Information:

1. The transmission transfers power from the: A) Wheels to engine B) Engine to wheels C) Battery to engine D) Engine to battery
2. What does EFI stand for? A) Electronic Fuel Injection B) Electric Fan Ignition C) Engine Fuel Indicator D) Emergency Fuel Injection
3. The thermostat regulates: A) Oil pressure B) Fuel flow C) Engine temperature D) Battery voltage
4. How many strokes does a 4-stroke engine have? A) 2 B) 4 C) 6 D) 8
5. The muffler is part of the: A) Cooling system B) Fuel system C) Exhaust system D) Electrical system
6. What does PS stand for in power steering? A) Power System B) Pressure System C) Power Steering D) Pump System
7. The fuel pump delivers fuel from the: A) Tank to carburetor/injectors B) Engine to tank C) Carburetor to engine D) Filter to tank
8. Anti-freeze prevents: A) Overheating only B) Freezing only C) Both freezing and overheating D) Rust only
9. The timing belt/chain synchronizes: A) Fuel injection B) Valve and piston movement C) Ignition timing D) Transmission shifting
10. What does CVT stand for? A) Constant Velocity Transmission B) Continuously Variable Transmission C) Central Valve Timing D) Computer Variable Timing
11. The master cylinder is part of the: A) Engine B) Transmission C) Brake system D) Steering system
12. What octane rating prevents engine knock? A) Lower octane B) Higher octane C) Any octane D) No octane
13. The serpentine belt drives: A) Only the alternator B) Multiple accessories C) Only the water pump D) Only the power steering

Shop Information: 14. A torque wrench is used to: A) Remove bolts B) Tighten to specific tension C) Cut threads D) Measure angles 15. Which saw is best for cutting curves? A) Circular saw B) Table saw C) Jigsaw D) Miter saw 16. A plumb bob is used to find: A) Horizontal level B) Vertical alignment C) Right angles D) Measurements 17. What grit sandpaper is coarsest? A) 60 grit B) 120 grit C) 220 grit D) 400 grit 18. A Robertson screw has a: A) Phillips head B) Flat slot C) Square socket D) Hexagonal socket 19. The strongest wood joint is: A) Butt joint B) Dado joint C) Mortise and tenon D) Lap joint 20. A rasp is used for: A) Fine sanding B) Rough shaping C) Drilling holes D) Measuring 21. Lumber size 2×4 actually measures: A) 2" × 4" B) 1.5" × 3.5" C) 2.5" × 4.5" D) 1.75" × 3.75" 22. A C-clamp is used to: A) Cut material B) Hold pieces together C) Measure angles D) Drive screws 23. The crosscut saw cuts: A) With the grain B) Against the grain C) Both directions D) Only curves 24. A try square checks for: A) 45° angles B) 90° angles C) 30° angles D) 60° angles 25. Which tool smooths wood surface? A) Chisel B) Rasp C) Plane D) Awl

Mechanical Comprehension (25 questions)

1. If gear A (10 teeth) drives gear B (30 teeth), the mechanical advantage is: A) 1:3 B) 3:1 C) 1:1 D) 10:30
2. In a second-class lever, the load is: A) Between fulcrum and effort B) At the fulcrum C) At the effort point D) Beyond the effort
3. A block and tackle with 6 supporting ropes has what mechanical advantage? A) 3 B) 6 C) 12 D) 18
4. Pressure in a fluid at rest depends on: A) Container shape B) Fluid depth C) Fluid color D) Container material
5. A 3:1 pulley system requires 30 pounds of input force to lift: A) 10 pounds B) 30 pounds C) 90 pounds D) 120 pounds
6. In hydraulics, if Area 1 = 2 sq in and Area 2 = 8 sq in, force multiplication is: A) 2:1 B) 4:1 C) 6:1 D) 8:1
7. A wheel 6 inches in diameter connected to an axle 2 inches in diameter has MA of: A) 2 B) 3 C) 4 D) 6
8. When water freezes, it: A) Contracts B) Expands C) Stays same volume D) Becomes denser
9. An object's center of gravity is the point where: A) It's heaviest B) It balances C) Gravity is strongest D) Mass is greatest
10. A screw with 4 threads per inch moved 1 inch requires: A) 2 turns B) 4 turns C) 6 turns D) 8 turns
11. A compressed spring has: A) Kinetic energy B) Potential energy C) No energy D) Heat energy
12. Lubricants reduce: A) Speed B) Weight C) Friction D) Force
13. In a gear train, smaller gear driving larger gear results in: A) Increased speed, decreased torque B) Decreased speed, increased torque C) Both increase D) Both decrease
14. An eccentric cam produces: A) Rotary motion B) Reciprocating motion C) No motion D) Random motion
15. Static friction is: A) Always less than kinetic B) Always greater than kinetic C) Equal to kinetic D) Independent of kinetic
16. The mechanical advantage of a ramp 12 feet long and 3 feet high is: A) 3 B) 4 C) 9 D) 12
17. As air moves faster over a wing, pressure: A) Increases above B) Decreases above C) Stays constant D) Reverses
18. A pendulum's frequency depends mainly on: A) Mass B) Length C) Amplitude D) Material
19. Four pulleys in a compound system give MA of: A) 4 B) 8 C) 12 D) 16
20. Archimedes' principle explains: A) Leverage B) Buoyancy C) Friction D) Momentum

21. Two meshing gears with 1:4 ratio, if input is 100 RPM, output is: A) 25 RPM B) 50 RPM C) 200 RPM D) 400 RPM
22. A gyroscope resists changes in: A) Speed B) Direction C) Weight D) Size
23. In a third-class lever: A) MA is always >1 B) MA is always <1 C) MA is always =1 D) MA varies widely
24. Water pressure at 20 feet depth is approximately: A) 8.7 psi B) 17.4 psi C) 26.1 psi D) 34.8 psi
25. A fixed pulley provides: A) No mechanical advantage B) 2:1 advantage C) 3:1 advantage D) Variable advantage

Test 8 Answer Key

General Science: 1-B, 2-B, 3-C, 4-C, 5-C, 6-B, 7-C, 8-B, 9-B, 10-C, 11-C, 12-C, 13-C, 14-C, 15-C, 16-B, 17-C, 18-A, 19-D, 20-C, 21-B, 22-A, 23-C, 24-B, 25-B

Arithmetic Reasoning: 1-C, 2-B, 3-C, 4-B, 5-B, 6-C, 7-B, 8-B, 9-A, 10-B, 11-A, 12-C, 13-C, 14-B, 15-B, 16-B, 17-B, 18-C, 19-D, 20-A, 21-A, 22-D, 23-B, 24-B, 25-C, 26-B, 27-B, 28-A, 29-A, 30-B

Word Knowledge: 1-B, 2-B, 3-B, 4-B, 5-B, 6-C, 7-B, 8-B, 9-B, 10-B, 11-B, 12-B, 13-B, 14-B, 15-B, 16-B, 17-B, 18-B, 19-B, 20-B, 21-B, 22-B, 23-B, 24-B, 25-B, 26-B, 27-B, 28-B, 29-B, 30-B, 31-B, 32-B, 33-B, 34-B, 35-B

Paragraph Comprehension: 1-B, 2-C, 3-B, 4-B, 5-B, 6-C, 7-B, 8-C, 9-B, 10-B, 11-B, 12-D, 13-A, 14-B, 15-C

Mathematics Knowledge: 1-B, 2-C, 3-B, 4-A, 5-A, 6-C, 7-B, 8-C, 9-A, 10-C, 11-A, 12-B, 13-B, 14-C, 15-A, 16-A, 17-A, 18-B, 19-B, 20-B, 21-C, 22-B, 23-C, 24-A, 25-B

Electronics Information: 1-A, 2-C, 3-C, 4-B, 5-B, 6-B, 7-B, 8-D, 9-A, 10-B, 11-B, 12-C, 13-C, 14-B, 15-B, 16-A, 17-B, 18-B, 19-C, 20-B

Auto & Shop Information: 1-B, 2-A, 3-C, 4-B, 5-C, 6-C, 7-A, 8-C, 9-B, 10-B, 11-C, 12-B, 13-B, 14-B, 15-C, 16-B, 17-A, 18-C, 19-C, 20-B, 21-B, 22-B, 23-B, 24-B, 25-C

Mechanical Comprehension: 1-B, 2-A, 3-B, 4-B, 5-C, 6-B, 7-B, 8-B, 9-B, 10-B, 11-B, 12-C, 13-B, 14-B, 15-B, 16-B, 17-B, 18-B, 19-B, 20-B, 21-A, 22-B, 23-B, 24-A, 25-A

Test 9

General Science (25 questions)

1. The process by which water vapor becomes liquid is called: A) Evaporation B) Condensation C) Sublimation D) Transpiration
2. Which planet is largest in our solar system? A) Earth B) Saturn C) Jupiter D) Neptune
3. What is the chemical symbol for sodium? A) So B) Sd C) Na D) S
4. The study of weather is called: A) Geology B) Meteorology C) Astronomy D) Biology
5. How many bones are in an adult human skeleton? A) 186 B) 206 C) 226 D) 246
6. What gas do plants absorb during photosynthesis? A) Oxygen B) Nitrogen C) Carbon dioxide D) Hydrogen
7. The smallest particle of an element is: A) Molecule B) Compound C) Atom D) Ion
8. Which blood vessels carry blood away from the heart? A) Veins B) Arteries C) Capillaries D) Ventricles
9. The force that opposes motion is: A) Gravity B) Magnetism C) Friction D) Inertia
10. What is the hardest mineral on Earth? A) Quartz B) Topaz C) Diamond D) Corundum
11. The Earth's core is mostly made of: A) Rock B) Ice C) Iron and nickel D) Magma
12. Which vitamin is essential for blood clotting? A) Vitamin A B) Vitamin C C) Vitamin D D) Vitamin K
13. Sound cannot travel through: A) Air B) Water C) Steel D) Vacuum
14. The main gas in the sun is: A) Oxygen B) Hydrogen C) Helium D) Nitrogen
15. What causes ocean tides? A) Wind B) Earth's rotation C) Moon's gravitational pull D) Solar radiation
16. The atomic number represents the number of: A) Neutrons B) Protons C) Electrons D) Nuclei
17. Which organ produces bile? A) Stomach B) Pancreas C) Liver D) Kidney
18. The speed of light is approximately: A) 186,000 mph B) 186,000 miles/second C) 300,000 mph D) 300,000 km/hour
19. What type of rock is formed from cooled magma? A) Sedimentary B) Metamorphic C) Igneous D) Limestone
20. The process of plants losing water through leaves is: A) Photosynthesis B) Respiration C) Transpiration D) Osmosis
21. Which element has the atomic symbol O? A) Gold B) Silver C) Oxygen D) Osmium
22. The ozone layer is located in the: A) Troposphere B) Stratosphere C) Mesosphere D) Thermosphere
23. How many chambers does a fish heart have? A) 2 B) 3 C) 4 D) 5
24. What is the study of fossils called? A) Archaeology B) Anthropology C) Paleontology D) Geology
25. The greenhouse effect is primarily caused by: A) Oxygen B) Nitrogen C) Carbon dioxide D) Argon

Arithmetic Reasoning (30 questions)

1. If a bicycle travels 15 miles in 45 minutes, what is its speed in mph? A) 15 mph B) 20 mph C) 25 mph D) 30 mph

2. A television costs $450. If the sales tax is 8%, what is the total cost? A) $486 B) $490 C) $495 D) $500
3. What is 22% of 150? A) 30 B) 33 C) 36 D) 39
4. If $5x + 3 = 28$, what is x? A) 4 B) 5 C) 6 D) 7
5. A recipe for 8 servings calls for 2 cups of flour. How much flour for 12 servings? A) 2.5 cups B) 3 cups C) 3.5 cups D) 4 cups
6. What is the next number in the sequence: 1, 4, 16, 64, ...? A) 128 B) 192 C) 256 D) 320
7. A worker earns $18 per hour for 35 hours. What is the total pay? A) $620 B) $630 C) $640 D) $650
8. If a rectangular garden is 20 feet by 15 feet, what is its area? A) 300 sq ft B) 350 sq ft C) 400 sq ft D) 450 sq ft
9. What is 3/4 + 2/3? A) 5/7 B) 17/12 C) 1 1/4 D) 1 5/12
10. A car travels 280 miles on 14 gallons of gas. What is the miles per gallon? A) 18 mpg B) 20 mpg C) 22 mpg D) 24 mpg
11. If 40% of a class of 35 students are girls, how many are boys? A) 14 B) 18 C) 21 D) 25
12. What is the perimeter of a square with sides of 9 inches? A) 18 inches B) 27 inches C) 36 inches D) 81 inches
13. A discount of 15% on a $60 item saves how much? A) $6 B) $9 C) $12 D) $15
14. If $x - 7 = 2x - 15$, what is x? A) 6 B) 7 C) 8 D) 9
15. A circular pool has a radius of 8 feet. What is its area? (Use $\pi = 3.14$) A) 200.96 sq ft B) 201.06 sq ft C) 201.62 sq ft D) 202.24 sq ft
16. What is the average of 76, 82, 90, 88, and 84? A) 82 B) 84 C) 86 D) 88
17. If 2/5 of a number is 18, what is the number? A) 40 B) 45 C) 50 D) 55
18. A store marks up items 30%. If the cost is $40, what is the selling price? A) $50 B) $52 C) $54 D) $56
19. What is $4^2 \times 2^3$? A) 64 B) 96 C) 128 D) 144
20. If a ladder 17 feet long reaches 15 feet up a wall, how far is the base from the wall? A) 6 feet B) 7 feet C) 8 feet D) 9 feet
21. A bag contains 6 red, 4 blue, and 5 green marbles. What's the probability of drawing blue? A) 4/15 B) 1/3 C) 2/5 D) 1/4
22. What is 25% of 40% of 160? A) 14 B) 16 C) 18 D) 20
23. If $y = 3x - 4$ and $x = 5$, what is y? A) 9 B) 11 C) 13 D) 15
24. A triangle has angles of 60° and 70°. What is the third angle? A) 40° B) 50° C) 60° D) 70°
25. What is 7/8 - 1/2? A) 3/8 B) 1/2 C) 5/8 D) 6/8
26. If an item costs $72 after a 20% discount, what was the original price? A) $85 B) $90 C) $95 D) $100
27. What is the median of: 12, 18, 15, 21, 9? A) 12 B) 15 C) 18 D) 21
28. A savings account earns 3% interest annually. What interest on $1,500? A) $40 B) $45 C) $50 D) $55
29. What is 5/6 × 3/4? A) 5/8 B) 15/24 C) 8/10 D) 5/6
30. If $3x - 2 = 4x + 5$, what is x? A) -7 B) -5 C) 5 D) 7

Word Knowledge (35 questions)

1. Affirmative means: A) Negative B) Positive C) Uncertain D) Neutral

2. Boundary means: A) Center B) Limit C) Opening D) Connection
3. Conceal means: A) Reveal B) Hide C) Display D) Show
4. Durable means: A) Fragile B) Temporary C) Lasting D) Weak
5. Eliminate means: A) Add B) Remove C) Keep D) Save
6. Flourish means: A) Decline B) Thrive C) Wither D) Fail
7. Generate means: A) Destroy B) Create C) Stop D) End
8. Humble means: A) Proud B) Modest C) Arrogant D) Boastful
9. Illuminate means: A) Darken B) Light up C) Shadow D) Hide
10. Justify means: A) Condemn B) Explain C) Confuse D) Question
11. Knowledgeable means: A) Ignorant B) Informed C) Confused D) Uncertain
12. Legitimate means: A) Illegal B) Valid C) False D) Wrong
13. Maintain means: A) Abandon B) Keep C) Destroy D) Lose
14. Neglect means: A) Care for B) Ignore C) Attend to D) Help
15. Omit means: A) Include B) Leave out C) Add D) Insert
16. Preserve means: A) Destroy B) Protect C) Damage D) Ruin
17. Qualify means: A) Disqualify B) Meet requirements C) Fail D) Reject
18. Reliable means: A) Untrustworthy B) Dependable C) Uncertain D) Questionable
19. Substitute means: A) Original B) Replacement C) Addition D) Extra
20. Tolerate means: A) Reject B) Accept C) Refuse D) Deny
21. Unique means: A) Common B) One of a kind C) Ordinary D) Typical
22. Variety means: A) Sameness B) Diversity C) Uniformity D) Similarity
23. Withdraw means: A) Deposit B) Remove C) Add D) Insert
24. Youthful means: A) Old B) Young C) Mature D) Ancient
25. Zeal means: A) Apathy B) Enthusiasm C) Boredom D) Laziness
26. Accurate means: A) Wrong B) Correct C) False D) Mistaken
27. Brief means: A) Long B) Short C) Detailed D) Extended
28. Cautious means: A) Reckless B) Careful C) Careless D) Bold
29. Delicate means: A) Rough B) Fragile C) Strong D) Tough
30. Eager means: A) Reluctant B) Enthusiastic C) Unwilling D) Hesitant
31. Final means: A) First B) Last C) Middle D) Beginning
32. Generous means: A) Selfish B) Giving C) Greedy D) Stingy
33. Honor means: A) Disgrace B) Respect C) Shame D) Dishonor
34. Ideal means: A) Imperfect B) Perfect C) Flawed D) Defective
35. Justice means: A) Injustice B) Fairness C) Bias D) Prejudice

Paragraph Comprehension (15 questions)

Passage 1: The ancient pyramids of Egypt were built as tombs for pharaohs and their families. The largest, the Great Pyramid of Giza, was constructed around 2580-2510 BCE and stands 481 feet tall. These monuments required enormous planning, workforce, and resources, demonstrating the advanced engineering capabilities of ancient Egyptian civilization.

1. The pyramids were built as: A) Temples B) Tombs C) Palaces D) Fortresses
2. The Great Pyramid stands how tall? A) 451 feet B) 471 feet C) 481 feet D) 491 feet

Passage 2: Antibiotics are medicines that fight bacterial infections by either killing bacteria or preventing their growth. However, they are ineffective against viral infections like the common cold or flu. The overuse of antibiotics has led to antibiotic resistance, where bacteria evolve to survive these medications.

3. Antibiotics fight: A) All infections B) Viral infections C) Bacterial infections D) Fungal infections
4. What problem has overuse of antibiotics caused? A) Viral resistance B) Antibiotic resistance C) Immune deficiency D) Allergic reactions

Passage 3: Renewable energy sources such as solar, wind, and hydroelectric power are becoming increasingly important as alternatives to fossil fuels. These sources produce clean energy without releasing greenhouse gases, helping to combat climate change while providing sustainable power for future generations.

5. Renewable energy sources mentioned include: A) Coal and oil B) Solar, wind, and hydroelectric C) Natural gas and nuclear D) Biomass and geothermal
6. Renewable energy helps combat: A) Pollution only B) Climate change C) Energy costs D) Power outages

Passage 4: The human immune system is a complex network of cells, tissues, and organs that work together to defend the body against harmful invaders like bacteria, viruses, and parasites. White blood cells are the primary defenders, with different types performing specialized functions in immune response.

7. The immune system defends against: A) Only bacteria B) Only viruses C) Harmful invaders D) All foreign substances
8. The primary defenders are: A) Red blood cells B) White blood cells C) Platelets D) Plasma

Passage 5: Urban planning involves designing and organizing urban areas to improve quality of life for residents. This includes planning transportation systems, housing, parks, and commercial areas. Good urban planning can reduce traffic congestion, improve air quality, and create more livable communities.

9. Urban planning involves designing: A) Only transportation B) Only housing C) Urban areas D) Rural areas
10. Good urban planning can reduce: A) Population B) Traffic congestion C) Economic growth D) Development

Passage 6: The water cycle is the continuous movement of water through the environment. Water evaporates from oceans, lakes, and rivers, forms clouds in the atmosphere, and returns to Earth as precipitation. This cycle is essential for maintaining freshwater supplies and supporting all life on Earth.

11. Water evaporates from: A) Only oceans B) Oceans, lakes, and rivers C) Only lakes D) Only rivers
12. The water cycle is essential for: A) Weather only B) Climate only C) Maintaining freshwater supplies D) Ocean currents

Passage 7: Regular exercise has numerous benefits for both physical and mental health. It strengthens the cardiovascular system, builds muscle mass, improves bone density, and can help prevent chronic diseases. Exercise also releases endorphins, which improve mood and reduce stress.

13. Exercise strengthens the: A) Nervous system B) Cardiovascular system C) Digestive system D) Respiratory system only
14. Endorphins help: A) Build muscle B) Strengthen bones C) Improve mood D) Prevent disease
15. Exercise can help prevent: A) Acute injuries B) Chronic diseases C) Genetic disorders D) Aging

Mathematics Knowledge (25 questions)

1. What is $\sqrt{225}$? A) 13 B) 14 C) 15 D) 16
2. If $x^2 = 100$, what is x? A) ±9 B) ±10 C) ±11 D) ±12
3. What is 2^5? A) 16 B) 25 C) 32 D) 64
4. The area of a rectangle with length 12 and width 5 is: A) 34 B) 60 C) 17 D) 24
5. What is the slope of $y = 4x - 3$? A) 4 B) -3 C) 7 D) 1
6. Factor: $x^2 - 25$ A) (x-5)(x-5) B) (x+5)(x+5) C) (x-5)(x+5) D) Cannot factor
7. What is $\log_{10} 100$? A) 1 B) 2 C) 10 D) 100
8. If $\tan \theta = 1$, what is θ? A) 30° B) 45° C) 60° D) 90°
9. The area of a circle with diameter 10 is: A) 25π B) 50π C) 100π D) 200π
10. What is 4! (4 factorial)? A) 16 B) 20 C) 24 D) 32
11. If $h(x) = x^2 + 2x - 3$, what is h(2)? A) 3 B) 5 C) 7 D) 9
12. The volume of a rectangular prism 4×3×6 is: A) 48 B) 60 C) 72 D) 84
13. What is the y-intercept of $4x + 2y = 8$? A) 2 B) 4 C) 6 D) 8
14. Solve: $4x - 5 = 3x + 2$ A) x = 5 B) x = 6 C) x = 7 D) x = 8
15. What is cos 0°? A) 0 B) 0.5 C) 0.707 D) 1
16. The solutions to $x^2 - 6x + 8 = 0$ are: A) x = 2, 4 B) x = 1, 8 C) x = -2, -4 D) x = 3, 6
17. The hypotenuse of a right triangle with legs 5 and 12 is: A) 13 B) 15 C) 17 D) 19
18. If $\cos \theta = 0.707$, what is θ? A) 30° B) 45° C) 60° D) 90°
19. The area of a triangle with base 10 and height 8 is: A) 18 B) 36 C) 40 D) 80
20. What is $\sqrt{(36 + 64)}$? A) 8 B) 10 C) 12 D) 14
21. The arithmetic sequence 5, 8, 11, 14, ... has common difference: A) 2 B) 3 C) 4 D) 5
22. What is 40% of 75% of 200? A) 50 B) 60 C) 70 D) 80
23. If $\log_2 x = 5$, what is x? A) 25 B) 32 C) 64 D) 128
24. The perimeter of a regular hexagon with side 6 is: A) 24 B) 30 C) 36 D) 42
25. What is the derivative of $2x^3$? A) $6x^2$ B) $2x^2$ C) $6x^3$ D) $2x^3$

Electronics Information (20 questions)

1. What does EMF stand for? A) Electrical Motor Force B) Electromotive Force C) Electronic Magnetic Force D) Electric Motor Function
2. The opposition to current flow is called: A) Voltage B) Current C) Resistance D) Power
3. A fuse protects a circuit from: A) Low voltage B) High voltage C) Overcurrent D) Under-current
4. Standard household current in the US is: A) AC B) DC C) Both D) Neither
5. A capacitor opposes changes in: A) Current B) Voltage C) Resistance D) Power
6. In a series circuit with three bulbs, if one burns out: A) All go out B) Two remain on C) Brightness increases D) Nothing happens
7. The neutral wire in household wiring is typically: A) Black B) White C) Green D) Red
8. A wattmeter measures: A) Voltage B) Current C) Resistance D) Power
9. What does BJT stand for? A) Bipolar Junction Transistor B) Binary Junction Transistor C) Bipolar Joint Transistor D) Binary Joint Transistor
10. A step-down transformer: A) Increases voltage B) Decreases voltage C) Maintains voltage D) Reverses polarity
11. In parallel circuits, voltage across each branch is: A) Different B) The same C) Zero D) Variable
12. Power equals: A) $V + I$ B) $V - I$ C) $V \times I$ D) $V \div I$
13. A conductor has: A) High resistance B) Low resistance C) No resistance D) Variable resistance
14. What does RMS stand for? A) Root Mean Square B) Relative Mean Standard C) Real Mean Signal D) Relative Maximum Standard
15. The frequency of household AC in Europe is: A) 50 Hz B) 60 Hz C) 100 Hz D) 120 Hz
16. A switch controls: A) Voltage level B) Current path C) Resistance value D) Power factor
17. If resistance doubles and voltage stays constant, current: A) Doubles B) Halves C) Stays same D) Quadruples
18. A function generator produces: A) DC only B) AC only C) Various waveforms D) Power only
19. The unit of capacitance is: A) Henry B) Farad C) Weber D) Tesla
20. A thermistor's resistance changes with: A) Voltage B) Current C) Temperature D) Frequency

Auto & Shop Information (25 questions)

Auto Information:

1. The crankshaft converts: A) Rotary to linear motion B) Linear to rotary motion C) AC to DC D) Mechanical to electrical
2. What does OBD stand for? A) On-Board Diagnostics B) Oil Burning Device C) Overhead Belt Drive D) Output Battery Display
3. The water pump circulates: A) Oil B) Fuel C) Coolant D) Air
4. In a 4-cylinder engine, firing order might be: A) 1-2-3-4 B) 1-3-4-2 C) 1-4-2-3 D) Any sequence
5. The air filter protects the: A) Fuel system B) Engine C) Exhaust D) Cooling system

6. What does DOHC stand for? A) Double Overhead Cam B) Direct Overhead Control C) Dual Oil Hydraulic Control D) Double Oil Head Chamber
7. The starter motor is part of the: A) Fuel system B) Cooling system C) Electrical system D) Exhaust system
8. Brake pads create friction against: A) Brake drums B) Brake rotors C) Brake lines D) Master cylinder
9. The flywheel connects the engine to the: A) Differential B) Transmission C) Alternator D) Radiator
10. What does TPMS stand for? A) Tire Pressure Monitoring System B) Transmission Power Management System C) Turbo Performance Monitoring System D) Throttle Position Monitoring System
11. The radiator cap controls: A) Temperature B) Pressure C) Flow rate D) Coolant level
12. High octane fuel: A) Burns faster B) Resists knock C) Has more energy D) Costs less
13. The CV joint is part of the: A) Brake system B) Steering system C) Drive system D) Fuel system

Shop Information: 14. A socket wrench is used with: A) Screws B) Nuts and bolts C) Nails D) Rivets 15. Which saw cuts metal best? A) Crosscut saw B) Rip saw C) Hacksaw D) Coping saw 16. A chalk line is used for: A) Measuring B) Marking straight lines C) Checking angles D) Testing materials 17. Fine sandpaper has: A) Low grit numbers B) High grit numbers C) No grit numbers D) Variable grit 18. A hex head screw requires: A) Phillips screwdriver B) Flat screwdriver C) Allen wrench D) Torx driver 19. The weakest wood joint is typically: A) Mortise and tenon B) Dovetail C) Butt joint D) Lap joint 20. A bastard file is: A) Very fine B) Medium cut C) Very coarse D) Smooth 21. Standard lumber thickness for a 2×6 is actually: A) 2" B) 1.75" C) 1.5" D) 1.25" 22. A pipe clamp is used to: A) Cut pipe B) Thread pipe C) Hold glued joints D) Bend pipe 23. A rip saw cuts: A) Across the grain B) With the grain C) Both directions D) Only curves 24. A framing square is used to check: A) Only 90° angles B) Various angles C) Only 45° angles D) Curves 25. Which tool creates the smoothest finish? A) Sandpaper B) File C) Rasp D) Grinder

Mechanical Comprehension (25 questions)

1. If gear A (15 teeth) drives gear B (45 teeth), gear B rotates: A) 3 times faster B) 3 times slower C) Same speed D) 1.5 times faster
2. In a first-class lever, if effort arm is 4 feet and load arm is 2 feet, MA is: A) 1/2 B) 2 C) 6 D) 8
3. A pulley system with 4 ropes supporting the load has MA of: A) 2 B) 4 C) 8 D) 16
4. Water pressure depends on: A) Container width B) Water temperature C) Depth below surface D) Container shape
5. To lift 120 pounds with a 4:1 mechanical advantage requires: A) 30 pounds B) 40 pounds C) 60 pounds D) 480 pounds
6. In a hydraulic press, if input piston area is 1 sq in and output is 10 sq in, force is multiplied by: A) 5 B) 10 C) 11 D) 100
7. A wheel of radius 12 inches driving an axle of radius 3 inches has MA of: A) 3 B) 4 C) 9 D) 15

8. When a gas is heated at constant pressure, it: A) Contracts B) Expands C) Maintains volume D) Condenses

9. The center of gravity of a uniform object is at its: A) Top B) Bottom C) Geometric center D) Heaviest point

10. A bolt with 8 threads per inch moved 2 inches requires: A) 4 turns B) 8 turns C) 16 turns D) 32 turns

11. A stretched spring stores: A) Kinetic energy B) Potential energy C) Heat energy D) No energy

12. Oil reduces friction by: A) Increasing weight B) Separating surfaces C) Adding pressure D) Cooling parts

13. Small gear driving large gear results in: A) More speed, less torque B) Less speed, more torque C) More of both D) Less of both

14. A cam with an off-center lobe produces: A) Continuous rotation B) Oscillating motion C) No motion D) Variable speed

15. Rolling friction is typically: A) Greater than sliding B) Less than sliding C) Equal to sliding D) Unrelated to sliding

16. An inclined plane 20 feet long raising load 4 feet has MA of: A) 4 B) 5 C) 16 D) 80

17. According to Bernoulli's principle, as fluid velocity increases: A) Pressure increases B) Pressure decreases C) Pressure stays constant D) Temperature increases

18. A simple pendulum's period depends on: A) Weight of bob B) Length of string C) Amplitude of swing D) All of the above

19. A compound pulley with 2 fixed and 2 movable pulleys has MA of: A) 2 B) 4 C) 6 D) 8

20. Pascal's principle states that pressure in a confined fluid: A) Varies with depth B) Is transmitted equally C) Decreases with temperature D) Increases with volume

21. Two gears with 2:1 ratio, if input gear turns at 60 RPM, output turns at: A) 30 RPM B) 60 RPM C) 120 RPM D) 240 RPM

22. A heavy flywheel helps an engine: A) Start easier B) Run smoother C) Use less fuel D) Produce more power

23. In a second-class lever, the mechanical advantage is always: A) Less than 1 B) Equal to 1 C) Greater than 1 D) Variable

24. Atmospheric pressure at sea level is approximately: A) 10.7 psi B) 14.7 psi C) 18.7 psi D) 22.7 psi

25. A movable pulley provides mechanical advantage of: A) 1 B) 2 C) 3 D) 4

Test 9 Answer Key

General Science: 1-B, 2-C, 3-C, 4-B, 5-B, 6-C, 7-C, 8-B, 9-C, 10-C, 11-C, 12-D, 13-D, 14-B, 15-C, 16-B, 17-C, 18-B, 19-C, 20-C, 21-C, 22-B, 23-A, 24-C, 25-C

Arithmetic Reasoning: 1-B, 2-A, 3-B, 4-B, 5-B, 6-C, 7-B, 8-A, 9-D, 10-B, 11-C, 12-C, 13-B, 14-C, 15-A, 16-B, 17-B, 18-B, 19-C, 20-C, 21-A, 22-B, 23-B, 24-B, 25-A, 26-B, 27-B, 28-B, 29-A, 30-A

Word Knowledge: 1-B, 2-B, 3-B, 4-C, 5-B, 6-B, 7-B, 8-B, 9-B, 10-B, 11-B, 12-B, 13-B, 14-B, 15-B, 16-B, 17-B, 18-B, 19-B, 20-B, 21-B, 22-B, 23-B, 24-B, 25-B, 26-B, 27-B, 28-B, 29-B, 30-B, 31-B, 32-B, 33-B, 34-B, 35-B

Paragraph Comprehension: 1-B, 2-C, 3-C, 4-B, 5-B, 6-B, 7-C, 8-B, 9-C, 10-B, 11-B, 12-C, 13-B, 14-C, 15-B

Mathematics Knowledge: 1-C, 2-B, 3-C, 4-B, 5-A, 6-C, 7-B, 8-B, 9-A, 10-C, 11-B, 12-C, 13-B, 14-C, 15-D, 16-A, 17-A, 18-B, 19-C, 20-B, 21-B, 22-B, 23-B, 24-C, 25-A

Electronics Information: 1-B, 2-C, 3-C, 4-A, 5-B, 6-A, 7-B, 8-D, 9-A, 10-B, 11-B, 12-C, 13-B, 14-A, 15-A, 16-B, 17-B, 18-C, 19-B, 20-C

Auto & Shop Information: 1-B, 2-A, 3-C, 4-B, 5-B, 6-A, 7-C, 8-B, 9-B, 10-A, 11-B, 12-B, 13-C, 14-B, 15-C, 16-B, 17-B, 18-C, 19-C, 20-B, 21-C, 22-C, 23-B, 24-B, 25-A

Mechanical Comprehension: 1-B, 2-B, 3-B, 4-C, 5-A, 6-B, 7-B, 8-B, 9-C, 10-C, 11-B, 12-B, 13-B, 14-B, 15-B, 16-B, 17-B, 18-B, 19-B, 20-B, 21-A, 22-B, 23-C, 24-B, 25-B

Test 10

General Science (25 questions)

1. The Earth's atmosphere is approximately what percent oxygen? A) 18% B) 21% C) 25% D) 28%
2. Which organ in the human body produces insulin? A) Liver B) Kidney C) Pancreas D) Spleen
3. What is the chemical formula for methane? A) CH_4 B) CO_2 C) H_2O D) NH_3
4. The study of earthquakes is called: A) Meteorology B) Seismology C) Oceanography D) Geology
5. How many chambers does a human heart have? A) 2 B) 3 C) 4 D) 5
6. Light travels fastest through: A) Water B) Glass C) Air D) Vacuum
7. The basic unit of heredity is the: A) Cell B) Gene C) Chromosome D) DNA
8. Which planet has the highest surface temperature? A) Mercury B) Venus C) Mars D) Jupiter
9. Photosynthesis converts light energy into: A) Heat energy B) Electrical energy C) Chemical energy D) Kinetic energy
10. The Mohs scale measures: A) Earthquake intensity B) Wind speed C) Mineral hardness D) Temperature
11. What is the most abundant element in the universe? A) Oxygen B) Carbon C) Hydrogen D) Helium
12. The process of liquid changing to gas is called: A) Condensation B) Evaporation C) Sublimation D) Precipitation
13. Which blood type is known as the universal recipient? A) Type A B) Type B C) Type AB D) Type O

14. Sound waves are examples of: A) Electromagnetic waves B) Longitudinal waves C) Transverse waves D) Light waves
15. The atomic number of carbon is: A) 4 B) 6 C) 8 D) 12
16. Which vitamin is synthesized by the skin when exposed to sunlight? A) Vitamin A B) Vitamin C C) Vitamin D D) Vitamin K
17. The Earth's magnetic field is generated by its: A) Crust B) Mantle C) Outer core D) Inner core
18. Acids have a pH: A) Greater than 7 B) Equal to 7 C) Less than 7 D) Between 7 and 14
19. The largest muscle in the human body is the: A) Heart B) Gluteus maximus C) Quadriceps D) Latissimus dorsi
20. Which gas is responsible for the greenhouse effect? A) Nitrogen B) Oxygen C) Carbon dioxide D) Argon
21. The speed of sound in air at room temperature is approximately: A) 343 m/s B) 300 m/s C) 400 m/s D) 500 m/s
22. Metamorphic rocks are formed by: A) Cooling magma B) Sediment accumulation C) Heat and pressure D) Erosion
23. The human brain uses approximately what percentage of the body's energy? A) 10% B) 15% C) 20% D) 25%
24. Which element has the symbol Fe? A) Fluorine B) Iron C) Lead D) Silver
25. The study of living organisms is called: A) Chemistry B) Physics C) Biology D) Geology

Arithmetic Reasoning (30 questions)

1. A train travels 350 miles in 5 hours. What is its average speed? A) 65 mph B) 70 mph C) 75 mph D) 80 mph
2. If a shirt originally costs $35 and is discounted 25%, what is the sale price? A) $24.25 B) $25.75 C) $26.25 D) $27.50
3. What is 16% of 225? A) 32 B) 34 C) 36 D) 38
4. If $6x - 9 = 33$, what is x? A) 6 B) 7 C) 8 D) 9
5. A recipe serves 4 people and uses 1.5 cups of rice. How much rice for 10 people? A) 3.25 cups B) 3.5 cups C) 3.75 cups D) 4 cups
6. What is the next number: 2, 8, 32, 128, ...? A) 256 B) 384 C) 512 D) 640
7. An employee works 42 hours at $16 per hour. If overtime (over 40 hours) is time-and-a-half, what is the total pay? A) $656 B) $672 C) $688 D) $704
8. The area of a circle with radius 9 is: (Use $\pi = 3.14$) A) 254.34 sq units B) 254.46 sq units C) 254.58 sq units D) 254.70 sq units
9. What is 5/6 - 1/3? A) 1/2 B) 4/6 C) 2/3 D) 4/3
10. A car gets 28 miles per gallon. How many gallons needed for a 420-mile trip? A) 12 gallons B) 15 gallons C) 18 gallons D) 21 gallons
11. In a class of 40 students, 60% are female. How many are male? A) 14 B) 16 C) 18 D) 20
12. What is the perimeter of a rectangle with length 14 and width 8? A) 22 B) 44 C) 112 D) 224
13. A 20% tip on a $45 meal is: A) $7 B) $8 C) $9 D) $10
14. If $2x + 3 = x + 12$, what is x? A) 7 B) 8 C) 9 D) 10
15. A square has an area of 64 square inches. What is its perimeter? A) 32 inches B) 36 inches C) 40 inches D) 44 inches

16. What is the average of 72, 84, 90, 78, and 86? A) 80 B) 82 C) 84 D) 86
17. If 3/8 of a number is 21, what is the number? A) 52 B) 54 C) 56 D) 58
18. A store buys an item for $30 and sells it for $45. What is the markup percentage? A) 40% B) 45% C) 50% D) 55%
19. What is $2^4 + 3^2$? A) 23 B) 25 C) 27 D) 29
20. A right triangle has legs of 9 and 12. What is the hypotenuse? A) 13 B) 15 C) 17 D) 19
21. A bag has 5 red, 7 blue, and 3 green marbles. What's the probability of drawing red? A) 1/3 B) 5/15 C) 7/15 D) 3/15
22. What is 35% of 20% of 400? A) 24 B) 26 C) 28 D) 30
23. If f(x) = 2x + 5 and x = 4, what is f(x)? A) 11 B) 13 C) 15 D) 17
24. The angles in a triangle are 45°, 60°, and what? A) 65° B) 70° C) 75° D) 80°
25. What is 2/3 ÷ 4/9? A) 1/2 B) 3/2 C) 8/27 D) 6/12
26. An item costs $85 after a 15% discount. What was the original price? A) $95 B) $98 C) $100 D) $102
27. What is the median of: 24, 18, 30, 15, 27? A) 21 B) 24 C) 27 D) 30
28. Simple interest on $2,000 at 4% for 3 years is: A) $220 B) $240 C) $260 D) $280
29. What is 3/4 × 8/9? A) 2/3 B) 24/36 C) 11/13 D) 32/36
30. If 5x - 8 = 3x + 10, what is x? A) 7 B) 8 C) 9 D) 10

Word Knowledge (35 questions)

1. Accelerate means: A) Slow down B) Speed up C) Stop D) Maintain speed
2. Beneficial means: A) Harmful B) Helpful C) Neutral D) Dangerous
3. Commence means: A) End B) Begin C) Continue D) Pause
4. Demonstrate means: A) Hide B) Show C) Question D) Doubt
5. Enhance means: A) Reduce B) Improve C) Maintain D) Damage
6. Formulate means: A) Destroy B) Create C) Copy D) Ignore
7. Gradual means: A) Sudden B) Slow C) Fast D) Immediate
8. Hereditary means: A) Acquired B) Inherited C) Learned D) Temporary
9. Implement means: A) Plan B) Execute C) Ignore D) Postpone
10. Jeopardize means: A) Protect B) Endanger C) Help D) Support
11. Kinetic means: A) Stationary B) Moving C) Potential D) Static
12. Lucrative means: A) Unprofitable B) Profitable C) Difficult D) Easy
13. Magnitude means: A) Direction B) Size C) Color D) Shape
14. Navigate means: A) Get lost B) Direct course C) Stop D) Wait
15. Obscure means: A) Clear B) Unclear C) Bright D) Obvious
16. Perpetual means: A) Temporary B) Continuous C) Brief D) Occasional
17. Quantify means: A) Estimate B) Measure C) Guess D) Ignore
18. Resilient means: A) Fragile B) Tough C) Weak D) Brittle
19. Subsequent means: A) Previous B) Following C) Simultaneous D) Unrelated
20. Terminate means: A) Begin B) End C) Continue D) Extend
21. Unanimous means: A) Divided B) United C) Partial D) Individual
22. Verify means: A) Deny B) Confirm C) Question D) Assume
23. Wager means: A) Certainty B) Bet C) Gift D) Loss
24. Yield means: A) Resist B) Give way C) Fight D) Oppose
25. Zealot means: A) Moderate B) Fanatic C) Indifferent D) Calm

26. Ample means: A) Insufficient B) Abundant C) Exact D) Minimal
27. Bleak means: A) Hopeful B) Grim C) Bright D) Cheerful
28. Compound means: A) Simple B) Complex C) Single D) Basic
29. Defiant means: A) Obedient B) Rebellious C) Cooperative D) Helpful
30. Eloquent means: A) Silent B) Articulate C) Confused D) Unclear
31. Fickle means: A) Constant B) Changeable C) Reliable D) Steady
32. Gregarious means: A) Antisocial B) Sociable C) Shy D) Lonely
33. Haphazard means: A) Organized B) Random C) Planned D) Systematic
34. Imminent means: A) Distant B) Approaching C) Past D) Delayed
35. Jubilant means: A) Sad B) Joyful C) Angry D) Worried

Paragraph Comprehension (15 questions)

Passage 1: Hurricanes are powerful tropical storms that form over warm ocean waters. They are characterized by strong winds, heavy rainfall, and low atmospheric pressure. The eye of a hurricane is a calm area at the center, surrounded by the eyewall where the strongest winds occur. Hurricanes are classified into categories 1-5 based on wind speed.

1. Hurricanes form over: A) Cold ocean waters B) Warm ocean waters C) Land masses D) Mountain areas
2. The strongest winds in a hurricane occur in the: A) Eye B) Eyewall C) Outer bands D) Upper atmosphere

Passage 2: DNA, or deoxyribonucleic acid, carries genetic information in all living organisms. It consists of two strands twisted into a double helix structure. The information is encoded in sequences of four chemical bases: adenine, thymine, guanine, and cytosine. This genetic code determines an organism's characteristics and is passed from parents to offspring.

3. DNA has how many chemical bases? A) 2 B) 3 C) 4 D) 5
4. DNA structure is described as a: A) Single strand B) Triple helix C) Double helix D) Circular loop

Passage 3: Solar panels convert sunlight directly into electricity through photovoltaic cells. These cells are typically made from silicon and generate direct current (DC) electricity. An inverter then converts this DC power to alternating current (AC) for use in homes and businesses. Solar energy is renewable and produces no greenhouse gas emissions during operation.

5. Solar panels generate what type of electricity? A) AC B) DC C) Both AC and DC D) Neither AC nor DC
6. Solar panels are typically made from: A) Aluminum B) Copper C) Silicon D) Steel

Passage 7: The Great Wall of China, built over many centuries, stretches approximately 13,000 miles across northern China. Originally constructed for defense against invasions, it's now one of the world's most famous tourist attractions. Despite popular belief, the wall is not visible from space with the naked eye, though this myth persists in popular culture.

7. The Great Wall stretches approximately: A) 1,300 miles B) 5,000 miles C) 13,000 miles D) 30,000 miles
8. The wall was originally built for: A) Tourism B) Defense C) Trade D) Transportation

Passage 8: Antibiotics revolutionized medicine by providing effective treatment for bacterial infections. However, the overuse and misuse of antibiotics has led to antibiotic resistance, where bacteria evolve to survive these drugs. This growing problem threatens to make some infections untreatable, emphasizing the importance of using antibiotics responsibly.

9. Antibiotics treat: A) Viral infections B) Bacterial infections C) All infections D) Genetic disorders
10. Antibiotic resistance occurs when: A) Antibiotics become stronger B) Bacteria evolve to survive drugs C) Patients become immune D) Doctors prescribe more

Passage 9: Photosynthesis is the process by which plants convert carbon dioxide and water into glucose using sunlight energy. This process occurs primarily in the leaves and releases oxygen as a byproduct. Photosynthesis is essential for life on Earth as it produces the oxygen we breathe and forms the foundation of most food chains.

11. Photosynthesis converts carbon dioxide and water into: A) Oxygen B) Chlorophyll C) Glucose D) Nitrogen
12. Photosynthesis primarily occurs in: A) Roots B) Stems C) Leaves D) Flowers

Passage 10: The human immune system is a complex defense network that protects the body from harmful pathogens like bacteria, viruses, and parasites. It includes both innate immunity, which provides immediate but general protection, and adaptive immunity, which creates specific responses and memory for future encounters with the same pathogen.

13. The immune system protects against: A) Only bacteria B) Only viruses C) Harmful pathogens D) All foreign substances
14. Adaptive immunity creates: A) General protection B) Specific responses and memory C) Immediate reactions D) Physical barriers
15. The immune system includes how many main types of immunity? A) 1 B) 2 C) 3 D) 4

Mathematics Knowledge (25 questions)

1. What is $\sqrt{289}$? A) 16 B) 17 C) 18 D) 19
2. If $x^2 = 121$, what is x? A) ± 10 B) ± 11 C) ± 12 D) ± 13
3. What is 3^6? A) 18 B) 216 C) 729 D) 1296
4. The area of a parallelogram with base 10 and height 6 is: A) 30 B) 32 C) 60 D) 120
5. What is the slope of $y = -3x + 8$? A) -3 B) 3 C) 8 D) -8
6. Factor: $x^2 - 49$ A) (x-7)(x-7) B) (x+7)(x+7) C) (x-7)(x+7) D) Cannot factor
7. What is $\log_{10} 1$? A) 0 B) 1 C) 10 D) Undefined
8. If $\sin \theta = 0.866$, what is θ? A) 30° B) 45° C) 60° D) 90°
9. The circumference of a circle with radius 4 is: A) 8π B) 12π C) 16π D) 32π
10. What is 5! (5 factorial)? A) 25 B) 60 C) 120 D) 240

11. If j(x) = 3x² - 2x + 1, what is j(3)? A) 22 B) 24 C) 26 D) 28
12. The surface area of a sphere with radius 3 is: A) 36π B) 9π C) 18π D) 12π
13. What is the x-intercept of y = 2x - 10? A) 2 B) 5 C) -5 D) 10
14. Solve: 5x + 4 = 2x + 19 A) x = 3 B) x = 4 C) x = 5 D) x = 6
15. What is tan 45°? A) 0 B) 0.5 C) 0.707 D) 1
16. The solutions to x² - 8x + 15 = 0 are: A) x = 3, 5 B) x = 1, 15 C) x = -3, -5 D) x = 2, 6
17. The area of a sector with central angle 90° and radius 6 is: A) 9π B) 18π C) 27π D) 36π
18. If tan θ = 0.577, what is θ? A) 30° B) 45° C) 60° D) 90°
19. The volume of a cone with radius 4 and height 9 is: A) 48π B) 36π C) 144π D) 432π
20. What is √(25 + 144)? A) 12 B) 13 C) 14 D) 15
21. An arithmetic sequence starts 7, 12, 17, ... What is the 10th term? A) 52 B) 57 C) 62 D) 67
22. What is 50% of 60% of 240? A) 60 B) 72 C) 84 D) 96
23. If log₃ x = 4, what is x? A) 64 B) 81 C) 243 D) 729
24. The area of a regular pentagon with side 8 is approximately: A) 110 B) 120 C) 130 D) 140
25. What is the integral of 3x²? A) x³ B) 6x C) 3x³ D) x³ + C

Electronics Information (20 questions)

1. What does AC stand for? A) Alternating Current B) Active Circuit C) Applied Current D) Automatic Control
2. Electrical power is measured in: A) Volts B) Amperes C) Ohms D) Watts
3. A circuit breaker trips when there is: A) Low voltage B) High voltage C) Excessive current D) No current
4. What is the voltage of a standard flashlight battery? A) 1.5V B) 3V C) 6V D) 9V
5. An inductor stores energy in a: A) Electric field B) Magnetic field C) Gravitational field D) Chemical bond
6. In a series circuit, current is: A) Different through each component B) Same through all components C) Zero D) Infinite
7. Ground wire color in US household wiring is typically: A) Black B) White C) Green D) Red
8. An ohmmeter measures: A) Voltage B) Current C) Resistance D) Power
9. What does FET stand for? A) Field Effect Transistor B) Fast Electronic Terminal C) Frequency Effect Transformer D) Fixed Electric Terminal
10. A transformer works on the principle of: A) Ohm's law B) Electromagnetic induction C) Coulomb's law D) Kirchhoff's law
11. In parallel circuits, the voltage across each branch is: A) Additive B) The same C) Divided equally D) Zero
12. Current equals: A) Voltage × Resistance B) Voltage ÷ Resistance C) Voltage + Resistance D) Voltage - Resistance
13. Copper is a good: A) Insulator B) Conductor C) Semiconductor D) Superconductor
14. What does PWM stand for? A) Pulse Width Modulation B) Power Wave Measurement C) Positive Wave Motion D) Parallel Wire Method
15. Standard AC frequency in North America is: A) 50 Hz B) 60 Hz C) 100 Hz D) 120 Hz
16. A potentiometer is a variable: A) Capacitor B) Inductor C) Resistor D) Transformer

17. As temperature increases, resistance in most metals: A) Increases B) Decreases C) Stays constant D) Becomes zero
18. A spectrum analyzer displays: A) Voltage vs time B) Current vs time C) Frequency vs amplitude D) Resistance vs time
19. The unit of inductance is: A) Farad B) Henry C) Weber D) Tesla
20. A photodiode converts: A) Light to electricity B) Heat to electricity C) Sound to electricity D) Magnetism to electricity

Auto & Shop Information (25 questions)

Auto Information:

1. The differential allows: A) Engine to start B) Wheels to turn at different speeds C) Transmission to shift D) Brakes to engage
2. What does VIN stand for? A) Vehicle Identification Number B) Valve Intake Number C) Variable Ignition Number D) Vacuum Intake Number
3. The thermostat controls: A) Oil pressure B) Fuel flow C) Engine temperature D) Electrical current
4. A turbocharger increases engine power by: A) Adding fuel B) Forcing more air into cylinders C) Cooling the engine D) Reducing friction
5. The alternator charges the: A) Spark plugs B) Fuel injectors C) Battery D) Radiator
6. What does ABS prevent? A) Engine overheating B) Fuel leaks C) Wheel lockup during braking D) Transmission slipping
7. The mass airflow sensor measures: A) Fuel quantity B) Air entering engine C) Exhaust gases D) Oil pressure
8. Coolant prevents: A) Only overheating B) Only freezing C) Both overheating and freezing D) Only corrosion
9. The camshaft operates the: A) Pistons B) Crankshaft C) Valves D) Transmission
10. What does ECU stand for? A) Engine Control Unit B) Electrical Control Unit C) Emergency Control Unit D) Electronic Control Unit
11. Brake fluid is: A) Compressible B) Incompressible C) Gaseous D) Solid
12. Higher octane fuel: A) Contains more energy B) Prevents engine knock C) Burns cooler D) Costs less
13. The oxygen sensor monitors: A) Air intake B) Exhaust gases C) Fuel pressure D) Oil quality

Shop Information: 14. A torque wrench measures: A) Length B) Angle C) Rotational force D) Weight 15. Which tool cuts internal threads? A) Die B) Tap C) Reamer D) Broach 16. A square is used to check: A) Circles B) 90° angles C) 45° angles D) Curves 17. Coarse sandpaper has: A) High grit number B) Low grit number C) No grit number D) Variable grit 18. A Torx screw has: A) Cross pattern B) Straight slot C) Star pattern D) Square pattern 19. The strongest wood joint is: A) Butt B) Lap C) Dovetail D) Simple splice 20. A mill file is used for: A) Rough work B) Fine finishing C) General purpose D) Sharpening only 21. A 2×8 actually measures: A) 2" × 8" B) 1.5" × 7.25" C) 1.75" × 7.5" D) 2.5" × 8.5" 22. A bar clamp is used to: A) Cut material B) Apply pressure over long distances C) Measure angles D) Hold round objects 23. A ripsaw is designed to cut: A) Across grain B) With the grain C) Metal D) Plastic 24. A combination square

can check: A) Only 90° angles B) Only 45° angles C) Both 90° and 45° angles D) Only curves
25. Which produces the finest surface? A) 80 grit sandpaper B) Rough file C) 220 grit sandpaper D) Coarse rasp

Mechanical Comprehension (25 questions)

1. If gear A (20 teeth) meshes with gear B (60 teeth), the speed ratio is: A) 1:3 B) 3:1 C) 1:1 D) 2:3
2. In a third-class lever, the effort is applied: A) At the fulcrum B) Between fulcrum and load C) Beyond the load D) At the load
3. A tackle system with 8 supporting ropes has mechanical advantage of: A) 4 B) 6 C) 8 D) 16
4. Hydraulic pressure depends on: A) Fluid type only B) Container size only C) Force and area D) Temperature only
5. A 6:1 lever requires 20 pounds input to lift: A) 120 pounds B) 100 pounds C) 80 pounds D) 60 pounds
6. In a hydraulic system with pistons of 2 sq in and 12 sq in, force multiplication is: A) 4:1 B) 6:1 C) 8:1 D) 10:1
7. A drive wheel 18 inches diameter connected to driven wheel 6 inches diameter has speed ratio of: A) 1:3 B) 3:1 C) 1:1 D) 2:1
8. When air is compressed, its temperature: A) Decreases B) Increases C) Stays constant D) Becomes zero
9. An object's center of gravity is where: A) Weight is concentrated B) Object balances C) Mass is greatest D) Density is highest
10. A screw with 6 threads per inch advanced 3 inches requires: A) 6 turns B) 9 turns C) 12 turns D) 18 turns
11. A coiled spring under tension has: A) No stored energy B) Kinetic energy C) Potential energy D) Heat energy
12. Ball bearings reduce friction by: A) Adding weight B) Rolling instead of sliding C) Increasing pressure D) Cooling surfaces
13. When a small gear drives a large gear: A) Speed increases, torque decreases B) Speed decreases, torque increases C) Both increase D) Both decrease
14. An oval cam produces: A) Uniform rotation B) Variable speed motion C) No motion D) Reverse motion
15. The coefficient of friction: A) Is always 1 B) Can exceed 1 C) Is always less than 1 D) Depends on speed only
16. A ramp 15 feet long raising a load 3 feet has mechanical advantage of: A) 3 B) 5 C) 12 D) 18
17. Venturi effect demonstrates that as fluid speed increases through a constriction: A) Pressure increases B) Pressure decreases C) Temperature increases D) Density increases
18. A pendulum's period is affected most by: A) Bob weight B) String length C) Release height D) Air resistance
19. A compound pulley system with 3 movable pulleys has mechanical advantage of: A) 3 B) 6 C) 9 D) 12
20. Buoyant force equals: A) Object's weight B) Weight of displaced fluid C) Fluid density D) Object's volume

21. If driving gear has 40 teeth and driven gear has 10 teeth, and input is 50 RPM, output is: A) 200 RPM B) 150 RPM C) 100 RPM D) 25 RPM
22. A gyroscope resists changes in: A) Speed B) Orientation C) Weight D) Temperature
23. In a first-class lever with equal arms, mechanical advantage is: A) Less than 1 B) Equal to 1 C) Greater than 1 D) Variable
24. Water pressure at 30 feet depth is approximately: A) 13 psi B) 17 psi C) 21 psi D) 25 psi
25. A single movable pulley provides mechanical advantage of: A) 1 B) 2 C) 3 D) 4

Test 10 Answer Key

General Science: 1-B, 2-C, 3-A, 4-B, 5-C, 6-D, 7-B, 8-B, 9-C, 10-C, 11-C, 12-B, 13-C, 14-B, 15-B, 16-C, 17-C, 18-C, 19-B, 20-C, 21-A, 22-C, 23-C, 24-B, 25-C

Arithmetic Reasoning: 1-B, 2-C, 3-C, 4-B, 5-C, 6-C, 7-C, 8-A, 9-A, 10-B, 11-B, 12-B, 13-C, 14-C, 15-A, 16-B, 17-C, 18-C, 19-B, 20-B, 21-A, 22-C, 23-B, 24-C, 25-B, 26-C, 27-B, 28-B, 29-A, 30-C

Word Knowledge: 1-B, 2-B, 3-B, 4-B, 5-B, 6-B, 7-B, 8-B, 9-B, 10-B, 11-B, 12-B, 13-B, 14-B, 15-B, 16-B, 17-B, 18-B, 19-B, 20-B, 21-B, 22-B, 23-B, 24-B, 25-B, 26-B, 27-B, 28-B, 29-B, 30-B, 31-B, 32-B, 33-B, 34-B, 35-B

Paragraph Comprehension: 1-B, 2-B, 3-C, 4-C, 5-B, 6-C, 7-C, 8-B, 9-B, 10-B, 11-C, 12-C, 13-C, 14-B, 15-B

Mathematics Knowledge: 1-B, 2-B, 3-C, 4-C, 5-A, 6-C, 7-A, 8-C, 9-A, 10-C, 11-A, 12-A, 13-B, 14-C, 15-D, 16-A, 17-A, 18-A, 19-A, 20-B, 21-B, 22-B, 23-B, 24-A, 25-D

Electronics Information: 1-A, 2-D, 3-C, 4-A, 5-B, 6-B, 7-C, 8-C, 9-A, 10-B, 11-B, 12-B, 13-B, 14-A, 15-B, 16-C, 17-A, 18-C, 19-B, 20-A

Auto & Shop Information: 1-B, 2-A, 3-C, 4-B, 5-C, 6-C, 7-B, 8-C, 9-C, 10-D, 11-B, 12-B, 13-B, 14-C, 15-B, 16-B, 17-B, 18-C, 19-C, 20-B, 21-B, 22-B, 23-B, 24-C, 25-C

Mechanical Comprehension: 1-B, 2-B, 3-C, 4-C, 5-A, 6-B, 7-B, 8-B, 9-B, 10-D, 11-C, 12-B, 13-B, 14-B, 15-B, 16-B, 17-B, 18-B, 19-B, 20-B, 21-A, 22-B, 23-B, 24-A, 25-B

Test 11

General Science (25 questions)

1. Which gas makes up most of the sun's mass? A) Helium B) Hydrogen C) Oxygen D) Carbon
2. The human body has how many pairs of chromosomes? A) 21 B) 22 C) 23 D) 24

3. What is the chemical symbol for potassium? A) P B) Po C) K D) Pt
4. Which force keeps satellites in orbit around Earth? A) Magnetism B) Gravity C) Centrifugal force D) Nuclear force
5. The smallest bone in the human body is located in the: A) Hand B) Foot C) Ear D) Spine
6. What type of energy is stored in a battery? A) Kinetic B) Potential C) Chemical D) Nuclear
7. The process by which plants lose water is called: A) Photosynthesis B) Respiration C) Transpiration D) Osmosis
8. Which planet has the most eccentric orbit? A) Mercury B) Venus C) Earth D) Mars
9. Sound cannot travel through: A) Air B) Water C) Wood D) Vacuum
10. The study of fungi is called: A) Botany B) Mycology C) Zoology D) Geology
11. What is the hardest substance known to man? A) Steel B) Titanium C) Diamond D) Graphite
12. The Earth's ozone layer protects us from: A) Meteors B) Cold temperatures C) Ultraviolet radiation D) Cosmic rays
13. Which blood component carries oxygen? A) Plasma B) White blood cells C) Red blood cells D) Platelets
14. The atomic number tells us the number of: A) Neutrons B) Protons C) Electrons D) Nuclei
15. What causes rust to form on iron? A) Heat B) Cold C) Oxidation D) Radiation
16. The human heart beats approximately how many times per minute at rest? A) 50-60 B) 60-100 C) 100-120 D) 120-140
17. Which type of rock is formed by volcanic activity? A) Sedimentary B) Metamorphic C) Igneous D) Limestone
18. The speed of light in a vacuum is approximately: A) 186,000 miles/second B) 300,000 miles/second C) 186,000 km/second D) 300,000 km/second
19. What is the main component of natural gas? A) Propane B) Butane C) Methane D) Ethane
20. The process of a solid changing directly to a gas is called: A) Evaporation B) Condensation C) Sublimation D) Deposition
21. Which vitamin is essential for night vision? A) Vitamin A B) Vitamin C C) Vitamin D D) Vitamin K
22. The Earth's magnetic North Pole is located near: A) Geographic North Pole B) Canada C) Alaska D) Greenland
23. What is the most abundant protein in the human body? A) Hemoglobin B) Insulin C) Collagen D) Keratin
24. The study of weather patterns is called: A) Geology B) Meteorology C) Astronomy D) Climatology
25. Which element is liquid at room temperature? A) Bromine B) Mercury C) Both A and B D) Neither A nor B

Arithmetic Reasoning (30 questions)

1. A plane flies 450 miles in 1.5 hours. What is its speed? A) 275 mph B) 300 mph C) 325 mph D) 350 mph

2. A computer costs $800. If the sales tax is 7.5%, what is the total cost? A) $860 B) $870 C) $880 D) $890
3. What is 28% of 175? A) 47 B) 49 C) 51 D) 53
4. If $7x + 5 = 47$, what is x? A) 5 B) 6 C) 7 D) 8
5. A recipe for 6 people calls for 4 cups of broth. How much for 9 people? A) 5 cups B) 6 cups C) 7 cups D) 8 cups
6. What is the next number: 5, 15, 45, 135, ...? A) 270 B) 305 C) 405 D) 540
7. A worker earns $22 per hour for 38 hours plus overtime at time-and-a-half for 6 hours. What is total pay? A) $1,034 B) $1,064 C) $1,094 D) $1,124
8. What is the area of a triangle with base 16 and height 9? A) 72 B) 144 C) 25 D) 50
9. What is 7/9 + 2/3? A) 9/12 B) 13/9 C) 1 4/9 D) 1 1/3
10. A car travels 315 miles using 15 gallons of gas. What is the mpg? A) 19 B) 20 C) 21 D) 22
11. In a survey of 250 people, 35% prefer tea. How many prefer coffee if those are the only choices? A) 162.5 B) 162 C) 163 D) 165
12. What is the circumference of a circle with diameter 21? (Use $\pi = 22/7$) A) 66 B) 68 C) 70 D) 72
13. A 15% gratuity on a $72 restaurant bill is: A) $10.20 B) $10.80 C) $11.40 D) $12.00
14. If $3x - 4 = 2x + 8$, what is x? A) 10 B) 11 C) 12 D) 13
15. A rectangular pool is 25 feet by 15 feet. What is its area? A) 350 sq ft B) 375 sq ft C) 400 sq ft D) 425 sq ft
16. What is the average of 68, 75, 82, 79, and 91? A) 78 B) 79 C) 80 D) 81
17. If 5/8 of a number is 35, what is the number? A) 52 B) 54 C) 56 D) 58
18. A retail store marks up merchandise 60% above cost. If an item costs $25, what is the selling price? A) $40 B) $42 C) $44 D) $46
19. What is $3^3 + 4^2$? A) 41 B) 43 C) 45 D) 47
20. A right triangle has legs of 8 and 15. What is the hypotenuse? A) 17 B) 19 C) 21 D) 23
21. A jar contains 4 red, 6 green, and 2 blue marbles. What's the probability of drawing green? A) 1/2 B) 1/3 C) 1/4 D) 1/6
22. What is 45% of 30% of 200? A) 25 B) 27 C) 29 D) 31
23. If $g(x) = x^2 - 3x + 2$ and $x = 4$, what is $g(x)$? A) 4 B) 5 C) 6 D) 7
24. In a triangle with angles 55° and 70°, what is the third angle? A) 50° B) 55° C) 60° D) 65°
25. What is 5/6 × 3/10? A) 1/4 B) 8/16 C) 15/60 D) 1/4
26. An item originally priced at $90 is reduced by 20%. What is the sale price? A) $70 B) $72 C) $74 D) $76
27. What is the median of: 34, 28, 41, 22, 35? A) 28 B) 32 C) 34 D) 35
28. Compound interest on $1,500 at 6% annually for 2 years is approximately: A) $180 B) $185 C) $190 D) $195
29. What is 2/3 ÷ 5/9? A) 10/27 B) 6/5 C) 5/6 D) 6/15
30. If $4x + 7 = 3x + 15$, what is x? A) 6 B) 7 C) 8 D) 9

Word Knowledge (35 questions)

1. Abate means: A) Increase B) Decrease C) Maintain D) Begin
2. Brevity means: A) Length B) Shortness C) Height D) Width

3. Candor means: A) Dishonesty B) Honesty C) Confusion D) Complexity
4. Diligent means: A) Lazy B) Hardworking C) Slow D) Careless
5. Eloquent means: A) Silent B) Articulate C) Confused D) Loud
6. Frugal means: A) Wasteful B) Economical C) Generous D) Expensive
7. Genial means: A) Unfriendly B) Friendly C) Serious D) Angry
8. Hasten means: A) Delay B) Hurry C) Stop D) Pause
9. Immerse means: A) Remove B) Submerge C) Dry D) Float
10. Jovial means: A) Sad B) Cheerful C) Angry D) Worried
11. Kindle means: A) Extinguish B) Ignite C) Cool D) Wet
12. Lament means: A) Celebrate B) Mourn C) Ignore D) Forget
13. Meager means: A) Abundant B) Scanty C) Sufficient D) Excessive
14. Nimble means: A) Clumsy B) Agile C) Slow D) Heavy
15. Opaque means: A) Transparent B) Not transparent C) Clear D) Bright
16. Ponder means: A) Act quickly B) Think carefully C) Ignore D) Forget
17. Quench means: A) Ignite B) Satisfy C) Increase D) Start
18. Robust means: A) Weak B) Strong C) Thin D) Fragile
19. Serene means: A) Chaotic B) Peaceful C) Loud D) Busy
20. Tedious means: A) Exciting B) Boring C) Quick D) Easy
21. Utter means: A) Partial B) Complete C) Silent D) Quiet
22. Vigilant means: A) Careless B) Watchful C) Sleepy D) Relaxed
23. Wither means: A) Grow B) Shrivel C) Bloom D) Strengthen
24. Yearn means: A) Reject B) Desire C) Ignore D) Forget
25. Zest means: A) Boredom B) Enthusiasm C) Tiredness D) Sadness
26. Ardent means: A) Cold B) Passionate C) Indifferent D) Calm
27. Brisk means: A) Slow B) Quick C) Lazy D) Tired
28. Cordial means: A) Rude B) Warm C) Cold D) Hostile
29. Docile means: A) Rebellious B) Submissive C) Aggressive D) Wild
30. Exempt means: A) Included B) Excused C) Required D) Obligated
31. Futile means: A) Successful B) Useless C) Helpful D) Effective
32. Grim means: A) Cheerful B) Stern C) Happy D) Bright
33. Hectic means: A) Calm B) Busy C) Peaceful D) Quiet
34. Inept means: A) Skilled B) Clumsy C) Talented D) Expert
35. Jaunty means: A) Sad B) Cheerful C) Worried D) Serious

Paragraph Comprehension (15 questions)

Passage 1: Coral reefs are among the most diverse ecosystems on Earth, supporting approximately 25% of all marine species despite covering less than 1% of the ocean floor. These underwater structures are built by tiny animals called coral polyps, which secrete calcium carbonate to form their skeletons. Rising ocean temperatures and acidification threaten these vital ecosystems.

1. Coral reefs support what percentage of marine species? A) 10% B) 25% C) 50% D) 75%
2. Coral reefs are built by: A) Fish B) Coral polyps C) Algae D) Bacteria

Passage 2: The invention of vaccines has been one of the greatest achievements in medical history. Vaccines work by introducing a weakened or inactive form of a disease-causing organism into the body, allowing the immune system to recognize and remember it. This prepares the body to fight the real disease if encountered later.

3. Vaccines introduce what into the body? A) Strong disease organisms B) Weakened or inactive organisms C) Antibiotics D) Vitamins
4. Vaccines help the immune system to: A) Fight all diseases B) Recognize and remember diseases C) Produce more blood D) Strengthen bones

Passage 3: Black holes are regions in space where gravity is so strong that nothing, not even light, can escape once it crosses the event horizon. They form when massive stars collapse at the end of their lives. Despite their name, black holes actually emit radiation through a process called Hawking radiation.

5. Nothing can escape a black hole once it crosses the: A) Event horizon B) Photon sphere C) Accretion disk D) Singularity
6. Black holes form from: A) Collapsed planets B) Collapsed massive stars C) Cosmic dust D) Dark matter

Passage 4: The water cycle is essential for distributing fresh water across the planet. Solar energy drives evaporation from oceans, lakes, and rivers. Water vapor rises and cools, forming clouds through condensation. Precipitation returns water to Earth's surface, where it flows back to water bodies or infiltrates into groundwater.

7. What drives the water cycle? A) Wind B) Solar energy C) Ocean currents D) Gravity
8. Water vapor forms clouds through: A) Evaporation B) Precipitation C) Condensation D) Infiltration

Passage 5: Artificial intelligence (AI) refers to computer systems that can perform tasks typically requiring human intelligence. Machine learning, a subset of AI, enables computers to learn and improve from experience without being explicitly programmed. AI applications include speech recognition, image analysis, and autonomous vehicles.

9. Machine learning is: A) The same as AI B) A subset of AI C) Unrelated to AI D) Opposite of AI
10. AI applications mentioned include: A) Only speech recognition B) Only image analysis C) Speech recognition, image analysis, and autonomous vehicles D) Only autonomous vehicles

Passage 6: Renewable energy sources are becoming increasingly cost-competitive with fossil fuels. Solar panel costs have dropped dramatically over the past decade, while wind energy capacity continues to expand globally. These technologies produce electricity without greenhouse gas emissions during operation.

11. Solar panel costs have: A) Increased B) Dropped dramatically C) Remained stable D) Fluctuated wildly
12. Renewable energy during operation produces: A) Some greenhouse gases B) Many greenhouse gases C) No greenhouse gases D) Only carbon dioxide

Passage 7: The human brain contains billions of neurons connected by trillions of synapses. Neuroplasticity refers to the brain's ability to reorganize and form new neural connections throughout life. This ability allows the brain to adapt to new experiences, learn new skills, and recover from injuries.

13. Neuroplasticity refers to the brain's ability to: A) Store memories B) Reorganize and form new connections C) Control body functions D) Process emotions
14. Neuroplasticity allows the brain to: A) Only learn new skills B) Only recover from injuries C) Adapt, learn, and recover D) Only adapt to experiences
15. The brain contains billions of: A) Synapses B) Neurons C) Memories D) Thoughts

Mathematics Knowledge (25 questions)

1. What is $\sqrt{361}$? A) 18 B) 19 C) 20 D) 21
2. If $x^2 = 169$, what is x? A) ± 12 B) ± 13 C) ± 14 D) ± 15
3. What is 4^4? A) 16 B) 64 C) 256 D) 1024
4. The area of a rhombus with diagonals 12 and 8 is: A) 48 B) 96 C) 20 D) 10
5. What is the slope of $y = (2/3)x - 5$? A) 2/3 B) -5 C) 3/2 D) 5
6. Factor: $x^2 - 36$ A) (x-6)(x-6) B) (x+6)(x+6) C) (x-6)(x+6) D) Cannot factor
7. What is $\log_{10} 0.01$? A) -2 B) -1 C) 0 D) 1
8. If $\cos \theta = 0.866$, what is θ? A) 30° B) 45° C) 60° D) 90°
9. The area of a circle with circumference 14π is: A) 49π B) 14π C) 7π D) 196π
10. What is $7! \div 5!$? A) 2 B) 42 C) 35 D) 7
11. If $k(x) = x^3 - 2x^2 + x - 3$, what is $k(2)$? A) -1 B) 1 C) 3 D) -3
12. The volume of a rectangular pyramid with base 6×4 and height 9 is: A) 72 B) 216 C) 54 D) 24
13. What is the y-intercept of $3x - 4y = 12$? A) 3 B) -3 C) 4 D) -4
14. Solve: $6x - 8 = 4x + 10$ A) x = 7 B) x = 8 C) x = 9 D) x = 10
15. What is sin 90°? A) 0 B) 0.5 C) 0.707 D) 1
16. The solutions to $x^2 + 2x - 15 = 0$ are: A) x = 3, -5 B) x = 5, -3 C) x = 1, -15 D) x = 15, -1
17. The length of arc with central angle 120° and radius 9 is: A) 6π B) 3π C) 18π D) 12π
18. If $\sin \theta = 0.5$, what is θ? A) 30° B) 45° C) 60° D) 90°
19. The surface area of a cylinder with radius 5 and height 8 is: A) 130π B) 65π C) 40π D) 200π
20. What is $\sqrt{(64 + 36)}$? A) 8 B) 9 C) 10 D) 11
21. A geometric sequence starts 3, 12, 48, ... What is the 6th term? A) 768 B) 1536 C) 3072 D) 6144
22. What is 60% of 80% of 150? A) 68 B) 70 C) 72 D) 74
23. If $\log_4 x = 3$, what is x? A) 12 B) 64 C) 81 D) 256
24. The area of a regular octagon with side 6 is approximately: A) 173 B) 173.8 C) 174 D) 175

25. What is the derivative of $4x^3 - 2x$? A) $12x^2 - 2$ B) $4x^2 - 2x$ C) $12x^3 - 2$ D) $x^4 - x^2$

Electronics Information (20 questions)

1. What does DC stand for? A) Direct Current B) Dynamic Circuit C) Digital Control D) Double Current
2. Electrical resistance is measured in: A) Volts B) Amperes C) Ohms D) Watts
3. A fuse is designed to: A) Increase current B) Store energy C) Protect from overcurrent D) Generate voltage
4. How many volts in a typical car battery? A) 6V B) 12V C) 24V D) 110V
5. A capacitor stores energy in: A) Magnetic field B) Electric field C) Chemical bonds D) Kinetic motion
6. In a parallel circuit, if one resistor fails: A) All current stops B) Other resistors continue working C) Voltage drops to zero D) Circuit overheats
7. Hot wire color in standard US wiring is: A) White B) Black C) Green D) Blue
8. A galvanometer measures: A) Voltage B) Small currents C) Resistance D) Power
9. What does IGBT stand for? A) Insulated Gate Bipolar Transistor B) Integrated Gate Binary Transistor C) Internal Gate Bipolar Transistor D) Isolated Gate Binary Transistor
10. An autotransformer: A) Has separate primary and secondary B) Has common primary and secondary C) Only steps up voltage D) Only steps down voltage
11. In series circuits, voltage: A) Is same across all components B) Divides across components C) Is zero D) Is infinite
12. Resistance equals: A) Voltage × Current B) Voltage ÷ Current C) Current ÷ Voltage D) Voltage + Current
13. Silicon is: A) A conductor B) An insulator C) A semiconductor D) A superconductor
14. What does AM stand for? A) Amplitude Modulation B) Angular Modulation C) Automatic Modulation D) Active Modulation
15. Power grid frequency in Japan is: A) 50 Hz B) 60 Hz C) Both 50 and 60 Hz D) 100 Hz
16. A rheostat is a: A) Fixed resistor B) Variable resistor C) Capacitor D) Inductor
17. When voltage increases and resistance stays constant, power: A) Decreases B) Increases C) Stays same D) Becomes zero
18. A signal generator produces: A) Only sine waves B) Only square waves C) Various waveforms D) Only DC signals
19. The unit of frequency is: A) Hertz B) Watt C) Joule D) Newton
20. A solar cell converts: A) Heat to electricity B) Light to electricity C) Motion to electricity D) Sound to electricity

Auto & Shop Information (25 questions)

Auto Information:

1. The crankcase contains: A) Transmission fluid B) Brake fluid C) Engine oil D) Coolant
2. What does OHV stand for? A) Overhead Valve B) Oil Hydraulic Valve C) Overhead Vent D) Oil Heating Valve
3. The fuel pump moves gasoline from: A) Engine to tank B) Tank to engine C) Carburetor to engine D) Filter to carburetor

4. A supercharger increases power by: A) Adding more fuel B) Compressing intake air C) Cooling the engine D) Reducing friction
5. The generator/alternator produces: A) Mechanical power B) Hydraulic pressure C) Electrical power D) Compressed air
6. What does ESP stand for? A) Electronic Stability Program B) Engine Speed Program C) Emergency Stop Program D) Electronic Suspension Program
7. The MAP sensor measures: A) Air temperature B) Manifold absolute pressure C) Miles per gallon D) Motor angular position
8. Antifreeze lowers the: A) Boiling point only B) Freezing point only C) Both freezing and boiling points D) Neither point
9. The timing belt/chain synchronizes: A) Fuel injection B) Crankshaft and camshaft C) Transmission shifting D) Brake application
10. What does TPMS monitor? A) Transmission pressure B) Tire pressure C) Throttle position D) Turbo pressure
11. Power steering fluid is: A) The same as brake fluid B) Hydraulic fluid C) Motor oil D) Transmission fluid
12. Premium fuel has: A) Higher octane rating B) More energy content C) Better fuel economy D) Longer shelf life
13. The PCV system controls: A) Power steering B) Crankcase ventilation C) Pollution control D) Power conversion

Shop Information: 14. An impact wrench is powered by: A) Manual force only B) Compressed air or electricity C) Hydraulic pressure only D) Steam power 15. Which blade cuts the finest? A) 14 TPI B) 18 TPI C) 24 TPI D) 32 TPI 16. A transit level is used for: A) Measuring angles B) Surveying elevations C) Checking squares D) Measuring thickness 17. What grit is considered very fine? A) 60 grit B) 120 grit C) 220 grit D) 400 grit 18. A Robertson screw has: A) Phillips head B) Flat head C) Square drive D) Hex head 19. The strongest corner joint is: A) Butt B) Miter C) Dado D) Rabbet 20. A smooth file is: A) Coarsest cut B) Medium cut C) Finest cut D) No cut 21. Kiln-dried lumber has: A) Higher moisture content B) Lower moisture content C) Same moisture content D) No moisture 22. A spring clamp applies: A) Light pressure B) Heavy pressure C) No pressure D) Variable pressure 23. A backsaw has: A) Flexible blade B) Reinforced back C) Curved blade D) Detachable blade 24. An engineer's square is used for: A) Only 90° angles B) Precision measurement C) Only 45° angles D) Circle measurement 25. Which creates smoothest surface? A) 100 grit sandpaper B) Bastard file C) 320 grit sandpaper D) Rough rasp

Mechanical Comprehension (25 questions)

1. If gear A (25 teeth) drives gear B (75 teeth), when A rotates 3 times, B rotates: A) 1 time B) 3 times C) 9 times D) 25 times
2. In a second-class lever, the load is located: A) At the fulcrum B) Between fulcrum and effort C) Beyond the effort point D) At the effort point
3. A pulley system with 6 supporting strands has mechanical advantage of: A) 3 B) 6 C) 12 D) 18
4. In a fluid, pressure at a given depth depends on: A) Container shape B) Fluid density and depth C) Container material D) Fluid temperature only

5. A 5:1 mechanical advantage system requires 40 pounds input to lift: A) 8 pounds B) 200 pounds C) 45 pounds D) 35 pounds
6. In a hydraulic jack with input area 1 sq in and output area 20 sq in, force is multiplied by: A) 19 B) 20 C) 21 D) 400
7. A belt drive where driving pulley diameter is 8 inches and driven pulley is 4 inches has speed ratio of: A) 1:2 B) 2:1 C) 1:1 D) 4:8
8. When a liquid is heated in a closed container, pressure: A) Decreases B) Increases C) Stays constant D) Becomes zero
9. The center of gravity of an irregular object is: A) Always at geometric center B) Where object balances C) At the heaviest point D) At the top
10. A bolt with 10 threads per inch turned 5 complete turns advances: A) 0.5 inch B) 2 inches C) 5 inches D) 50 inches
11. A spring under compression stores: A) Kinetic energy B) Potential energy C) Heat energy D) Chemical energy
12. Roller bearings reduce friction by: A) Adding lubricant B) Rolling contact instead of sliding C) Increasing surface area D) Reducing weight
13. When a large gear drives a small gear: A) Speed decreases, torque increases B) Speed increases, torque decreases C) Both increase D) Both decrease
14. A heart-shaped cam produces: A) Uniform motion B) Variable motion C) No motion D) Circular motion
15. Kinetic friction is usually: A) Greater than static friction B) Less than static friction C) Equal to static friction D) Unrelated to static friction
16. An inclined plane 24 feet long raising load 4 feet has mechanical advantage of: A) 4 B) 6 C) 20 D) 96
17. The Bernoulli effect explains: A) Why airplanes fly B) How hydraulics work C) Gear ratios D) Lever mechanics
18. A pendulum's period depends primarily on: A) Bob mass B) String length C) Release angle D) Air density
19. A block and tackle with 4 movable pulleys has mechanical advantage of: A) 4 B) 8 C) 12 D) 16
20. Archimedes' principle explains: A) Leverage B) Floating and sinking C) Gear ratios D) Friction
21. Two gears with ratio 3:1, if input gear turns 90 RPM, output gear turns: A) 30 RPM B) 90 RPM C) 270 RPM D) 360 RPM
22. A flywheel smooths: A) Power delivery B) Gear changes C) Brake application D) Steering input
23. In levers, mechanical advantage equals: A) Effort arm ÷ Load arm B) Load arm ÷ Effort arm C) Effort arm × Load arm D) Effort arm + Load arm
24. Gauge pressure plus atmospheric pressure equals: A) Vacuum B) Absolute pressure C) Relative pressure D) Differential pressure
25. A compound pulley combines: A) Only fixed pulleys B) Only movable pulleys C) Fixed and movable pulleys D) Gears and pulleys

Test 11 Answer Key

General Science: 1-B, 2-C, 3-C, 4-B, 5-C, 6-C, 7-C, 8-A, 9-D, 10-B, 11-C, 12-C, 13-C, 14-B, 15-C, 16-B, 17-C, 18-A, 19-C, 20-C, 21-A, 22-B, 23-C, 24-B, 25-C

Arithmetic Reasoning: 1-B, 2-A, 3-B, 4-B, 5-B, 6-C, 7-C, 8-A, 9-B, 10-C, 11-C, 12-A, 13-B, 14-C, 15-B, 16-B, 17-C, 18-A, 19-B, 20-A, 21-A, 22-B, 23-C, 24-B, 25-A, 26-B, 27-C, 28-C, 29-B, 30-C

Word Knowledge: 1-B, 2-B, 3-B, 4-B, 5-B, 6-B, 7-B, 8-B, 9-B, 10-B, 11-B, 12-B, 13-B, 14-B, 15-B, 16-B, 17-B, 18-B, 19-B, 20-B, 21-B, 22-B, 23-B, 24-B, 25-B, 26-B, 27-B, 28-B, 29-B, 30-B, 31-B, 32-B, 33-B, 34-B, 35-B

Paragraph Comprehension: 1-B, 2-B, 3-B, 4-B, 5-A, 6-B, 7-B, 8-C, 9-B, 10-C, 11-B, 12-C, 13-B, 14-C, 15-B

Mathematics Knowledge: 1-B, 2-B, 3-C, 4-A, 5-A, 6-C, 7-A, 8-A, 9-A, 10-B, 11-A, 12-A, 13-B, 14-C, 15-D, 16-A, 17-A, 18-A, 19-A, 20-C, 21-A, 22-C, 23-B, 24-A, 25-A

Electronics Information: 1-A, 2-C, 3-C, 4-B, 5-B, 6-B, 7-B, 8-B, 9-A, 10-B, 11-B, 12-B, 13-C, 14-A, 15-C, 16-B, 17-B, 18-C, 19-A, 20-B

Auto & Shop Information: 1-C, 2-A, 3-B, 4-B, 5-C, 6-A, 7-B, 8-B, 9-B, 10-B, 11-B, 12-A, 13-B, 14-B, 15-D, 16-B, 17-D, 18-C, 19-C, 20-C, 21-B, 22-A, 23-B, 24-B, 25-C

Mechanical Comprehension: 1-A, 2-B, 3-B, 4-B, 5-B, 6-B, 7-B, 8-B, 9-B, 10-A, 11-B, 12-B, 13-B, 14-B, 15-B, 16-B, 17-A, 18-B, 19-B, 20-B, 21-A, 22-A, 23-A, 24-B, 25-C

Test 15

General Science (25 questions)

1. Which gas is most abundant in Earth's atmosphere? A) Oxygen B) Carbon dioxide C) Nitrogen D) Argon
2. What is the powerhouse of the cell? A) Nucleus B) Mitochondria C) Ribosome D) Cytoplasm
3. The process by which green plants make food using sunlight is: A) Respiration B) Photosynthesis C) Digestion D) Transpiration
4. Which planet has the strongest gravitational pull? A) Earth B) Mars C) Jupiter D) Saturn
5. What is the chemical formula for table salt? A) $NaCl$ B) H_2O C) CO_2 D) $CaCl_2$
6. How many chambers does a human heart have? A) 2 B) 3 C) 4 D) 5
7. The study of weather patterns is called: A) Geology B) Meteorology C) Astronomy D) Seismology

8. Which vitamin is produced when skin is exposed to sunlight? A) Vitamin A B) Vitamin C C) Vitamin D D) Vitamin K
9. What is the basic unit of heredity? A) Chromosome B) Gene C) DNA D) RNA
10. The Earth's magnetic field protects us from: A) Gravity B) Solar radiation C) Earthquakes D) Volcanoes
11. What type of bond holds water molecules together? A) Ionic B) Covalent C) Metallic D) Hydrogen
12. Which organ produces bile? A) Pancreas B) Liver C) Kidney D) Spleen
13. The process by which rocks change form due to heat and pressure is: A) Erosion B) Weathering C) Metamorphism D) Sedimentation
14. What is the speed of light in a vacuum? A) 300,000 km/s B) 150,000 km/s C) 450,000 km/s D) 600,000 km/s
15. Which blood cells are responsible for clotting? A) Red blood cells B) White blood cells C) Platelets D) Plasma
16. The ozone layer is located in which atmospheric layer? A) Troposphere B) Stratosphere C) Mesosphere D) Thermosphere
17. What is the most common element in the human body? A) Carbon B) Nitrogen C) Oxygen D) Hydrogen
18. The process of liquid changing to gas at the surface is: A) Condensation B) Evaporation C) Sublimation D) Freezing
19. Which scientist proposed the theory of continental drift? A) Darwin B) Einstein C) Wegener D) Newton
20. What causes the phases of the moon? A) Earth's rotation B) Moon's rotation C) Earth's shadow D) Sun's position relative to Earth and Moon
21. The smallest particle of an element that retains its properties is: A) Molecule B) Atom C) Proton D) Electron
22. Which gas is essential for cellular respiration? A) Nitrogen B) Carbon dioxide C) Oxygen D) Hydrogen
23. The asteroid belt is located between: A) Earth and Mars B) Mars and Jupiter C) Jupiter and Saturn D) Venus and Earth
24. What is the pH of pure water? A) 6 B) 7 C) 8 D) 9
25. The force that keeps planets in orbit around the sun is: A) Magnetism B) Friction C) Gravity D) Centrifugal force

Arithmetic Reasoning (30 questions)

1. A laptop costs $850 with a 15% discount. What is the sale price? A) $722.50 B) $732.50 C) $742.50 D) $752.50
2. If a recipe serves 6 people and calls for 2 cups of flour, how much flour is needed to serve 9 people? A) 2.5 cups B) 3 cups C) 3.5 cups D) 4 cups
3. A car travels 350 miles in 5 hours. What is its average speed? A) 65 mph B) 70 mph C) 75 mph D) 80 mph
4. Tom buys 3 books at $14.95 each and 2 magazines at $4.50 each. What is his total cost? A) $53.85 B) $54.85 C) $55.85 D) $56.85
5. A rectangular garden is 18 feet long and 12 feet wide. What is its area? A) 206 sq ft B) 216 sq ft C) 226 sq ft D) 236 sq ft

6. If 15 apples cost $6.75, what is the cost per apple? A) $0.40 B) $0.45 C) $0.50 D) $0.55
7. The temperature rose from 58°F to 79°F. What was the increase? A) 19°F B) 21°F C) 23°F D) 25°F
8. If y + 18 = 35, what is y? A) 15 B) 17 C) 19 D) 21
9. A circle has a radius of 5 inches. What is its circumference? (Use π = 3.14) A) 31.4 inches B) 15.7 inches C) 78.5 inches D) 25.12 inches
10. Lisa earns $16 per hour and works 32 hours. How much does she earn? A) $512 B) $522 C) $532 D) $542
11. What is 30% of 180? A) 52 B) 54 C) 56 D) 58
12. If a train travels 480 miles in 8 hours, how far will it travel in 5 hours at the same speed? A) 280 miles B) 300 miles C) 320 miles D) 340 miles
13. The sum of two numbers is 73. If one number is 28, what is the other? A) 43 B) 45 C) 47 D) 49
14. A rectangle has a perimeter of 42 feet and a width of 9 feet. What is its length? A) 10 feet B) 11 feet C) 12 feet D) 13 feet
15. If 4/7 of a number is 32, what is the number? A) 54 B) 56 C) 58 D) 60
16. A ladder 20 feet long leans against a wall. The bottom is 12 feet from the wall. How high up does it reach? A) 14 feet B) 15 feet C) 16 feet D) 17 feet
17. Sarah's test scores are 89, 94, 87, and 90. What is her average? A) 89 B) 90 C) 91 D) 92
18. If you buy 8 items at $5.75 each and get a 12% discount, what do you pay? A) $40.48 B) $40.94 C) $41.36 D) $41.82
19. If 6x - 18 = 30, what is x? A) 6 B) 7 C) 8 D) 9
20. The ratio of dogs to cats at a shelter is 4:7. If there are 20 dogs, how many cats are there? A) 28 B) 30 C) 32 D) 35
21. A store marks up items 45% above cost. If an item costs $20, what is the selling price? A) $27 B) $28 C) $29 D) $30
22. If a factory produces 216 parts in 9 hours, how many parts per hour? A) 22 B) 24 C) 26 D) 28
23. The area of a square is 144 square inches. What is the length of each side? A) 11 inches B) 12 inches C) 13 inches D) 14 inches
24. If 3/5 of a class of 45 students passed a test, how many failed? A) 16 B) 17 C) 18 D) 19
25. A number decreased by 25% becomes 60. What was the original number? A) 75 B) 80 C) 85 D) 90
26. The perimeter of a triangle with sides 13, 17, and 19 is: A) 47 B) 48 C) 49 D) 50
27. If you travel 420 miles and use 15 gallons of gas, what is your mpg? A) 26 B) 28 C) 30 D) 32
28. The average of 6 numbers is 35. If five numbers are 32, 38, 34, 36, and 39, what is the sixth? A) 31 B) 32 C) 33 D) 34
29. A circular pool has a diameter of 24 feet. What is its area? (Use π = 3.14) A) 452.16 sq ft B) 462.16 sq ft C) 472.16 sq ft D) 482.16 sq ft
30. If a 20% discount saves $18, what was the original price? A) $85 B) $90 C) $95 D) $100

Word Knowledge (35 questions)

1. Accessible most nearly means: A) Blocked B) Available C) Hidden D) Distant
2. Bellicose most nearly means: A) Peaceful B) Warlike C) Friendly D) Calm

3. Coherent most nearly means: A) Confused B) Clear C) Scattered D) Mixed
4. Deceptive most nearly means: A) Honest B) Misleading C) Truthful D) Reliable
5. Eccentric most nearly means: A) Normal B) Unusual C) Common D) Typical
6. Feasible most nearly means: A) Impossible B) Practical C) Difficult D) Complex
7. Gregarious most nearly means: A) Antisocial B) Sociable C) Shy D) Quiet
8. Haphazard most nearly means: A) Organized B) Random C) Planned D) Systematic
9. Immaculate most nearly means: A) Dirty B) Spotless C) Stained D) Messy
10. Judicious most nearly means: A) Foolish B) Wise C) Careless D) Hasty
11. Kinetic most nearly means: A) Still B) Moving C) Stationary D) Fixed
12. Lucrative most nearly means: A) Unprofitable B) Profitable C) Costly D) Expensive
13. Meager most nearly means: A) Abundant B) Scanty C) Plentiful D) Excessive
14. Nostalgic most nearly means: A) Forward-looking B) Sentimental C) Modern D) Progressive
15. Opulent most nearly means: A) Poor B) Wealthy C) Simple D) Plain
16. Pervasive most nearly means: A) Limited B) Widespread C) Rare D) Absent
17. Quaint most nearly means: A) Modern B) Charming C) Ugly D) New
18. Resolute most nearly means: A) Uncertain B) Determined C) Hesitant D) Weak
19. Sporadic most nearly means: A) Continuous B) Irregular C) Constant D) Regular
20. Turbulent most nearly means: A) Calm B) Stormy C) Peaceful D) Quiet
21. Unprecedented most nearly means: A) Common B) Unique C) Usual D) Typical
22. Vigilant most nearly means: A) Careless B) Watchful C) Lazy D) Inattentive
23. Whimsical most nearly means: A) Serious B) Playful C) Stern D) Harsh
24. Xenophobic most nearly means: A) Welcoming B) Fearful of foreigners C) Friendly D) Open-minded
25. Yielding most nearly means: A) Rigid B) Flexible C) Hard D) Stiff
26. Apathetic most nearly means: A) Enthusiastic B) Indifferent C) Excited D) Passionate
27. Boisterous most nearly means: A) Quiet B) Rowdy C) Calm D) Peaceful
28. Caustic most nearly means: A) Gentle B) Harsh C) Mild D) Soothing
29. Dubious most nearly means: A) Certain B) Doubtful C) Sure D) Confident
30. Eloquent most nearly means: A) Silent B) Articulate C) Unclear D) Confused
31. Futile most nearly means: A) Successful B) Useless C) Effective D) Productive
32. Garrulous most nearly means: A) Silent B) Talkative C) Quiet D) Reserved
33. Heinous most nearly means: A) Good B) Evil C) Kind D) Pleasant
34. Insipid most nearly means: A) Flavorful B) Bland C) Spicy D) Tasty
35. Jocular most nearly means: A) Serious B) Humorous C) Sad D) Gloomy

Paragraph Comprehension (15 questions)

Passage 1: Effective time management is crucial for success in both personal and professional life. By prioritizing tasks, setting realistic goals, and eliminating distractions, individuals can accomplish more in less time. Time management also reduces stress and improves work-life balance. Simple techniques such as creating to-do lists, breaking large projects into smaller tasks, and using calendars can significantly improve productivity and reduce feelings of being overwhelmed.

1. According to the passage, effective time management: A) Only benefits professional life B) Reduces stress and improves work-life balance C) Is impossible to learn D) Requires expensive tools
2. The passage suggests that breaking large projects into smaller tasks: A) Wastes time B) Improves productivity C) Creates more stress D) Is unnecessary
3. Time management techniques mentioned include: A) Only creating calendars B) Creating to-do lists and using calendars C) Hiring assistants D) Working longer hours

Passage 2: Coral reefs are among the most diverse ecosystems on Earth, supporting about 25% of all marine species despite covering less than 1% of the ocean floor. These underwater structures are built by tiny animals called coral polyps that secrete calcium carbonate to form their skeletons. Unfortunately, coral reefs face numerous threats including climate change, pollution, and overfishing. Rising ocean temperatures cause coral bleaching, a stress response that can lead to coral death if prolonged.

4. Coral reefs support approximately what percentage of marine species? A) 10% B) 25% C) 50% D) 75%
5. Coral reefs are built by: A) Fish B) Coral polyps C) Algae D) Sea plants
6. Coral bleaching is caused by: A) Pollution only B) Overfishing only C) Rising ocean temperatures D) Too much sunlight

Passage 3: The invention of the internet has transformed global communication and commerce. Originally developed for military and academic use, the internet now connects billions of people worldwide, enabling instant communication, online shopping, and access to vast amounts of information. Social media platforms have revolutionized how people interact and share information, while e-commerce has changed the way businesses operate and consumers shop.

7. The internet was originally developed for: A) Commercial use B) Military and academic use C) Entertainment D) Social media
8. According to the passage, the internet has changed: A) Only communication B) Only commerce C) Both communication and commerce D) Only entertainment
9. E-commerce has changed: A) How businesses operate and consumers shop B) Only how businesses operate C) Only how consumers shop D) Neither business nor consumer behavior

Passage 4: Regular physical exercise provides numerous health benefits including improved cardiovascular health, stronger bones and muscles, and better mental health. Exercise helps control weight, reduces the risk of chronic diseases such as diabetes and heart disease, and can improve mood and cognitive function. Health experts recommend at least 150 minutes of moderate-intensity exercise per week for adults, which can include activities like brisk walking, swimming, or cycling.

10. Exercise helps control: A) Only weight B) Weight and reduces disease risk C) Only mood D) Only bone strength
11. Health experts recommend how much exercise per week for adults? A) 75 minutes B) 100 minutes C) 150 minutes D) 200 minutes

12. The passage states that exercise improves: A) Only physical health B) Only mental health C) Both physical and mental health D) Neither physical nor mental health

Passage 5: Renewable energy technologies are becoming increasingly cost-competitive with traditional fossil fuels. Solar panel prices have dropped dramatically over the past decade, while wind turbine efficiency has improved significantly. Many countries are investing heavily in renewable energy infrastructure to reduce greenhouse gas emissions and achieve energy independence. Battery storage technology is also advancing rapidly, addressing the challenge of storing renewable energy for use when the sun isn't shining or wind isn't blowing.

13. Solar panel prices have: A) Increased dramatically B) Dropped dramatically C) Remained the same D) Fluctuated wildly
14. Countries are investing in renewable energy to: A) Reduce emissions and achieve energy independence B) Only reduce emissions C) Only achieve energy independence D) Create jobs only
15. Battery storage technology addresses: A) The cost of renewable energy B) The efficiency of solar panels C) Storing renewable energy for later use D) Wind turbine maintenance

Mathematics Knowledge (25 questions)

1. What is 22% of 350? A) 75 B) 77 C) 79 D) 81
2. If $z + 11 = 28$, then $z = $? A) 15 B) 17 C) 19 D) 21
3. What is the square root of 196? A) 12 B) 13 C) 14 D) 15
4. In a right triangle with legs 8 and 15, what is the hypotenuse? A) 17 B) 18 C) 19 D) 20
5. What is 2^6? A) 32 B) 48 C) 64 D) 72
6. If a circle has an area of 78.5, what is its radius? (Use $\pi = 3.14$) A) 4 B) 5 C) 6 D) 7
7. What is $8! \div 6!$? A) 48 B) 54 C) 56 D) 62
8. Solve: $7x + 21 = 49$ A) 3 B) 4 C) 5 D) 6
9. What is the area of a trapezoid with parallel sides 8 and 12, and height 5? A) 48 B) 50 C) 52 D) 54
10. If $5z - 10 = 4z + 8$, then $z = $? A) 16 B) 17 C) 18 D) 19
11. What is 40% of 125? A) 48 B) 50 C) 52 D) 54
12. In $g(x) = 5x - 3$, what is $g(4)$? A) 15 B) 16 C) 17 D) 18
13. What is the surface area of a cube with side length 6? A) 216 B) 196 C) 186 D) 176
14. An equilateral triangle has a perimeter of 27. What is the length of each side? A) 8 B) 9 C) 10 D) 11
15. What is $|-18|$? A) -18 B) 0 C) 18 D) 36
16. Solve: $9x - 36 = 27$ A) 6 B) 7 C) 8 D) 9
17. What is $15^2 - 11^2$? A) 104 B) 106 C) 108 D) 110
18. If $p = 5$ and $q = 2$, what is $3p^2 - 4q^2$? A) 59 B) 61 C) 63 D) 65
19. What is the slope of the line through (3,7) and (7,15)? A) 1 B) 2 C) 3 D) 4
20. What is $4/7 + 1/3$? A) 5/10 B) 19/21 C) 11/21 D) 5/21
21. If $\log_5(x) = 2$, then $x = $? A) 10 B) 20 C) 25 D) 32
22. What is the median of 4, 9, 2, 7, 6, 8, 5? A) 5 B) 6 C) 7 D) 8
23. Solve: $x^2 - 36 = 0$ A) ±5 B) ±6 C) ±7 D) ±8
24. What is $\sin(30°)$? A) 1/3 B) 1/2 C) $\sqrt{3}/2$ D) $\sqrt{2}/2$

25. If $k(x) = 2x^2 + 3x - 1$, what is $k(3)$? A) 24 B) 26 C) 28 D) 30

Electronics Information (20 questions)

1. What is the unit of magnetic field strength? A) Tesla B) Weber C) Henry D) Gauss
2. Which component opposes changes in current? A) Resistor B) Capacitor C) Inductor D) Diode
3. In a series-parallel circuit: A) All components are in series B) All components are in parallel C) Some components are in series, others in parallel D) Components change configuration
4. What does RF stand for? A) Radio Frequency B) Reverse Flow C) Resistance Factor D) Rapid Function
5. A thyristor is a type of: A) Resistor B) Controlled switch C) Capacitor D) Inductor
6. The unit of electrical energy is: A) Watt B) Joule C) Ampere D) Volt
7. Admittance is the reciprocal of: A) Resistance B) Capacitance C) Impedance D) Inductance
8. Which element is used in semiconductor devices? A) Copper B) Silicon C) Iron D) Aluminum
9. A step-down transformer: A) Increases voltage B) Decreases voltage C) Maintains voltage D) Converts DC to AC
10. Faraday's law relates to: A) Resistance B) Electromagnetic induction C) Static electricity D) Magnetic fields only
11. What does PCB stand for? A) Power Control Board B) Printed Circuit Board C) Positive Current Board D) Primary Component Board
12. Magnetic field strength around a current-carrying wire: A) Increases with distance B) Decreases with distance C) Remains constant D) Is zero
13. A varactor diode is used for: A) Rectification B) Voltage regulation C) Variable capacitance D) Current amplification
14. The unit of electrical conductance is: A) Ohm B) Siemens C) Farad D) Henry
15. In a full-wave rectifier: A) Only positive half-cycles are used B) Both half-cycles are used C) Only negative half-cycles are used D) AC is amplified
16. What is susceptance? A) Imaginary part of admittance B) Real part of impedance C) Magnetic permeability D) Electrical resistance
17. A spectrum analyzer displays: A) Time domain signals B) Frequency domain signals C) Only DC levels D) Only AC levels
18. A trimmer capacitor is used for: A) High power applications B) Fine tuning C) Energy storage D) Current limiting
19. Which device converts electrical energy to light? A) Photodiode B) LED C) Resistor D) Inductor
20. The Q factor of a circuit indicates: A) Power consumption B) Selectivity C) Voltage gain D) Current capacity

Auto & Shop Information (25 questions)

1. The ECU in a car stands for: A) Engine Control Unit B) Electronic Control Unit C) Either A or B D) Emergency Control Unit

2. What tool measures cylinder bore diameter? A) Caliper B) Micrometer C) Bore gauge D) Feeler gauge
3. The timing belt controls: A) Ignition timing B) Valve timing C) Fuel timing D) Transmission timing
4. Which system provides power assistance for braking? A) ABS B) Power brake booster C) EBD D) Traction control
5. A Robertson screwdriver has a: A) Square tip B) Phillips tip C) Flat tip D) Hexagonal tip
6. The MAP sensor measures: A) Air temperature B) Manifold absolute pressure C) Mass airflow D) Throttle position
7. What does OBD stand for? A) On-Board Diagnostics B) Oil Burn Detection C) Oxygen Balance Device D) Output Boost Driver
8. A tap and die set is used for: A) Cutting holes B) Creating threads C) Measuring angles D) Joining metals
9. The oxygen sensor: A) Measures air intake B) Monitors exhaust gases C) Controls fuel injection D) Regulates engine temperature
10. What produces the high voltage for spark plugs? A) Battery B) Alternator C) Ignition coil D) Starter
11. Which tool cuts internal threads? A) Die B) Tap C) Reamer D) Drill
12. The limited slip differential: A) Locks both wheels B) Allows different wheel speeds C) Prevents wheel spin D) All of the above
13. MIG welding uses: A) Stick electrodes B) Wire feed and gas C) Oxy-acetylene D) Arc welding only
14. The expansion tank: A) Stores extra fuel B) Allows coolant expansion C) Holds transmission fluid D) Contains brake fluid
15. A dial indicator measures: A) Electrical current B) Small movements or runout C) Temperature D) Pressure
16. What controls idle speed? A) Throttle body B) IAC valve C) Fuel pump D) ECU
17. Emery cloth is used for: A) Cleaning glass B) Polishing metal C) Cutting wood D) Measuring thickness
18. The knock sensor detects: A) Engine vibration B) Abnormal combustion C) Low oil pressure D) High temperature
19. A tap wrench is used to: A) Hold dies B) Turn taps C) Cut pipes D) Bend metal
20. Variable valve timing: A) Changes when valves open/close B) Controls fuel injection C) Regulates oil pressure D) Adjusts compression ratio
21. Which gauge measures tire tread depth? A) Depth gauge B) Tread depth gauge C) Both A and B D) Pressure gauge
22. The crankshaft position sensor: A) Measures engine speed B) Determines piston position C) Both A and B D) Controls timing
23. "Torque-to-yield" bolts: A) Can be reused indefinitely B) Must be replaced after removal C) Are used only in transmissions D) Don't require specific torque
24. A countersink is used to: A) Mark centers B) Create angled holes C) Cut threads D) Measure depths
25. Direct injection systems: A) Inject fuel into intake ports B) Inject fuel directly into cylinders C) Use carburetors D) Only work with diesel

Mechanical Comprehension (25 questions)

1. If a 20-pound weight is placed 2 feet from a fulcrum, what weight is needed 8 feet away to balance? A) 5 pounds B) 6 pounds C) 7 pounds D) 8 pounds
2. Which simple machine multiplies force most effectively? A) Lever B) Pulley C) Inclined plane D) Compound pulley system
3. If a 16-tooth gear drives a 64-tooth gear, the output gear rotates: A) 4 times faster B) 4 times slower C) 2 times faster D) 2 times slower
4. Fluid pressure in a container: A) Varies with depth only B) Is equal in all directions at any point C) Only acts downward D) Depends on container shape
5. A screw is an inclined plane wrapped around: A) A wheel B) A cylinder C) A cone D) A sphere
6. If you triple the effort arm length of a lever: A) Mechanical advantage triples B) Mechanical advantage is halved C) No change in advantage D) Force doubles
7. In a hydraulic system, if input piston area is 4 sq in and output area is 36 sq in, force multiplication is: A) 6 B) 8 C) 9 D) 12
8. A ramp 30 feet long rising 6 # ASVAB Practice Tests 12-25

Test 12

General Science (25 questions)

1. Which blood type is considered the universal donor? A) A B) B C) AB D) O
2. What is the hardest natural substance? A) Quartz B) Diamond C) Steel D) Iron
3. The process by which plants make food is called: A) Respiration B) Photosynthesis C) Digestion D) Fermentation
4. Which planet is closest to the Sun? A) Venus B) Earth C) Mercury D) Mars
5. What gas makes up about 78% of Earth's atmosphere? A) Oxygen B) Carbon dioxide C) Nitrogen D) Hydrogen
6. The smallest unit of matter is: A) Molecule B) Atom C) Cell D) Electron
7. What type of rock is formed by cooling magma? A) Sedimentary B) Metamorphic C) Igneous D) Fossil
8. Which organ produces insulin? A) Liver B) Kidney C) Pancreas D) Heart
9. The speed of light is approximately: A) 186,000 miles/sec B) 93,000 miles/sec C) 300,000 miles/sec D) 150,000 miles/sec
10. What is the chemical symbol for gold? A) Go B) Gd C) Au D) Ag
11. Which vitamin is produced when skin is exposed to sunlight? A) Vitamin A B) Vitamin C C) Vitamin D D) Vitamin K
12. The study of earthquakes is called: A) Geology B) Seismology C) Meteorology D) Astronomy
13. What is the normal human body temperature? A) 96.8°F B) 98.6°F C) 100.4°F D) 102.2°F
14. Which gas is produced during photosynthesis? A) Carbon dioxide B) Nitrogen C) Oxygen D) Hydrogen
15. The largest organ in the human body is: A) Liver B) Brain C) Lungs D) Skin
16. What causes tides? A) Wind B) Earth's rotation C) Moon's gravity D) Sun's heat

17. Which element has the atomic number 1? A) Helium B) Hydrogen C) Lithium D) Carbon
18. The process of water changing from liquid to gas is: A) Condensation B) Evaporation C) Precipitation D) Sublimation
19. Which blood vessels carry blood away from the heart? A) Veins B) Arteries C) Capillaries D) Ventricles
20. What is the study of weather called? A) Geology B) Biology C) Meteorology D) Astronomy
21. Which type of energy is stored in food? A) Kinetic B) Potential C) Chemical D) Thermal
22. The center of an atom is called: A) Electron B) Proton C) Neutron D) Nucleus
23. Which planet has the most moons? A) Jupiter B) Saturn C) Uranus D) Neptune
24. What is the main component of natural gas? A) Propane B) Butane C) Methane D) Ethane
25. The force that opposes motion is: A) Gravity B) Friction C) Magnetism D) Inertia

Arithmetic Reasoning (30 questions)

1. If a shirt costs $24 and is on sale for 25% off, what is the sale price? A) $18 B) $20 C) $22 D) $16
2. A recipe calls for 3 cups of flour to make 12 cookies. How many cups are needed for 36 cookies? A) 6 B) 9 C) 12 D) 15
3. If a car travels 240 miles in 4 hours, what is its average speed? A) 50 mph B) 60 mph C) 70 mph D) 80 mph
4. John has $125. He spends $45 on groceries and $28 on gas. How much does he have left? A) $52 B) $62 C) $72 D) $82
5. A rectangular garden is 15 feet long and 8 feet wide. What is its area? A) 100 sq ft B) 120 sq ft C) 140 sq ft D) 160 sq ft
6. If 5 pencils cost $2.50, how much do 12 pencils cost? A) $5.00 B) $6.00 C) $7.50 D) $8.00
7. Sarah earns $12 per hour. If she works 35 hours, how much does she earn? A) $420 B) $440 C) $460 D) $480
8. A pizza is cut into 8 equal slices. If Tom eats 3 slices, what fraction of the pizza remains? A) 3/8 B) 5/8 C) 1/2 D) 2/3
9. The temperature was 72°F at noon and dropped 15°F by evening. What was the evening temperature? A) 57°F B) 62°F C) 67°F D) 87°F
10. If a train travels 300 miles in 5 hours, how far will it travel in 8 hours at the same speed? A) 480 miles B) 500 miles C) 520 miles D) 540 miles
11. A store has 144 items. If they sell 3/4 of them, how many items are left? A) 24 B) 36 C) 48 D) 54
12. Mike's test scores are 85, 92, 78, and 89. What is his average score? A) 84 B) 86 C) 88 D) 90
13. If a book costs $18 and the tax is 8%, what is the total cost? A) $18.80 B) $19.20 C) $19.44 D) $19.80
14. A ladder is leaning against a wall. The bottom is 6 feet from the wall and the ladder is 10 feet long. How high up the wall does it reach? A) 6 feet B) 8 feet C) 10 feet D) 12 feet
15. If $2x + 5 = 15$, what is x? A) 5 B) 10 C) 15 D) 20

16. A swimming pool holds 15,000 gallons. If it's being filled at 250 gallons per hour, how long will it take to fill? A) 50 hours B) 60 hours C) 70 hours D) 80 hours
17. The ratio of boys to girls in a class is 3:4. If there are 12 boys, how many girls are there? A) 9 B) 12 C) 16 D) 20
18. If a discount of 30% reduces the price by $21, what was the original price? A) $60 B) $70 C) $80 D) $90
19. A rectangle has a perimeter of 24 feet and a length of 8 feet. What is its width? A) 2 feet B) 4 feet C) 6 feet D) 8 feet
20. If you buy 3 items for $2.40 each and 2 items for $1.80 each, what is the total cost? A) $10.80 B) $11.20 C) $11.60 D) $12.00
21. A number increased by 25% becomes 150. What was the original number? A) 120 B) 125 C) 130 D) 135
22. If a machine produces 240 widgets in 8 hours, how many does it produce per hour? A) 25 B) 30 C) 35 D) 40
23. The sum of three consecutive integers is 48. What is the middle integer? A) 15 B) 16 C) 17 D) 18
24. If 4 workers can complete a job in 6 days, how many days will it take 3 workers? A) 6 days B) 7 days C) 8 days D) 9 days
25. A circle has a radius of 7 inches. What is its circumference? (Use $\pi = 22/7$) A) 44 inches B) 42 inches C) 40 inches D) 38 inches
26. If the sales tax rate is 6% and the tax on an item is $3.60, what is the item's price before tax? A) $50 B) $55 C) $60 D) $65
27. A bag contains 5 red marbles and 3 blue marbles. What is the probability of drawing a red marble? A) 3/8 B) 5/8 C) 3/5 D) 5/3
28. If a car's value depreciates 20% each year and is worth $16,000 after one year, what was its original value? A) $19,200 B) $20,000 C) $20,800 D) $21,600
29. The average of 5 numbers is 24. If four of the numbers are 20, 22, 25, and 28, what is the fifth number? A) 23 B) 24 C) 25 D) 26
30. If 3/4 of a number is 18, what is 2/3 of that number? A) 12 B) 14 C) 16 D) 18

Word Knowledge (35 questions)

1. Abundant most nearly means: A) Scarce B) Plentiful C) Ordinary D) Expensive
2. Conceal most nearly means: A) Reveal B) Hide C) Discover D) Show
3. Frigid most nearly means: A) Hot B) Warm C) Cold D) Mild
4. Genuine most nearly means: A) Fake B) Real C) Copied D) Artificial
5. Hazardous most nearly means: A) Safe B) Dangerous C) Easy D) Simple
6. Immense most nearly means: A) Tiny B) Small C) Huge D) Medium
7. Jovial most nearly means: A) Sad B) Angry C) Cheerful D) Quiet
8. Keen most nearly means: A) Dull B) Sharp C) Blunt D) Broken
9. Lavish most nearly means: A) Simple B) Plain C) Extravagant D) Cheap
10. Meager most nearly means: A) Abundant B) Scarce C) Plenty D) Excessive
11. Nimble most nearly means: A) Clumsy B) Slow C) Agile D) Heavy
12. Obscure most nearly means: A) Clear B) Obvious C) Hidden D) Bright
13. Perilous most nearly means: A) Safe B) Dangerous C) Easy D) Comfortable
14. Quaint most nearly means: A) Modern B) New C) Old-fashioned D) Ugly

15. Robust most nearly means: A) Weak B) Strong C) Sick D) Tired
16. Serene most nearly means: A) Noisy B) Chaotic C) Peaceful D) Busy
17. Tedious most nearly means: A) Exciting B) Boring C) Quick D) Easy
18. Unique most nearly means: A) Common B) Ordinary C) One-of-a-kind D) Similar
19. Verbose most nearly means: A) Quiet B) Wordy C) Brief D) Silent
20. Wary most nearly means: A) Trusting B) Cautious C) Careless D) Naive
21. Zealous most nearly means: A) Lazy B) Enthusiastic C) Indifferent D) Tired
22. Amplify most nearly means: A) Reduce B) Increase C) Maintain D) Ignore
23. Benevolent most nearly means: A) Evil B) Kind C) Selfish D) Cruel
24. Complacent most nearly means: A) Worried B) Self-satisfied C) Anxious D) Active
25. Diligent most nearly means: A) Lazy B) Careless C) Hardworking D) Slow
26. Eloquent most nearly means: A) Silent B) Articulate C) Confused D) Unclear
27. Frugal most nearly means: A) Wasteful B) Thrifty C) Generous D) Careless
28. Gregarious most nearly means: A) Shy B) Sociable C) Quiet D) Lonely
29. Harmony most nearly means: A) Discord B) Agreement C) Conflict D) Noise
30. Inhibit most nearly means: A) Encourage B) Restrain C) Help D) Support
31. Jeopardy most nearly means: A) Safety B) Danger C) Security D) Protection
32. Kinetic most nearly means: A) Still B) Moving C) Quiet D) Stable
33. Luminous most nearly means: A) Dark B) Bright C) Dull D) Hidden
34. Malevolent most nearly means: A) Kind B) Evil C) Helpful D) Generous
35. Nomadic most nearly means: A) Settled B) Wandering C) Stationary D) Fixed

Paragraph Comprehension (15 questions)

Passage 1: The Internet has revolutionized how we communicate, work, and access information. What began as a military research project has become an essential part of daily life for billions of people. Social media platforms connect friends and family across great distances, while online education makes learning accessible to anyone with an internet connection. However, this digital age also brings challenges, including privacy concerns, cyberbullying, and information overload.

1. According to the passage, the Internet originally began as: A) A social media platform B) An educational tool C) A military research project D) A communication device
2. The passage suggests that online education: A) Is only for young people B) Makes learning more accessible C) Is less effective than traditional education D) Requires expensive equipment
3. Which of the following is NOT mentioned as a challenge of the digital age? A) Privacy concerns B) Cyberbullying C) Information overload D) Lack of internet access

Passage 2: Regular exercise provides numerous health benefits beyond just physical fitness. Studies show that consistent physical activity can improve mental health by reducing symptoms of depression and anxiety. Exercise also enhances cognitive function, helping with memory and concentration. Additionally, people who exercise regularly tend to sleep better and have more energy throughout the day. The key is finding activities you enjoy, whether it's walking, swimming, dancing, or playing sports.

4. The main idea of this passage is that: A) Exercise is only good for physical health B) Exercise provides many health benefits C) Only certain types of exercise are beneficial D) Exercise is difficult to maintain
5. According to the passage, exercise can help with: A) Memory and concentration B) Only physical strength C) Sleeping problems only D) Social skills
6. The passage suggests that the most important factor in exercise is: A) Intensity B) Duration C) Cost D) Enjoyment

Passage 3: Climate change refers to long-term shifts in global temperatures and weather patterns. While climate variations are natural, scientific evidence shows that human activities have been the main driver of climate change since the 1800s. The burning of fossil fuels releases greenhouse gases that trap heat in the atmosphere. Rising temperatures affect weather patterns, ocean levels, and ecosystems worldwide. Many countries are working together to reduce greenhouse gas emissions and develop cleaner energy sources.

7. Climate change is primarily caused by: A) Natural variations only B) Human activities since the 1800s C) Ocean currents D) Solar radiation
8. Greenhouse gases: A) Cool the atmosphere B) Have no effect on temperature C) Trap heat in the atmosphere D) Only affect ocean temperatures
9. The passage indicates that addressing climate change requires: A) Individual action only B) Government regulation only C) International cooperation D) New technology only

Passage 4: The human brain is remarkably adaptable, a quality scientists call neuroplasticity. This means the brain can form new neural connections and reorganize itself throughout life. When we learn new skills or information, our brains create new pathways. This adaptability helps us recover from injuries, adapt to changes, and continue learning as we age. Brain training exercises, learning new languages, and playing musical instruments are all activities that can help maintain and improve brain function.

10. Neuroplasticity refers to: A) The brain's ability to adapt and change B) The brain's fixed structure C) Brain damage D) Memory loss
11. According to the passage, the brain forms new pathways when we: A) Sleep B) Exercise C) Learn new things D) Eat healthy food
12. Which activity is mentioned as beneficial for brain function? A) Watching television B) Playing musical instruments C) Sleeping more D) Eating certain foods

Passage 5: Renewable energy sources like solar, wind, and hydroelectric power are becoming increasingly important as alternatives to fossil fuels. These energy sources are considered "renewable" because they are naturally replenished and don't run out like coal, oil, and natural gas. Solar panels convert sunlight into electricity, wind turbines harness wind power, and hydroelectric plants use flowing water to generate energy. As technology improves and costs decrease, renewable energy is becoming more competitive with traditional energy sources.

13. Renewable energy sources are called "renewable" because they: A) Are expensive to produce B) Are naturally replenished C) Require special equipment D) Are only available in certain locations

14. According to the passage, what is happening to renewable energy costs? A) They are increasing B) They are decreasing C) They remain the same D) They are unpredictable
15. The passage mentions all of the following renewable energy sources EXCEPT: A) Solar B) Wind C) Nuclear D) Hydroelectric

Mathematics Knowledge (25 questions)

1. What is 15% of 240? A) 32 B) 36 C) 40 D) 44
2. If $x + 7 = 15$, then $x = $? A) 6 B) 7 C) 8 D) 9
3. What is the square root of 144? A) 10 B) 11 C) 12 D) 13
4. In a right triangle, if one leg is 3 and the other leg is 4, what is the hypotenuse? A) 5 B) 6 C) 7 D) 8
5. What is $2^3 \times 3^2$? A) 36 B) 48 C) 54 D) 72
6. If a circle has a diameter of 14, what is its radius? A) 6 B) 7 C) 8 D) 9
7. What is the value of 4! (4 factorial)? A) 16 B) 20 C) 24 D) 32
8. Solve for x: $3x - 9 = 12$ A) 5 B) 6 C) 7 D) 8
9. What is the area of a triangle with base 8 and height 6? A) 20 B) 24 C) 28 D) 32
10. If $2x + 5 = 3x - 2$, then $x = $? A) 5 B) 6 C) 7 D) 8
11. What is 25% of 80? A) 15 B) 18 C) 20 D) 25
12. In the equation $y = 2x + 3$, what is y when $x = 4$? A) 9 B) 10 C) 11 D) 12
13. What is the circumference of a circle with radius 5? (Use $\pi \approx 3.14$) A) 31.4 B) 15.7 C) 78.5 D) 25.12
14. If a rectangle has length 12 and width 5, what is its perimeter? A) 32 B) 34 C) 36 D) 38
15. What is the value of $|-8|$? A) -8 B) 0 C) 8 D) 16
16. Solve: $5x + 10 = 35$ A) 3 B) 4 C) 5 D) 6
17. What is $8^2 - 5^2$? A) 39 B) 41 C) 43 D) 45
18. If $a = 3$ and $b = 4$, what is $a^2 + b^2$? A) 20 B) 23 C) 25 D) 28
19. What is the slope of the line passing through (2,3) and (4,7)? A) 1 B) 2 C) 3 D) 4
20. What is $3/4 + 2/3$? A) 5/7 B) 17/12 C) 5/12 D) 11/12
21. If $\log_2(x) = 3$, then $x = $? A) 6 B) 8 C) 9 D) 12
22. What is the median of 5, 8, 3, 9, 7? A) 6 B) 7 C) 8 D) 9
23. Solve: $x^2 - 9 = 0$ A) ±2 B) ±3 C) ±4 D) ±5
24. What is $\sin(30°)$? A) 1/3 B) 1/2 C) $\sqrt{3}/2$ D) $\sqrt{2}/2$
25. If $f(x) = 2x - 1$, what is $f(5)$? A) 8 B) 9 C) 10 D) 11

Electronics Information (20 questions)

1. The unit of electrical resistance is: A) Ampere B) Volt C) Ohm D) Watt
2. Which component stores electrical energy? A) Resistor B) Capacitor C) Transistor D) Diode
3. In a parallel circuit, if one component fails: A) All components stop working B) Other components continue working C) The circuit becomes a series circuit D) Voltage increases
4. What does AC stand for? A) Automatic Current B) Alternating Current C) Additional Current D) Applied Current

5. A fuse is designed to: A) Increase current B) Store energy C) Protect against overcurrent D) Amplify signals
6. The positive terminal of a battery is called: A) Cathode B) Anode C) Electrode D) Terminal
7. What is the relationship between voltage, current, and resistance? A) $V = I \times R$ B) $V = I \div R$ C) $V = R \div I$ D) $V = I + R$
8. Which material is the best conductor of electricity? A) Rubber B) Glass C) Silver D) Wood
9. A transformer is used to: A) Store electricity B) Generate electricity C) Change voltage levels D) Measure current
10. In a series circuit, the total resistance is: A) Less than the smallest resistor B) Equal to the average of all resistors C) The sum of all resistances D) Equal to the largest resistor
11. What does LED stand for? A) Light Emitting Diode B) Low Energy Device C) Large Electronic Display D) Linear Electric Driver
12. The flow of electrons is called: A) Voltage B) Current C) Resistance D) Power
13. Which component allows current to flow in only one direction? A) Capacitor B) Resistor C) Diode D) Inductor
14. What is the unit of electrical power? A) Ampere B) Volt C) Ohm D) Watt
15. A ground wire is typically: A) Red B) Black C) White D) Green
16. The opposition to the flow of alternating current is: A) Resistance B) Reactance C) Impedance D) Conductance
17. What type of current flows from a battery? A) AC B) DC C) Both D) Neither
18. A potentiometer is a type of: A) Fixed resistor B) Variable resistor C) Capacitor D) Inductor
19. Which component can amplify signals? A) Resistor B) Capacitor C) Transistor D) Diode
20. The unit of frequency is: A) Hertz B) Ampere C) Volt D) Ohm

Auto & Shop Information (25 questions)

1. The alternator in a car: A) Starts the engine B) Charges the battery C) Controls the brakes D) Steers the wheels
2. What tool is used to measure tire pressure? A) Multimeter B) Pressure gauge C) Caliper D) Micrometer
3. The crankshaft converts: A) Electrical energy to mechanical B) Linear motion to rotational C) Chemical energy to heat D) Potential energy to kinetic
4. Which fluid is used in the brake system? A) Motor oil B) Transmission fluid C) Brake fluid D) Coolant
5. A Phillips head screwdriver has a: A) Flat tip B) Cross-shaped tip C) Hexagonal tip D) Star-shaped tip
6. The carburetor's main function is to: A) Cool the engine B) Filter air C) Mix fuel and air D) Generate electricity
7. What does MPG stand for? A) Miles Per Gallon B) Maximum Power Generated C) Motor Performance Grade D) Minimum Pressure Gauge
8. A socket wrench is used with: A) Screws B) Bolts and nuts C) Nails D) Rivets
9. The radiator in a car: A) Generates power B) Stores fuel C) Cools the engine D) Filters oil

10. What is the purpose of a spark plug? A) Cool the engine B) Ignite the fuel mixture C) Filter air D) Pump fuel
11. Which tool is used to cut metal? A) Wood saw B) Hacksaw C) Coping saw D) Jigsaw
12. The differential allows: A) Steering B) Braking C) Wheels to turn at different speeds D) Engine cooling
13. What type of joint is created by welding? A) Temporary B) Adjustable C) Permanent D) Flexible
14. The transmission: A) Starts the engine B) Steers the car C) Changes gear ratios D) Cools the engine
15. A torque wrench is used to: A) Remove bolts B) Tighten bolts to specific tension C) Cut threads D) Measure angles
16. What does the thermostat control? A) Fuel flow B) Air flow C) Coolant flow D) Oil flow
17. Sandpaper grit numbers indicate: A) Size of abrasive particles B) Type of material C) Color of paper D) Strength of backing
18. The exhaust system: A) Brings air into the engine B) Removes waste gases C) Cools the engine D) Stores fuel
19. A center punch is used to: A) Cut holes B) Make starting marks for drilling C) Measure distances D) File metal
20. What is the function of motor oil? A) Clean the air filter B) Lubricate engine parts C) Cool the radiator D) Charge the battery
21. Which tool measures small distances accurately? A) Ruler B) Tape measure C) Caliper D) Level
22. The starter motor: A) Charges the battery B) Cranks the engine C) Controls idle speed D) Filters fuel
23. What does "torque" refer to? A) Speed B) Twisting force C) Pressure D) Temperature
24. A ball-peen hammer has: A) Two flat faces B) A flat face and rounded face C) A claw D) A cross-shaped face
25. The fuel pump: A) Filters fuel B) Burns fuel C) Delivers fuel to the engine D) Stores fuel

Mechanical Comprehension (25 questions)

1. If a 10-pound weight is placed 2 feet from the fulcrum of a lever, how much weight is needed 4 feet on the other side to balance it? A) 5 pounds B) 10 pounds C) 15 pounds D) 20 pounds
2. Which pulley system provides the greatest mechanical advantage? A) Fixed pulley B) Movable pulley C) Block and tackle D) Single pulley
3. In a gear system, if the driving gear has 20 teeth and the driven gear has 40 teeth, the driven gear will turn: A) Twice as fast B) Half as fast C) At the same speed D) Four times as fast
4. Water pressure increases with: A) Temperature B) Depth C) Surface area D) Container size
5. A screw is essentially a: A) Lever B) Pulley C) Inclined plane D) Wedge
6. If you increase the length of a lever arm, you: A) Decrease mechanical advantage B) Increase mechanical advantage C) Have no effect D) Double the weight

7. In a hydraulic system, if the input piston has an area of 1 square inch and the output piston has an area of 10 square inches, a force of 10 pounds on the input will produce how much force on the output? A) 1 pound B) 10 pounds C) 100 pounds D) 1000 pounds
8. The mechanical advantage of an inclined plane is determined by: A) Its height B) Its length C) The ratio of length to height D) Its width
9. When a force is applied to move an object up an inclined plane: A) Less force is needed but greater distance B) More force is needed but less distance C) Same force and distance D) No force is needed
10. In a wheel and axle, if the wheel has a radius of 6 inches and the axle has a radius of 2 inches, the mechanical advantage is: A) 2 B) 3 C) 4 D) 6
11. Which simple machine is a doorknob an example of? A) Lever B) Pulley C) Wheel and axle D) Inclined plane
12. If two gears are meshed together, they rotate in: A) The same direction B) Opposite directions C) Random directions D) No direction
13. The center of gravity of an object is: A) Always at its geometric center B) The point where it balances C) The heaviest point D) The lightest point
14. In a compound pulley system with 4 supporting ropes, the mechanical advantage is: A) 2 B) 4 C) 6 D) 8
15. A wedge works by: A) Rotating motion B) Converting downward force to sideways force C) Lifting objects D) Storing energy
16. The efficiency of a machine is always: A) Greater than 100% B) Equal to 100% C) Less than 100% D) Variable
17. If a machine has a mechanical advantage of 4 and you apply 25 pounds of force, the output force is: A) 25 pounds B) 50 pounds C) 75 pounds D) 100 pounds
18. In a first-class lever: A) The fulcrum is between the effort and load B) The load is between the fulcrum and effort C) The effort is between the fulcrum and load D) All three are at the same point
19. The amount of work done is calculated by: A) Force × Time B) Force × Distance C) Mass × Acceleration D) Power × Time
20. If you push with 50 pounds of force through a distance of 10 feet, the work done is: A) 5 foot-pounds B) 50 foot-pounds C) 500 foot-pounds D) 5000 foot-pounds
21. A nail is an example of a: A) Lever B) Screw C) Wedge D) Pulley
22. In a second-class lever: A) The fulcrum is between the effort and load B) The load is between the fulcrum and effort C) The effort is between the fulcrum and load D) The mechanical advantage is always 1
23. The force needed to overcome friction depends on: A) The speed of movement B) The normal force and coefficient of friction C) The size of the object D) The temperature
24. A fixed pulley changes: A) The amount of force needed B) The direction of force C) Both force and direction D) Neither force nor direction
25. Power is defined as: A) Force × Distance B) Work ÷ Time C) Mass × Velocity D) Energy × Time

Answer Key - Test 12

General Science:

1. D 2. B 3. B 4. C 5. C 6. B 7. C 8. C 9. A 10. C
2. C 12. B 13. B 14. C 15. D 16. C 17. B 18. B 19. B 20. C
3. C 22. D 23. B 24. C 25. B

Arithmetic Reasoning:

1. A 2. B 3. B 4. A 5. B 6. B 7. A 8. B 9. A 10. A
2. B 12. B 13. C 14. B 15. A 16. B 17. C 18. B 19. B 20. D
3. A 22. B 23. B 24. C 25. A 26. C 27. B 28. B 29. C 30. C

Word Knowledge:

1. B 2. B 3. C 4. B 5. B 6. C 7. C 8. B 9. C 10. B
2. C 12. C 13. B 14. C 15. B 16. C 17. B 18. C 19. B 20. B
3. B 22. B 23. B 24. B 25. C 26. B 27. B 28. B 29. B 30. B
4. B 32. B 33. B 34. B 35. B

Paragraph Comprehension:

1. C 2. B 3. D 4. B 5. A 6. D 7. B 8. C 9. C 10. A
2. C 12. B 13. B 14. B 15. C

Mathematics Knowledge:

1. B 2. C 3. C 4. A 5. D 6. B 7. C 8. C 9. B 10. C
2. C 12. C 13. A 14. B 15. C 16. C 17. A 18. C 19. B 20. B
3. B 22. B 23. B 24. B 25. B

Electronics Information:

1. C 2. B 3. B 4. B 5. C 6. B 7. A 8. C 9. C 10. C
2. A 12. B 13. C 14. D 15. D 16. C 17. B 18. B 19. C 20. A

Auto & Shop Information:

1. B 2. B 3. B 4. C 5. B 6. C 7. A 8. B 9. C 10. B
2. B 12. C 13. C 14. C 15. B 16. C 17. A 18. B 19. B 20. B
3. C 22. B 23. B 24. B 25. C

Mechanical Comprehension:

1. A 2. C 3. B 4. B 5. C 6. B 7. C 8. C 9. A 10. B
2. C 12. B 13. B 14. B 15. B 16. C 17. D 18. A 19. B 20. C
3. C 22. B 23. B 24. B 25. B

Test 13

General Science (25 questions)

1. What is the main gas found in the air we breathe? A) Oxygen B) Carbon dioxide C) Nitrogen D) Hydrogen
2. Which planet is known as the "Red Planet"? A) Venus B) Mars C) Jupiter D) Saturn
3. What is the process called when a liquid turns into a gas? A) Condensation B) Evaporation C) Sublimation D) Freezing
4. The human heart has how many chambers? A) 2 B) 3 C) 4 D) 5
5. What is the chemical formula for water? A) H_2O B) CO_2 C) NaCl D) O_2
6. Which type of blood cell fights infection? A) Red blood cells B) White blood cells C) Platelets D) Plasma
7. The Earth's core is primarily made of: A) Rock B) Ice C) Iron and nickel D) Gas
8. What is the smallest bone in the human body? A) Femur B) Tibia C) Stapes D) Radius
9. Which gas is essential for photosynthesis? A) Oxygen B) Nitrogen C) Carbon dioxide D) Hydrogen
10. The study of heredity is called: A) Biology B) Genetics C) Anatomy D) Physiology
11. What causes lightning? A) Wind B) Rain C) Electrical discharge D) Temperature changes
12. Which organ filters waste from the blood? A) Liver B) Heart C) Kidney D) Lungs
13. The speed of sound in air is approximately: A) 186,000 miles/sec B) 1,100 feet/sec C) 300,000 km/sec D) 500 mph
14. What is the most abundant element in the universe? A) Oxygen B) Carbon C) Hydrogen D) Helium
15. Which part of the eye controls the amount of light entering? A) Cornea B) Lens C) Iris D) Retina
16. The process by which rocks are broken down by weather is: A) Erosion B) Weathering C) Sedimentation D) Metamorphism
17. What is the normal range for human blood pressure? A) 80/40 B) 120/80 C) 160/100 D) 200/120
18. Which scientist developed the theory of evolution? A) Einstein B) Newton C) Darwin D) Galileo
19. The ozone layer protects Earth from: A) Meteorites B) Cold temperatures C) Ultraviolet radiation D) Cosmic rays
20. What is the hardest substance in the human body? A) Bone B) Tooth enamel C) Cartilage D) Nail
21. The process of cell division is called: A) Meiosis B) Mitosis C) Both A and B D) Neither A nor B
22. Which element is essential for healthy bones and teeth? A) Iron B) Calcium C) Potassium D) Sodium
23. The asteroid belt is located between: A) Earth and Mars B) Mars and Jupiter C) Jupiter and Saturn D) Saturn and Uranus
24. What is the function of hemoglobin? A) Fight infection B) Carry oxygen C) Clot blood D) Digest food

25. The greenhouse effect is caused by: A) Water vapor B) Carbon dioxide C) Methane D) All of the above

Arithmetic Reasoning (30 questions)

1. A store sells apples for $1.20 per pound. How much do 3.5 pounds cost? A) $4.00 B) $4.20 C) $4.40 D) $4.60
2. If a rectangle has a length of 12 feet and width of 7 feet, what is its perimeter? A) 19 feet B) 38 feet C) 84 feet D) 42 feet
3. Tom scored 85%, 92%, and 78% on three tests. What is his average score? A) 83% B) 85% C) 87% D) 89%
4. A car travels 280 miles using 14 gallons of gas. How many miles per gallon does it get? A) 18 mpg B) 20 mpg C) 22 mpg D) 24 mpg
5. If 12 pencils cost $3.60, what is the cost per pencil? A) $0.25 B) $0.30 C) $0.35 D) $0.40
6. A pizza has 8 slices. If you eat 3 slices, what fraction of the pizza is left? A) 3/8 B) 5/8 C) 1/2 D) 2/3
7. The temperature rose from 65°F to 82°F. What was the increase? A) 15°F B) 17°F C) 19°F D) 21°F
8. If 4 workers can paint a fence in 6 hours, how long will it take 3 workers? A) 6 hours B) 7 hours C) 8 hours D) 9 hours
9. A shirt costs $25. With a 20% discount, what is the sale price? A) $18 B) $20 C) $22 D) $24
10. If x - 8 = 15, what is x? A) 7 B) 15 C) 23 D) 25
11. A circular garden has a radius of 4 feet. What is its area? (Use π = 3.14) A) 25.12 sq ft B) 50.24 sq ft C) 12.56 sq ft D) 100.48 sq ft
12. The ratio of boys to girls in a class is 2:3. If there are 8 boys, how many girls are there? A) 10 B) 12 C) 14 D) 16
13. If you save $50 per month for 18 months, how much will you have saved? A) $800 B) $850 C) $900 D) $950
14. A ladder 13 feet long leans against a wall. The bottom is 5 feet from the wall. How high up the wall does it reach? A) 8 feet B) 10 feet C) 12 feet D) 15 feet
15. What is 15% of 160? A) 20 B) 22 C) 24 D) 26
16. If a train travels 450 miles in 6 hours, what is its average speed? A) 70 mph B) 75 mph C) 80 mph D) 85 mph
17. The sum of two numbers is 45. If one number is 18, what is the other? A) 25 B) 27 C) 29 D) 31
18. A rectangle has an area of 72 square feet and a width of 8 feet. What is its length? A) 8 feet B) 9 feet C) 10 feet D) 12 feet
19. If 3x + 7 = 22, what is x? A) 3 B) 5 C) 7 D) 9
20. A box contains 24 items. If 1/3 are defective, how many are good? A) 8 B) 12 C) 16 D) 18
21. The price of gas increased from $2.40 to $2.88 per gallon. What was the percent increase? A) 15% B) 18% C) 20% D) 25%
22. If you buy 5 items at $3.25 each and 3 items at $2.50 each, what is the total cost? A) $22.50 B) $23.75 C) $24.00 D) $24.25

23. A number decreased by 30% becomes 42. What was the original number? A) 54 B) 58 C) 60 D) 64
24. If a machine produces 180 parts in 9 hours, how many parts does it produce per hour? A) 18 B) 20 C) 22 D) 24
25. The average of 4 numbers is 28. If three numbers are 25, 30, and 32, what is the fourth number? A) 21 B) 23 C) 25 D) 27
26. A swimming pool is 25 meters long and 15 meters wide. What is its perimeter? A) 70 meters B) 80 meters C) 90 meters D) 100 meters
27. If 2/5 of a number is 18, what is the number? A) 36 B) 40 C) 42 D) 45
28. A store marks up items 40% above cost. If an item costs $15, what is the selling price? A) $19 B) $21 C) $23 D) $25
29. The perimeter of a square is 36 inches. What is its area? A) 64 sq in B) 81 sq in C) 100 sq in D) 121 sq in
30. If a discount of 25% saves $12, what was the original price? A) $44 B) $48 C) $52 D) $56

Word Knowledge (35 questions)

1. Adequate most nearly means: A) Insufficient B) Sufficient C) Excessive D) Minimal
2. Belligerent most nearly means: A) Peaceful B) Hostile C) Friendly D) Calm
3. Conspicuous most nearly means: A) Hidden B) Obvious C) Quiet D) Small
4. Durable most nearly means: A) Fragile B) Temporary C) Lasting D) Weak
5. Enhance most nearly means: A) Reduce B) Improve C) Damage D) Ignore
6. Feasible most nearly means: A) Impossible B) Possible C) Difficult D) Easy
7. Gracious most nearly means: A) Rude B) Kind C) Harsh D) Selfish
8. Hostile most nearly means: A) Friendly B) Unfriendly C) Neutral D) Helpful
9. Imminent most nearly means: A) Distant B) Approaching C) Past D) Unlikely
10. Jeopardize most nearly means: A) Protect B) Endanger C) Help D) Support
11. Kindle most nearly means: A) Extinguish B) Ignite C) Cool D) Freeze
12. Lucid most nearly means: A) Confused B) Clear C) Dark D) Complicated
13. Meticulous most nearly means: A) Careless B) Careful C) Quick D) Slow
14. Notable most nearly means: A) Ordinary B) Remarkable C) Hidden D) Small
15. Optimistic most nearly means: A) Pessimistic B) Hopeful C) Worried D) Sad
16. Persistent most nearly means: A) Giving up B) Determined C) Lazy D) Weak
17. Quarantine most nearly means: A) Release B) Isolate C) Mix D) Combine
18. Reluctant most nearly means: A) Eager B) Unwilling C) Happy D) Excited
19. Sturdy most nearly means: A) Weak B) Strong C) Flexible D) Soft
20. Timid most nearly means: A) Bold B) Shy C) Loud D) Confident
21. Universal most nearly means: A) Local B) General C) Specific D) Limited
22. Vivid most nearly means: A) Dull B) Bright C) Dark D) Pale
23. Wary most nearly means: A) Careless B) Cautious C) Trusting D) Naive
24. Yearn most nearly means: A) Reject B) Long for C) Ignore D) Forget
25. Zeal most nearly means: A) Laziness B) Enthusiasm C) Boredom D) Indifference
26. Abrupt most nearly means: A) Gradual B) Sudden C) Slow D) Smooth
27. Benign most nearly means: A) Harmful B) Harmless C) Dangerous D) Threatening
28. Cordial most nearly means: A) Cold B) Warm C) Angry D) Sad

29. Diverse most nearly means: A) Similar B) Varied C) Same D) Identical
30. Elaborate most nearly means: A) Simple B) Detailed C) Plain D) Basic
31. Flourish most nearly means: A) Decline B) Thrive C) Fail D) Wither
32. Generous most nearly means: A) Selfish B) Giving C) Greedy D) Stingy
33. Humble most nearly means: A) Proud B) Modest C) Arrogant D) Boastful
34. Illusion most nearly means: A) Reality B) Deception C) Truth D) Fact
35. Jovial most nearly means: A) Sad B) Cheerful C) Angry D) Worried

Paragraph Comprehension (15 questions)

Passage 1: Sleep plays a crucial role in physical and mental health. During sleep, the body repairs tissues, consolidates memories, and releases important hormones. Adults typically need 7-9 hours of sleep per night, while teenagers require 8-10 hours. Poor sleep quality can lead to weakened immune function, difficulty concentrating, and increased risk of chronic diseases. Maintaining good sleep hygiene, such as keeping a regular sleep schedule and avoiding screens before bedtime, can improve sleep quality.

1. According to the passage, adults typically need: A) 6-8 hours of sleep B) 7-9 hours of sleep C) 8-10 hours of sleep D) 9-11 hours of sleep
2. Poor sleep quality can lead to: A) Better concentration B) Stronger immune function C) Weakened immune function D) Decreased disease risk
3. The passage suggests that good sleep hygiene includes: A) Using screens before bed B) Irregular sleep schedules C) Avoiding screens before bedtime D) Sleeping less than 6 hours

Passage 2: Recycling is an important environmental practice that helps reduce waste and conserve natural resources. When materials like paper, plastic, glass, and metal are recycled, they can be processed and made into new products rather than being sent to landfills. This process saves energy, reduces pollution, and helps preserve raw materials for future generations. Many communities have established recycling programs to make it easier for residents to participate in this environmental effort.

4. The main purpose of recycling is to: A) Create jobs B) Reduce waste and conserve resources C) Make money D) Increase pollution
5. According to the passage, recycling helps: A) Increase waste B) Waste energy C) Save energy D) Damage the environment
6. Recycling programs are established to: A) Make recycling more difficult B) Make recycling easier for residents C) Increase landfill use D) Reduce community involvement

Passage 3: The invention of the printing press in the 15th century revolutionized the spread of information. Before the printing press, books were hand-copied by scribes, making them expensive and rare. Johannes Gutenberg's printing press allowed books to be produced quickly and cheaply, leading to increased literacy rates and the rapid spread of ideas. This innovation played a crucial role in the Renaissance, the Reformation, and the Scientific Revolution.

7. Before the printing press, books were: A) Printed by machines B) Hand-copied by scribes C) Not available D) Free to everyone
8. The printing press allowed books to be: A) More expensive B) Produced quickly and cheaply C) Hand-written only D) Available to scribes only
9. The passage states that the printing press played a role in: A) Only the Renaissance B) The Renaissance, Reformation, and Scientific Revolution C) Only the Reformation D) Only the Scientific Revolution

Passage 4: Physical exercise has numerous benefits for mental health. Regular physical activity can reduce symptoms of depression and anxiety, improve mood, and boost self-esteem. Exercise releases endorphins, which are natural mood elevators, and can also improve sleep quality and cognitive function. Even moderate activities like walking, swimming, or dancing can provide these mental health benefits. Health experts recommend at least 150 minutes of moderate exercise per week.

10. Exercise releases chemicals called: A) Antibodies B) Endorphins C) Hormones D) Proteins
11. According to the passage, exercise can improve: A) Only physical health B) Only mental health C) Both physical and mental health D) Neither physical nor mental health
12. Health experts recommend: A) 150 minutes of moderate exercise per week B) 150 minutes of intense exercise per day C) 50 minutes of exercise per week D) No specific amount of exercise

Passage 5: Wind energy is a clean, renewable source of power that harnesses the kinetic energy of moving air. Wind turbines convert this energy into electricity through rotating blades that turn a generator. Wind farms, consisting of multiple turbines, are often located in areas with consistent wind patterns, such as coastal regions or open plains. As technology advances, wind energy is becoming more efficient and cost-effective, making it an increasingly important part of the global energy mix.

13. Wind turbines convert wind energy into electricity using: A) Solar panels B) Rotating blades and generators C) Water wheels D) Steam engines
14. Wind farms are typically located: A) In cities B) Underground C) In areas with consistent wind patterns D) In forests
15. The passage suggests that wind energy is: A) Becoming less efficient B) Becoming more efficient and cost-effective C) Only useful in certain seasons D) Harmful to the environment

Mathematics Knowledge (25 questions)

1. What is 20% of 150? A) 25 B) 30 C) 35 D) 40
2. Solve for x: $x + 12 = 25$ A) 11 B) 12 C) 13 D) 14
3. What is the square root of 169? A) 12 B) 13 C) 14 D) 15
4. If a right triangle has legs of 5 and 12, what is the hypotenuse? A) 13 B) 14 C) 15 D) 16
5. What is 3^4? A) 64 B) 81 C) 100 D) 125
6. A circle has a radius of 6. What is its diameter? A) 10 B) 12 C) 14 D) 16

7. What is 6! (6 factorial)? A) 120 B) 360 C) 720 D) 1440
8. Solve: 4x + 8 = 28 A) 4 B) 5 C) 6 D) 7
9. What is the area of a rectangle with length 9 and width 7? A) 56 B) 63 C) 70 D) 77
10. If 3x - 6 = 2x + 4, then x = ? A) 8 B) 10 C) 12 D) 14
11. What is 30% of 120? A) 30 B) 36 C) 40 D) 45
12. In y = 3x - 2, what is y when x = 5? A) 11 B) 13 C) 15 D) 17
13. What is the area of a circle with radius 4? (Use $\pi \approx 3.14$) A) 50.24 B) 25.12 C) 12.56 D) 100.48
14. A square has a perimeter of 28. What is its area? A) 49 B) 56 C) 64 D) 81
15. What is |-12|? A) -12 B) 0 C) 12 D) 24
16. Solve: 6x - 15 = 21 A) 4 B) 5 C) 6 D) 7
17. What is $9^2 + 4^2$? A) 97 B) 85 C) 81 D) 65
18. If a = 2 and b = 5, what is 3a + 2b? A) 16 B) 18 C) 20 D) 22
19. What is the slope of the line through (1,2) and (3,8)? A) 2 B) 3 C) 4 D) 5
20. What is 2/3 + 1/4? A) 3/7 B) 11/12 C) 5/12 D) 7/12
21. If $\log_3(x) = 2$, then x = ? A) 6 B) 8 C) 9 D) 12
22. What is the mode of 3, 7, 5, 7, 9, 7, 4? A) 5 B) 6 C) 7 D) 9
23. Solve: $x^2 - 16 = 0$ A) ±3 B) ±4 C) ±5 D) ±6
24. What is cos(60°)? A) 1/2 B) √3/2 C) √2/2 D) 1
25. If g(x) = 3x + 4, what is g(2)? A) 8 B) 10 C) 12 D) 14

Electronics Information (20 questions)

1. What is the unit of electrical current? A) Volt B) Ampere C) Ohm D) Watt
2. A device that opposes the flow of current is a: A) Capacitor B) Resistor C) Inductor D) Transformer
3. In a series circuit, the current is: A) Different through each component B) The same through all components C) Zero D) Infinite
4. What does DC stand for? A) Direct Current B) Dynamic Current C) Dual Current D) Digital Current
5. A circuit breaker is designed to: A) Increase voltage B) Store energy C) Protect against overcurrent D) Amplify signals
6. The negative terminal of a battery is called: A) Anode B) Cathode C) Electrode D) Terminal
7. Power is calculated as: A) $P = V \times I$ B) $P = V \div I$ C) $P = I \div V$ D) $P = V + I$
8. Which material is an insulator? A) Copper B) Silver C) Rubber D) Aluminum
9. An inductor stores energy in: A) Electric field B) Magnetic field C) Both fields D) Neither field
10. In a parallel circuit, the voltage across each branch is: A) Different B) The same C) Zero D) Infinite
11. What does CRT stand for? A) Current Resistance Technology B) Cathode Ray Tube C) Computer Related Terminal D) Circuit Resistance Tester
12. The rate of flow of electric charge is: A) Voltage B) Current C) Resistance D) Power
13. A semiconductor allows current to flow: A) Always B) Never C) Under certain conditions D) Only in AC circuits
14. What is the unit of inductance? A) Farad B) Henry C) Coulomb D) Tesla

15. A hot wire in household wiring is typically: A) Green B) White C) Black D) Blue
16. What is impedance? A) AC resistance B) DC resistance C) Capacitance D) Inductance
17. A rectifier converts: A) AC to DC B) DC to AC C) Low voltage to high voltage D) High voltage to low voltage
18. A rheostat is used to: A) Measure current B) Control current C) Store energy D) Generate electricity
19. What amplifies electrical signals? A) Resistor B) Capacitor C) Amplifier D) Inductor
20. The unit of capacitance is: A) Henry B) Farad C) Ohm D) Volt

Auto & Shop Information (25 questions)

1. The battery in a car provides: A) Mechanical power B) Electrical power C) Hydraulic power D) Pneumatic power
2. What tool is used to remove lug nuts from wheels? A) Screwdriver B) Lug wrench C) Pliers D) Hammer
3. The pistons in an engine move: A) In circles B) Up and down C) Side to side D) Diagonally
4. Which system stops the car? A) Steering B) Suspension C) Brake D) Exhaust
5. A flathead screwdriver has a: A) Cross-shaped tip B) Star-shaped tip C) Flat tip D) Hexagonal tip
6. The fuel injection system: A) Cools the engine B) Delivers fuel to cylinders C) Filters air D) Removes exhaust
7. What does ABS stand for? A) Auto Brake System B) Anti-lock Brake System C) Advanced Brake System D) Automatic Brake System
8. A wrench is used to: A) Cut materials B) Turn nuts and bolts C) Measure distances D) Mark materials
9. The muffler is part of the: A) Engine B) Transmission C) Exhaust system D) Cooling system
10. What ignites the fuel in the cylinder? A) Fuel injector B) Spark plug C) Piston D) Valve
11. Which saw is used for cutting curves? A) Circular saw B) Hacksaw C) Jigsaw D) Table saw
12. The clutch is found in: A) Automatic transmissions B) Manual transmissions C) Both transmissions D) Neither transmission
13. Brazing joins metals using: A) Mechanical fasteners B) Heat and filler metal C) Glue D) Pressure only
14. The cooling system prevents: A) Fuel leaks B) Engine overheating C) Electrical problems D) Brake failure
15. A level is used to: A) Measure weight B) Check if surfaces are horizontal C) Cut materials D) Drive screws
16. What controls the flow of coolant? A) Water pump B) Thermostat C) Radiator D) Fan
17. Different sandpaper grits are used for: A) Different colors B) Different materials only C) Different levels of roughness D) Different tools
18. The muffler: A) Increases engine power B) Reduces exhaust noise C) Filters fuel D) Cools the engine
19. A chisel is used to: A) Measure angles B) Cut or shape materials C) Join materials D) Lift heavy objects

20. Engine oil: A) Cools the radiator B) Lubricates moving parts C) Powers the alternator D) Filters air
21. Which tool provides the most accurate measurement? A) Ruler B) Tape measure C) Micrometer D) Level
22. The flywheel: A) Steers the car B) Smooths engine operation C) Cools the engine D) Filters oil
23. "Horsepower" measures: A) Vehicle weight B) Engine power C) Fuel efficiency D) Top speed
24. A file is used to: A) Join materials B) Smooth and shape materials C) Measure thickness D) Mark locations
25. The power steering system: A) Makes steering easier B) Stops the car C) Cools the engine D) Charges the battery

Mechanical Comprehension (25 questions)

1. A lever with a mechanical advantage of 3 means: A) Input force is tripled B) Output force is tripled C) Distance is tripled D) Speed is tripled
2. Which type of pulley changes only the direction of force? A) Fixed pulley B) Movable pulley C) Compound pulley D) Block and tackle
3. If a gear with 30 teeth drives a gear with 15 teeth, the smaller gear turns: A) Half as fast B) Twice as fast C) Three times as fast D) At the same speed
4. Pressure in a liquid increases with: A) Temperature only B) Depth only C) Both temperature and depth D) Neither temperature nor depth
5. A bolt is a type of: A) Lever B) Inclined plane C) Wedge D) Screw
6. Increasing the effort distance in a lever: A) Decreases mechanical advantage B) Increases mechanical advantage C) Has no effect D) Doubles the load
7. In a hydraulic jack, if the input area is 2 sq in and output area is 20 sq in, what is the mechanical advantage? A) 5 B) 10 C) 15 D) 20
8. The mechanical advantage of a ramp depends on: A) Its height only B) Its length only C) The ratio of length to height D) Its width only
9. An inclined plane reduces: A) The work needed B) The force needed C) Both work and force D) Neither work nor force
10. A wheel with radius 8 inches connected to an axle with radius 2 inches has a mechanical advantage of: A) 2 B) 4 C) 6 D) 8
11. A screwdriver is an example of a: A) Lever B) Pulley C) Wheel and axle D) Inclined plane
12. Two meshing gears always turn: A) In the same direction B) In opposite directions C) At the same speed D) Randomly
13. An object's center of gravity is: A) Always at its top B) The point where it balances C) Always at its bottom D) Its heaviest point
14. A pulley system with 6 supporting ropes has a mechanical advantage of: A) 3 B) 6 C) 9 D) 12
15. A knife blade works as a: A) Lever B) Pulley C) Wedge D) Screw
16. Real machines have efficiency: A) Greater than 100% B) Equal to 100% C) Less than 100% D) That varies randomly

17. If you apply 30 pounds of force to a machine with mechanical advantage 5, the output force is: A) 6 pounds B) 25 pounds C) 35 pounds D) 150 pounds
18. In a third-class lever: A) The fulcrum is between effort and load B) The load is between fulcrum and effort C) The effort is between fulcrum and load D) All points are the same
19. Work equals: A) Force + Distance B) Force - Distance C) Force × Distance D) Force ÷ Distance
20. If you apply 40 pounds through 8 feet, the work done is: A) 5 foot-pounds B) 48 foot-pounds C) 320 foot-pounds D) 360 foot-pounds
21. An axe is an example of a: A) Lever B) Screw C) Wedge D) Pulley
22. In a first-class lever, the mechanical advantage can be: A) Less than 1 B) Equal to 1 C) Greater than 1 D) All of the above
23. Friction force depends on: A) Speed only B) Surface area only C) Normal force and surface type D) Temperature only
24. A movable pulley provides: A) Force advantage only B) Distance advantage only C) Both force and distance advantage D) Direction change only
25. Power equals: A) Work × Time B) Work ÷ Time C) Force × Time D) Energy ÷ Distance

Answer Key - Test 13

General Science:

1. C 2. B 3. B 4. C 5. A 6. B 7. C 8. C 9. C 10. B
2. C 12. C 13. B 14. C 15. C 16. B 17. B 18. C 19. C 20. B
3. C 22. B 23. B 24. B 25. D

Arithmetic Reasoning:

1. B 2. B 3. B 4. B 5. B 6. B 7. B 8. C 9. B 10. C
2. B 12. B 13. C 14. C 15. C 16. B 17. B 18. B 19. B 20. C
3. C 22. B 23. C 24. B 25. B 26. B 27. D 28. B 29. B 30. B

Word Knowledge:

1. B 2. B 3. B 4. C 5. B 6. B 7. B 8. B 9. B 10. B
2. B 12. B 13. B 14. B 15. B 16. B 17. B 18. B 19. B 20. B
3. B 22. B 23. B 24. B 25. B 26. B 27. B 28. B 29. B 30. B
4. B 32. B 33. B 34. B 35. B

Paragraph Comprehension:

1. B 2. C 3. C 4. B 5. C 6. B 7. B 8. B 9. B 10. B
2. C 12. A 13. B 14. C 15. B

Mathematics Knowledge:

1. B 2. C 3. B 4. A 5. B 6. B 7. C 8. B 9. B 10. B

2. B 12. B 13. A 14. A 15. C 16. C 17. A 18. A 19. B 20. B
3. C 22. C 23. B 24. A 25. B

Electronics Information:

1. B 2. B 3. B 4. A 5. C 6. B 7. A 8. C 9. B 10. B
2. B 12. B 13. C 14. B 15. C 16. A 17. A 18. B 19. C 20. B

Auto & Shop Information:

1. B 2. B 3. B 4. C 5. C 6. B 7. B 8. B 9. C 10. B
2. C 12. B 13. B 14. B 15. B 16. B 17. C 18. B 19. B 20. B
3. C 22. B 23. B 24. B 25. A

Mechanical Comprehension:

1. B 2. A 3. B 4. B 5. D 6. B 7. B 8. C 9. B 10. B
2. C 12. B 13. B 14. B 15. C 16. C 17. D 18. C 19. C 20. C
3. C 22. D 23. C 24. A 25. B

Test 14

General Science (25 questions)

1. What is the chemical symbol for sodium? A) So B) S C) Na D) N
2. Which layer of the atmosphere contains the ozone layer? A) Troposphere B) Stratosphere C) Mesosphere D) Thermosphere
3. The process of splitting atoms is called: A) Fusion B) Fission C) Combustion D) Oxidation
4. How many pairs of chromosomes do humans have? A) 21 B) 22 C) 23 D) 24
5. What gas do plants absorb during photosynthesis? A) Oxygen B) Nitrogen C) Carbon dioxide D) Hydrogen
6. The largest planet in our solar system is: A) Saturn B) Jupiter C) Neptune D) Uranus
7. Which bone protects the brain? A) Femur B) Ribs C) Skull D) Spine
8. The study of fossils is called: A) Geology B) Paleontology C) Archaeology D) Biology
9. What is the main component of the sun? A) Helium B) Oxygen C) Hydrogen D) Carbon
10. Which blood type is the universal recipient? A) A B) B C) O D) AB
11. Lightning is caused by: A) Static electricity B) Magnetism C) Gravity D) Heat
12. The smallest unit of life is: A) Organ B) Tissue C) Cell D) Atom
13. What is the boiling point of water at sea level? A) 100°C B) 90°C C) 110°C D) 120°C
14. Which vitamin prevents scurvy? A) Vitamin A B) Vitamin B C) Vitamin C D) Vitamin D
15. The force that pulls objects toward Earth is: A) Magnetism B) Friction C) Gravity D) Inertia
16. What type of rock is formed from sediments? A) Igneous B) Metamorphic C) Sedimentary D) Volcanic

17. The human body has how many lungs? A) 1 B) 2 C) 3 D) 4
18. Which planet is closest to Earth? A) Mars B) Venus C) Mercury D) Jupiter
19. The pH scale measures: A) Temperature B) Pressure C) Acidity D) Density
20. What is the largest organ inside the human body? A) Brain B) Heart C) Liver D) Kidneys
21. Sound travels fastest through: A) Air B) Water C) Steel D) Vacuum
22. The process where water vapor becomes liquid is: A) Evaporation B) Condensation C) Sublimation D) Precipitation
23. Which element has the symbol Fe? A) Fluorine B) Iron C) Lead D) Gold
24. The Earth rotates on its axis once every: A) 12 hours B) 24 hours C) 48 hours D) 72 hours
25. What is the hardest mineral on Earth? A) Quartz B) Topaz C) Diamond D) Sapphire

Arithmetic Reasoning (30 questions)

1. A book costs $16.80. If the sales tax is 5%, what is the total cost? A) $17.64 B) $17.80 C) $18.00 D) $18.24
2. If a car travels 315 miles in 7 hours, what is its average speed? A) 40 mph B) 45 mph C) 50 mph D) 55 mph
3. Jenny bought 4 shirts at $12.50 each and 2 pairs of pants at $18.75 each. What was her total cost? A) $87.50 B) $90.00 C) $92.50 D) $95.00
4. A rectangular room is 14 feet long and 10 feet wide. How many square feet of carpet are needed? A) 120 B) 140 C) 160 D) 180
5. If 8 oranges cost $3.20, how much do 15 oranges cost? A) $5.60 B) $6.00 C) $6.40 D) $6.80
6. The temperature dropped from 78°F to 61°F. What was the decrease? A) 15°F B) 17°F C) 19°F D) 21°F
7. If $x + 15 = 32$, what is x? A) 15 B) 17 C) 19 D) 21
8. A pizza is divided into 12 equal slices. If 5 slices are eaten, what fraction remains? A) 5/12 B) 7/12 C) 1/2 D) 2/3
9. Sarah earns $14 per hour and works 28 hours. How much does she earn? A) $392 B) $420 C) $448 D) $476
10. If a rectangle has a perimeter of 32 feet and a length of 10 feet, what is its width? A) 4 feet B) 6 feet C) 8 feet D) 10 feet
11. What is 25% of 240? A) 50 B) 55 C) 60 D) 65
12. A train travels 420 miles in 6 hours. How far will it travel in 9 hours at the same speed? A) 580 miles B) 600 miles C) 620 miles D) 630 miles
13. The sum of three consecutive even numbers is 48. What is the middle number? A) 14 B) 16 C) 18 D) 20
14. If 3/5 of a number is 24, what is the number? A) 35 B) 40 C) 45 D) 50
15. A ladder 17 feet long leans against a wall. If the bottom is 8 feet from the wall, how high up does it reach? A) 12 feet B) 13 feet C) 15 feet D) 16 feet
16. Mike's test scores are 88, 92, 85, and 91. What is his average? A) 88 B) 89 C) 90 D) 91
17. If you buy 6 items for $4.25 each and get a 10% discount, what do you pay? A) $22.95 B) $23.50 C) $24.00 D) $25.50
18. A swimming pool is being filled at 120 gallons per hour. How long will it take to fill an 8,400-gallon pool? A) 65 hours B) 70 hours C) 75 hours D) 80 hours

19. If 4x - 12 = 20, what is x? A) 6 B) 7 C) 8 D) 9
20. The ratio of cats to dogs at a shelter is 3:5. If there are 15 cats, how many dogs are there? A) 20 B) 25 C) 30 D) 35
21. A store marks down prices by 35%. If an item was $80, what is the sale price? A) $48 B) $52 C) $56 D) $60
22. If a machine produces 144 widgets in 8 hours, how many does it produce per hour? A) 16 B) 18 C) 20 D) 22
23. The perimeter of a square is 44 inches. What is the length of each side? A) 10 inches B) 11 inches C) 12 inches D) 13 inches
24. If 2/3 of a class of 36 students are present, how many students are absent? A) 10 B) 12 C) 14 D) 16
25. A number increased by 40% becomes 84. What was the original number? A) 55 B) 60 C) 65 D) 70
26. The area of a triangle with base 14 inches and height 8 inches is: A) 48 sq in B) 52 sq in C) 56 sq in D) 60 sq in
27. If you travel 240 miles and use 12 gallons of gas, what is your miles per gallon? A) 18 mpg B) 20 mpg C) 22 mpg D) 24 mpg
28. The average of 5 numbers is 32. If four numbers are 28, 35, 31, and 36, what is the fifth? A) 28 B) 30 C) 32 D) 34
29. A circular garden has a diameter of 20 feet. What is its radius? A) 8 feet B) 10 feet C) 12 feet D) 15 feet
30. If a discount of 20% saves $15, what was the original price? A) $65 B) $70 C) $75 D) $80

Word Knowledge (35 questions)

1. Abolish most nearly means: A) Create B) Eliminate C) Support D) Maintain
2. Brevity most nearly means: A) Length B) Shortness C) Width D) Height
3. Candid most nearly means: A) Dishonest B) Honest C) Confused D) Secretive
4. Debilitate most nearly means: A) Strengthen B) Weaken C) Support D) Build
5. Elaborate most nearly means: A) Simple B) Complex C) Small D) Quick
6. Frugal most nearly means: A) Wasteful B) Thrifty C) Generous D) Careless
7. Gullible most nearly means: A) Suspicious B) Easily deceived C) Smart D) Careful
8. Hinder most nearly means: A) Help B) Obstruct C) Support D) Encourage
9. Imperative most nearly means: A) Optional B) Essential C) Unnecessary D) Trivial
10. Jeopardy most nearly means: A) Safety B) Danger C) Security D) Protection
11. Keen most nearly means: A) Dull B) Sharp C) Blunt D) Thick
12. Lethargic most nearly means: A) Energetic B) Sluggish C) Active D) Quick
13. Marginal most nearly means: A) Central B) Borderline C) Important D) Major
14. Negligent most nearly means: A) Careful B) Careless C) Thoughtful D) Responsible
15. Obsolete most nearly means: A) Modern B) Outdated C) New D) Current
16. Pessimistic most nearly means: A) Optimistic B) Negative C) Hopeful D) Positive
17. Quell most nearly means: A) Encourage B) Suppress C) Start D) Begin
18. Robust most nearly means: A) Weak B) Strong C) Sick D) Frail
19. Scrutinize most nearly means: A) Ignore B) Examine C) Overlook D) Miss
20. Tangible most nearly means: A) Abstract B) Concrete C) Imaginary D) Theoretical

21. Unanimous most nearly means: A) Divided B) In agreement C) Conflicted D) Partial
22. Versatile most nearly means: A) Limited B) Adaptable C) Restricted D) Specialized
23. Wander most nearly means: A) Stay B) Roam C) Remain D) Settle
24. Yield most nearly means: A) Resist B) Give way C) Fight D) Oppose
25. Zealous most nearly means: A) Indifferent B) Passionate C) Lazy D) Uninterested
26. Amiable most nearly means: A) Unfriendly B) Friendly C) Hostile D) Mean
27. Boisterous most nearly means: A) Quiet B) Noisy C) Calm D) Peaceful
28. Contemplate most nearly means: A) Ignore B) Consider C) Reject D) Dismiss
29. Diligent most nearly means: A) Lazy B) Hardworking C) Careless D) Slow
30. Elated most nearly means: A) Sad B) Joyful C) Angry D) Worried
31. Fickle most nearly means: A) Constant B) Changeable C) Steady D) Reliable
32. Gregarious most nearly means: A) Antisocial B) Sociable C) Shy D) Withdrawn
33. Harmonious most nearly means: A) Discordant B) Agreeable C) Conflicting D) Chaotic
34. Inept most nearly means: A) Skilled B) Incompetent C) Able D) Talented
35. Jovial most nearly means: A) Sad B) Cheerful C) Depressed D) Gloomy

Paragraph Comprehension (15 questions)

Passage 1: The human brain contains approximately 86 billion neurons, each capable of forming thousands of connections with other neurons. This vast network allows for complex thought processes, memory formation, and emotional responses. Scientists have discovered that the brain continues to develop and form new connections throughout life, a process called neuroplasticity. This adaptability means that people can learn new skills, recover from injuries, and adapt to changes even in old age.

1. According to the passage, the human brain contains approximately: A) 86 million neurons B) 86 billion neurons C) 68 billion neurons D) 68 million neurons
2. Neuroplasticity refers to: A) The brain's inability to change B) The brain's ability to adapt and form new connections C) Brain damage D) Memory loss
3. The passage suggests that learning new skills: A) Is only possible in youth B) Becomes impossible with age C) Is possible throughout life D) Requires surgery

Passage 2: Renewable energy sources are becoming increasingly important as countries seek to reduce their carbon footprint and dependence on fossil fuels. Solar panels convert sunlight directly into electricity, while wind turbines harness the kinetic energy of moving air. Hydroelectric plants use the force of flowing water to generate power. These clean energy technologies produce no harmful emissions during operation and use naturally replenishing resources.

4. The main advantage of renewable energy mentioned is: A) Lower cost B) No harmful emissions during operation C) Easier installation D) Better appearance
5. According to the passage, solar panels convert: A) Wind into electricity B) Water into electricity C) Sunlight into electricity D) Heat into electricity
6. Renewable energy sources use: A) Non-renewable resources B) Naturally replenishing resources C) Fossil fuels D) Nuclear materials

Passage 3: Regular reading has numerous cognitive benefits beyond entertainment and information gathering. Studies show that reading improves vocabulary, enhances concentration, and strengthens analytical thinking skills. Reading fiction, in particular, has been linked to increased empathy as readers experience different perspectives and emotions through characters. Additionally, reading before bed can help reduce stress and improve sleep quality.

7. According to the passage, reading fiction can increase: A) Vocabulary only B) Empathy C) Sleep problems D) Stress levels
8. Reading before bed can: A) Increase stress B) Reduce stress and improve sleep C) Cause insomnia D) Increase anxiety
9. The passage states that reading improves: A) Only vocabulary B) Only concentration C) Vocabulary, concentration, and analytical thinking D) Only entertainment value

Passage 4: The water cycle is a continuous process that circulates water throughout Earth's atmosphere, land, and oceans. Evaporation occurs when the sun heats water in oceans, lakes, and rivers, turning it into water vapor that rises into the atmosphere. As the vapor cools at higher altitudes, it condenses into clouds. When conditions are right, precipitation occurs, returning water to Earth's surface as rain, snow, or sleet.

10. The water cycle is described as: A) A one-time event B) A continuous process C) Occurring only in oceans D) Happening only in winter
11. Evaporation occurs when: A) Water freezes B) The sun heats water C) Clouds form D) Rain falls
12. Precipitation returns water to Earth as: A) Only rain B) Only snow C) Rain, snow, or sleet D) Only sleet

Passage 5: Effective communication involves both speaking clearly and listening actively. Active listening means giving full attention to the speaker, asking clarifying questions, and providing feedback to show understanding. Non-verbal communication, such as body language and facial expressions, also plays a crucial role in conveying messages. Good communicators adapt their style to their audience and situation, ensuring their message is understood and well-received.

13. Active listening involves: A) Only hearing words B) Giving full attention and asking questions C) Interrupting frequently D) Thinking about your response
14. Non-verbal communication includes: A) Only words B) Body language and facial expressions C) Only facial expressions D) Only gestures
15. Good communicators: A) Use the same style with everyone B) Adapt their style to their audience C) Speak as quickly as possible D) Avoid asking questions

Mathematics Knowledge (25 questions)

1. What is 18% of 250? A) 40 B) 42 C) 45 D) 48
2. If y - 9 = 14, then y = ? A) 21 B) 23 C) 25 D) 27
3. What is the square root of 225? A) 13 B) 14 C) 15 D) 16
4. In a right triangle with legs 9 and 12, what is the hypotenuse? A) 15 B) 16 C) 17 D) 18

5. What is $5^3 \times 2^2$? A) 480 B) 500 C) 520 D) 540
6. If a circle has a circumference of 31.4, what is its radius? (Use $\pi = 3.14$) A) 4 B) 5 C) 6 D) 7
7. What is $7! \div 5!$? A) 35 B) 42 C) 48 D) 56
8. Solve: $5x + 15 = 40$ A) 4 B) 5 C) 6 D) 7
9. What is the area of a parallelogram with base 11 and height 6? A) 60 B) 64 C) 66 D) 68
10. If $4y + 8 = 3y + 15$, then y = ? A) 5 B) 6 C) 7 D) 8
11. What is 35% of 160? A) 52 B) 54 C) 56 D) 58
12. In $f(x) = 4x + 1$, what is $f(3)$? A) 11 B) 12 C) 13 D) 14
13. What is the volume of a cube with side length 4? A) 48 B) 56 C) 64 D) 72
14. A triangle has a perimeter of 36 and two sides of length 12 and 15. What is the third side? A) 7 B) 8 C) 9 D) 10
15. What is $|-15|$? A) -15 B) 0 C) 15 D) 30
16. Solve: $8x - 24 = 32$ A) 6 B) 7 C) 8 D) 9
17. What is $12^2 - 8^2$? A) 70 B) 75 C) 80 D) 85
18. If $m = 4$ and $n = 3$, what is $2m^2 + n^2$? A) 41 B) 43 C) 45 D) 47
19. What is the slope of the line through (2,5) and (6,13)? A) 1 B) 2 C) 3 D) 4
20. What is $3/5 + 2/7$? A) 5/12 B) 31/35 C) 5/35 D) 17/35
21. If $\log_2(x) = 4$, then x = ? A) 8 B) 12 C) 16 D) 20
22. What is the range of 2, 8, 3, 9, 5, 7? A) 6 B) 7 C) 8 D) 9
23. Solve: $x^2 - 25 = 0$ A) ± 4 B) ± 5 C) ± 6 D) ± 7
24. What is $\tan(45°)$? A) 0 B) 1/2 C) 1 D) $\sqrt{3}$
25. If $h(x) = x^2 - 3x + 2$, what is $h(4)$? A) 4 B) 5 C) 6 D) 7

Electronics Information (20 questions)

1. What is the unit of frequency? A) Ampere B) Volt C) Hertz D) Watt
2. Which component stores electrical charge? A) Resistor B) Capacitor C) Inductor D) Transformer
3. In an AC circuit, current: A) Flows in one direction B) Alternates direction C) Remains constant D) Flows randomly
4. What does EMF stand for? A) Electric Motor Force B) Electromotive Force C) Electronic Measuring Force D) Electrical Magnetic Force
5. A relay is: A) An electronic switch B) A measuring device C) A power source D) A type of wire
6. The unit of electrical charge is: A) Ampere B) Volt C) Coulomb D) Ohm
7. Conductance is the opposite of: A) Voltage B) Current C) Resistance D) Power
8. Which metal is the best conductor? A) Copper B) Silver C) Gold D) Aluminum
9. A step-up transformer: A) Decreases voltage B) Increases voltage C) Maintains voltage D) Converts AC to DC
10. Kirchhoff's current law states that current: A) Always increases B) Is conserved at a junction C) Always decreases D) Is random
11. What does PWM stand for? A) Power Wave Modulation B) Pulse Width Modulation C) Primary Wire Method D) Positive Wave Mode
12. Electric field strength is measured in: A) Volts per meter B) Amperes per meter C) Ohms per meter D) Watts per meter

13. A Zener diode is used for: A) Amplification B) Voltage regulation C) Current amplification D) Signal mixing
14. The unit of magnetic flux is: A) Tesla B) Weber C) Henry D) Gauss
15. In a bridge rectifier circuit: A) Only half the AC waveform is used B) The full AC waveform is used C) DC is converted to AC D) Voltage is stepped up
16. What is reactance? A) DC resistance B) AC opposition C) Power dissipation D) Energy storage
17. An oscilloscope measures: A) Only voltage B) Only current C) Voltage over time D) Only power
18. A variable capacitor is used to: A) Control voltage B) Control current C) Tune circuits D) Generate power
19. Which device converts light to electricity? A) LED B) Photodiode C) Transistor D) Resistor
20. The bandwidth of a filter is measured in: A) Volts B) Amperes C) Hertz D) Ohms

Auto & Shop Information (25 questions)

1. The alternator in a car: A) Starts the engine B) Generates electrical power C) Filters oil D) Cools the engine
2. What tool is used to check engine compression? A) Multimeter B) Compression gauge C) Torque wrench D) Feeler gauge
3. The camshaft controls: A) Fuel injection B) Valve timing C) Ignition timing D) Transmission shifting
4. Which fluid is used in power steering? A) Brake fluid B) Transmission fluid C) Power steering fluid D) Engine oil
5. A torx screwdriver has a: A) Flat tip B) Cross tip C) Star-shaped tip D) Hexagonal tip
6. The EGR valve: A) Controls air flow B) Recirculates exhaust gases C) Filters fuel D) Regulates oil pressure
7. What does CVT stand for? A) Constant Velocity Transmission B) Continuously Variable Transmission C) Central Valve Timing D) Computer Variable Timing
8. A socket set is used with: A) Screws only B) Nuts and bolts C) Nails D) Rivets only
9. The catalytic converter: A) Increases power B) Reduces emissions C) Improves fuel economy D) Cools exhaust
10. What creates the spark in a spark plug? A) Compression B) Fuel injection C) Electrical arc D) Heat
11. Which saw cuts metal most effectively? A) Wood saw B) Hacksaw C) Circular saw D) Hand saw
12. The CV joint allows: A) Steering B) Braking C) Power transfer during steering D) Engine cooling
13. Soldering joins metals using: A) Heat only B) Pressure only C) Heat and low-temperature metal D) Glue
14. The radiator cap: A) Decorates the radiator B) Maintains cooling system pressure C) Filters coolant D) Measures temperature
15. A square is used to: A) Measure length B) Check right angles C) Mark circles D) Cut materials

16. What regulates engine temperature? A) Oil pump B) Thermostat C) Fuel pump D) Alternator
17. Steel wool is graded by: A) Color B) Coarseness C) Length D) Weight
18. The PCV valve: A) Controls air conditioning B) Manages crankcase ventilation C) Regulates fuel flow D) Controls transmission
19. A drift punch is used to: A) Start holes B) Drive out pins C) Measure gaps D) Cut threads
20. Automatic transmission fluid: A) Lubricates the engine B) Operates transmission hydraulics C) Cools the radiator D) Powers the alternator
21. Which tool measures very small gaps? A) Ruler B) Feeler gauge C) Tape measure D) Square
22. The mass airflow sensor: A) Measures fuel flow B) Measures air entering the engine C) Controls emissions D) Regulates oil pressure
23. "Displacement" in engines refers to: A) Engine weight B) Cylinder volume C) Fuel capacity D) Power output
24. A reamer is used to: A) Cut threads B) Enlarge holes precisely C) Mark metal D) Measure angles
25. The serpentine belt drives: A) Only the alternator B) Multiple engine accessories C) Only the air conditioning D) The transmission

Mechanical Comprehension (25 questions)

1. If a 15-pound force is applied 3 feet from a fulcrum, what force is needed 5 feet on the other side? A) 7 pounds B) 9 pounds C) 11 pounds D) 13 pounds
2. Which pulley arrangement provides the greatest force advantage? A) Single fixed B) Single movable C) Multiple pulley system D) All provide equal advantage
3. If a 24-tooth gear drives a 48-tooth gear, the larger gear rotates: A) Twice as fast B) Half as fast C) Three times as fast D) At the same speed
4. In a liquid, pressure at any depth acts: A) Only downward B) Only upward C) In all directions D) Only sideways
5. A wedge converts: A) Rotational motion to linear B) Downward force to sideways force C) Linear motion to rotational D) Small force to large force
6. Doubling the effort arm of a lever: A) Halves the mechanical advantage B) Doubles the mechanical advantage C) Has no effect D) Quadruples the force
7. In Pascal's principle, if input area is 3 sq in and output area is 27 sq in, the force multiplication is: A) 3 B) 6 C) 9 D) 12
8. An inclined plane 20 feet long and 4 feet high has a mechanical advantage of: A) 4 B) 5 C) 16 D) 20
9. Work is reduced by using an inclined plane: A) True B) False C) Only sometimes D) Only for heavy objects
10. A wheel with diameter 12 inches and axle diameter 3 inches has mechanical advantage: A) 3 B) 4 C) 9 D) 12
11. A bottle opener is an example of a: A) First-class lever B) Second-class lever C) Third-class lever D) Pulley
12. In a gear train, if one gear turns clockwise, the next gear turns: A) Clockwise B) Counterclockwise C) Either direction D) It depends on size

13. The center of mass of an object is: A) Always at the geometric center B) Where the object balances C) The heaviest point D) Always at the bottom
14. A block and tackle with 4 rope segments supporting the load has mechanical advantage: A) 2 B) 4 C) 6 D) 8
15. A chisel works as a: A) Lever B) Inclined plane C) Wedge D) Screw
16. The efficiency of any real machine is: A) Always 100% B) Greater than 100% C) Less than 100% D) Variable and unpredictable
17. A machine with mechanical advantage 6 that applies 20 pounds input produces: A) 26 pounds B) 100 pounds C) 120 pounds D) 140 pounds
18. In a wheelbarrow (second-class lever): A) Load is between fulcrum and effort B) Effort is between fulcrum and load C) Fulcrum is between load and effort D) All points are equal
19. The formula for work is: A) W = F + d B) W = F - d C) W = F × d D) W = F ÷ d
20. If 25 pounds of force moves an object 12 feet, work done is: A) 13 ft-lbs B) 37 ft-lbs C) 300 ft-lbs D) 312 ft-lbs
21. A crowbar is primarily used as a: A) Screw B) Wedge C) Lever D) Inclined plane
22. Mechanical advantage can be: A) Only greater than 1 B) Only less than 1 C) Only equal to 1 D) Greater than, less than, or equal to 1
23. Rolling friction is: A) Greater than sliding friction B) Less than sliding friction C) Equal to sliding friction D) Unrelated to sliding friction
24. A fixed pulley changes: A) Force magnitude B) Force direction C) Both magnitude and direction D) Neither magnitude nor direction
25. Power is: A) Force times distance B) Work divided by time C) Energy times velocity D) Mass times acceleration

Answer Key - Test 14

General Science:

1. C 2. B 3. B 4. C 5. C 6. B 7. C 8. B 9. C 10. D
2. A 12. C 13. A 14. C 15. C 16. C 17. B 18. B 19. C 20. C
3. C 22. B 23. B 24. B 25. C

Arithmetic Reasoning:

1. A 2. B 3. A 4. B 5. B 6. B 7. B 8. B 9. A 10. B
2. C 12. D 13. B 14. B 15. C 16. B 17. A 18. B 19. C 20. B
3. B 22. B 23. B 24. B 25. B 26. C 27. B 28. B 29. B 30. C

Word Knowledge:

1. B 2. B 3. B 4. B 5. B 6. B 7. B 8. B 9. B 10. B
2. B 12. B 13. B 14. B 15. B 16. B 17. B 18. B 19. B 20. B
3. B 22. B 23. B 24. B 25. B 26. B 27. B 28. B 29. B 30. B
4. B 32. B 33. B 34. B 35. B

Paragraph Comprehension:

1. B 2. B 3. C 4. B 5. C 6. B 7. B 8. B 9. C 10. B
2. B 12. C 13. B 14. B 15. B

Mathematics Knowledge:

1. C 2. B 3. C 4. A 5. B 6. B 7. B 8. B 9. C 10. C
2. C 12. C 13. C 14. C 15. C 16. B 17. C 18. A 19. B 20. B
3. C 22. B 23. B 24. C 25. C

Electronics Information:

1. C 2. B 3. B 4. B 5. A 6. C 7. C 8. B 9. B 10. B
2. B 12. A 13. B 14. B 15. B 16. B 17. C 18. C 19. B 20. C

Auto & Shop Information:

1. B 2. B 3. B 4. C 5. C 6. B 7. B 8. B 9. B 10. C
2. B 12. C 13. C 14. B 15. B 16. B 17. B 18. B 19. B 20. B
3. B 22. B 23. B 24. B 25. B

Mechanical Comprehension:

1. B 2. C 3. B 4. C 5. B 6. B 7. C 8. B 9. B 10. B
2. A 12. B 13. B 14. B 15. C 16. C 17. C 18. A 19. C 20. C
3. C 22. D 23. B 24. B 25. B

TEST 15

GENERAL SCIENCE (25 questions)

1. The smallest unit of matter that retains chemical properties is: a) Atom b) Molecule c) Electron d) Proton
2. Which gas makes up approximately 78% of Earth's atmosphere? a) Oxygen b) Carbon dioxide c) Nitrogen d) Argon
3. The process by which plants make food using sunlight is called: a) Respiration b) Photosynthesis c) Transpiration d) Germination
4. Which of these is NOT a type of blood vessel? a) Artery b) Vein c) Capillary d) Nephron
5. The hardest natural substance on Earth is: a) Quartz b) Diamond c) Steel d) Iron
6. Which planet is closest to the Sun? a) Venus b) Earth c) Mercury d) Mars
7. The study of earthquakes is called: a) Meteorology b) Seismology c) Geology d) Oceanography
8. Which element has the chemical symbol "Au"? a) Silver b) Aluminum c) Gold d) Argon
9. The human body has how many chambers in the heart? a) 2 b) 3 c) 4 d) 6
10. Which type of rock is formed by cooling magma? a) Sedimentary b) Metamorphic c) Igneous d) Composite

11. The process of water changing from liquid to gas is: a) Condensation b) Evaporation c) Precipitation d) Sublimation
12. Which organelle is known as the "powerhouse of the cell"? a) Nucleus b) Ribosome c) Mitochondria d) Vacuole
13. The pH scale measures: a) Temperature b) Pressure c) Acidity/Alkalinity d) Density
14. Which force keeps planets in orbit around the Sun? a) Magnetism b) Friction c) Gravity d) Centrifugal force
15. The largest organ in the human body is: a) Liver b) Brain c) Lungs d) Skin
16. Which gas do plants release during photosynthesis? a) Carbon dioxide b) Nitrogen c) Oxygen d) Hydrogen
17. The speed of light is approximately: a) 186,000 miles per second b) 300,000 km per hour c) 100,000 miles per hour d) 500,000 km per second
18. Which blood type is considered the universal donor? a) A b) B c) AB d) O
19. The process of cell division is called: a) Meiosis b) Mitosis c) Both a and b d) Osmosis
20. Which layer of the atmosphere contains the ozone layer? a) Troposphere b) Stratosphere c) Mesosphere d) Thermosphere
21. The chemical formula for water is: a) H_2O_2 b) HO_2 c) H_2O d) H_3O
22. Which instrument measures atmospheric pressure? a) Thermometer b) Barometer c) Hygrometer d) Anemometer
23. The study of heredity is called: a) Ecology b) Biology c) Genetics d) Anatomy
24. Which metal is liquid at room temperature? a) Lead b) Mercury c) Tin d) Zinc
25. The asteroid belt is located between which two planets? a) Earth and Mars b) Mars and Jupiter c) Jupiter and Saturn d) Venus and Earth

ARITHMETIC REASONING (30 questions)

1. If a car travels 240 miles in 4 hours, what is its average speed? a) 50 mph b) 60 mph c) 70 mph d) 80 mph
2. Sarah has $85. She spends $23 on groceries and $15 on gas. How much money does she have left? a) $47 b) $52 c) $57 d) $62
3. A recipe calls for 3/4 cup of flour. If you want to make 2/3 of the recipe, how much flour do you need? a) 1/2 cup b) 2/3 cup c) 3/8 cup d) 1/4 cup
4. What is 15% of 200? a) 25 b) 30 c) 35 d) 40
5. If 5 pencils cost $2.50, what is the cost of 8 pencils? a) $3.50 b) $4.00 c) $4.50 d) $5.00
6. A box contains 24 apples. If 1/3 are red and 1/4 are green, how many are neither red nor green? a) 8 b) 10 c) 12 d) 14
7. Tom's test scores were 85, 92, 78, and 89. What is his average score? a) 84 b) 86 c) 88 d) 90
8. If a rectangle is 12 feet long and 8 feet wide, what is its area? a) 96 sq ft b) 104 sq ft c) 112 sq ft d) 120 sq ft
9. A store offers a 20% discount on a $75 item. What is the sale price? a) $55 b) $60 c) $65 d) $70
10. If you work 40 hours at $12 per hour, how much do you earn? a) $460 b) $480 c) $500 d) $520
11. A train travels 300 miles in 5 hours. At this rate, how long will it take to travel 450 miles? a) 6.5 hours b) 7 hours c) 7.5 hours d) 8 hours

12. What is 2/3 × 3/4? a) 1/2 b) 5/12 c) 6/12 d) 5/7
13. If 3x + 7 = 22, what is x? a) 3 b) 4 c) 5 d) 6
14. A circle has a radius of 6 inches. What is its circumference? (Use $\pi = 3.14$) a) 36.68 inches b) 37.68 inches c) 38.68 inches d) 39.68 inches
15. If you buy 3 items for $4.50 each and pay with a $20 bill, how much change do you receive? a) $6.50 b) $7.00 c) $6.00 d) $5.50
16. What is 0.75 expressed as a fraction in lowest terms? a) 3/4 b) 7/10 c) 75/100 d) 15/20
17. A bag contains 15 marbles: 6 red, 4 blue, and 5 green. What is the probability of drawing a blue marble? a) 4/15 b) 4/11 c) 1/4 d) 1/3
18. If a car depreciates 15% each year and is worth $20,000 now, what will it be worth in one year? a) $15,000 b) $16,000 c) $17,000 d) $18,000
19. How many minutes are in 2.5 hours? a) 120 minutes b) 130 minutes c) 140 minutes d) 150 minutes
20. If 4y - 3 = 17, what is y? a) 4 b) 5 c) 6 d) 7
21. A rectangular garden is 15 feet by 20 feet. What is its perimeter? a) 60 feet b) 70 feet c) 80 feet d) 90 feet
22. What is 45% of 80? a) 32 b) 34 c) 36 d) 38
23. If you save $25 per week, how much will you save in 18 weeks? a) $400 b) $425 c) $450 d) $475
24. What is the square root of 144? a) 11 b) 12 c) 13 d) 14
25. A pizza is cut into 8 equal slices. If you eat 3 slices, what fraction of the pizza remains? a) 3/8 b) 5/8 c) 1/2 d) 2/3
26. If gas costs $3.20 per gallon and you buy 12 gallons, what is the total cost? a) $38.40 b) $38.80 c) $39.20 d) $39.60
27. What is $7^2 - 3^2$? a) 30 b) 35 c) 40 d) 45
28. If a shirt originally costs $40 and is marked up 25%, what is the new price? a) $45 b) $48 c) $50 d) $52
29. A book has 480 pages. If you read 60 pages per day, how many days will it take to finish? a) 6 days b) 7 days c) 8 days d) 9 days
30. What is 1/3 + 1/4? a) 2/7 b) 5/12 c) 7/12 d) 1/2

WORD KNOWLEDGE (35 questions)

1. ABUNDANT most nearly means: a) Scarce b) Plentiful c) Average d) Moderate
2. CANDID most nearly means: a) Sweet b) Honest c) Angry d) Confused
3. DECIPHER most nearly means: a) Encode b) Decode c) Ignore d) Memorize
4. ELATED most nearly means: a) Sad b) Tired c) Joyful d) Angry
5. FRAGILE most nearly means: a) Strong b) Heavy c) Delicate d) Large
6. GENUINE most nearly means: a) Fake b) Real c) Old d) New
7. HOSTILE most nearly means: a) Friendly b) Neutral c) Unfriendly d) Happy
8. IMMENSE most nearly means: a) Tiny b) Huge c) Medium d) Narrow
9. JOVIAL most nearly means: a) Sad b) Cheerful c) Serious d) Quiet
10. KEEN most nearly means: a) Dull b) Sharp c) Soft d) Rough
11. LUCID most nearly means: a) Confused b) Dark c) Clear d) Bright
12. MEAGER most nearly means: a) Abundant b) Scanty c) Heavy d) Light
13. NOVICE most nearly means: a) Expert b) Beginner c) Teacher d) Student

14. OBSOLETE most nearly means: a) Modern b) Outdated c) New d) Popular
15. PECULIAR most nearly means: a) Normal b) Strange c) Common d) Regular
16. QUAINT most nearly means: a) Modern b) Charming c) Ugly d) Large
17. RELUCTANT most nearly means: a) Eager b) Unwilling c) Ready d) Quick
18. SERENE most nearly means: a) Noisy b) Peaceful c) Busy d) Chaotic
19. TEDIOUS most nearly means: a) Exciting b) Boring c) Quick d) Easy
20. UNIQUE most nearly means: a) Common b) One-of-a-kind c) Multiple d) Similar
21. VIVID most nearly means: a) Dull b) Bright c) Dark d) Faded
22. WARY most nearly means: a) Careless b) Cautious c) Bold d) Reckless
23. ZEAL most nearly means: a) Laziness b) Enthusiasm c) Boredom d) Tiredness
24. ARID most nearly means: a) Wet b) Dry c) Cold d) Hot
25. BENIGN most nearly means: a) Harmful b) Harmless c) Dangerous d) Toxic
26. CORDIAL most nearly means: a) Rude b) Friendly c) Cold d) Distant
27. DIMINISH most nearly means: a) Increase b) Decrease c) Maintain d) Double
28. ELABORATE most nearly means: a) Simple b) Detailed c) Quick d) Easy
29. FUTILE most nearly means: a) Useful b) Useless c) Helpful d) Productive
30. GRATITUDE most nearly means: a) Anger b) Thankfulness c) Sadness d) Fear
31. HINDER most nearly means: a) Help b) Obstruct c) Encourage d) Support
32. INTRICATE most nearly means: a) Simple b) Complex c) Easy d) Clear
33. JEOPARDY most nearly means: a) Safety b) Danger c) Security d) Protection
34. KINDLE most nearly means: a) Extinguish b) Ignite c) Cool d) Freeze
35. LEGITIMATE most nearly means: a) Illegal b) Legal c) Wrong d) False

PARAGRAPH COMPREHENSION (15 questions)

Passage 1: The invention of the printing press by Johannes Gutenberg in the 15th century revolutionized the way information was shared. Before this invention, books were copied by hand, making them expensive and rare. The printing press allowed for mass production of books, making knowledge more accessible to the general population. This development played a crucial role in the Renaissance and the spread of literacy throughout Europe.

1. According to the passage, what made books expensive before the printing press? a) High demand b) Hand copying c) Paper costs d) Transportation
2. The printing press contributed to: a) The Renaissance b) Higher book prices c) Less literacy d) Fewer books

Passage 2: Photosynthesis is the process by which green plants convert sunlight, water, and carbon dioxide into glucose and oxygen. This process occurs primarily in the leaves, where chlorophyll captures light energy. The glucose produced serves as food for the plant, while oxygen is released into the atmosphere. This process is essential for life on Earth as it provides oxygen for animals and removes carbon dioxide from the air.

3. Chlorophyll's main function in photosynthesis is to: a) Produce glucose b) Capture light energy c) Release oxygen d) Remove carbon dioxide
4. According to the passage, photosynthesis is essential because it: a) Feeds animals b) Produces glucose c) Provides oxygen and removes CO_2 d) Occurs in leaves

Passage 3: Regular exercise has numerous benefits for both physical and mental health. Physically, exercise strengthens the heart, improves circulation, and helps maintain a healthy weight. Mentally, exercise releases endorphins, which are natural mood elevators that can help reduce stress and anxiety. Studies have shown that people who exercise regularly tend to have better sleep patterns and higher self-esteem than those who don't.

5. According to the passage, endorphins: a) Strengthen the heart b) Improve circulation c) Elevate mood d) Help maintain weight
6. People who exercise regularly tend to have: a) Better sleep and higher self-esteem b) More stress c) Lower self-esteem d) Poor circulation

Passage 4: The water cycle is a continuous process that circulates water throughout the Earth's atmosphere, land, and oceans. Evaporation occurs when the sun heats water in lakes, rivers, and oceans, turning it into water vapor. This vapor rises into the atmosphere, where it cools and condenses into clouds. Eventually, the water falls back to Earth as precipitation in the form of rain, snow, or sleet.

7. The water cycle begins with: a) Condensation b) Precipitation c) Evaporation d) Cloud formation
8. Water vapor in the atmosphere: a) Heats up b) Cools and condenses c) Disappears d) Becomes ice

Passage 5: Renewable energy sources, such as solar, wind, and hydroelectric power, are becoming increasingly important as alternatives to fossil fuels. Unlike coal and oil, renewable energy sources don't produce harmful emissions and won't run out over time. Solar panels convert sunlight directly into electricity, while wind turbines harness the power of moving air. Hydroelectric plants use flowing water to generate power.

9. What makes renewable energy sources different from fossil fuels? a) They're more expensive b) They don't produce harmful emissions c) They're harder to use d) They're less efficient
10. According to the passage, solar panels: a) Use flowing water b) Harness wind power c) Convert sunlight to electricity d) Produce emissions

Passage 6: Sleep plays a vital role in physical health and mental well-being. During sleep, the body repairs tissues, consolidates memories, and releases important hormones. Adults typically need 7-9 hours of sleep per night for optimal health. Sleep deprivation can lead to decreased concentration, weakened immune system, and increased risk of accidents. Maintaining good sleep hygiene, such as keeping a regular sleep schedule and creating a comfortable sleep environment, can improve sleep quality.

11. During sleep, the body: a) Only rests b) Repairs tissues and consolidates memories c) Produces stress d) Decreases hormone production
12. Sleep deprivation can cause: a) Better concentration b) Stronger immune system c) Decreased concentration and weakened immunity d) Improved memory

Passage 7: The Great Wall of China, one of the most famous landmarks in the world, was built over many centuries by different Chinese dynasties. Construction began in the 7th century BC and continued through the Ming Dynasty (1368-1644 AD). The wall was built primarily for defense against invasions from northern tribes. Contrary to popular belief, the Great Wall is not visible from space with the naked eye, although this myth persists.

13. The Great Wall was built primarily for: a) Tourism b) Defense c) Transportation d) Communication
14. According to the passage, the myth about the Great Wall is that it's: a) Very old b) In China c) Visible from space d) Built by dynasties

Passage 8: Coral reefs are among the most diverse ecosystems on Earth, providing habitat for thousands of marine species. These underwater structures are formed by tiny animals called coral polyps, which secrete calcium carbonate to create hard skeletons. However, coral reefs are under threat from climate change, pollution, and overfishing. Rising ocean temperatures cause coral bleaching, a phenomenon where corals expel the algae living in their tissues, often leading to coral death.

15. Coral bleaching occurs when: a) Corals eat too much b) Ocean temperatures rise c) There's too much pollution d) Fish overeat

MATHEMATICS KNOWLEDGE (25 questions)

1. What is the value of $3^2 + 4^2$? a) 25 b) 24 c) 23 d) 22
2. If x = 5, what is the value of 2x + 3? a) 11 b) 12 c) 13 d) 14
3. What is the area of a triangle with base 8 and height 6? a) 24 b) 48 c) 14 d) 28
4. Solve for y: 3y - 4 = 11 a) 5 b) 6 c) 7 d) 8
5. What is 25% of 160? a) 35 b) 40 c) 45 d) 50
6. If a = 3 and b = 4, what is $a^2 + b^2$? a) 24 b) 25 c) 26 d) 27
7. What is the circumference of a circle with radius 5? (Use $\pi = 3.14$) a) 31.4 b) 15.7 c) 78.5 d) 25
8. Simplify: 2(x + 3) - 4 a) 2x + 2 b) 2x + 6 c) 2x - 4 d) 2x + 10
9. What is the slope of the line passing through points (1, 2) and (3, 6)? a) 1 b) 2 c) 3 d) 4
10. If 2x + 5 = 15, what is x? a) 4 b) 5 c) 6 d) 7
11. What is the volume of a cube with side length 4? a) 16 b) 48 c) 64 d) 12
12. Simplify: $\sqrt{36} + \sqrt{49}$ a) 11 b) 12 c) 13 d) 14
13. What is the value of $|-8|$? a) -8 b) 8 c) 0 d) 16
14. If f(x) = 2x + 1, what is f(3)? a) 6 b) 7 c) 8 d) 9
15. What is 3/4 × 8/9? a) 2/3 b) 24/36 c) 1/2 d) 11/13
16. Solve: $x^2 = 36$ a) x = 6 only b) x = ±6 c) x = 18 d) x = 72
17. What is the perimeter of a rectangle with length 7 and width 5? a) 24 b) 35 c) 12 d) 22
18. If $\log_2(8) = x$, what is x? a) 2 b) 3 c) 4 d) 6
19. What is the sum of the interior angles of a triangle? a) 90° b) 180° c) 270° d) 360°
20. Simplify: $(x^3)^2$ a) x^5 b) x^6 c) x^9 d) $2x^3$
21. What is the distance between points (0, 0) and (3, 4)? a) 5 b) 6 c) 7 d) 12
22. If $5^x = 125$, what is x? a) 2 b) 3 c) 4 d) 5

23. What is the median of: 3, 7, 5, 9, 1? a) 5 b) 6 c) 7 d) 9
24. Simplify: 2x + 3x - x a) 4x b) 5x c) 6x d) x
25. What is sin(30°)? a) 1/2 b) √2/2 c) √3/2 d) 1

ELECTRONICS INFORMATION (20 questions)

1. The unit of electrical resistance is the: a) Volt b) Ampere c) Ohm d) Watt
2. In a series circuit, the total resistance is: a) Less than the smallest resistor b) Equal to the average resistance c) The sum of all resistances d) The product of all resistances
3. What does AC stand for in electrical terms? a) Actual Current b) Alternating Current c) Additional Current d) Active Current
4. A device that stores electrical energy is a: a) Resistor b) Capacitor c) Inductor d) Transformer
5. The flow of electrons in a circuit is called: a) Voltage b) Current c) Resistance d) Power
6. Which material is the best conductor of electricity? a) Rubber b) Wood c) Silver d) Glass
7. In Ohm's Law, V = I × R, what does I represent? a) Voltage b) Current c) Resistance d) Power
8. A transformer is used to: a) Store energy b) Change voltage levels c) Create resistance d) Generate current
9. The positive terminal of a battery is called the: a) Cathode b) Anode c) Electrode d) Terminal
10. What happens to current in a parallel circuit when more branches are added? a) Decreases b) Stays the same c) Increases d) Becomes zero
11. A fuse is designed to: a) Increase current b) Store energy c) Protect circuits from overcurrent d) Change voltage
12. The unit of electrical power is the: a) Ohm b) Volt c) Ampere d) Watt
13. In a DC circuit, current flows: a) In both directions b) In one direction only c) In alternating directions d) Not at all
14. A semiconductor has electrical conductivity: a) Greater than a conductor b) Less than an insulator c) Between a conductor and insulator d) Equal to a conductor
15. The device that converts AC to DC is called a: a) Transformer b) Capacitor c) Rectifier d) Inductor
16. Ground in an electrical circuit represents: a) High voltage b) Zero voltage reference c) Maximum current d) Infinite resistance
17. An LED stands for: a) Light Emitting Diode b) Low Energy Device c) Linear Electronic Display d) Large Electrical Detector
18. In a circuit diagram, a zigzag line represents a: a) Battery b) Switch c) Resistor d) Wire
19. The frequency of standard household AC power in the US is: a) 50 Hz b) 60 Hz c) 100 Hz d) 120 Hz
20. A multimeter can measure: a) Only voltage b) Only current c) Only resistance d) Voltage, current, and resistance

AUTO & SHOP INFORMATION (25 questions)

1. The engine component that mixes air and fuel is the: a) Piston b) Carburetor c) Cylinder d) Crankshaft

2. Which tool is used to measure the diameter of a pipe? a) Ruler b) Calipers c) Level d) Square
3. The cooling system component that regulates engine temperature is the: a) Radiator b) Thermostat c) Water pump d) Fan
4. What type of screwdriver is used for screws with a star-shaped head? a) Phillips b) Flathead c) Torx d) Robertson
5. The transmission component that allows wheels to turn at different speeds is the: a) Clutch b) Differential c) Flywheel d) Driveshaft
6. Which saw is best for cutting curves in wood? a) Circular saw b) Table saw c) Jigsaw d) Miter saw
7. The electrical system component that starts the engine is the: a) Alternator b) Battery c) Starter d) Generator
8. A wrench with a box end and an open end is called: a) Adjustable wrench b) Combination wrench c) Socket wrench d) Pipe wrench
9. The brake system component that applies friction to stop the vehicle is the: a) Brake fluid b) Brake pad c) Master cylinder d) Brake line
10. Which abrasive has the finest grit? a) 60 grit b) 120 grit c) 220 grit d) 400 grit
11. The engine's compression ratio compares: a) Fuel to air b) Cylinder volume at bottom vs. top of stroke c) Power to torque d) RPM to horsepower
12. A chisel is primarily used for: a) Drilling holes b) Cutting and shaping c) Measuring d) Smoothing surfaces
13. Anti-lock braking systems (ABS) prevent: a) Brake fade b) Wheel lockup c) Brake fluid loss d) Pad wear
14. The woodworking joint where two pieces meet at right angles is called: a) Butt joint b) Miter joint c) Dovetail joint d) Mortise and tenon
15. The camshaft operates the: a) Pistons b) Crankshaft c) Valves d) Transmission
16. Which fastener is designed to be used only once? a) Bolt b) Screw c) Rivet d) Nut
17. The fuel injection system is controlled by the: a) Carburetor b) ECU/PCM c) Fuel pump d) Air filter
18. The angle of a drill bit point is typically: a) 90 degrees b) 118 degrees c) 135 degrees d) 150 degrees
19. Power steering fluid helps: a) Stop the vehicle b) Steer more easily c) Shift gears d) Cool the engine
20. Which type of file cuts on the push stroke only? a) Double-cut file b) Single-cut file c) Rasp d) All files cut both ways
21. The catalytic converter reduces: a) Fuel consumption b) Engine noise c) Harmful emissions d) Engine temperature
22. The measurement across the flats of a hex nut determines: a) Thread pitch b) Wrench size needed c) Material strength d) Installation torque
23. Hydraulic brake systems work because liquids: a) Compress easily b) Are incompressible c) Expand when heated d) Flow quickly
24. The kerf of a saw blade refers to: a) Number of teeth b) Width of cut c) Blade length d) Cutting speed
25. The alternator charges the battery when the engine is: a) Off b) Idling only c) Running d) Being started

MECHANICAL COMPREHENSION (25 questions)

1. If gear A has 20 teeth and gear B has 40 teeth, when gear A makes 2 complete turns, gear B makes: a) 1 turn b) 2 turns c) 4 turns d) 8 turns
2. A first-class lever has the fulcrum positioned: a) At one end b) Between the effort and load c) At the load end d) Away from the lever
3. In a pulley system, using more wheels: a) Decreases mechanical advantage b) Increases the distance you must pull c) Both b and decreases required force d) None of the above
4. Water pressure at the bottom of a tank is determined by: a) Total volume of water b) Shape of tank c) Height of water d) Width of tank
5. If you apply 10 pounds of force to a lever with a mechanical advantage of 4, the output force is: a) 2.5 pounds b) 14 pounds c) 40 pounds d) 6 pounds
6. In a hydraulic system, if the input piston has an area of 2 sq in and the output piston has an area of 8 sq in, the mechanical advantage is: a) 2 b) 4 c) 6 d) 16
7. An inclined plane reduces the force needed to lift an object by: a) Decreasing the weight b) Increasing the distance c) Changing direction d) Adding wheels
8. The center of gravity of an object is the point where: a) It weighs the most b) It's perfectly balanced c) It's strongest d) It touches the ground
9. If a wheel is 3 feet in diameter, how far does it travel in one complete revolution? a) 3 feet b) 6 feet c) 9.42 feet d) 12 feet
10. In a gear train, if the input gear rotates clockwise, the next gear in contact rotates: a) Clockwise b) Counterclockwise c) At the same speed d) Faster
11. A screw is essentially an inclined plane wrapped around a: a) Circle b) Cylinder c) Cone d) Sphere
12. The mechanical advantage of a wedge depends on its: a) Weight b) Length and thickness c) Color d) Material
13. In a block and tackle system with 4 supporting ropes, the mechanical advantage is: a) 2 b) 4 c) 8 d) 16
14. Ball bearings in machinery are used to: a) Increase weight b) Reduce friction c) Add strength d) Improve appearance
15. If you increase the diameter of a drive pulley while keeping the driven pulley the same size: a) Speed increases b) Speed decreases c) Torque increases d) No change occurs
16. The amount of work done equals: a) Force × time b) Force × distance c) Distance × time d) Force × speed
17. A cam converts: a) Linear motion to rotary motion b) Rotary motion to linear motion c) Fast motion to slow motion d) Clockwise to counterclockwise motion
18. In a simple machine, if you increase mechanical advantage, you must: a) Apply force over a greater distance b) Use more force c) Work faster d) Use less energy
19. The efficiency of a machine is: a) Work output ÷ work input b) Work input ÷ work output c) Force × distance d) Always 100%
20. A flywheel stores: a) Electrical energy b) Potential energy c) Kinetic energy d) Chemical energy
21. In a spring scale, the amount of stretch is proportional to: a) Time b) Temperature c) Applied force d) Spring length
22. The law of conservation of energy states that energy: a) Always increases b) Cannot be created or destroyed c) Decreases over time d) Only exists in motion

23. Archimedes' principle explains why objects: a) Fall to earth b) Float or sink c) Rotate d) Expand when heated
24. If two gears have the same number of teeth and one rotates at 100 RPM, the other rotates at: a) 50 RPM b) 100 RPM c) 200 RPM d) 400 RPM
25. A governor on an engine controls: a) Fuel mixture b) Engine speed c) Oil pressure d) Cooling temperature

ANSWER KEY - TEST 15

General Science: 1-b, 2-c, 3-b, 4-d, 5-b, 6-c, 7-b, 8-c, 9-c, 10-c, 11-b, 12-c, 13-c, 14-c, 15-d, 16-c, 17-a, 18-d, 19-c, 20-b, 21-c, 22-b, 23-c, 24-b, 25-b

Arithmetic Reasoning: 1-b, 2-a, 3-a, 4-b, 5-b, 6-b, 7-b, 8-a, 9-b, 10-b, 11-c, 12-a, 13-c, 14-b, 15-d, 16-a, 17-a, 18-c, 19-d, 20-b, 21-b, 22-c, 23-c, 24-b, 25-b, 26-a, 27-c, 28-c, 29-c, 30-c

Word Knowledge: 1-b, 2-b, 3-b, 4-c, 5-c, 6-b, 7-c, 8-b, 9-b, 10-b, 11-c, 12-b, 13-b, 14-b, 15-b, 16-b, 17-b, 18-b, 19-b, 20-b, 21-b, 22-b, 23-b, 24-b, 25-b, 26-b, 27-b, 28-b, 29-b, 30-b, 31-b, 32-b, 33-b, 34-b, 35-b

Paragraph Comprehension: 1-b, 2-a, 3-b, 4-c, 5-c, 6-a, 7-c, 8-b, 9-b, 10-c, 11-b, 12-c, 13-b, 14-c, 15-b

Mathematics Knowledge: 1-a, 2-c, 3-a, 4-a, 5-b, 6-b, 7-a, 8-a, 9-b, 10-b, 11-c, 12-c, 13-b, 14-b, 15-a, 16-b, 17-a, 18-b, 19-b, 20-b, 21-a, 22-b, 23-a, 24-a, 25-a

Electronics Information: 1-c, 2-c, 3-b, 4-b, 5-b, 6-c, 7-b, 8-b, 9-b, 10-c, 11-c, 12-d, 13-b, 14-c, 15-c, 16-b, 17-a, 18-c, 19-b, 20-d

Auto & Shop Information: 1-b, 2-b, 3-b, 4-c, 5-b, 6-c, 7-c, 8-b, 9-b, 10-d, 11-b, 12-b, 13-b, 14-a, 15-c, 16-c, 17-b, 18-b, 19-b, 20-b, 21-c, 22-b, 23-b, 24-b, 25-c

Mechanical Comprehension: 1-a, 2-b, 3-c, 4-c, 5-c, 6-b, 7-b, 8-b, 9-c, 10-b, 11-b, 12-b, 13-b, 14-b, 15-a, 16-b, 17-b, 18-a, 19-a, 20-c, 21-c, 22-b, 23-b, 24-b, 25-b

TEST 16

GENERAL SCIENCE (25 questions)

1. Which of the following is NOT a fossil fuel? a) Coal b) Oil c) Natural gas d) Wind
2. The chemical symbol for sodium is: a) So b) S c) Na d) N
3. Which blood cells are responsible for carrying oxygen? a) White blood cells b) Red blood cells c) Platelets d) Plasma cells

4. The process by which rocks are broken down by wind and water is called: a) Erosion b) Weathering c) Deposition d) Sedimentation
5. What is the closest star to Earth? a) Alpha Centauri b) Polaris c) Sirius d) The Sun
6. Which gas is produced when fossil fuels are burned? a) Oxygen b) Nitrogen c) Carbon dioxide d) Hydrogen
7. The basic unit of heredity is the: a) Cell b) Chromosome c) Gene d) DNA
8. Which planet has the most moons? a) Jupiter b) Saturn c) Neptune d) Uranus
9. The study of weather is called: a) Astronomy b) Geology c) Meteorology d) Biology
10. Which of these is an example of a chemical change? a) Ice melting b) Paper burning c) Water boiling d) Glass breaking
11. The instrument used to measure earthquakes is a: a) Barometer b) Seismograph c) Thermometer d) Anemometer
12. Which part of the atom has a positive charge? a) Electron b) Neutron c) Proton d) Nucleus
13. The process by which plants lose water through their leaves is: a) Photosynthesis b) Respiration c) Transpiration d) Germination
14. Which type of energy is stored in food? a) Kinetic b) Potential c) Chemical d) Nuclear
15. The largest planet in our solar system is: a) Earth b) Saturn c) Neptune d) Jupiter
16. Which mineral is the hardest on the Mohs scale? a) Quartz b) Topaz c) Diamond d) Corundum
17. The human skeleton has approximately how many bones? a) 106 b) 206 c) 306 d) 406
18. Which gas makes up most of the air we breathe? a) Oxygen b) Carbon dioxide c) Nitrogen d) Argon
19. The change of state from gas to liquid is called: a) Evaporation b) Condensation c) Sublimation d) Freezing
20. Which of these is NOT a renewable energy source? a) Solar b) Wind c) Nuclear d) Hydroelectric
21. The study of living things is called: a) Physics b) Chemistry c) Biology d) Geology
22. Which blood type is considered the universal recipient? a) A b) B c) AB d) O
23. The force that pulls objects toward Earth is: a) Magnetism b) Friction c) Gravity d) Centripetal force
24. Which of these elements is a noble gas? a) Oxygen b) Nitrogen c) Helium d) Hydrogen
25. The smallest bone in the human body is located in the: a) Foot b) Hand c) Ear d) Nose

ARITHMETIC REASONING (30 questions)

1. A store sells apples for $1.25 per pound. How much do 4 pounds cost? a) $4.00 b) $4.50 c) $5.00 d) $5.50
2. If a rectangle has a length of 15 inches and width of 8 inches, what is its perimeter? a) 46 inches b) 120 inches c) 23 inches d) 31 inches
3. What is 30% of 250? a) 65 b) 70 c) 75 d) 80
4. If you drive 180 miles in 3 hours, what is your average speed? a) 50 mph b) 55 mph c) 60 mph d) 65 mph
5. A pizza has 12 slices. If you eat 1/3 of the pizza, how many slices did you eat? a) 3 b) 4 c) 5 d) 6
6. What is 2/5 + 1/3? a) 3/8 b) 11/15 c) 7/15 d) 1/2

7. If a shirt costs $35 and is on sale for 20% off, what is the sale price? a) $28 b) $30 c) $32 d) $33

8. A classroom has 28 students. If 3/4 of them are present, how many students are absent? a) 6 b) 7 c) 8 d) 9

9. What is the area of a circle with radius 4 inches? (Use $\pi = 3.14$) a) 12.56 sq in b) 25.12 sq in c) 50.24 sq in d) 100.48 sq in

10. If you save $15 per week for 12 weeks, how much will you have saved? a) $160 b) $170 c) $180 d) $190

11. A box contains 36 pencils. If you use 2/9 of them, how many pencils are left? a) 24 b) 26 c) 28 d) 30

12. What is $45 \div 9 + 3 \times 2$? a) 9 b) 11 c) 13 d) 15

13. If $4x + 8 = 32$, what is x? a) 4 b) 5 c) 6 d) 7

14. A train travels 420 miles in 7 hours. How long will it take to travel 300 miles at the same speed? a) 4 hours b) 5 hours c) 6 hours d) 7 hours

15. What is 0.6 expressed as a fraction in lowest terms? a) 6/10 b) 3/5 c) 12/20 d) 60/100

16. If you buy 5 items at $3.75 each and pay with $25, how much change do you receive? a) $6.25 b) $6.50 c) $6.75 d) $7.00

17. What is the square root of 81? a) 8 b) 9 c) 10 d) 11

18. A recipe for 4 people calls for 2 cups of flour. How much flour is needed for 6 people? a) 2.5 cups b) 3 cups c) 3.5 cups d) 4 cups

19. If $y = 2x + 3$ and $x = 4$, what is y? a) 9 b) 10 c) 11 d) 12

20. What is 25% of 80% of 200? a) 30 b) 35 c) 40 d) 45

21. A car's value depreciates 12% each year. If it's worth $25,000 now, what will it be worth next year? a) $22,000 b) $22,500 c) $23,000 d) $23,500

22. What is $7 + 3 \times 4 - 2$? a) 15 b) 17 c) 19 d) 38

23. If a triangle has angles of 60° and 70°, what is the third angle? a) 40° b) 45° c) 50° d) 55°

24. How many seconds are in 2.5 minutes? a) 120 seconds b) 130 seconds c) 140 seconds d) 150 seconds

25. What is $3/8 \times 2/3$? a) 1/4 b) 5/11 c) 6/24 d) 1/2

26. If a book has 360 pages and you read 45 pages per day, how many days will it take to finish? a) 7 days b) 8 days c) 9 days d) 10 days

27. What is $12^2 - 10^2$? a) 44 b) 46 c) 48 d) 50

28. A jacket originally costs $60 and is marked up 30%. What is the new price? a) $75 b) $78 c) $80 d) $82

29. If $3y - 5 = 13$, what is y? a) 4 b) 5 c) 6 d) 7

30. What is the perimeter of a square with area 64 square feet? a) 28 feet b) 30 feet c) 32 feet d) 34 feet

WORD KNOWLEDGE (35 questions)

1. AMPLIFY most nearly means: a) Reduce b) Enlarge c) Clarify d) Simplify

2. BIZARRE most nearly means: a) Normal b) Strange c) Large d) Small

3. CAUTIOUS most nearly means: a) Careless b) Careful c) Quick d) Slow

4. DETOUR most nearly means: a) Direct route b) Alternate route c) Fast route d) Main route

5. ENDURE most nearly means: a) Begin b) End c) Last d) Start

6. FLAW most nearly means: a) Perfection b) Defect c) Strength d) Beauty
7. GLOOMY most nearly means: a) Bright b) Dark c) Happy d) Colorful
8. HARSH most nearly means: a) Gentle b) Severe c) Soft d) Kind
9. IDLE most nearly means: a) Busy b) Active c) Inactive d) Working
10. JUSTIFY most nearly means: a) Condemn b) Explain c) Hide d) Ignore
11. KEEN most nearly means: a) Dull b) Sharp c) Slow d) Lazy
12. LOYAL most nearly means: a) Disloyal b) Faithful c) Unreliable d) Dishonest
13. MERGE most nearly means: a) Separate b) Combine c) Divide d) Split
14. NIMBLE most nearly means: a) Clumsy b) Agile c) Slow d) Heavy
15. OPPOSE most nearly means: a) Support b) Resist c) Help d) Agree
16. PERIL most nearly means: a) Safety b) Danger c) Peace d) Calm
17. QUEST most nearly means: a) Answer b) Search c) Find d) Solution
18. RIGID most nearly means: a) Flexible b) Stiff c) Soft d) Loose
19. SUMMIT most nearly means: a) Bottom b) Peak c) Middle d) Valley
20. TIMID most nearly means: a) Bold b) Shy c) Loud d) Confident
21. URGENT most nearly means: a) Delayed b) Pressing c) Calm d) Relaxed
22. VAGUE most nearly means: a) Clear b) Unclear c) Specific d) Exact
23. WEARY most nearly means: a) Energetic b) Tired c) Fresh d) Alert
24. YEARN most nearly means: a) Dislike b) Long for c) Avoid d) Reject
25. ZEALOUS most nearly means: a) Lazy b) Enthusiastic c) Bored d) Tired
26. ABRUPT most nearly means: a) Gradual b) Sudden c) Slow d) Smooth
27. BRILLIANT most nearly means: a) Dull b) Bright c) Dark d) Dim
28. CRITICAL most nearly means: a) Unimportant b) Important c) Minor d) Trivial
29. DEVISE most nearly means: a) Destroy b) Create c) Copy d) Imitate
30. EVIDENT most nearly means: a) Hidden b) Obvious c) Secret d) Unclear
31. FICTION most nearly means: a) Truth b) Fantasy c) Reality d) Fact
32. GENEROUS most nearly means: a) Selfish b) Giving c) Greedy d) Stingy
33. HUMBLE most nearly means: a) Proud b) Modest c) Arrogant d) Boastful
34. IDENTICAL most nearly means: a) Different b) Same c) Opposite d) Unique
35. JUVENILE most nearly means: a) Adult b) Young c) Old d) Senior

PARAGRAPH COMPREHENSION (15 questions)

Passage 1: Regular physical exercise is essential for maintaining good health. Exercise strengthens the heart muscle, improves circulation, and helps control weight. It also releases endorphins, which are natural chemicals that make you feel good and reduce stress. People who exercise regularly report better sleep quality and higher energy levels throughout the day. Health experts recommend at least 30 minutes of moderate exercise most days of the week.

1. According to the passage, endorphins: a) Strengthen the heart b) Make you feel good c) Control weight d) Improve circulation
2. Health experts recommend exercising for at least: a) 20 minutes daily b) 30 minutes most days c) 1 hour daily d) 30 minutes weekly

Passage 2: The Amazon rainforest, often called the "lungs of the Earth," produces about 20% of the world's oxygen. This vast forest covers over 2 million square miles and is home to millions of species of plants and animals. Many medicines come from plants found in the Amazon. Unfortunately, deforestation threatens this vital ecosystem. Scientists estimate that an area the size of a football field is cleared every minute.

3. The Amazon rainforest is called the "lungs of the Earth" because it: a) Covers 2 million square miles b) Is home to many species c) Produces oxygen d) Contains medicine plants
4. According to the passage, deforestation in the Amazon occurs at a rate of: a) One football field per hour b) One football field per minute c) Two football fields per minute d) One football field per day

Passage 3: Nutrition labels on food packages provide important information about the contents of the food. The label shows the serving size, number of calories, and amounts of various nutrients like fat, sodium, and vitamins. Understanding these labels can help people make healthier food choices. For example, foods high in saturated fat and sodium should be consumed in moderation, while foods rich in fiber and vitamins are generally beneficial.

5. Nutrition labels help people: a) Cook food properly b) Store food safely c) Make healthier choices d) Determine food cost
6. According to the passage, which nutrients should be consumed in moderation? a) Fiber and vitamins b) Saturated fat and sodium c) Calories and serving size d) Protein and carbohydrates

Passage 4: The invention of the telephone by Alexander Graham Bell in 1876 revolutionized communication. Before the telephone, long-distance communication relied on written messages sent by mail or telegraph. The telephone allowed people to have real-time conversations across great distances. This invention paved the way for modern communication technologies, including cell phones and the internet.

7. Before the telephone, long-distance communication used: a) Only mail b) Only telegraph c) Mail and telegraph d) Smoke signals
8. The telephone allowed people to: a) Send written messages b) Have real-time conversations c) Use the internet d) Send telegraphs

Passage 5: Recycling is the process of converting waste materials into new products. This practice helps reduce the amount of waste sent to landfills and conserves natural resources. Common recyclable materials include paper, plastic, glass, and metal. Recycling also saves energy because it often requires less energy to make products from recycled materials than from raw materials. Many communities have curbside recycling programs to make recycling convenient for residents.

9. Recycling helps by: a) Only reducing waste b) Only conserving resources c) Reducing waste and conserving resources d) Only saving energy
10. According to the passage, making products from recycled materials: a) Uses more energy b) Uses less energy c) Uses the same energy d) Doesn't affect energy use

Passage 6: Volcanoes are openings in the Earth's crust where molten rock, ash, and gases can escape from below the surface. There are three main types of volcanoes: active, dormant, and extinct. Active volcanoes have erupted recently and may erupt again. Dormant volcanoes haven't erupted recently but could become active again. Extinct volcanoes are not expected to erupt again. Volcanic eruptions can be dangerous but also create fertile soil for farming.

11. Dormant volcanoes are those that: a) Have never erupted b) Haven't erupted recently but could c) Will never erupt again d) Are currently erupting
12. Volcanic eruptions can: a) Only be dangerous b) Only create fertile soil c) Be dangerous and create fertile soil d) Never be beneficial

Passage 7: Photosynthesis is crucial for life on Earth. During this process, plants use sunlight, carbon dioxide from the air, and water from the soil to produce glucose (sugar) and oxygen. The glucose provides energy for the plant to grow, while the oxygen is released into the atmosphere. Without photosynthesis, there would be no oxygen for animals to breathe, and no food chain could exist.

13. During photosynthesis, plants produce: a) Only glucose b) Only oxygen c) Glucose and oxygen d) Carbon dioxide and water
14. Without photosynthesis: a) Plants couldn't grow b) There would be no oxygen for animals c) No food chain could exist d) All of the above

Passage 8: The water cycle is a continuous process that moves water around the Earth. The sun heats water in oceans, lakes, and rivers, causing it to evaporate and rise as water vapor. As the vapor rises higher in the atmosphere, it cools and condenses into tiny water droplets that form clouds. When the droplets become too heavy, they fall as precipitation (rain, snow, or sleet). This water then flows back to the oceans or soaks into the ground, completing the cycle.

15. In the water cycle, precipitation occurs when: a) Water evaporates b) Vapor condenses c) Droplets become too heavy d) Water soaks into ground

MATHEMATICS KNOWLEDGE (25 questions)

1. What is the value of $5^2 - 3^2$? a) 14 b) 16 c) 18 d) 20
2. If $x = -3$, what is the value of $x^2 + 2x$? a) 3 b) 6 c) 9 d) 15
3. What is the area of a rectangle with length 12 and width 7? a) 38 b) 84 c) 19 d) 76
4. Solve for a: $2a + 5 = 17$ a) 5 b) 6 c) 7 d) 8
5. What is 40% of 150? a) 50 b) 55 c) 60 d) 65
6. If $y = 2x - 1$ and $x = 5$, what is y? a) 8 b) 9 c) 10 d) 11
7. What is the perimeter of a triangle with sides 5, 7, and 9? a) 19 b) 20 c) 21 d) 22
8. Simplify: $3(2x + 4) - 6$ a) 6x + 6 b) 6x + 12 c) 6x - 6 d) 6x + 18
9. What is the slope of the line passing through (2, 3) and (4, 7)? a) 1 b) 2 c) 3 d) 4
10. If $3z - 8 = 19$, what is z? a) 7 b) 8 c) 9 d) 10
11. What is the volume of a rectangular box with dimensions $4 \times 5 \times 6$? a) 110 b) 120 c) 130 d) 140
12. Simplify: $\sqrt{64} - \sqrt{16}$ a) 2 b) 3 c) 4 d) 6

13. What is the value of |-5| + |3|? a) 2 b) 8 c) -8 d) -2
14. If g(x) = 3x - 2, what is g(4)? a) 8 b) 9 c) 10 d) 11
15. What is 2/3 ÷ 4/5? a) 5/6 b) 8/15 c) 10/12 d) 8/12
16. Solve: x^2 = 49 a) x = 7 only b) x = ±7 c) x = 24.5 d) x = 98
17. What is the circumference of a circle with diameter 10? (Use π = 3.14) a) 31.4 b) 15.7 c) 62.8 d) 78.5
18. If $\log_3(27)$ = x, what is x? a) 2 b) 3 c) 9 d) 81
19. What is the sum of angles in a quadrilateral? a) 180° b) 270° c) 360° d) 450°
20. Simplify: $(a^2)^3$ a) a^5 b) a^6 c) a^8 d) $3a^2$
21. What is the distance between points (1, 2) and (4, 6)? a) 4 b) 5 c) 6 d) 7
22. If 2^x = 32, what is x? a) 4 b) 5 c) 6 d) 16
23. What is the mode of: 4, 7, 4, 9, 6, 4, 8? a) 4 b) 6 c) 7 d) 9
24. Simplify: 5x - 2x + 3x a) 6x b) 5x c) 4x d) 3x
25. What is cos(60°)? a) 1/2 b) √2/2 c) √3/2 d) 1

ELECTRONICS INFORMATION (20 questions)

1. The opposition to current flow in a circuit is called: a) Voltage b) Power c) Resistance d) Frequency
2. In a parallel circuit, voltage across each branch is: a) Different b) The same c) Zero d) Infinite
3. What does DC stand for? a) Direct Current b) Digital Current c) Dynamic Current d) Double Current
4. A device that allows current to flow in only one direction is a: a) Resistor b) Capacitor c) Diode d) Transformer
5. Electric power is measured in: a) Volts b) Amperes c) Ohms d) Watts
6. Which material is commonly used as an insulator? a) Copper b) Aluminum c) Rubber d) Silver
7. In the formula P = I × V, what does P represent? a) Pressure b) Power c) Potential d) Pulse
8. An inductor opposes changes in: a) Voltage b) Current c) Resistance d) Power
9. The negative terminal of a battery is called the: a) Anode b) Cathode c) Electrode d) Terminal
10. What happens to total resistance when resistors are added in parallel? a) Increases b) Decreases c) Stays the same d) Becomes infinite
11. A circuit breaker is designed to: a) Increase voltage b) Store energy c) Protect from overcurrent d) Reduce resistance
12. Electrical energy is measured in: a) Watts b) Watt-hours c) Volts d) Amperes
13. In an AC circuit, current changes: a) Direction only b) Magnitude only c) Both direction and magnitude d) Neither
14. A resistor's value is indicated by: a) Size b) Color bands c) Weight d) Temperature
15. The device that steps up or steps down AC voltage is a: a) Capacitor b) Resistor c) Transformer d) Inductor
16. Earth ground serves as a: a) Current source b) Voltage reference c) Power supply d) Load
17. A potentiometer is a type of: a) Fixed resistor b) Variable resistor c) Capacitor d) Inductor

18. In a schematic, a circle with a "+" and "-" represents: a) Resistor b) Capacitor c) Battery d) Switch
19. The standard voltage for household outlets in the US is: a) 110V b) 120V c) 220V d) 240V
20. An oscilloscope is used to measure: a) Only voltage b) Only current c) Only resistance d) Voltage over time

AUTO & SHOP INFORMATION (25 questions)

1. The part of the engine that converts up and down motion to rotary motion is the: a) Piston b) Connecting rod c) Crankshaft d) Camshaft
2. Which tool is used to cut internal threads? a) Die b) Tap c) Reamer d) Drill bit
3. The system that removes heat from the engine is the: a) Exhaust system b) Cooling system c) Fuel system d) Ignition system
4. What type of joint is formed when two pieces of wood are cut at 45-degree angles? a) Butt joint b) Miter joint c) Lap joint d) Dovetail joint
5. The component that allows the engine to start is the: a) Alternator b) Starter motor c) Generator d) Distributor
6. Which sandpaper grit would be used for rough sanding? a) 220 grit b) 120 grit c) 60 grit d) 400 grit
7. The device that ignites the fuel mixture in the cylinder is the: a) Fuel injector b) Spark plug c) Glow plug d) Carburetor
8. A Phillips head screwdriver has a: a) Flat blade b) Star-shaped tip c) Cross-shaped tip d) Hexagonal tip
9. Anti-freeze in the cooling system prevents: a) Overheating only b) Freezing only c) Both freezing and overheating d) Corrosion only
10. The woodworking tool used to make smooth, flat surfaces is a: a) Saw b) Drill c) Plane d) Chisel
11. The transmission allows the engine to: a) Start b) Cool down c) Change speed and torque d) Generate electricity
12. Which type of screw head requires a square-shaped driver? a) Phillips b) Flathead c) Robertson d) Torx
13. The exhaust system removes: a) Heat from the engine b) Waste gases from the engine c) Oil from the engine d) Fuel from the engine
14. A file that cuts on both the push and pull strokes is called: a) Single-cut b) Double-cut c) Mill file d) Bastard file
15. The oil pump circulates oil to: a) Cool the engine b) Lubricate moving parts c) Clean the fuel d) Ignite the mixture
16. Which saw is best for making straight cuts in lumber? a) Coping saw b) Hacksaw c) Crosscut saw d) Keyhole saw
17. The differential allows: a) The engine to start b) Wheels to turn at different speeds c) Brakes to work d) Steering to function
18. The measurement of a drill bit's cutting diameter is its: a) Length b) Shank size c) Bit size d) Point angle
19. Brake fluid is: a) Compressible b) Incompressible c) A gas d) Solid at room temperature

20. A countersink is used to: a) Enlarge holes b) Make holes for screw heads c) Thread holes d) Clean holes
21. The air filter prevents: a) Fuel contamination b) Oil contamination c) Air contamination d) Dirt from entering the engine
22. The cutting edge angle of a chisel is typically: a) 15 degrees b) 25 degrees c) 45 degrees d) 90 degrees
23. Power steering uses: a) Engine vacuum b) Hydraulic pressure c) Electric motors only d) Manual force only
24. Sandpaper with 320 grit would be used for: a) Rough sanding b) Medium sanding c) Fine sanding d) Paint removal
25. The fuel injection system is controlled by: a) The carburetor b) The fuel pump c) The ECU/computer d) The air filter

MECHANICAL COMPREHENSION (25 questions)

1. If gear A has 30 teeth and gear B has 15 teeth, when gear A makes 1 turn, gear B makes: a) 1/2 turn b) 1 turn c) 2 turns d) 3 turns
2. A second-class lever has the load positioned: a) At the fulcrum b) Between the fulcrum and effort c) At the effort end d) Beyond the effort
3. Using a block and tackle with 3 supporting ropes, if you pull the rope 6 feet, the load moves: a) 6 feet b) 3 feet c) 2 feet d) 18 feet
4. Pressure in a liquid increases with: a) Temperature only b) Depth only c) Volume only d) Container shape
5. If you apply 20 pounds of force to a lever with mechanical advantage of 3, the output force is: a) 23 pounds b) 17 pounds c) 60 pounds d) 6.7 pounds
6. In a hydraulic jack, if the input piston has area 1 sq in and output piston has area 10 sq in, applying 50 pounds of force produces: a) 5 pounds b) 50 pounds c) 500 pounds d) 5000 pounds
7. An inclined plane that is longer will: a) Require more force b) Require less force c) Not change force needed d) Be harder to use
8. The center of gravity of a uniform rod is located: a) At one end b) At the middle c) Closer to the heavier end d) At the bottom
9. A wheel with diameter 4 feet will travel how far in one revolution? a) 4 feet b) 8 feet c) 12.56 feet d) 16 feet
10. Two meshing gears always rotate in: a) The same direction b) Opposite directions c) Random directions d) No specific pattern
11. A jackscrew converts: a) Rotary motion to linear motion b) Linear motion to rotary motion c) Fast motion to slow motion d) Heavy loads to light loads
12. The mechanical advantage of a wedge is determined by: a) Its weight b) Its material c) The ratio of length to thickness d) Its color
13. In a simple pulley system with 2 supporting ropes, the mechanical advantage is: a) 1 b) 2 c) 4 d) 1/2
14. Roller bearings are used to: a) Increase friction b) Reduce friction c) Add weight d) Slow rotation
15. If you double the diameter of a drive pulley while keeping the driven pulley constant: a) Speed doubles b) Speed halves c) Torque doubles d) No change

16. Work is calculated as: a) Force ÷ distance b) Force + distance c) Force × distance d) Distance ÷ force
17. A connecting rod changes: a) Rotary to linear motion b) Linear to rotary motion c) Speed d) Direction only
18. If mechanical advantage increases, you must apply force over: a) A shorter distance b) A greater distance c) The same distance d) No distance
19. Machine efficiency is always: a) 100% b) Greater than 100% c) Less than 100% d) 50%
20. A flywheel smooths out: a) Electrical pulses b) Power fluctuations c) Temperature changes d) Pressure variations
21. In a lever, if the effort arm is twice as long as the load arm, the mechanical advantage is: a) 1/2 b) 1 c) 2 d) 4
22. Pascal's principle applies to: a) Gases only b) Liquids only c) Both gases and liquids d) Solids only
23. Buoyancy depends on: a) Object weight only b) Fluid density only c) Volume of displaced fluid d) Object color
24. If gear A rotates at 200 RPM and has 20 teeth, and gear B has 40 teeth, gear B rotates at: a) 100 RPM b) 200 RPM c) 400 RPM d) 800 RPM
25. A thermostat controls temperature by: a) Generating heat b) Sensing and regulating c) Cooling only d) Heating only

ANSWER KEY - TEST 16

General Science: 1-d, 2-c, 3-b, 4-b, 5-d, 6-c, 7-c, 8-b, 9-c, 10-b, 11-b, 12-c, 13-c, 14-c, 15-d, 16-c, 17-b, 18-c, 19-b, 20-c, 21-c, 22-c, 23-c, 24-c, 25-c

Arithmetic Reasoning: 1-c, 2-a, 3-c, 4-c, 5-b, 6-b, 7-a, 8-b, 9-c, 10-c, 11-c, 12-b, 13-c, 14-b, 15-b, 16-a, 17-b, 18-b, 19-c, 20-c, 21-a, 22-b, 23-c, 24-d, 25-a, 26-b, 27-a, 28-b, 29-c, 30-c

Word Knowledge: 1-b, 2-b, 3-b, 4-b, 5-c, 6-b, 7-b, 8-b, 9-c, 10-b, 11-b, 12-b, 13-b, 14-b, 15-b, 16-b, 17-b, 18-b, 19-b, 20-b, 21-b, 22-b, 23-b, 24-b, 25-b, 26-b, 27-b, 28-b, 29-b, 30-b, 31-b, 32-b, 33-b, 34-b, 35-b

Paragraph Comprehension: 1-b, 2-b, 3-c, 4-b, 5-c, 6-b, 7-c, 8-b, 9-c, 10-b, 11-b, 12-c, 13-c, 14-d, 15-c

Mathematics Knowledge: 1-b, 2-a, 3-b, 4-b, 5-c, 6-b, 7-c, 8-a, 9-b, 10-c, 11-b, 12-c, 13-b, 14-c, 15-a, 16-b, 17-a, 18-b, 19-c, 20-b, 21-b, 22-b, 23-a, 24-a, 25-a

Electronics Information: 1-c, 2-b, 3-a, 4-c, 5-d, 6-c, 7-b, 8-b, 9-b, 10-b, 11-c, 12-b, 13-c, 14-b, 15-c, 16-b, 17-b, 18-c, 19-b, 20-d

Auto & Shop Information: 1-c, 2-b, 3-b, 4-b, 5-b, 6-c, 7-b, 8-c, 9-c, 10-c, 11-c, 12-c, 13-b, 14-b, 15-b, 16-c, 17-b, 18-c, 19-b, 20-b, 21-d, 22-b, 23-b, 24-c, 25-c

TEST 17

GENERAL SCIENCE (25 questions)

1. Which type of energy is stored in a compressed spring? a) Kinetic b) Potential c) Chemical d) Nuclear
2. The chemical formula for table salt is: a) NaCl b) NaOH c) $CaCl_2$ d) KCl
3. Which organ produces insulin in the human body? a) Liver b) Kidney c) Pancreas d) Stomach
4. The process by which sedimentary rock changes to metamorphic rock is caused by: a) Wind b) Water c) Heat and pressure d) Ice
5. Which planet is known as the "Red Planet"? a) Venus b) Mars c) Jupiter d) Saturn
6. During cellular respiration, glucose is broken down to release: a) Oxygen b) Carbon dioxide c) Energy d) Water
7. The study of fossils is called: a) Geology b) Paleontology c) Archaeology d) Biology
8. Which element has the atomic number 6? a) Nitrogen b) Oxygen c) Carbon d) Boron
9. The human circulatory system includes: a) Heart only b) Blood vessels only c) Heart and blood vessels d) Lungs only
10. Which type of cloud produces thunderstorms? a) Cirrus b) Stratus c) Cumulus d) Cumulonimbus
11. The process by which liquid water becomes water vapor is: a) Condensation b) Evaporation c) Precipitation d) Sublimation
12. Which part of the cell controls what enters and leaves? a) Nucleus b) Cell membrane c) Cytoplasm d) Mitochondria
13. The pH of pure water is: a) 5 b) 6 c) 7 d) 8
14. Which force opposes motion between two surfaces? a) Gravity b) Magnetism c) Friction d) Tension
15. The largest artery in the human body is the: a) Pulmonary artery b) Carotid artery c) Aorta d) Coronary artery
16. Which gas is released when plants undergo cellular respiration? a) Oxygen b) Nitrogen c) Carbon dioxide d) Hydrogen
17. The speed of sound in air at room temperature is approximately: a) 186,000 miles per second b) 1,100 feet per second c) 300,000 km per second d) 500 miles per hour
18. Which blood component helps clot blood? a) Red blood cells b) White blood cells c) Platelets d) Plasma
19. The division of the nucleus during cell reproduction is called: a) Meiosis b) Mitosis c) Photosynthesis d) Respiration
20. Which layer of the atmosphere is closest to Earth's surface? a) Stratosphere b) Troposphere c) Mesosphere d) Thermosphere
21. The chemical formula for carbon dioxide is: a) CO b) CO_2 c) C_2O d) C_2O_2
22. Which instrument measures wind speed? a) Barometer b) Thermometer c) Hygrometer d) Anemometer

23. The science that studies the relationships between organisms and their environment is: a) Biology b) Ecology c) Geology d) Chemistry
24. Which element is essential for thyroid function? a) Iron b) Calcium c) Iodine d) Potassium
25. The asteroid belt is located between: a) Mercury and Venus b) Earth and Mars c) Mars and Jupiter d) Jupiter and Saturn

ARITHMETIC REASONING (30 questions)

1. If a bicycle wheel has a diameter of 26 inches, what is its circumference? (Use $\pi = 3.14$) a) 81.64 inches b) 82.64 inches c) 83.64 inches d) 84.64 inches
2. Maria earns $12.50 per hour. If she works 35 hours in a week, how much does she earn? a) $437.50 b) $447.50 c) $457.50 d) $467.50
3. What is 5/8 - 1/4? a) 3/8 b) 4/8 c) 1/2 d) 3/4
4. If a car travels 45 miles on 1.5 gallons of gas, how many miles per gallon does it get? a) 25 mpg b) 28 mpg c) 30 mpg d) 32 mpg
5. A rectangle has an area of 96 square feet and a width of 8 feet. What is its length? a) 10 feet b) 11 feet c) 12 feet d) 14 feet
6. What is 18% of 350? a) 60 b) 63 c) 66 d) 69
7. If you buy 6 items at $4.25 each and pay 8% sales tax, what is the total cost? a) $27.54 b) $27.84 c) $28.04 d) $28.54
8. A class has 32 students. If 3/8 of them are absent, how many students are present? a) 18 b) 20 c) 22 d) 24
9. What is the volume of a cylinder with radius 3 inches and height 8 inches? (Use $\pi = 3.14$) a) 226.08 cubic inches b) 235.08 cubic inches c) 245.08 cubic inches d) 255.08 cubic inches
10. If you invest $500 at 6% simple interest for 3 years, how much interest do you earn? a) $80 b) $85 c) $90 d) $95
11. A bag contains 45 marbles. If 2/5 are blue and 1/3 are red, how many are other colors? a) 8 b) 10 c) 12 d) 14
12. What is 24 ÷ 4 + 5 × 3? a) 18 b) 20 c) 21 d) 23
13. If 5x - 3 = 27, what is x? a) 5 b) 6 c) 7 d) 8
14. A plane travels 1,800 miles in 4 hours. At this speed, how long will it take to travel 2,700 miles? a) 5 hours b) 6 hours c) 7 hours d) 8 hours
15. What is 0.125 expressed as a fraction in lowest terms? a) 1/8 b) 125/1000 c) 1/4 d) 5/40
16. If you purchase 4 books at $8.95 each and receive a $5 discount, what is the total cost? a) $30.80 b) $31.80 c) $32.80 d) $33.80
17. What is the square root of 169? a) 12 b) 13 c) 14 d) 15
18. A recipe for 8 servings calls for 3 cups of rice. How much rice is needed for 12 servings? a) 4 cups b) 4.5 cups c) 5 cups d) 5.5 cups
19. If m = 3n + 2 and n = 4, what is m? a) 12 b) 13 c) 14 d) 15
20. What is 35% of 60% of 400? a) 80 b) 84 c) 88 d) 92
21. A house value appreciates 8% per year. If it's worth $200,000 now, what will it be worth next year? a) $208,000 b) $212,000 c) $216,000 d) $220,000
22. What is 15 - 4 × 2 + 8? a) 15 b) 18 c) 20 d) 30
23. If a triangle has angles of 45° and 55°, what is the third angle? a) 70° b) 75° c) 80° d) 85°

24. How many minutes are in 3.25 hours? a) 185 minutes b) 190 minutes c) 195 minutes d) 200 minutes
25. What is 5/6 × 3/10? a) 1/4 b) 15/60 c) 1/2 d) 8/16
26. If a swimming pool holds 18,000 gallons and drains at 150 gallons per hour, how long will it take to empty? a) 110 hours b) 115 hours c) 120 hours d) 125 hours
27. What is $9^2 + 5^2$? a) 96 b) 100 c) 104 d) 106
28. A computer originally costs $800 and is marked up 15%. What is the new price? a) $900 b) $920 c) $940 d) $960
29. If 4y + 7 = 31, what is y? a) 5 b) 6 c) 7 d) 8
30. What is the area of a circle with radius 6 feet? (Use $\pi = 3.14$) a) 113.04 sq ft b) 113.44 sq ft c) 113.84 sq ft d) 114.04 sq ft

WORD KNOWLEDGE (35 questions)

1. ABOLISH most nearly means: a) Create b) Eliminate c) Support d) Improve
2. BENEVOLENT most nearly means: a) Selfish b) Kind c) Mean d) Lazy
3. COLLABORATE most nearly means: a) Compete b) Work together c) Argue d) Separate
4. DELICATE most nearly means: a) Strong b) Fragile c) Heavy d) Rough
5. ELABORATE most nearly means: a) Simple b) Detailed c) Quick d) Small
6. FABRICATE most nearly means: a) Destroy b) Make c) Find d) Lose
7. GRACIOUS most nearly means: a) Rude b) Courteous c) Angry d) Sad
8. HESITATE most nearly means: a) Rush b) Pause c) Continue d) Start
9. IMITATE most nearly means: a) Create b) Copy c) Destroy d) Ignore
10. JOVIAL most nearly means: a) Sad b) Cheerful c) Angry d) Tired
11. KNOWLEDGEABLE most nearly means: a) Ignorant b) Informed c) Confused d) Simple
12. LENIENT most nearly means: a) Strict b) Tolerant c) Harsh d) Mean
13. MAGNIFICENT most nearly means: a) Ordinary b) Splendid c) Small d) Ugly
14. NURTURE most nearly means: a) Neglect b) Care for c) Ignore d) Abandon
15. OPTIMISTIC most nearly means: a) Negative b) Hopeful c) Sad d) Worried
16. PERCEPTIVE most nearly means: a) Blind b) Aware c) Confused d) Ignorant
17. QUARANTINE most nearly means: a) Release b) Isolate c) Unite d) Mix
18. RATIONAL most nearly means: a) Emotional b) Logical c) Crazy d) Wild
19. SUBSTANTIAL most nearly means: a) Small b) Large c) Empty d) Light
20. TEMPORARY most nearly means: a) Permanent b) Brief c) Forever d) Long
21. UNANIMOUS most nearly means: a) Divided b) In complete agreement c) Partial d) Confused
22. VIGILANT most nearly means: a) Careless b) Watchful c) Sleepy d) Lazy
23. WANDER most nearly means: a) Stay b) Roam c) Stop d) Rest
24. EXAGGERATE most nearly means: a) Minimize b) Overstate c) Ignore d) Understand
25. YIELD most nearly means: a) Resist b) Give way c) Fight d) Push
26. ARCHIVE most nearly means: a) Destroy b) Store c) Lose d) Forget
27. BRIEF most nearly means: a) Long b) Short c) Detailed d) Complex
28. COMPREHENSIVE most nearly means: a) Partial b) Complete c) Simple d) Easy
29. DILIGENT most nearly means: a) Lazy b) Hardworking c) Careless d) Slow
30. EFFICIENT most nearly means: a) Wasteful b) Effective c) Slow d) Careless

31. FLEXIBLE most nearly means: a) Rigid b) Adaptable c) Broken d) Hard
32. GRADUAL most nearly means: a) Sudden b) Step-by-step c) Fast d) Immediate
33. HOSTILE most nearly means: a) Friendly b) Unfriendly c) Kind d) Helpful
34. IMMINENT most nearly means: a) Distant b) About to happen c) Never d) Past
35. JEOPARDIZE most nearly means: a) Protect b) Endanger c) Help d) Support

PARAGRAPH COMPREHENSION (15 questions)

Passage 1: Sleep is essential for both physical and mental health. During sleep, the body repairs tissues, consolidates memories, and releases growth hormones. Adults need 7-9 hours of sleep per night for optimal health. Sleep deprivation can lead to weakened immune function, poor concentration, and increased risk of accidents. Good sleep hygiene includes maintaining a regular sleep schedule, avoiding caffeine before bedtime, and creating a comfortable sleep environment.

1. According to the passage, during sleep the body: a) Only repairs tissues b) Only consolidates memories c) Repairs tissues and consolidates memories d) Only releases hormones
2. Sleep deprivation can cause: a) Better concentration b) Stronger immune function c) Weakened immune function d) Fewer accidents

Passage 2: Global warming refers to the long-term increase in Earth's average surface temperature due to human activities. The primary cause is the emission of greenhouse gases, particularly carbon dioxide from burning fossil fuels. These gases trap heat in the atmosphere, leading to climate change effects such as melting ice caps, rising sea levels, and more frequent extreme weather events. Reducing greenhouse gas emissions is crucial for addressing this global challenge.

3. The primary cause of global warming is: a) Natural climate cycles b) Solar radiation c) Greenhouse gas emissions d) Ocean currents
4. Effects of global warming include: a) Only melting ice caps b) Only rising sea levels c) Melting ice caps and rising sea levels d) Cooler temperatures

Passage 3: The human immune system is a complex network of cells, tissues, and organs that work together to defend the body against harmful substances. White blood cells are the key players in immune response, identifying and destroying foreign invaders like bacteria and viruses. The immune system also has memory, allowing it to respond more quickly to previously encountered threats. Vaccines work by training the immune system to recognize specific pathogens without causing disease.

5. White blood cells function to: a) Carry oxygen b) Identify and destroy foreign invaders c) Clot blood d) Digest food
6. Vaccines work by: a) Destroying all bacteria b) Training the immune system c) Replacing white blood cells d) Eliminating the immune system

Passage 4: Renewable energy sources are becoming increasingly important as alternatives to fossil fuels. Solar energy harnesses the power of sunlight through photovoltaic cells or solar thermal systems. Wind energy uses turbines to convert wind motion into electricity. Hydroelectric power generates electricity from flowing water. These renewable sources produce little to no pollution and are sustainable for long-term use.

7. Solar energy can be harnessed through: a) Only photovoltaic cells b) Only solar thermal systems c) Photovoltaic cells or solar thermal systems d) Wind turbines
8. Renewable energy sources are important because they: a) Are expensive b) Produce little to no pollution c) Are difficult to use d) Require fossil fuels

Passage 5: The process of digestion breaks down food into nutrients that the body can absorb and use. Digestion begins in the mouth, where saliva starts breaking down starches. In the stomach, acid and enzymes continue the breakdown process. The small intestine is where most nutrient absorption occurs, while the large intestine absorbs water and forms waste products. The entire digestive process typically takes 24-72 hours.

9. Most nutrient absorption occurs in the: a) Mouth b) Stomach c) Small intestine d) Large intestine
10. The digestive process typically takes: a) 2-6 hours b) 12-24 hours c) 24-72 hours d) 3-7 days

Passage 6: Erosion is the process by which rocks and soil are worn away and transported by natural forces such as wind, water, and ice. While erosion is a natural geological process, human activities can accelerate it significantly. Deforestation, farming, and construction can remove protective vegetation, making soil more vulnerable to erosion. This can lead to loss of fertile topsoil, reduced agricultural productivity, and environmental problems.

11. Human activities that can accelerate erosion include: a) Only deforestation b) Only farming c) Deforestation, farming, and construction d) Only construction
12. Accelerated erosion can lead to: a) Better soil quality b) Loss of fertile topsoil c) Increased agricultural productivity d) No environmental impact

Passage 7: The water cycle is driven by energy from the sun. Solar energy causes water to evaporate from oceans, lakes, and rivers. The water vapor rises into the atmosphere, where it cools and condenses into clouds. When the water droplets in clouds become too heavy, they fall as precipitation. This water then flows back to bodies of water or soaks into the ground, completing the cycle.

13. The water cycle is driven by: a) Wind energy b) Solar energy c) Geothermal energy d) Nuclear energy
14. Water vapor in the atmosphere: a) Heats up b) Stays the same temperature c) Cools and condenses d) Disappears

Passage 8: Antibiotics are medicines that fight bacterial infections by killing bacteria or preventing their growth. However, they are not effective against viral infections like the common cold or flu. The overuse and misuse of antibiotics has led to the development of antibiotic-resistant bacteria, which are much more difficult to treat. It's important to take antibiotics exactly as prescribed and to complete the entire course, even if you feel better.

15. Antibiotics are effective against: a) All infections b) Viral infections c) Bacterial infections d) Fungal infections

MATHEMATICS KNOWLEDGE (25 questions)

1. What is the value of $6^2 - 4^2$? a) 18 b) 20 c) 22 d) 24
2. If x = -2, what is the value of $3x^2 - 4x$? a) 8 b) 12 c) 16 d) 20
3. What is the area of a triangle with base 10 and height 8? a) 36 b) 40 c) 44 d) 48
4. Solve for b: 3b - 7 = 14 a) 6 b) 7 c) 8 d) 9
5. What is 35% of 200? a) 60 b) 65 c) 70 d) 75
6. If a = 4 and b = 5, what is 2a + 3b? a) 21 b) 22 c) 23 d) 24
7. What is the perimeter of a rectangle with length 15 and width 9? a) 44 b) 46 c) 48 d) 50
8. Simplify: 4(x - 3) + 8 a) 4x - 4 b) 4x - 12 c) 4x + 8 d) 4x - 8
9. What is the slope of the line passing through (1, 4) and (5, 12)? a) 1 b) 2 c) 3 d) 4
10. If 4z + 6 = 26, what is z? a) 4 b) 5 c) 6 d) 7
11. What is the volume of a cube with side length 5? a) 100 b) 125 c) 150 d) 175
12. Simplify: $\sqrt{100} + \sqrt{25}$ a) 12 b) 13 c) 14 d) 15
13. What is the value of $|-12| - |5|$? a) 5 b) 7 c) 17 d) -7
14. If h(x) = 2x + 5, what is h(6)? a) 15 b) 16 c) 17 d) 18
15. What is $3/5 \times 5/6$? a) 1/2 b) 8/11 c) 15/30 d) 3/6
16. Solve: $x^2 = 64$ a) x = 8 only b) x = ±8 c) x = 32 d) x = 128
17. What is the area of a circle with radius 8? (Use $\pi = 3.14$) a) 200.96 b) 201.06 c) 201.16 d) 201.26
18. If $\log_4(16) = x$, what is x? a) 2 b) 3 c) 4 d) 8
19. What is the sum of interior angles in a pentagon? a) 540° b) 360° c) 720° d) 900°
20. Simplify: $(x^4)^2$ a) x^6 b) x^8 c) x^{16} d) $2x^4$
21. What is the distance between points (2, 1) and (6, 4)? a) 4 b) 5 c) 6 d) 7
22. If 3^x = 81, what is x? a) 3 b) 4 c) 5 d) 27
23. What is the mean of: 6, 8, 10, 12, 14? a) 8 b) 9 c) 10 d) 11
24. Simplify: 7x - 3x + 2x a) 4x b) 5x c) 6x d) 12x
25. What is tan(45°)? a) 0 b) 1/2 c) 1 d) $\sqrt{3}$

ELECTRONICS INFORMATION (20 questions)

1. Electrical current is measured in: a) Volts b) Amperes c) Ohms d) Watts
2. In a series circuit, current through each component is: a) Different b) The same c) Zero d) Infinite
3. What does EMF stand for? a) Electric Motor Force b) Electromotive Force c) Electronic Magnetic Field d) Electric Magnetic Force
4. A capacitor stores: a) Current b) Resistance c) Electrical charge d) Inductance
5. The unit of electrical power is: a) Volt b) Ampere c) Ohm d) Watt

6. Which material has the highest electrical conductivity? a) Gold b) Copper c) Silver d) Aluminum
7. In the equation $P = V \times I$, what does V represent? a) Power b) Current c) Voltage d) Resistance
8. A device that opposes changes in current is an: a) Resistor b) Capacitor c) Inductor d) Transformer
9. The positive electrode in an electrochemical cell is the: a) Cathode b) Anode c) Terminal d) Conductor
10. When resistors are connected in parallel, total resistance: a) Increases b) Decreases c) Stays the same d) Becomes zero
11. A device that protects circuits from excessive current is a: a) Resistor b) Fuse c) Capacitor d) Inductor
12. Electrical frequency is measured in: a) Volts b) Amperes c) Hertz d) Ohms
13. In a DC circuit, current flows: a) In alternating directions b) In one direction c) In both directions d) Randomly
14. A diode allows current to flow: a) In both directions b) In one direction only c) In no direction d) In alternating directions
15. The device used to change AC voltage levels is a: a) Resistor b) Capacitor c) Transformer d) Diode
16. Common ground in a circuit provides: a) High voltage b) Zero voltage reference c) Maximum current d) Infinite resistance
17. An ammeter measures: a) Voltage b) Current c) Resistance d) Power
18. In a circuit diagram, two parallel lines represent a: a) Resistor b) Battery c) Capacitor d) Switch
19. The power factor in an AC circuit is the ratio of: a) Voltage to current b) Real power to apparent power c) Current to resistance d) Frequency to voltage
20. A voltmeter should be connected: a) In series b) In parallel c) Either way d) Not connected

AUTO & SHOP INFORMATION (25 questions)

1. The component that converts linear motion of pistons to rotary motion is the: a) Connecting rod b) Crankshaft c) Camshaft d) Flywheel
2. Which tool is used to cut external threads on a rod? a) Tap b) Die c) Reamer d) Counterbore
3. The system that reduces harmful exhaust emissions is the: a) Cooling system b) Fuel system c) Emission control system d) Lubrication system
4. A rabbet joint is commonly used in: a) Metalworking b) Woodworking c) Plumbing d) Electrical work
5. The device that converts chemical energy to electrical energy in a vehicle is the: a) Alternator b) Starter c) Battery d) Generator
6. Which abrasive would be used for the smoothest finish? a) 80 grit b) 150 grit c) 220 grit d) 400 grit
7. The component that opens and closes the intake and exhaust ports is the: a) Piston b) Valve c) Connecting rod d) Crankshaft

8. A hex key is also known as a: a) Phillips screwdriver b) Allen wrench c) Torx driver d) Robertson driver
9. The cooling system prevents engine: a) Starting b) Overheating c) Lubrication d) Ignition
10. Which type of saw produces the smoothest cut in wood? a) Rip saw b) Crosscut saw c) Backsaw d) Coping saw
11. The device that increases battery voltage for ignition is the: a) Distributor b) Ignition coil c) Spark plug d) Condenser
12. The threads per inch on a bolt determine the: a) Length b) Diameter c) Thread pitch d) Head size
13. Power steering reduces the effort needed to: a) Brake b) Accelerate c) Steer d) Shift gears
14. A mortise and tenon joint is held together by: a) Screws b) Nails c) Glue and fit d) Bolts
15. The lubrication system reduces: a) Power b) Friction c) Cooling d) Ignition
16. Which fastener cannot be removed and reused? a) Bolt b) Screw c) Rivet d) Nut
17. The automatic transmission uses: a) Manual shifting b) Hydraulic pressure c) Gear ratios only d) Clutch only
18. The point angle on a standard twist drill is: a) 90° b) 118° c) 135° d) 150°
19. Brake pads create friction against the: a) Brake drum b) Brake rotor c) Brake line d) Master cylinder
20. A spokeshave is used for: a) Drilling holes b) Shaping curved surfaces c) Cutting threads d) Measuring angles
21. The PCV system controls: a) Fuel mixture b) Ignition timing c) Crankcase ventilation d) Exhaust flow
22. The bevel on a chisel is typically ground at: a) 15° b) 25° c) 45° d) 60°
23. ABS prevents: a) Engine stalling b) Brake lock-up c) Power steering failure d) Transmission slipping
24. Cross-cut teeth on a saw blade cut: a) With the grain b) Against the grain c) Both directions d) Only metal
25. Fuel injectors are controlled by the: a) Carburetor b) Fuel pump c) Engine computer d) Air filter

MECHANICAL COMPREHENSION (25 questions)

1. If gear A has 40 teeth and gear B has 20 teeth, when gear A makes 1 turn, gear B makes: a) 1/2 turn b) 1 turn c) 2 turns d) 4 turns
2. A third-class lever has the effort applied: a) At the fulcrum b) At the load end c) Between fulcrum and load d) Beyond the load
3. In a compound pulley system with 4 supporting ropes, pulling the rope 8 feet moves the load: a) 2 feet b) 4 feet c) 8 feet d) 32 feet
4. Water pressure depends primarily on: a) Container width b) Container length c) Water depth d) Water temperature
5. A lever with mechanical advantage of 5 requires 25 pounds of effort to lift: a) 5 pounds b) 25 pounds c) 125 pounds d) 250 pounds
6. In a hydraulic press, if input force is 100 pounds and mechanical advantage is 8, output force is: a) 12.5 pounds b) 108 pounds c) 800 pounds d) 8000 pounds
7. A steeper inclined plane requires: a) Less force but more distance b) More force but less distance c) Same force and distance d) No force

8. An object's center of gravity is where its: a) Weight is concentrated b) Mass is evenly distributed c) Weight appears to act d) Density is highest
9. A wheel with radius 2 feet travels what distance in one revolution? a) 4 feet b) 6.28 feet c) 12.56 feet d) 8 feet
10. In gear trains, adjacent gears always rotate: a) In the same direction b) In opposite directions c) At the same speed d) Randomly
11. A screw thread converts: a) Rotary to linear motion b) Linear to rotary motion c) Fast to slow motion d) Small to large force
12. The efficiency of a wedge depends on: a) Its weight b) Its material c) Its angle d) Its color
13. A block and tackle with 6 supporting ropes has mechanical advantage of: a) 3 b) 6 c) 12 d) 36
14. Lubrication reduces: a) Speed b) Friction c) Weight d) Power
15. Increasing the diameter of a driving pulley while keeping the driven pulley constant: a) Increases driven speed b) Decreases driven speed c) Maintains same speed d) Stops motion
16. The formula for work is: a) Force × time b) Force × distance c) Distance × time d) Power × time
17. A cam mechanism converts: a) Linear to rotary motion b) Rotary to linear motion c) Steady to variable motion d) All of the above
18. In simple machines, increasing force output requires: a) Increasing force input b) Decreasing distance input c) Increasing distance input d) No change
19. No machine can have efficiency of: a) 50% b) 75% c) 95% d) 100%
20. A flywheel stores energy in the form of: a) Potential energy b) Kinetic energy c) Chemical energy d) Electrical energy
21. If effort arm is 3 times the load arm, mechanical advantage is: a) 1/3 b) 1 c) 3 d) 9
22. Hydraulic systems work because liquids are: a) Compressible b) Incompressible c) Light d) Heavy
23. Objects float when their density is: a) Greater than water b) Less than water c) Equal to water d) Independent of water
24. Two identical gears meshing together will rotate at: a) Different speeds b) The same speed c) Proportional speeds d) Inverse speeds
25. A bimetallic strip bends when heated because: a) Metals expand differently b) All metals expand equally c) Metals don't expand d) Heat makes metal soft

ANSWER KEY - TEST 17

General Science: 1-b, 2-a, 3-c, 4-c, 5-b, 6-c, 7-b, 8-c, 9-c, 10-d, 11-b, 12-b, 13-c, 14-c, 15-c, 16-c, 17-b, 18-c, 19-b, 20-b, 21-b, 22-d, 23-b, 24-c, 25-c

Arithmetic Reasoning: 1-a, 2-a, 3-a, 4-c, 5-c, 6-b, 7-a, 8-b, 9-a, 10-c, 11-b, 12-c, 13-b, 14-b, 15-a, 16-b, 17-b, 18-b, 19-c, 20-b, 21-c, 22-a, 23-c, 24-c, 25-a, 26-c, 27-d, 28-b, 29-b, 30-a

Word Knowledge: 1-b, 2-b, 3-b, 4-b, 5-b, 6-b, 7-b, 8-b, 9-b, 10-b, 11-b, 12-b, 13-b, 14-b, 15-b, 16-b, 17-b, 18-b, 19-b, 20-b, 21-b, 22-b, 23-b, 24-b, 25-b, 26-b, 27-b, 28-b, 29-b, 30-b, 31-b, 32-b, 33-b, 34-b, 35-b

Paragraph Comprehension: 1-c, 2-c, 3-c, 4-c, 5-b, 6-b, 7-c, 8-b, 9-c, 10-c, 11-c, 12-b, 13-b, 14-c, 15-c

Mathematics Knowledge: 1-b, 2-d, 3-b, 4-b, 5-c, 6-c, 7-c, 8-a, 9-b, 10-b, 11-b, 12-d, 13-b, 14-c, 15-a, 16-b, 17-a, 18-a, 19-a, 20-b, 21-b, 22-b, 23-c, 24-c, 25-c

Electronics Information: 1-b, 2-b, 3-b, 4-c, 5-d, 6-c, 7-c, 8-c, 9-b, 10-b, 11-b, 12-c, 13-b, 14-b, 15-c, 16-b, 17-b, 18-c, 19-b, 20-b

Auto & Shop Information: 1-b, 2-b, 3-c, 4-b, 5-c, 6-d, 7-b, 8-b, 9-b, 10-c, 11-b, 12-c, 13-c, 14-c, 15-b, 16-c, 17-b, 18-b, 19-b, 20-b, 21-c, 22-b, 23-b, 24-b, 25-c

Mechanical Comprehension: 1-c, 2-c, 3-a, 4-c, 5-c, 6-c, 7-b, 8-c, 9-c, 10-b, 11-a, 12-c, 13-b, 14-b, 15-a, 16-b, 17-d, 18-c, 19-d, 20-b, 21-c, 22-b, 23-b, 24-b, 25-a

Test 18

General Science (25 questions)

1. The process by which plants convert light energy into chemical energy is called: A) Respiration B) Photosynthesis C) Transpiration D) Germination
2. Which planet is known as the "Red Planet"? A) Venus B) Jupiter C) Mars D) Saturn
3. The smallest unit of matter that retains chemical properties is: A) Atom B) Molecule C) Ion D) Electron
4. Which blood type is considered the universal donor? A) A B) B C) AB D) O
5. The study of earthquakes is called: A) Geology B) Seismology C) Meteorology D) Oceanography
6. What is the hardest natural substance on Earth? A) Quartz B) Diamond C) Granite D) Steel
7. Which gas makes up approximately 78% of Earth's atmosphere? A) Oxygen B) Carbon dioxide C) Nitrogen D) Argon
8. The process of cell division that produces gametes is: A) Mitosis B) Meiosis C) Binary fission D) Budding
9. Which element has the chemical symbol Fe? A) Fluorine B) Iron C) Francium D) Fermium
10. The largest organ in the human body is: A) Liver B) Lungs C) Brain D) Skin
11. What type of rock is formed from cooled magma? A) Sedimentary B) Metamorphic C) Igneous D) Fossilized
12. Which vitamin is produced when skin is exposed to sunlight? A) Vitamin A B) Vitamin C C) Vitamin D D) Vitamin K

13. The speed of light in a vacuum is approximately: A) 186,000 miles per second B) 300,000 km per second C) Both A and B D) Neither A nor B
14. Which part of the brain controls balance and coordination? A) Cerebrum B) Cerebellum C) Medulla D) Hypothalamus
15. The pH scale measures: A) Temperature B) Pressure C) Acidity/Alkalinity D) Density
16. Which type of cloud is associated with thunderstorms? A) Cirrus B) Stratus C) Cumulus D) Cumulonimbus
17. The process by which water changes from liquid to gas is: A) Condensation B) Evaporation C) Precipitation D) Sublimation
18. Which organelle is responsible for protein synthesis? A) Nucleus B) Mitochondria C) Ribosome D) Golgi apparatus
19. The measure of how much matter is in an object is: A) Weight B) Mass C) Volume D) Density
20. Which planet has the most moons? A) Jupiter B) Saturn C) Uranus D) Neptune
21. The study of heredity is called: A) Genetics B) Evolution C) Ecology D) Taxonomy
22. Which force keeps planets in orbit around the sun? A) Magnetic force B) Gravitational force C) Nuclear force D) Electrical force
23. The chemical formula for water is: A) H_2O B) CO_2 C) NaCl D) CH_4
24. Which part of the eye controls the amount of light entering? A) Cornea B) Lens C) Pupil D) Retina
25. The process by which plants lose water through their leaves is: A) Photosynthesis B) Respiration C) Transpiration D) Absorption

Arithmetic Reasoning (30 questions)

1. If a car travels 60 miles in 1.5 hours, what is its average speed? A) 30 mph B) 40 mph C) 45 mph D) 50 mph
2. A recipe calls for 2/3 cup of flour. If you want to make 3 batches, how much flour do you need? A) 1 cup B) 1.5 cups C) 2 cups D) 2.5 cups
3. If 15% of a number is 45, what is the number? A) 200 B) 250 C) 300 D) 350
4. A store offers a 25% discount on a $80 item. What is the sale price? A) $55 B) $60 C) $65 D) $70
5. If you earn $12 per hour and work 37.5 hours per week, what is your weekly gross pay? A) $450 B) $475 C) $500 D) $525
6. A box contains 24 chocolates. If 3/8 of them are dark chocolate, how many are dark chocolate? A) 6 B) 8 C) 9 D) 12
7. If the ratio of boys to girls in a class is 3:4 and there are 21 students total, how many are girls? A) 9 B) 12 C) 15 D) 18
8. A rectangular garden is 15 feet long and 10 feet wide. What is its area? A) 25 sq ft B) 50 sq ft C) 150 sq ft D) 300 sq ft
9. If you buy 3 shirts for $25 each and 2 ties for $15 each, what is the total cost? A) $95 B) $100 C) $105 D) $110
10. A train travels 240 miles in 4 hours. At the same rate, how far will it travel in 6 hours? A) 320 miles B) 360 miles C) 400 miles D) 480 miles
11. If 40% of a class of 30 students are absent, how many students are present? A) 12 B) 15 C) 18 D) 20

12. A ladder is leaning against a wall. The bottom of the ladder is 3 feet from the wall and the ladder is 5 feet long. How high up the wall does the ladder reach? A) 3 feet B) 4 feet C) 5 feet D) 6 feet
13. If you save $50 per month, how much will you have saved after 2 years? A) $1,000 B) $1,100 C) $1,200 D) $1,300
14. A pizza is cut into 8 equal slices. If you eat 3 slices, what fraction of the pizza remains? A) 3/8 B) 5/8 C) 1/2 D) 2/3
15. If the temperature drops from 75°F to 58°F, by how many degrees did it drop? A) 13° B) 15° C) 17° D) 19°
16. A car's fuel tank holds 15 gallons. If it's currently 1/3 full, how many gallons are needed to fill it? A) 5 gallons B) 8 gallons C) 10 gallons D) 12 gallons
17. If you work 8 hours a day for 5 days, then 6 hours on Saturday, how many total hours did you work? A) 44 hours B) 46 hours C) 48 hours D) 50 hours
18. A rectangular room is 12 feet by 14 feet. How many square feet of carpet are needed? A) 156 sq ft B) 168 sq ft C) 180 sq ft D) 196 sq ft
19. If 5 apples cost $2.50, how much do 12 apples cost? A) $5.00 B) $5.50 C) $6.00 D) $6.50
20. A student scores 85, 92, 78, and 89 on four tests. What is the average score? A) 84 B) 85 C) 86 D) 87
21. If a 20-foot rope is cut into pieces that are each 2.5 feet long, how many pieces will there be? A) 6 B) 7 C) 8 D) 9
22. A bakery sells muffins for $1.25 each or $13.50 per dozen. How much do you save per muffin by buying a dozen? A) $0.25 B) $0.50 C) $0.75 D) $1.00
23. If you drive 45 miles per hour for 2.5 hours, how far do you travel? A) 110.5 miles B) 112.5 miles C) 115 miles D) 117.5 miles
24. A circle has a radius of 7 inches. What is its circumference? (Use $\pi = 22/7$) A) 22 inches B) 44 inches C) 154 inches D) 308 inches
25. If you have $100 and spend 35% of it, how much money do you have left? A) $60 B) $65 C) $70 D) $75
26. A recipe serves 6 people and calls for 4 cups of flour. How much flour is needed to serve 9 people? A) 5 cups B) 6 cups C) 7 cups D) 8 cups
27. If a bus travels 300 miles in 5 hours, what is its average speed? A) 50 mph B) 55 mph C) 60 mph D) 65 mph
28. A rectangular field is 80 yards long and 60 yards wide. What is its perimeter? A) 140 yards B) 240 yards C) 280 yards D) 320 yards
29. If you earn $15 per hour and work 32 hours per week, what is your monthly gross pay (assume 4 weeks per month)? A) $1,800 B) $1,900 C) $1,920 D) $2,000
30. A store has 120 items. If 25% are on sale, how many items are NOT on sale? A) 80 B) 85 C) 90 D) 95

Word Knowledge (35 questions)

1. Meticulous most nearly means: A) Careful B) Quick C) Lazy D) Confused
2. Plausible most nearly means: A) Impossible B) Believable C) Strange D) Obvious
3. Candid most nearly means: A) Sweet B) Honest C) Bitter D) Fake
4. Resilient most nearly means: A) Fragile B) Tough C) Smooth D) Rough
5. Brevity most nearly means: A) Length B) Shortness C) Width D) Height

6. Ambiguous most nearly means: A) Clear B) Vague C) Bright D) Dark
7. Zealous most nearly means: A) Lazy B) Enthusiastic C) Tired D) Bored
8. Redundant most nearly means: A) Necessary B) Unique C) Unnecessary D) Important
9. Benevolent most nearly means: A) Evil B) Kind C) Angry D) Sad
10. Tenacious most nearly means: A) Weak B) Persistent C) Flexible D) Gentle
11. Serene most nearly means: A) Noisy B) Peaceful C) Busy D) Chaotic
12. Trivial most nearly means: A) Important B) Unimportant C) Large D) Small
13. Exuberant most nearly means: A) Sad B) Excited C) Calm D) Tired
14. Skeptical most nearly means: A) Trusting B) Doubting C) Happy D) Angry
15. Frugal most nearly means: A) Wasteful B) Generous C) Thrifty D) Rich
16. Articulate most nearly means: A) Silent B) Clear-speaking C) Loud D) Quiet
17. Superficial most nearly means: A) Deep B) Shallow C) Wide D) Narrow
18. Diligent most nearly means: A) Lazy B) Hardworking C) Slow D) Fast
19. Modest most nearly means: A) Boastful B) Humble C) Loud D) Proud
20. Tangible most nearly means: A) Invisible B) Touchable C) Imaginary D) Abstract
21. Volatile most nearly means: A) Stable B) Unstable C) Solid D) Liquid
22. Eloquent most nearly means: A) Silent B) Well-spoken C) Rude D) Quiet
23. Malevolent most nearly means: A) Kind B) Evil C) Neutral D) Friendly
24. Pragmatic most nearly means: A) Idealistic B) Practical C) Theoretical D) Emotional
25. Lucid most nearly means: A) Confused B) Clear C) Dark D) Bright
26. Adamant most nearly means: A) Flexible B) Stubborn C) Soft D) Weak
27. Gregarious most nearly means: A) Shy B) Sociable C) Quiet D) Lonely
28. Mundane most nearly means: A) Exciting B) Ordinary C) Special D) Unique
29. Innate most nearly means: A) Learned B) Natural C) Taught D) Acquired
30. Verbose most nearly means: A) Brief B) Wordy C) Silent D) Clear
31. Cordial most nearly means: A) Rude B) Friendly C) Cold D) Harsh
32. Ephemeral most nearly means: A) Permanent B) Temporary C) Solid D) Heavy
33. Austere most nearly means: A) Luxurious B) Plain C) Colorful D) Decorated
34. Vindictive most nearly means: A) Forgiving B) Vengeful C) Kind D) Generous
35. Fortuitous most nearly means: A) Unlucky B) Lucky C) Planned D) Expected

Paragraph Comprehension (15 questions)

Passage 1: The honeybee is one of nature's most industrious creatures. A single bee colony can contain up to 80,000 bees during peak season. Worker bees, which are all female, perform various tasks including foraging for nectar, caring for young, and maintaining the hive. The queen bee's sole purpose is to lay eggs, producing up to 2,000 eggs per day during peak season. Drones, the male bees, exist primarily to mate with queens from other colonies.

1. According to the passage, worker bees are: A) All male B) All female C) Both male and female D) Neither male nor female
2. The queen bee's main function is to: A) Forage for nectar B) Care for young C) Lay eggs D) Maintain the hive
3. How many eggs can a queen bee lay per day during peak season? A) 1,000 B) 1,500 C) 2,000 D) 2,500

Passage 2: Solar energy is becoming increasingly popular as a renewable energy source. Solar panels convert sunlight directly into electricity through photovoltaic cells. Unlike fossil fuels, solar energy produces no harmful emissions during operation. However, the initial cost of installing solar panels can be high, and their efficiency depends on weather conditions and geographic location. Despite these challenges, many homeowners are choosing solar energy to reduce their electricity bills and environmental impact.

4. Solar panels convert sunlight into electricity using: A) Thermal cells B) Photovoltaic cells C) Chemical cells D) Mechanical cells
5. What is mentioned as a disadvantage of solar energy? A) It produces harmful emissions B) It's not renewable C) High initial installation cost D) It works only at night
6. The efficiency of solar panels depends on: A) The type of roof B) Weather and location C) The brand of panels D) The size of the house

Passage 3: The ancient city of Pompeii was buried under volcanic ash when Mount Vesuvius erupted in 79 AD. This catastrophic event preserved the city in remarkable detail, providing archaeologists with an unprecedented glimpse into daily life in ancient Rome. The ash acted as a natural preservative, maintaining buildings, artifacts, and even the shapes of victims. Today, Pompeii is a UNESCO World Heritage Site and one of Italy's most popular tourist destinations.

7. Mount Vesuvius erupted in: A) 69 AD B) 79 AD C) 89 AD D) 99 AD
8. The volcanic ash preserved Pompeii by acting as a: A) Destroyer B) Natural preservative C) Heat source D) Water source
9. Pompeii is now designated as a: A) National Park B) UNESCO World Heritage Site C) Private Museum D) Archaeological School

Passage 4: Regular exercise provides numerous health benefits for people of all ages. Physical activity strengthens the heart, improves circulation, and helps maintain healthy weight. Exercise also releases endorphins, which are natural mood elevators that can reduce stress and anxiety. Additionally, regular physical activity can improve sleep quality, boost immune function, and increase overall energy levels. Health experts recommend at least 150 minutes of moderate exercise per week.

10. According to the passage, endorphins are: A) Artificial mood elevators B) Natural mood elevators C) Heart medications D) Sleep aids
11. How many minutes of moderate exercise do health experts recommend per week? A) 100 B) 125 C) 150 D) 175
12. Regular exercise can improve all of the following EXCEPT: A) Sleep quality B) Immune function C) Hair growth D) Energy levels

Passage 5: The Internet has revolutionized how we communicate, learn, and conduct business. Email, social media, and video conferencing have made it possible to connect with people around the world instantly. Online education has made learning more accessible, allowing students to take courses from anywhere. E-commerce has transformed retail, enabling businesses to reach global markets and consumers to shop from home. However, the Internet has also created new challenges, including cybersecurity threats, privacy concerns, and the spread of misinformation.

13. According to the passage, online education has made learning more: A) Expensive B) Difficult C) Accessible D) Time-consuming
14. E-commerce has transformed retail by: A) Making it more expensive B) Limiting market reach C) Enabling global markets D) Reducing product variety
15. The passage mentions all of the following as Internet challenges EXCEPT: A) Cybersecurity threats B) Privacy concerns C) High costs D) Misinformation

Mathematics Knowledge (25 questions)

1. If $x + 7 = 15$, then x = A) 6 B) 7 C) 8 D) 9
2. What is $3^2 \times 2^3$? A) 36 B) 54 C) 72 D) 108
3. The square root of 144 is: A) 10 B) 11 C) 12 D) 13
4. If $3x = 21$, then x = A) 6 B) 7 C) 8 D) 9
5. What is 25% of 80? A) 15 B) 20 C) 25 D) 30
6. The area of a rectangle with length 8 and width 5 is: A) 13 B) 26 C) 40 D) 45
7. If $y - 4 = 11$, then y = A) 7 B) 15 C) 17 D) 19
8. What is the value of $2x + 3$ when $x = 4$? A) 10 B) 11 C) 12 D) 13
9. The perimeter of a square with side length 6 is: A) 12 B) 18 C) 24 D) 36
10. If $2x + 5 = 17$, then x = A) 4 B) 5 C) 6 D) 7
11. What is 0.75 expressed as a fraction in lowest terms? A) 3/4 B) 7/10 C) 75/100 D) 15/20
12. The circumference of a circle with radius 3 is: (Use $\pi = 3.14$) A) 9.42 B) 18.84 C) 28.26 D) 37.68
13. If $4x - 3 = 13$, then x = A) 3 B) 4 C) 5 D) 6
14. What is the slope of the line passing through points (2, 3) and (4, 7)? A) 1 B) 2 C) 3 D) 4
15. The volume of a cube with side length 4 is: A) 12 B) 16 C) 48 D) 64
16. If $5x + 2 = 3x + 10$, then x = A) 2 B) 3 C) 4 D) 5
17. What is the area of a triangle with base 6 and height 8? A) 24 B) 28 C) 32 D) 48
18. If $x^2 = 25$, then x = A) ±3 B) ±4 C) ±5 D) ±6
19. The distance between points (1, 2) and (4, 6) is: A) 3 B) 4 C) 5 D) 6
20. If $3(x + 2) = 15$, then x = A) 1 B) 2 C) 3 D) 4
21. What is the value of $|-8|$? A) -8 B) 0 C) 8 D) 16
22. The area of a circle with radius 5 is: (Use $\pi = 3.14$) A) 31.4 B) 78.5 C) 157 D) 314
23. If $2x - 7 = x + 5$, then x = A) 10 B) 11 C) 12 D) 13
24. What is the greatest common factor of 24 and 36? A) 6 B) 8 C) 12 D) 18
25. If $f(x) = 2x + 1$, what is $f(3)$? A) 5 B) 6 C) 7 D) 8

Electronics Information (20 questions)

1. The unit of electrical resistance is the: A) Volt B) Amp C) Ohm D) Watt
2. In a parallel circuit, if one bulb burns out: A) All bulbs go out B) The other bulbs stay on C) The fuse blows D) The circuit shorts
3. What does AC stand for in electrical terms? A) Automatic Current B) Alternating Current C) Active Current D) Additional Current

4. The primary function of a fuse is to: A) Increase voltage B) Store electricity C) Protect against overcurrent D) Convert AC to DC
5. In Ohm's Law, V = I × R, what does R represent? A) Resistance B) Voltage C) Current D) Power
6. A capacitor is used to: A) Increase current B) Store electrical energy C) Reduce voltage D) Create heat
7. The symbol for a resistor in a circuit diagram is: A) A straight line B) A zigzag line C) A circle D) A triangle
8. What is the voltage of a standard household outlet in the US? A) 110V B) 120V C) 220V D) 240V
9. A transformer is used to: A) Store electricity B) Change voltage levels C) Measure current D) Create resistance
10. The flow of electrons in a circuit is called: A) Voltage B) Current C) Resistance D) Power
11. What does LED stand for? A) Light Emitting Diode B) Low Energy Device C) Laser Electronic Display D) Linear Electric Driver
12. In a series circuit, the total resistance is: A) Less than the smallest resistor B) Equal to the average of all resistors C) The sum of all resistances D) Equal to the largest resistor
13. A multimeter is used to measure: A) Only voltage B) Only current C) Only resistance D) Voltage, current, and resistance
14. The positive terminal of a battery is called the: A) Cathode B) Anode C) Electrode D) Terminal
15. What type of current flows in only one direction? A) Alternating current B) Direct current C) Pulsed current D) Variable current
16. A relay is an electrically operated: A) Resistor B) Capacitor C) Switch D) Transformer
17. The ground wire in household wiring is typically: A) Black B) White C) Green D) Red
18. What is the purpose of a circuit breaker? A) To increase voltage B) To store power C) To protect against overcurrent D) To measure electricity
19. In electrical terms, what does EMF stand for? A) Electrical Motor Force B) Electromagnetic Field C) Electromotive Force D) Electronic Measurement Factor
20. A semiconductor material commonly used in electronics is: A) Copper B) Aluminum C) Silicon D) Iron

Auto & Shop Information (25 questions)

1. The part of an engine that converts the up-and-down motion of pistons into rotary motion is the: A) Camshaft B) Crankshaft C) Connecting rod D) Flywheel
2. What tool is used to measure the gap between spark plug electrodes? A) Caliper B) Micrometer C) Feeler gauge D) Torque wrench
3. The cooling system component that regulates engine temperature is the: A) Radiator B) Water pump C) Thermostat D) Fan
4. What type of wrench is best for working in tight spaces? A) Open-end wrench B) Box-end wrench C) Combination wrench D) Adjustable wrench
5. The device that changes the engine's rotational speed to wheel speed is the: A) Differential B) Transmission C) Clutch D) Flywheel
6. What tool is used to cut internal threads? A) Die B) Tap C) Reamer D) Drill bit

7. The electrical component that provides high voltage to spark plugs is the: A) Alternator B) Starter C) Ignition coil D) Battery
8. A Phillips head screwdriver is designed for screws with: A) Straight slots B) Cross-shaped slots C) Hexagonal holes D) Square holes
9. What causes engine knock? A) Low oil pressure B) Worn spark plugs C) Premature ignition D) Clogged air filter
10. The tool used to measure torque is a: A) Torque wrench B) Impact wrench C) Socket wrench D) Combination wrench
11. The part of the braking system that creates friction to stop the car is the: A) Brake fluid B) Brake pad C) Brake line D) Brake booster
12. What type of saw is best for cutting curves in wood? A) Circular saw B) Table saw C) Jigsaw D) Miter saw
13. The component that filters air entering the engine is the: A) Fuel filter B) Oil filter C) Air filter D) Cabin filter
14. A wood chisel is primarily used for: A) Cutting curves B) Making holes C) Shaping wood D) Measuring angles
15. What does ABS stand for in automotive terms? A) Automatic Brake System B) Anti-lock Braking System C) Advanced Brake System D) Auxiliary Brake System
16. The tool used to hold work pieces while drilling is a: A) Vise B) Clamp C) Chuck D) Arbor
17. The part that stores electrical energy in a car is the: A) Alternator B) Battery C) Starter D) Distributor
18. What tool is used to remove damaged bolts? A) Extractor B) Tap C) Die D) Reamer
19. The system that removes exhaust gases from the engine is the: A) Intake system B) Exhaust system C) Cooling system D) Fuel system
20. A miter box is used with what tool? A) Drill B) Saw C) Chisel D) Plane
21. What fluid is used to transfer power in automatic transmissions? A) Engine oil B) Brake fluid C) Transmission fluid D) Coolant
22. The tool used to measure outside dimensions accurately is a: A) Ruler B) Caliper C) Square D) Level
23. The component that mixes air and fuel in older engines is the: A) Fuel injector B) Carburetor C) Throttle body D) Intake manifold
24. What type of hammer is used for metalworking? A) Claw hammer B) Ball peen hammer C) Sledgehammer D) Rubber mallet
25. The safety device that prevents wheels from locking during hard braking is: A) ABS B) Traction control C) Stability control D) Brake assist

Mechanical Comprehension (25 questions)

1. If gear A has 20 teeth and gear B has 40 teeth, and gear A makes 10 revolutions, how many revolutions does gear B make? A) 5 B) 10 C) 20 D) 40
2. A lever is 6 feet long. If the fulcrum is 2 feet from one end, what is the mechanical advantage? A) 2:1 B) 3:1 C) 1:2 D) 1:3
3. In a pulley system, if you pull 4 feet of rope to lift an object 1 foot, what is the mechanical advantage? A) 1:4 B) 4:1 C) 1:1 D) 2:1

4. Water flows fastest through a pipe at: A) The top B) The bottom C) The center D) The sides
5. If a 10-pound weight is placed 5 feet from a fulcrum, what weight is needed 2 feet on the other side to balance it? A) 20 pounds B) 25 pounds C) 30 pounds D) 35 pounds
6. In a hydraulic system, if the input piston has an area of 2 square inches and the output piston has an area of 8 square inches, what is the force advantage? A) 2:1 B) 4:1 C) 6:1 D) 8:1
7. A wheel and axle has a wheel radius of 12 inches and an axle radius of 3 inches. What is the mechanical advantage? A) 3:1 B) 4:1 C) 9:1 D) 12:1
8. In which direction will wheel B turn if wheel A turns clockwise? A) Clockwise B) Counterclockwise C) It won't turn D) Cannot be determined
9. If a screw has 8 threads per inch, how far will it advance with one complete turn? A) 1/8 inch B) 1/4 inch C) 1/2 inch D) 1 inch
10. A pendulum will swing fastest when: A) It's longest B) It's shortest C) The weight is heaviest D) The weight is lightest
11. In a gear train, if the driver gear has 30 teeth and the driven gear has 10 teeth, the driven gear will turn: A) 3 times slower B) 3 times faster C) At the same speed D) 10 times faster
12. The mechanical advantage of an inclined plane depends on: A) The weight of the object B) The surface friction C) The length and height D) The angle only
13. In a block and tackle system with 4 supporting ropes, what is the theoretical mechanical advantage? A) 2:1 B) 3:1 C) 4:1 D) 8:1
14. Which requires more force to turn? A) A long wrench B) A short wrench C) Both require the same force D) It depends on the bolt
15. If pressure increases in a closed container of gas, the temperature will: A) Increase B) Decrease C) Stay the same D) Become unpredictable
16. A cam rotates to create: A) Circular motion B) Reciprocating motion C) Rotary motion D) Oscillating motion
17. In a differential gear system, if both wheels turn at the same speed, the differential: A) Turns slowly B) Turns quickly C) Doesn't turn D) Reverses direction
18. The efficiency of a machine is always: A) Greater than 100% B) Equal to 100% C) Less than 100% D) Variable
19. A flywheel is used to: A) Increase speed B) Store energy C) Reduce friction D) Change direction
20. In a compound gear train, the overall ratio is found by: A) Adding all ratios B) Subtracting ratios C) Multiplying ratios D) Dividing ratios
21. A governor controls: A) Direction B) Speed C) Force D) Temperature
22. The advantage of a worm gear is: A) High speed B) High torque C) Low friction D) Reversibility
23. In a centrifugal pump, fluid is moved by: A) Pressure B) Centrifugal force C) Vacuum D) Gravity
24. A clutch is used to: A) Increase speed B) Change direction C) Engage/disengage power D) Reduce noise
25. The mechanical advantage of a jackscrew depends on: A) The thread pitch B) The handle length C) Both A and B D) Neither A nor B

Test 18 Answer Key:

- **General Science:** 1-B, 2-C, 3-B, 4-D, 5-B, 6-B, 7-C, 8-B, 9-B, 10-D, 11-C, 12-C, 13-C, 14-B, 15-C, 16-D, 17-B, 18-C, 19-B, 20-B, 21-A, 22-B, 23-A, 24-C, 25-C
- **Arithmetic Reasoning:** 1-B, 2-C, 3-C, 4-B, 5-A, 6-C, 7-B, 8-C, 9-C, 10-B, 11-C, 12-B, 13-C, 14-B, 15-C, 16-C, 17-B, 18-B, 19-C, 20-C, 21-C, 22-A, 23-B, 24-B, 25-B, 26-B, 27-C, 28-C, 29-C, 30-C
- **Word Knowledge:** 1-A, 2-B, 3-B, 4-B, 5-B, 6-B, 7-B, 8-C, 9-B, 10-B, 11-B, 12-B, 13-B, 14-B, 15-C, 16-B, 17-B, 18-B, 19-B, 20-B, 21-B, 22-B, 23-B, 24-B, 25-B, 26-B, 27-B, 28-B, 29-B, 30-B, 31-B, 32-B, 33-B, 34-B, 35-B
- **Paragraph Comprehension:** 1-B, 2-C, 3-C, 4-B, 5-C, 6-B, 7-B, 8-B, 9-B, 10-B, 11-C, 12-C, 13-C, 14-C, 15-C
- **Mathematics Knowledge:** 1-C, 2-C, 3-C, 4-B, 5-B, 6-C, 7-B, 8-B, 9-C, 10-C, 11-A, 12-B, 13-B, 14-B, 15-D, 16-C, 17-A, 18-C, 19-C, 20-C, 21-C, 22-B, 23-C, 24-C, 25-C
- **Electronics Information:** 1-C, 2-B, 3-B, 4-C, 5-A, 6-B, 7-B, 8-B, 9-B, 10-B, 11-A, 12-C, 13-D, 14-B, 15-B, 16-C, 17-C, 18-C, 19-C, 20-C
- **Auto & Shop Information:** 1-B, 2-C, 3-C, 4-B, 5-B, 6-B, 7-C, 8-B, 9-C, 10-A, 11-B, 12-C, 13-C, 14-C, 15-B, 16-A, 17-B, 18-A, 19-B, 20-B, 21-C, 22-B, 23-B, 24-B, 25-A
- **Mechanical Comprehension:** 1-A, 2-C, 3-B, 4-C, 5-B, 6-B, 7-B, 8-B, 9-A, 10-B, 11-B, 12-C, 13-C, 14-B, 15-A, 16-B, 17-C, 18-C, 19-B, 20-C, 21-B, 22-B, 23-B, 24-C, 25-C

Test 19

General Science (25 questions)

1. Which organelle is known as the "powerhouse of the cell"? A) Nucleus B) Mitochondria C) Ribosome D) Golgi apparatus
2. The process by which rocks are broken down by wind and water is called: A) Erosion B) Weathering C) Sedimentation D) Metamorphism
3. What is the most abundant gas in Earth's atmosphere? A) Oxygen B) Carbon dioxide C) Nitrogen D) Argon
4. The study of fossils is called: A) Geology B) Paleontology C) Archaeology D) Anthropology
5. Which vitamin is essential for blood clotting? A) Vitamin A B) Vitamin C C) Vitamin D D) Vitamin K
6. The force that opposes motion between two surfaces is: A) Gravity B) Friction C) Magnetism D) Inertia
7. What type of bond forms when electrons are shared between atoms? A) Ionic bond B) Covalent bond C) Metallic bond D) Hydrogen bond
8. The smallest bone in the human body is located in the: A) Finger B) Toe C) Ear D) Nose
9. Which planet is closest to the Sun? A) Venus B) Earth C) Mercury D) Mars
10. The process by which green plants make their own food is: A) Respiration B) Photosynthesis C) Digestion D) Fermentation
11. What is the chemical symbol for gold? A) Go B) Au C) Ag D) Gd

12. The layer of the atmosphere closest to Earth is the: A) Stratosphere B) Mesosphere C) Troposphere D) Thermosphere
13. Which blood vessels carry blood away from the heart? A) Veins B) Arteries C) Capillaries D) Venules
14. The measure of how much space an object occupies is: A) Mass B) Weight C) Volume D) Density
15. What causes the phases of the Moon? A) Earth's rotation B) Moon's rotation C) Earth's shadow D) Moon's orbit around Earth
16. The basic unit of heredity is the: A) Chromosome B) Gene C) DNA D) Nucleus
17. Which element is essential for plant growth and has the symbol N? A) Nickel B) Nitrogen C) Neon D) Sodium
18. The process by which water vapor becomes liquid is: A) Evaporation B) Condensation C) Precipitation D) Sublimation
19. What is the hardest mineral on the Mohs scale? A) Quartz B) Topaz C) Diamond D) Corundum
20. The study of the structure and function of living organisms is: A) Physiology B) Anatomy C) Biology D) Ecology
21. Which gas is produced during photosynthesis? A) Carbon dioxide B) Oxygen C) Nitrogen D) Hydrogen
22. The center of an atom is called the: A) Electron B) Proton C) Neutron D) Nucleus
23. What type of rock is formed from existing rocks under heat and pressure? A) Igneous B) Sedimentary C) Metamorphic D) Volcanic
24. The organ that produces insulin is the: A) Liver B) Kidney C) Pancreas D) Spleen
25. Which force keeps planets in orbit around the Sun? A) Magnetic force B) Gravitational force C) Electric force D) Nuclear force

Arithmetic Reasoning (30 questions)

1. If a train travels 180 miles in 3 hours, what is its average speed? A) 50 mph B) 55 mph C) 60 mph D) 65 mph
2. A recipe calls for 3/4 cup of sugar. If you want to make 4 batches, how much sugar do you need? A) 2 cups B) 2.5 cups C) 3 cups D) 3.5 cups
3. If 20% of a number is 60, what is the number? A) 250 B) 280 C) 300 D) 320
4. A store offers a 30% discount on a $120 item. What is the sale price? A) $80 B) $84 C) $90 D) $96
5. If you earn $14 per hour and work 40 hours per week, what is your weekly gross pay? A) $540 B) $560 C) $580 D) $600
6. A pizza is cut into 12 equal slices. If you eat 5 slices, what fraction of the pizza is left? A) 5/12 B) 7/12 C) 1/2 D) 2/3
7. If the ratio of red marbles to blue marbles is 2:3 and there are 30 marbles total, how many are blue? A) 12 B) 15 C) 18 D) 20
8. A rectangular pool is 20 feet long and 15 feet wide. What is its area? A) 250 sq ft B) 300 sq ft C) 350 sq ft D) 400 sq ft
9. If you buy 4 books for $12 each and 3 magazines for $5 each, what is the total cost? A) $58 B) $60 C) $63 D) $65

10. A car travels 320 miles in 5 hours. At the same rate, how far will it travel in 8 hours? A) 480 miles B) 512 miles C) 540 miles D) 560 miles

11. If 35% of a class of 40 students passed the test, how many students failed? A) 14 B) 24 C) 26 D) 28

12. A ladder is 13 feet long and is leaning against a wall. If the bottom is 5 feet from the wall, how high up the wall does it reach? A) 8 feet B) 10 feet C) 12 feet D) 15 feet

13. If you save $75 per month, how much will you have saved after 18 months? A) $1,200 B) $1,300 C) $1,350 D) $1,400

14. A circle has a diameter of 14 inches. What is its radius? A) 6 inches B) 7 inches C) 8 inches D) 9 inches

15. If the temperature rises from 42°F to 68°F, by how many degrees did it rise? A) 24° B) 26° C) 28° D) 30°

16. A car's gas tank holds 18 gallons. If it's currently 2/3 full, how many gallons does it contain? A) 10 gallons B) 12 gallons C) 14 gallons D) 16 gallons

17. If you work 7.5 hours a day for 6 days, how many total hours did you work? A) 42 hours B) 45 hours C) 48 hours D) 50 hours

18. A square garden has a perimeter of 48 feet. What is the length of each side? A) 10 feet B) 12 feet C) 14 feet D) 16 feet

19. If 8 pencils cost $3.20, how much do 15 pencils cost? A) $5.50 B) $6.00 C) $6.50 D) $7.00

20. A student scores 78, 85, 92, and 81 on four tests. What is the average score? A) 82 B) 83 C) 84 D) 85

21. If a 15-foot board is cut into pieces that are each 1.5 feet long, how many pieces will there be? A) 8 B) 9 C) 10 D) 12

22. A store sells apples for $0.80 each or $8.50 per dozen. How much do you save per apple by buying a dozen? A) $0.09 B) $0.10 C) $0.11 D) $0.12

23. If you drive 55 miles per hour for 3.5 hours, how far do you travel? A) 185.5 miles B) 192.5 miles C) 195 miles D) 197.5 miles

24. A rectangle has a length of 12 inches and a width of 8 inches. What is its perimeter? A) 32 inches B) 40 inches C) 48 inches D) 56 inches

25. If you have $150 and spend 40% of it, how much money do you have left? A) $85 B) $90 C) $95 D) $100

26. A recipe serves 8 people and calls for 6 cups of broth. How much broth is needed to serve 12 people? A) 8 cups B) 9 cups C) 10 cups D) 12 cups

27. If a plane travels 450 miles in 1.5 hours, what is its average speed? A) 280 mph B) 300 mph C) 320 mph D) 350 mph

28. A triangular flag has a base of 10 inches and a height of 8 inches. What is its area? A) 35 sq in B) 40 sq in C) 45 sq in D) 50 sq in

29. If you earn $16 per hour and work 35 hours per week, what is your monthly gross pay (assume 4 weeks per month)? A) $2,100 B) $2,200 C) $2,240 D) $2,300

30. A school has 180 students. If 60% are girls, how many are boys? A) 70 B) 72 C) 75 D) 80

Word Knowledge (35 questions)

1. Vivid most nearly means: A) Dull B) Bright C) Dark D) Faded

2. Contemplate most nearly means: A) Ignore B) Consider C) Reject D) Forget
3. Arduous most nearly means: A) Easy B) Difficult C) Quick D) Simple
4. Diminish most nearly means: A) Increase B) Decrease C) Maintain D) Expand
5. Jovial most nearly means: A) Sad B) Cheerful C) Angry D) Tired
6. Tedious most nearly means: A) Exciting B) Boring C) Quick D) Easy
7. Perplexed most nearly means: A) Clear B) Confused C) Happy D) Angry
8. Abundant most nearly means: A) Scarce B) Plentiful C) Small D) Rare
9. Meager most nearly means: A) Plentiful B) Scanty C) Generous D) Large
10. Robust most nearly means: A) Weak B) Strong C) Thin D) Fragile
11. Wary most nearly means: A) Trusting B) Cautious C) Careless D) Bold
12. Replenish most nearly means: A) Empty B) Refill C) Waste D) Destroy
13. Somber most nearly means: A) Cheerful B) Serious C) Bright D) Funny
14. Cordial most nearly means: A) Rude B) Friendly C) Cold D) Harsh
15. Stagnant most nearly means: A) Moving B) Still C) Fast D) Flowing
16. Inevitable most nearly means: A) Avoidable B) Unavoidable C) Possible D) Unlikely
17. Conventional most nearly means: A) Unusual B) Traditional C) Modern D) Unique
18. Adverse most nearly means: A) Favorable B) Unfavorable C) Neutral D) Positive
19. Coherent most nearly means: A) Confused B) Clear C) Complicated D) Twisted
20. Prominent most nearly means: A) Hidden B) Noticeable C) Small D) Unimportant
21. Dormant most nearly means: A) Active B) Inactive C) Busy D) Moving
22. Agile most nearly means: A) Clumsy B) Nimble C) Slow D) Heavy
23. Versatile most nearly means: A) Limited B) Adaptable C) Rigid D) Inflexible
24. Obsolete most nearly means: A) Modern B) Outdated C) New D) Current
25. Subtle most nearly means: A) Obvious B) Slight C) Loud D) Clear
26. Impartial most nearly means: A) Biased B) Neutral C) Unfair D) Prejudiced
27. Tentative most nearly means: A) Definite B) Uncertain C) Permanent D) Fixed
28. Lethal most nearly means: A) Harmless B) Deadly C) Gentle D) Safe
29. Perpetual most nearly means: A) Temporary B) Continuous C) Occasional D) Intermittent
30. Arbitrary most nearly means: A) Planned B) Random C) Organized D) Systematic
31. Feasible most nearly means: A) Impossible B) Possible C) Difficult D) Unlikely
32. Legitimate most nearly means: A) Illegal B) Valid C) False D) Fake
33. Tranquil most nearly means: A) Noisy B) Peaceful C) Chaotic D) Busy
34. Flourish most nearly means: A) Decline B) Thrive C) Fail D) Struggle
35. Erratic most nearly means: A) Consistent B) Unpredictable C) Regular D) Steady

Paragraph Comprehension (15 questions)

Passage 1: Recycling is an important practice that helps protect our environment. When materials like paper, plastic, glass, and metal are recycled, they are processed and turned into new products instead of being thrown away. This process reduces the amount of waste that goes to landfills and conserves natural resources. For example, recycling one ton of paper can save 17 trees, 7,000 gallons of water, and enough energy to power an average home for six months.

1. According to the passage, recycling helps protect the environment by: A) Creating new jobs B) Reducing landfill waste C) Increasing production D) Lowering costs

2. Recycling one ton of paper can save: A) 15 trees B) 17 trees C) 19 trees D) 21 trees
3. The passage states that recycling conserves: A) Money B) Time C) Natural resources D) Space

Passage 2: The Great Wall of China is one of the most impressive architectural achievements in human history. Built over many centuries, the wall stretches approximately 13,000 miles across northern China. It was constructed to protect Chinese territories from invasions by northern tribes. The wall is not actually a single continuous structure but rather a series of walls and fortifications built by different dynasties. Today, it attracts millions of tourists from around the world and is recognized as a UNESCO World Heritage Site.

4. The Great Wall of China was built primarily to: A) Attract tourists B) Protect from invasions C) Show architectural skill D) Mark boundaries
5. The Great Wall stretches approximately: A) 10,000 miles B) 12,000 miles C) 13,000 miles D) 15,000 miles
6. The wall is described as: A) A single continuous structure B) A series of walls and fortifications C) A modern construction D) A religious monument

Passage 3: Regular reading has numerous benefits for people of all ages. It improves vocabulary, enhances critical thinking skills, and increases knowledge about various subjects. Reading also helps reduce stress by providing an escape from daily pressures. Studies have shown that reading for just 30 minutes a day can significantly improve cognitive function and memory. Additionally, reading before bedtime can help improve sleep quality by relaxing the mind.

7. According to the passage, reading helps reduce: A) Vocabulary B) Stress C) Knowledge D) Memory
8. How much daily reading can significantly improve cognitive function? A) 15 minutes B) 20 minutes C) 30 minutes D) 45 minutes
9. Reading before bedtime can help improve: A) Vocabulary B) Critical thinking C) Sleep quality D) Memory

Passage 4: The invention of the printing press by Johannes Gutenberg in the 15th century revolutionized the spread of information. Before this invention, books were copied by hand, making them expensive and rare. The printing press allowed books to be produced quickly and cheaply, making knowledge accessible to more people. This technological advance played a crucial role in the Renaissance, the Reformation, and the Scientific Revolution by enabling the rapid spread of new ideas.

10. The printing press was invented by: A) Martin Luther B) Johannes Gutenberg C) Leonardo da Vinci D) William Shakespeare
11. Before the printing press, books were: A) Printed on machines B) Copied by hand C) Mass produced D) Electronically copied
12. The printing press contributed to all of the following EXCEPT: A) The Renaissance B) The Reformation C) The Scientific Revolution D) The Industrial Revolution

Passage 5: Climate change refers to long-term shifts in global temperatures and weather patterns. While climate variations are natural, scientific evidence shows that human activities since the Industrial Revolution have been the primary driver of climate change. The burning of fossil fuels releases greenhouse gases into the atmosphere, which trap heat and cause global temperatures to rise. This warming trend is leading to melting ice caps, rising sea levels, and more frequent extreme weather events.

13. According to the passage, the primary driver of climate change since the Industrial Revolution has been: A) Natural variations B) Solar activity C) Human activities D) Volcanic eruptions
14. Greenhouse gases in the atmosphere: A) Cool the planet B) Trap heat C) Create oxygen D) Reduce pollution
15. Climate change is leading to all of the following EXCEPT: A) Melting ice caps B) Rising sea levels C) Extreme weather events D) Decreasing temperatures

Mathematics Knowledge (25 questions)

1. If $x - 5 = 12$, then $x =$ A) 7 B) 15 C) 17 D) 19
2. What is $4^3 + 2^2$? A) 68 B) 72 C) 76 D) 80
3. The square root of 169 is: A) 11 B) 12 C) 13 D) 14
4. If $4x = 28$, then $x =$ A) 6 B) 7 C) 8 D) 9
5. What is 30% of 120? A) 30 B) 36 C) 40 D) 45
6. The area of a triangle with base 10 and height 6 is: A) 16 B) 20 C) 30 D) 60
7. If $y + 8 = 23$, then $y =$ A) 15 B) 17 C) 19 D) 21
8. What is the value of $3x - 4$ when $x = 5$? A) 9 B) 11 C) 13 D) 15
9. The circumference of a circle with diameter 8 is: (Use $\pi = 3.14$) A) 24.12 B) 25.12 C) 26.12 D) 27.12
10. If $3x + 7 = 22$, then $x =$ A) 3 B) 4 C) 5 D) 6
11. What is 0.6 expressed as a fraction in lowest terms? A) 3/5 B) 6/10 C) 12/20 D) 60/100
12. The area of a circle with radius 4 is: (Use $\pi = 3.14$) A) 50.24 B) 52.24 C) 54.24 D) 56.24
13. If $5x - 2 = 18$, then $x =$ A) 3 B) 4 C) 5 D) 6
14. What is the slope of the line passing through points (1, 2) and (3, 8)? A) 2 B) 3 C) 4 D) 5
15. The volume of a rectangular prism with length 5, width 3, and height 4 is: A) 48 B) 52 C) 56 D) 60
16. If $6x + 3 = 4x + 11$, then $x =$ A) 2 B) 3 C) 4 D) 5
17. What is the perimeter of a rectangle with length 9 and width 5? A) 24 B) 26 C) 28 D) 30
18. If $x^2 = 36$, then $x =$ A) ±4 B) ±5 C) ±6 D) ±7
19. The distance between points (0, 0) and (3, 4) is: A) 4 B) 5 C) 6 D) 7
20. If $2(x + 3) = 14$, then $x =$ A) 2 B) 3 C) 4 D) 5
21. What is the value of $|-6|$? A) -6 B) 0 C) 6 D) 12
22. The area of a square with side length 7 is: A) 28 B) 35 C) 42 D) 49
23. If $3x - 5 = 2x + 7$, then $x =$ A) 10 B) 11 C) 12 D) 13
24. What is the least common multiple of 6 and 8? A) 12 B) 18 C) 24 D) 48
25. If $g(x) = 3x - 2$, what is $g(4)$? A) 8 B) 9 C) 10 D) 11

Electronics Information (20 questions)

1. The unit of electrical power is the: A) Volt B) Amp C) Ohm D) Watt
2. In a series circuit, if one component fails: A) Other components work normally B) The entire circuit stops working C) Only nearby components fail D) The voltage increases
3. What does DC stand for in electrical terms? A) Direct Current B) Dual Current C) Dynamic Current D) Distributed Current
4. The primary function of a resistor is to: A) Store energy B) Limit current flow C) Increase voltage D) Generate heat
5. In Ohm's Law, $P = V \times I$, what does P represent? A) Pressure B) Power C) Potential D) Pulse
6. An inductor is used to: A) Store electrical energy in a magnetic field B) Store electrical energy in an electric field C) Convert AC to DC D) Increase resistance
7. The symbol for a capacitor in a circuit diagram is: A) Two parallel lines B) A coil C) A zigzag line D) A circle with a cross
8. Standard household current in the US is: A) Direct current B) Alternating current C) Pulsed current D) Variable current
9. A rectifier is used to: A) Increase voltage B) Decrease voltage C) Convert AC to DC D) Convert DC to AC
10. The opposition to current flow in a circuit is called: A) Voltage B) Current C) Resistance D) Power
11. What does LCD stand for? A) Light Control Display B) Liquid Crystal Display C) Low Current Device D) Linear Circuit Display
12. In a parallel circuit, the total current is: A) Less than the smallest branch current B) Equal to each branch current C) The sum of all branch currents D) Equal to the largest branch current
13. An oscilloscope is used to: A) Measure only voltage B) Measure only current C) Display electrical waveforms D) Generate electrical signals
14. The negative terminal of a battery is called the: A) Anode B) Cathode C) Electrode D) Terminal
15. What type of current changes direction periodically? A) Direct current B) Alternating current C) Pulsed current D) Static current
16. A transistor can be used as: A) Only an amplifier B) Only a switch C) Both an amplifier and a switch D) Neither an amplifier nor a switch
17. The hot wire in household wiring is typically colored: A) Black B) White C) Green D) Red
18. What is the primary function of a surge protector? A) To increase voltage B) To decrease voltage C) To protect against voltage spikes D) To measure electrical usage
19. In electrical terms, what does RMS stand for? A) Root Mean Square B) Resistive Magnetic Signal C) Rapid Measurement System D) Remote Monitoring System
20. A diode allows current to flow in: A) Both directions equally B) One direction only C) No direction D) Multiple directions

Auto & Shop Information (25 questions)

1. The part of an engine that seals the combustion chamber is the: A) Piston B) Cylinder head C) Piston ring D) Valve
2. What tool is used to measure the thickness of brake rotors? A) Caliper B) Micrometer C) Feeler gauge D) Depth gauge
3. The component that stores and releases hydraulic pressure in a brake system is the: A) Master cylinder B) Brake booster C) Accumulator D) Brake line
4. What type of file is used for rough shaping of metal? A) Smooth file B) Bastard file C) Dead smooth file D) Single cut file
5. The device that controls the air-fuel mixture entering the engine is the: A) Carburetor B) Fuel pump C) Air filter D) Throttle body
6. What tool is used to cut external threads on a rod? A) Tap B) Die C) Reamer D) Broach
7. The component that converts the engine's mechanical energy into electrical energy is the: A) Starter B) Alternator C) Battery D) Distributor
8. A center punch is used to: A) Make holes B) Mark drilling points C) Cut threads D) Measure angles
9. What causes a car to pull to one side while driving? A) Low tire pressure B) Wheel misalignment C) Worn shocks D) All of the above
10. The tool used to measure the internal diameter of a cylinder is: A) Outside caliper B) Inside caliper C) Micrometer D) Ruler
11. The component that multiplies braking force applied by the driver is the: A) Master cylinder B) Brake booster C) Brake pad D) Brake caliper
12. What type of saw blade is best for cutting metal? A) Wood cutting blade B) Fine-tooth blade C) Coarse-tooth blade D) Carbide-tip blade
13. The component that removes harmful gases from engine exhaust is the: A) Muffler B) Catalytic converter C) Exhaust pipe D) Resonator
14. A ball peen hammer is used primarily for: A) Driving nails B) Metalworking C) Demolition D) Framing
15. What does EFI stand for in automotive terms? A) Electronic Fuel Injection B) Engine Fire Ignition C) Electric Fan Induction D) Emergency Fuel Indicator
16. The tool used to hold round stock while turning on a lathe is a: A) Chuck B) Vise C) Clamp D) Fixture
17. The part that prevents the engine from overheating is the: A) Oil pump B) Water pump C) Fuel pump D) Air pump
18. What tool is used to remove broken screws? A) Screw extractor B) Tap C) Die D) Punch
19. The system that reduces harmful exhaust emissions is the: A) Cooling system B) Emission control system C) Lubrication system D) Fuel system
20. A hand plane is used to: A) Cut curves B) Make holes C) Smooth wood surfaces D) Join wood pieces
21. What type of oil is typically used in automatic transmissions? A) Motor oil B) Gear oil C) Transmission fluid D) Hydraulic oil
22. The tool used to measure angles accurately is a: A) Square B) Level C) Protractor D) Compass
23. The component that prevents engine oil from leaking is the: A) Oil filter B) Oil pan C) Oil seal D) Oil pump

24. What type of joint is strongest for joining two pieces of wood end-to-end? A) Butt joint B) Lap joint C) Mortise and tenon D) Dovetail joint
25. The safety system that prevents wheel lockup during emergency braking is: A) Power brakes B) ABS C) Traction control D) Stability control

Mechanical Comprehension (25 questions)

1. If gear A has 15 teeth and gear B has 45 teeth, and gear A makes 12 revolutions, how many revolutions does gear B make? A) 3 B) 4 C) 6 D) 8
2. A lever is 8 feet long. If the fulcrum is 3 feet from one end, what is the mechanical advantage? A) 5:3 B) 3:5 C) 8:3 D) 3:8
3. In a pulley system, if you pull 6 feet of rope to lift an object 2 feet, what is the mechanical advantage? A) 2:1 B) 3:1 C) 6:1 D) 1:3
4. Air flows fastest through a pipe where the pipe is: A) Widest B) Narrowest C) Horizontal D) Vertical
5. If a 15-pound weight is placed 4 feet from a fulcrum, what weight is needed 3 feet on the other side to balance it? A) 15 pounds B) 18 pounds C) 20 pounds D) 24 pounds
6. In a hydraulic system, if the input piston has an area of 3 square inches and the output piston has an area of 12 square inches, what is the force advantage? A) 3:1 B) 4:1 C) 9:1 D) 12:1
7. A wheel and axle has a wheel radius of 15 inches and an axle radius of 5 inches. What is the mechanical advantage? A) 2:1 B) 3:1 C) 5:1 D) 10:1
8. In which direction will wheel C turn if wheel A turns clockwise? A) Clockwise B) Counterclockwise C) It won't turn D) Cannot be determined
9. If a screw has 10 threads per inch, how far will it advance with one complete turn? A) 1/10 inch B) 1/8 inch C) 1/5 inch D) 1 inch
10. A pendulum will have the shortest period when it is: A) Longest B) Shortest C) Heaviest D) Lightest
11. In a gear train, if the driver gear has 40 teeth and the driven gear has 8 teeth, the driven gear will turn: A) 5 times slower B) 5 times faster C) 8 times faster D) At the same speed
12. The mechanical advantage of an inclined plane increases as: A) The angle increases B) The angle decreases C) The weight increases D) The length decreases
13. In a block and tackle system with 6 supporting ropes, what is the theoretical mechanical advantage? A) 3:1 B) 6:1 C) 12:1 D) 36:1
14. To apply the greatest turning force to a bolt, use: A) A long wrench B) A short wrench C) Your hands D) A hammer
15. If temperature decreases in a closed container of gas at constant volume, the pressure will: A) Increase B) Decrease C) Stay the same D) Become zero
16. A eccentric cam produces: A) Uniform circular motion B) Variable linear motion C) Constant speed D) No motion
17. In a planetary gear system, the sun gear is: A) Stationary B) The fastest rotating C) The largest gear D) The center gear
18. The efficiency of a simple machine can never be: A) 50% B) 75% C) 90% D) 110%
19. A flywheel stores energy in the form of: A) Potential energy B) Kinetic energy C) Chemical energy D) Electrical energy

20. In a compound gear train, to find the overall gear ratio: A) Add all individual ratios B) Subtract the ratios C) Multiply all individual ratios D) Divide the largest by smallest
21. A centrifugal governor regulates: A) Temperature B) Pressure C) Speed D) Direction
22. The main advantage of a worm gear is its: A) High speed ratio B) High efficiency C) Reversibility D) Low cost
23. In a centrifugal pump, the impeller: A) Moves up and down B) Rotates to move fluid C) Stays stationary D) Vibrates
24. A universal joint allows: A) Linear motion only B) Rotational motion at angles C) No motion D) Vertical motion only
25. The mechanical advantage of a screw jack depends on: A) The thread pitch only B) The handle length only C) Both thread pitch and handle length D) The weight being lifted

Test 19 Answer Key:

- **General Science:** 1-B, 2-B, 3-C, 4-B, 5-D, 6-B, 7-B, 8-C, 9-C, 10-B, 11-B, 12-C, 13-B, 14-C, 15-D, 16-B, 17-B, 18-B, 19-C, 20-C, 21-B, 22-D, 23-C, 24-C, 25-B
- **Arithmetic Reasoning:** 1-C, 2-C, 3-C, 4-B, 5-B, 6-B, 7-C, 8-B, 9-C, 10-B, 11-C, 12-C, 13-C, 14-B, 15-B, 16-B, 17-B, 18-B, 19-B, 20-C, 21-C, 22-A, 23-B, 24-B, 25-B, 26-B, 27-B, 28-B, 29-C, 30-B
- **Word Knowledge:** 1-B, 2-B, 3-B, 4-B, 5-B, 6-B, 7-B, 8-B, 9-B, 10-B, 11-B, 12-B, 13-B, 14-B, 15-B, 16-B, 17-B, 18-B, 19-B, 20-B, 21-B, 22-B, 23-B, 24-B, 25-B, 26-B, 27-B, 28-B, 29-B, 30-B, 31-B, 32-B, 33-B, 34-B, 35-B
- **Paragraph Comprehension:** 1-B, 2-B, 3-C, 4-B, 5-C, 6-B, 7-B, 8-C, 9-C, 10-B, 11-B, 12-D, 13-C, 14-B, 15-D
- **Mathematics Knowledge:** 1-C, 2-A, 3-C, 4-B, 5-B, 6-C, 7-A, 8-B, 9-B, 10-C, 11-A, 12-A, 13-B, 14-B, 15-D, 16-C, 17-C, 18-C, 19-B, 20-C, 21-C, 22-D, 23-C, 24-C, 25-C
- **Electronics Information:** 1-D, 2-B, 3-A, 4-B, 5-B, 6-A, 7-A, 8-B, 9-C, 10-C, 11-B, 12-C, 13-C, 14-B, 15-B, 16-C, 17-A, 18-C, 19-A, 20-B
- **Auto & Shop Information:** 1-C, 2-B, 3-C, 4-B, 5-A, 6-B, 7-B, 8-B, 9-D, 10-B, 11-B, 12-B, 13-B, 14-B, 15-A, 16-A, 17-B, 18-A, 19-B, 20-C, 21-C, 22-C, 23-C, 24-C, 25-B
- **Mechanical Comprehension:** 1-B, 2-A, 3-B, 4-B, 5-C, 6-B, 7-B, 8-B, 9-A, 10-B, 11-B, 12-B, 13-B, 14-A, 15-B, 16-B, 17-D, 18-D, 19-B, 20-C, 21-C, 22-A, 23-B, 24-B, 25-C

Test 21

General Science (25 questions)

1. The organelle that controls cell activities is the: A) Mitochondria B) Nucleus C) Ribosome D) Vacuole
2. What type of plate boundary causes earthquakes in California? A) Convergent B) Divergent C) Transform D) Subduction
3. The gas that makes up about 21% of Earth's atmosphere is: A) Nitrogen B) Oxygen C) Carbon dioxide D) Argon
4. Animals that are active at night are called: A) Diurnal B) Nocturnal C) Crepuscular D) Arboreal

5. Which element has the symbol Ca? A) Carbon B) Calcium C) Cadmium D) Cesium
6. The force that acts on moving objects in a fluid is: A) Gravity B) Friction C) Drag D) Tension
7. What type of electromagnetic radiation has the longest wavelength? A) Gamma rays B) X-rays C) Visible light D) Radio waves
8. The organ that produces bile is the: A) Pancreas B) Liver C) Gallbladder D) Stomach
9. Which planet is known for its Great Red Spot? A) Mars B) Jupiter C) Saturn D) Neptune
10. The process by which cells obtain energy without oxygen is: A) Aerobic respiration B) Anaerobic respiration C) Photosynthesis D) Fermentation
11. What is the chemical formula for table salt? A) NaCl B) KCl C) CaCl2 D) MgCl2
12. The layer of the atmosphere where weather occurs is the: A) Stratosphere B) Troposphere C) Mesosphere D) Thermosphere
13. Which component of blood carries oxygen? A) Plasma B) White blood cells C) Red blood cells D) Platelets
14. The measure of matter's resistance to acceleration is: A) Weight B) Mass C) Volume D) Density
15. What causes day and night on Earth? A) Earth's revolution B) Earth's rotation C) Moon's orbit D) Sun's movement
16. The molecule that carries genetic information is: A) RNA B) DNA C) Protein D) Lipid
17. Which noble gas is most abundant in the atmosphere? A) Helium B) Neon C) Argon D) Krypton
18. The process by which gas becomes liquid is: A) Evaporation B) Condensation C) Sublimation D) Melting
19. What type of chemical reaction releases energy? A) Endothermic B) Exothermic C) Catalytic D) Synthesis
20. The study of life in the oceans is called: A) Geology B) Meteorology C) Marine biology D) Astronomy
21. Which part of a plant conducts water upward? A) Phloem B) Xylem C) Cambium D) Epidermis
22. The particle with a positive charge is the: A) Electron B) Neutron C) Proton D) Photon
23. What type of rock forms from layers of sediment? A) Igneous B) Metamorphic C) Sedimentary D) Magmatic
24. The part of the nervous system that controls reflexes is the: A) Brain B) Spinal cord C) Nerves D) Neurons
25. Which type of energy is stored in chemical bonds? A) Kinetic energy B) Potential energy C) Thermal energy D) Chemical energy

Arithmetic Reasoning (30 questions)

1. If a machine produces 150 widgets in 3 hours, how many widgets will it produce in 8 hours? A) 350 B) 400 C) 450 D) 500
2. A recipe calls for 2/5 cup of butter. If you want to make 5 batches, how much butter do you need? A) 1.5 cups B) 2 cups C) 2.5 cups D) 3 cups
3. If 35% of a number is 105, what is the number? A) 250 B) 275 C) 300 D) 325
4. A jacket originally costs $180. If it's marked down 25%, what is the sale price? A) $125 B) $130 C) $135 D) $140

5. If you earn $15.75 per hour and work 32 hours per week, what is your weekly gross pay?
   A) $500 B) $504 C) $508 D) $512
6. A basket contains 42 fruits. If 2/7 of them are apples, how many are apples? A) 10 B) 12
   C) 14 D) 16
7. If the ratio of fiction to non-fiction books is 5:3 and there are 48 books total, how many
   are fiction? A) 28 B) 30 C) 32 D) 35
8. A rectangular garden is 28 feet long and 16 feet wide. What is its area? A) 448 sq ft B)
   464 sq ft C) 480 sq ft D) 496 sq ft
9. If you buy 6 shirts for $18 each and 4 belts for $12 each, what is the total cost? A) $148
   B) $152 C) $156 D) $160
10. A truck travels 420 miles in 6 hours. At the same rate, how far will it travel in 9 hours?
    A) 600 miles B) 620 miles C) 630 miles D) 650 miles
11. If 55% of a group of 80 people are adults, how many are children? A) 32 B) 34 C) 36 D)
    38
12. A right triangle has legs of 15 and 20 units. What is the length of the hypotenuse? A) 22
    units B) 24 units C) 25 units D) 27 units
13. If you invest $120 per month, how much will you have invested after 20 months? A)
    $2,300 B) $2,350 C) $2,400 D) $2,450
14. A circle has a radius of 9 inches. What is its area? (Use π = 3.14) A) 254.34 sq in B)
    256.34 sq in C) 258.34 sq in D) 260.34 sq in
15. If the temperature rises from 38°F to 67°F, by how many degrees did it rise? A) 27° B)
    29° C) 31° D) 33°
16. A swimming pool holds 24 gallons. If it's currently 5/8 full, how many gallons does it
    contain? A) 12 gallons B) 15 gallons C) 18 gallons D) 20 gallons
17. If you work 9 hours a day for 4 days, then 6 hours on Friday, how many total hours did
    you work? A) 40 hours B) 42 hours C) 44 hours D) 46 hours
18. A square playground has a perimeter of 160 feet. What is the length of each side? A) 35
    feet B) 38 feet C) 40 feet D) 42 feet
19. If 9 magazines cost $4.05, how much do 15 magazines cost? A) $6.50 B) $6.75 C) $7.00
    D) $7.25
20. A student scores 84, 91, 87, and 94 on four tests. What is the average score? A) 87 B) 88
    C) 89 D) 90
21. If a 30-foot cable is cut into pieces that are each 2.5 feet long, how many pieces will there
    be? A) 10 B) 11 C) 12 D) 13
22. A store sells erasers for $0.45 each or $4.80 per dozen. How much do you save per eraser
    by buying a dozen? A) $0.05 B) $0.06 C) $0.08 D) $0.10
23. If you drive 70 miles per hour for 4.5 hours, how far do you travel? A) 305 miles B) 310
    miles C) 315 miles D) 320 miles
24. A parallelogram has a base of 16 inches and a height of 9 inches. What is its area? A) 140
    sq in B) 144 sq in C) 148 sq in D) 152 sq in
25. If you have $250 and spend 28% of it, how much money do you have left? A) $175 B)
    $180 C) $185 D) $190
26. A recipe serves 6 people and calls for 4.5 cups of flour. How much flour is needed to
    serve 16 people? A) 11 cups B) 12 cups C) 13 cups D) 14 cups
27. If a bicycle travels 480 miles in 8 hours, what is its average speed? A) 58 mph B) 60 mph
    C) 62 mph D) 65 mph

28. A rectangular field is 150 yards long and 100 yards wide. What is its perimeter? A) 450 yards B) 480 yards C) 500 yards D) 520 yards
29. If you earn $22 per hour and work 30 hours per week, what is your monthly gross pay (assume 4 weeks per month)? A) $2,580 B) $2,620 C) $2,640 D) $2,680
30. A bookstore has 320 books. If 45% are paperbacks, how many are hardcover? A) 172 B) 174 C) 176 D) 178

Word Knowledge (35 questions)

1. Astute most nearly means: A) Foolish B) Clever C) Slow D) Confused
2. Elaborate most nearly means: A) Simple B) Detailed C) Brief D) Plain
3. Hazardous most nearly means: A) Safe B) Dangerous C) Easy D) Helpful
4. Deteriorate most nearly means: A) Improve B) Worsen C) Maintain D) Repair
5. Serene most nearly means: A) Agitated B) Calm C) Noisy D) Excited
6. Archaic most nearly means: A) Modern B) Ancient C) New D) Current
7. Perplexed most nearly means: A) Certain B) Puzzled C) Clear D) Confident
8. Copious most nearly means: A) Scarce B) Abundant C) Limited D) Few
9. Listless most nearly means: A) Energetic B) Lethargic C) Active D) Busy
10. Durable most nearly means: A) Fragile B) Lasting C) Weak D) Temporary
11. Vigilant most nearly means: A) Careless B) Watchful C) Sleepy D) Negligent
12. Renovate most nearly means: A) Destroy B) Restore C) Neglect D) Abandon
13. Morose most nearly means: A) Happy B) Gloomy C) Cheerful D) Excited
14. Amiable most nearly means: A) Unfriendly B) Pleasant C) Rude D) Harsh
15. Inert most nearly means: A) Active B) Inactive C) Moving D) Energetic
16. Mandatory most nearly means: A) Optional B) Required C) Forbidden D) Suggested
17. Contemporary most nearly means: A) Ancient B) Modern C) Old D) Historical
18. Detrimental most nearly means: A) Helpful B) Harmful C) Neutral D) Beneficial
19. Opaque most nearly means: A) Transparent B) Not transparent C) Clear D) See-through
20. Renowned most nearly means: A) Unknown B) Famous C) Ordinary D) Unpopular
21. Passive most nearly means: A) Active B) Inactive C) Aggressive D) Energetic
22. Agile most nearly means: A) Slow B) Quick C) Clumsy D) Heavy
23. Rigid most nearly means: A) Flexible B) Stiff C) Soft D) Bendable
24. Recent most nearly means: A) Old B) New C) Ancient D) Historical
25. Fragile most nearly means: A) Strong B) Breakable C) Tough D) Durable
26. Biased most nearly means: A) Fair B) Prejudiced C) Neutral D) Impartial
27. Definite most nearly means: A) Uncertain B) Clear C) Vague D) Doubtful
28. Dangerous most nearly means: A) Safe B) Risky C) Secure D) Protected
29. Continuous most nearly means: A) Broken B) Unbroken C) Interrupted D) Stopped
30. Predictable most nearly means: A) Random B) Expected C) Surprising D) Unusual
31. Impossible most nearly means: A) Possible B) Unachievable C) Easy D) Simple
32. Sound most nearly means: A) Broken B) Solid C) Damaged D) Faulty
33. Chaotic most nearly means: A) Organized B) Disorderly C) Peaceful D) Calm
34. Decline most nearly means: A) Accept B) Refuse C) Agree D) Approve
35. Consistent most nearly means: A) Variable B) Uniform C) Changing D) Different

Paragraph Comprehension (15 questions)

Passage 1: Artificial intelligence (AI) is rapidly transforming many aspects of modern life. From virtual assistants in our smartphones to recommendation algorithms on streaming platforms, AI systems are becoming increasingly sophisticated. Machine learning, a subset of AI, allows computers to learn from data without being explicitly programmed for every task. This technology has applications in healthcare, finance, transportation, and entertainment. However, as AI becomes more prevalent, questions about privacy, job displacement, and ethical considerations continue to arise.

1. According to the passage, machine learning allows computers to: A) Replace human workers B) Learn from data C) Make ethical decisions D) Protect privacy
2. The passage mentions AI applications in all of the following EXCEPT: A) Healthcare B) Finance C) Agriculture D) Transportation
3. As AI becomes more prevalent, the passage notes concerns about: A) Cost B) Privacy and ethics C) Speed D) Complexity

Passage 2: The Amazon rainforest, often called the "lungs of the Earth," covers over 2.1 million square miles across nine countries in South America. Brazil contains about 60% of the rainforest. This ecosystem is home to an estimated 10% of the world's known species, including jaguars, sloths, and thousands of bird species. The rainforest plays a crucial role in regulating global climate by absorbing carbon dioxide and producing oxygen. Unfortunately, deforestation threatens this vital ecosystem, with significant areas cleared for agriculture and development.

4. The Amazon rainforest is often called the: A) Heart of South America B) Lungs of the Earth C) Green Paradise D) Carbon Sink
5. Brazil contains approximately what percentage of the Amazon rainforest? A) 50% B) 55% C) 60% D) 65%
6. According to the passage, the rainforest is home to an estimated what percentage of the world's known species? A) 8% B) 10% C) 12% D) 15%

Passage 3: Vaccines are one of the greatest achievements in public health history.

General Science (25 questions)

1. The process by which organisms maintain internal stability is called: A) Evolution B) Homeostasis C) Metabolism D) Reproduction
2. Which layer of the Earth is liquid? A) Crust B) Mantle C) Outer core D) Inner core
3. The gas that plants absorb from the atmosphere during photosynthesis is: A) Oxygen B) Nitrogen C) Carbon dioxide D) Hydrogen
4. What is the term for animals that eat only plants? A) Carnivores B) Herbivores C) Omnivores D) Decomposers
5. Which element has the atomic number 1? A) Helium B) Hydrogen C) Lithium D) Carbon
6. The force that pulls objects toward the center of the Earth is: A) Magnetism B) Friction C) Gravity D) Inertia

7. What type of radiation has the shortest wavelength? A) Radio waves B) Microwaves C) X-rays D) Gamma rays
8. The organ that filters waste from the blood is the: A) Liver B) Lung C) Kidney D) Heart
9. Which planet has rings visible from Earth? A) Mars B) Jupiter C) Saturn D) Uranus
10. The process by which bacteria reproduce is called: A) Mitosis B) Meiosis C) Binary fission D) Budding
11. What is the chemical formula for carbon dioxide? A) CO B) CO2 C) C2O D) C2O2
12. The part of the atmosphere that contains the ozone layer is the: A) Troposphere B) Stratosphere C) Mesosphere D) Thermosphere
13. Which type of blood cell fights infection? A) Red blood cells B) White blood cells C) Platelets D) Plasma
14. The measure of the average kinetic energy of particles in matter is: A) Heat B) Temperature C) Pressure D) Volume
15. What causes tides on Earth? A) Earth's rotation B) Moon's gravitational pull C) Sun's heat D) Ocean currents
16. The basic unit of life is the: A) Organ B) Tissue C) Cell D) Organism
17. Which gas is most abundant in the Sun? A) Helium B) Hydrogen C) Oxygen D) Nitrogen
18. The process by which liquid becomes a gas at the surface is: A) Condensation B) Evaporation C) Sublimation D) Precipitation
19. What type of bond forms between a metal and a nonmetal? A) Covalent bond B) Ionic bond C) Metallic bond D) Hydrogen bond
20. The study of weather is called: A) Geology B) Meteorology C) Astronomy D) Biology
21. Which vitamin is produced by bacteria in the intestines? A) Vitamin C B) Vitamin D C) Vitamin K D) Vitamin B12
22. The center of the solar system is the: A) Earth B) Moon C) Sun D) Jupiter
23. What type of rock is limestone? A) Igneous B) Metamorphic C) Sedimentary D) Volcanic
24. The part of the brain that controls breathing is the: A) Cerebrum B) Cerebellum C) Medulla oblongata D) Hypothalamus
25. Which particle has no electric charge? A) Proton B) Electron C) Neutron D) Ion

Arithmetic Reasoning (30 questions)

1. If a bicycle wheel makes 200 revolutions to travel 400 feet, how far will it travel in 300 revolutions? A) 500 feet B) 600 feet C) 700 feet D) 800 feet
2. A recipe calls for 1/3 cup of oil. If you want to make 6 batches, how much oil do you need? A) 1.5 cups B) 2 cups C) 2.5 cups D) 3 cups
3. If 25% of a number is 75, what is the number? A) 250 B) 275 C) 300 D) 325
4. A store offers a 20% discount on a $150 item. What is the sale price? A) $115 B) $120 C) $125 D) $130
5. If you earn $13.50 per hour and work 36 hours per week, what is your weekly gross pay? A) $480 B) $486 C) $490 D) $495
6. A bag contains 35 marbles. If 3/7 of them are red, how many are red? A) 12 B) 15 C) 18 D) 21
7. If the ratio of cats to dogs in a shelter is 4:5 and there are 36 animals total, how many are dogs? A) 16 B) 18 C) 20 D) 22

8. A rectangular yard is 25 feet long and 18 feet wide. What is its area? A) 400 sq ft B) 425 sq ft C) 450 sq ft D) 475 sq ft

9. If you buy 5 notebooks for $8 each and 3 pens for $3 each, what is the total cost? A) $47 B) $49 C) $51 D) $53

10. A bus travels 280 miles in 4 hours. At the same rate, how far will it travel in 7 hours? A) 460 miles B) 480 miles C) 490 miles D) 500 miles

11. If 45% of a class of 60 students are absent, how many students are present? A) 27 B) 30 C) 33 D) 36

12. A right triangle has legs of 9 and 12 units. What is the length of the hypotenuse? A) 13 units B) 15 units C) 17 units D) 19 units

13. If you save $85 per month, how much will you have saved after 15 months? A) $1,200 B) $1,225 C) $1,275 D) $1,300

14. A circle has a circumference of 31.4 inches. What is its diameter? (Use $\pi = 3.14$) A) 8 inches B) 9 inches C) 10 inches D) 11 inches

15. If the temperature drops from 85°F to 62°F, by how many degrees did it drop? A) 21° B) 23° C) 25° D) 27°

16. A car's fuel tank holds 16 gallons. If it's currently 3/4 full, how many gallons does it contain? A) 10 gallons B) 12 gallons C) 14 gallons D) 15 gallons

17. If you work 8.5 hours a day for 5 days, then 4 hours on Saturday, how many total hours did you work? A) 46.5 hours B) 47.5 hours C) 48.5 hours D) 49.5 hours

18. A square tile has an area of 144 square inches. What is the length of each side? A) 10 inches B) 11 inches C) 12 inches D) 13 inches

19. If 6 oranges cost $2.40, how much do 10 oranges cost? A) $3.60 B) $3.80 C) $4.00 D) $4.20

20. A student scores 88, 76, 94, and 82 on four tests. What is the average score? A) 84 B) 85 C) 86 D) 87

21. If a 24-foot rope is cut into pieces that are each 3.2 feet long, how many pieces will there be? A) 7 B) 7.5 C) 8 D) 8.5

22. A bakery sells bagels for $0.75 each or $8.50 per dozen. How much do you save per bagel by buying a dozen? A) $0.04 B) $0.05 C) $0.08 D) $0.10

23. If you drive 65 miles per hour for 2.5 hours, how far do you travel? A) 160.5 miles B) 162.5 miles C) 165 miles D) 167.5 miles

24. A triangle has a base of 14 inches and a height of 10 inches. What is its area? A) 65 sq in B) 70 sq in C) 75 sq in D) 80 sq in

25. If you have $200 and spend 35% of it, how much money do you have left? A) $120 B) $125 C) $130 D) $135

26. A recipe serves 4 people and calls for 3 cups of rice. How much rice is needed to serve 14 people? A) 9.5 cups B) 10 cups C) 10.5 cups D) 11 cups

27. If a train travels 540 miles in 6 hours, what is its average speed? A) 85 mph B) 90 mph C) 95 mph D) 100 mph

28. A rectangular field is 120 yards long and 80 yards wide. What is its perimeter? A) 360 yards B) 380 yards C) 400 yards D) 420 yards

29. If you earn $18 per hour and work 28 hours per week, what is your monthly gross pay (assume 4 weeks per month)? A) $1,980 B) $2,000 C) $2,016 D) $2,040

30. A library has 240 books. If 65% are fiction, how many are non-fiction? A) 80 B) 84 C) 88 D) 92

Word Knowledge (35 questions)

1. Novice most nearly means: A) Expert B) Beginner C) Professional D) Teacher
2. Scrutinize most nearly means: A) Ignore B) Examine C) Accept D) Reject
3. Perilous most nearly means: A) Safe B) Dangerous C) Easy D) Simple
4. Enhance most nearly means: A) Weaken B) Improve C) Destroy D) Ignore
5. Tranquil most nearly means: A) Noisy B) Peaceful C) Busy D) Chaotic
6. Obsolete most nearly means: A) Modern B) Outdated C) New D) Advanced
7. Baffled most nearly means: A) Clear B) Confused C) Certain D) Confident
8. Ample most nearly means: A) Insufficient B) Adequate C) Small D) Tiny
9. Sluggish most nearly means: A) Quick B) Slow C) Active D) Energetic
10. Sturdy most nearly means: A) Weak B) Strong C) Fragile D) Delicate
11. Cautious most nearly means: A) Reckless B) Careful C) Careless D) Bold
12. Restore most nearly means: A) Destroy B) Repair C) Break D) Damage
13. Gloomy most nearly means: A) Bright B) Dark C) Cheerful D) Happy
14. Hostile most nearly means: A) Friendly B) Unfriendly C) Kind D) Gentle
15. Stationary most nearly means: A) Moving B) Still C) Fast D) Active
16. Compulsory most nearly means: A) Optional B) Required C) Voluntary D) Free
17. Traditional most nearly means: A) Modern B) Conventional C) New D) Revolutionary
18. Beneficial most nearly means: A) Harmful B) Helpful C) Useless D) Dangerous
19. Transparent most nearly means: A) Opaque B) Clear C) Dark D) Solid
20. Notorious most nearly means: A) Unknown B) Famous for bad reasons C) Respected D) Honored
21. Active most nearly means: A) Passive B) Energetic C) Lazy D) Tired
22. Nimble most nearly means: A) Clumsy B) Quick C) Slow D) Heavy
23. Flexible most nearly means: A) Rigid B) Bendable C) Hard D) Stiff
24. Ancient most nearly means: A) Modern B) Old C) New D) Recent
25. Delicate most nearly means: A) Rough B) Fragile C) Strong D) Tough
26. Neutral most nearly means: A) Biased B) Impartial C) Partial D) Prejudiced
27. Uncertain most nearly means: A) Sure B) Doubtful C) Confident D) Positive
28. Harmless most nearly means: A) Dangerous B) Safe C) Risky D) Threatening
29. Endless most nearly means: A) Limited B) Infinite C) Short D) Brief
30. Random most nearly means: A) Planned B) Unpredictable C) Organized D) Systematic
31. Possible most nearly means: A) Impossible B) Achievable C) Unlikely D) Unrealistic
32. Valid most nearly means: A) Invalid B) Sound C) False D) Wrong
33. Peaceful most nearly means: A) Violent B) Calm C) Aggressive D) Hostile
34. Thrive most nearly means: A) Struggle B) Prosper C) Decline D) Fail
35. Irregular most nearly means: A) Regular B) Uneven C) Smooth D) Consistent

Paragraph Comprehension (15 questions)

Passage 1: Renewable energy sources are becoming increasingly important as the world seeks to reduce its dependence on fossil fuels. Wind power has emerged as one of the most promising renewable technologies. Modern wind turbines can generate electricity efficiently even in moderate wind conditions. Wind farms, both onshore and offshore, are being developed worldwide. The main advantages of wind power include its renewable nature, low operating costs, and minimal environmental impact during operation.

1. According to the passage, wind power is considered: A) Unreliable B) Expensive C) Promising D) Outdated
2. Modern wind turbines can generate electricity efficiently in: A) Strong winds only B) Moderate wind conditions C) No wind D) Storms only
3. The passage mentions all of the following advantages of wind power EXCEPT: A) Renewable nature B) Low operating costs C) Minimal environmental impact D) Easy installation

Passage 2: The human brain is one of the most complex organs in the body. It contains approximately 86 billion neurons that communicate through electrical and chemical signals. The brain is divided into several regions, each responsible for different functions. The cerebrum controls conscious thought and voluntary movements, while the cerebellum coordinates balance and fine motor skills. The brain stem regulates vital functions such as breathing, heart rate, and blood pressure.

4. The human brain contains approximately how many neurons? A) 86 million B) 86 billion C) 86 trillion D) 86 thousand
5. The cerebellum is responsible for: A) Conscious thought B) Balance and fine motor skills C) Breathing D) Heart rate
6. Vital functions such as breathing are regulated by the: A) Cerebrum B) Cerebellum C) Brain stem D) Neurons

Passage 3: The Great Barrier Reef, located off the coast of Australia, is the world's largest coral reef system. It stretches over 1,400 miles and consists of nearly 3,000 individual reefs and 900 islands. This natural wonder is home to an incredible diversity of marine life, including over 1,500 species of fish and 400 types of coral. However, the reef faces serious threats from climate change, pollution, and coastal development. Conservation efforts are underway to protect this UNESCO World Heritage Site.

7. The Great Barrier Reef stretches over: A) 1,200 miles B) 1,300 miles C) 1,400 miles D) 1,500 miles
8. The reef is home to over how many species of fish? A) 1,200 B) 1,300 C) 1,400 D) 1,500
9. According to the passage, the reef faces threats from all EXCEPT: A) Climate change B) Pollution C) Coastal development D) Tourism

Passage 4: Regular physical exercise is essential for maintaining good health throughout life. Exercise strengthens the cardiovascular system, improves muscle tone, and helps maintain healthy bone density. It also has mental health benefits, including reducing stress and improving mood through the release of endorphins. Additionally, regular exercise can help prevent chronic diseases such as diabetes, heart disease, and certain types of cancer. Health professionals recommend at least 30 minutes of moderate exercise most days of the week.

10. According to the passage, exercise helps maintain healthy: A) Sleep patterns B) Bone density C) Appetite D) Memory
11. Exercise improves mood through the release of: A) Insulin B) Adrenaline C) Endorphins D) Cortisol
12. Health professionals recommend at least how many minutes of moderate exercise most days? A) 20 minutes B) 25 minutes C) 30 minutes D) 45 minutes

Passage 5: The invention of the wheel around 3500 BCE was one of humanity's most significant technological achievements. Initially used for pottery making, the wheel was later adapted for transportation, revolutionizing trade and travel. The wheel's simple yet effective design – a circular disk that rotates around a central axis – has remained largely unchanged for thousands of years. Today, wheels are essential components in countless machines and vehicles, from bicycles and cars to industrial equipment and spacecraft.

13. The wheel was initially used for: A) Transportation B) Pottery making C) Construction D) Agriculture
14. The wheel was invented around: A) 3000 BCE B) 3500 BCE C) 4000 BCE D) 4500 BCE
15. According to the passage, the wheel's design has: A) Changed dramatically B) Remained largely unchanged C) Become more complex D) Been completely redesigned

Mathematics Knowledge (25 questions)

1. If $x + 9 = 20$, then $x =$ A) 9 B) 10 C) 11 D) 12
2. What is $5^2 - 3^2$? A) 14 B) 16 C) 18 D) 20
3. The square root of 196 is: A) 12 B) 13 C) 14 D) 15
4. If $6x = 42$, then $x =$ A) 6 B) 7 C) 8 D) 9
5. What is 40% of 150? A) 50 B) 55 C) 60 D) 65
6. The area of a rectangle with length 12 and width 7 is: A) 38 B) 76 C) 84 D) 91
7. If $y - 6 = 18$, then $y =$ A) 22 B) 24 C) 26 D) 28
8. What is the value of $4x + 5$ when $x = 3$? A) 15 B) 17 C) 19 D) 21
9. The perimeter of a rectangle with length 11 and width 8 is: A) 36 B) 38 C) 40 D) 42
10. If $4x + 6 = 26$, then $x =$ A) 4 B) 5 C) 6 D) 7
11. What is 0.8 expressed as a fraction in lowest terms? A) 4/5 B) 8/10 C) 16/20 D) 80/100
12. The area of a circle with radius 6 is: (Use $\pi = 3.14$) A) 113.04 B) 115.04 C) 117.04 D) 119.04
13. If $6x - 4 = 20$, then $x =$ A) 3 B) 4 C) 5 D) 6
14. What is the slope of the line passing through points (2, 1) and (6, 9)? A) 1 B) 2 C) 3 D) 4
15. The volume of a cube with side length 5 is: A) 100 B) 115 C) 125 D) 135
16. If $7x + 4 = 5x + 16$, then $x =$ A) 4 B) 5 C) 6 D) 7
17. What is the area of a triangle with base 8 and height 12? A) 46 B) 48 C) 50 D) 52
18. If $x^2 = 49$, then $x =$ A) ±6 B) ±7 C) ±8 D) ±9
19. The distance between points (2, 1) and (6, 4) is: A) 4 B) 5 C) 6 D) 7
20. If $3(x + 4) = 21$, then $x =$ A) 1 B) 2 C) 3 D) 4
21. What is the value of $|-12|$? A) -12 B) 0 C) 12 D) 24
22. The circumference of a circle with diameter 10 is: (Use $\pi = 3.14$) A) 31.4 B) 32.4 C) 33.4 D) 34.4

23. If 4x - 8 = 2x + 6, then x = A) 5 B) 6 C) 7 D) 8
24. What is the greatest common factor of 30 and 45? A) 10 B) 12 C) 15 D) 18
25. If h(x) = 4x - 3, what is h(5)? A) 15 B) 16 C) 17 D) 18

Electronics Information (20 questions)

1. The unit of electrical frequency is the: A) Volt B) Hertz C) Ohm D) Watt
2. In a parallel circuit, voltage across each branch is: A) Different B) The same C) Zero D) Infinite
3. What does RF stand for in electronics? A) Radio Frequency B) Resistive Force C) Reactive Factor D) Rapid Flow
4. The primary function of an amplifier is to: A) Reduce signal strength B) Increase signal strength C) Filter signals D) Generate signals
5. In Ohm's Law, I = V/R, what does I represent? A) Impedance B) Current C) Inductance D) Intensity
6. A battery is an example of: A) AC source B) DC source C) RF source D) Signal source
7. The symbol for an inductor in a circuit diagram is: A) Parallel lines B) Coil or spiral C) Zigzag line D) Triangle
8. The frequency of standard AC power in the US is: A) 50 Hz B) 60 Hz C) 100 Hz D) 120 Hz
9. An inverter is used to: A) Convert AC to DC B) Convert DC to AC C) Increase voltage D) Decrease voltage
10. The total resistance in a series circuit is: A) Less than the smallest resistor B) Equal to the largest resistor C) The sum of all resistances D) The average of all resistances
11. What does CRT stand for? A) Current Resistance Test B) Cathode Ray Tube C) Circuit Relay Timer D) Constant Rate Transformer
12. In a parallel circuit, if one resistor burns out: A) Total resistance increases B) Total resistance decreases C) Total resistance stays the same D) Current stops flowing
13. A voltmeter is connected in: A) Series with the circuit B) Parallel with the circuit C) Series with the load D) Any configuration
14. The unit of electrical charge is the: A) Volt B) Amp C) Coulomb D) Watt
15. What type of current flows in a battery circuit? A) Alternating current B) Direct current C) Pulsed current D) Radio frequency current
16. A semiconductor has conductivity: A) Greater than a conductor B) Less than a conductor but greater than an insulator C) Equal to an insulator D) Equal to a conductor
17. The neutral wire in household wiring is typically colored: A) Black B) White C) Green D) Red
18. What is the primary purpose of a filter circuit? A) To amplify signals B) To remove unwanted frequencies C) To generate power D) To measure voltage
19. In electrical terms, what does PWM stand for? A) Power Wave Modulation B) Pulse Width Modulation C) Phase Wave Management D) Positive Wire Measurement
20. A Zener diode is primarily used for: A) Amplification B) Switching C) Voltage regulation D) Current limiting

Auto & Shop Information (25 questions)

1. The component that connects the piston to the crankshaft is the: A) Cam B) Connecting rod C) Pushrod D) Timing belt
2. What tool is used to measure valve clearance? A) Thickness gauge B) Feeler gauge C) Depth gauge D) Pressure gauge
3. The component that stores brake fluid under pressure is the: A) Brake line B) Master cylinder C) Brake caliper D) Accumulator
4. What type of chisel is used for cutting metal? A) Wood chisel B) Cold chisel C) Hot chisel D) Stone chisel
5. The device that advances ignition timing as engine speed increases is the: A) Distributor B) Timing advance mechanism C) Spark plug D) Coil
6. What tool is used to cut internal threads in a hole? A) Die B) Tap C) Drill D) Reamer
7. The component that converts low voltage to high voltage for ignition is the: A) Battery B) Alternator C) Ignition coil D) Starter
8. A socket wrench is also known as a: A) Box wrench B) Open-end wrench C) Ratchet wrench D) Torque wrench
9. What causes engine dieseling (running on after ignition is turned off)? A) Low octane fuel B) High compression C) Carbon deposits D) All of the above
10. The tool used to measure small distances accurately is a: A) Ruler B) Tape measure C) Micrometer D) Caliper
11. The component that increases braking force is the: A) Brake pedal B) Brake booster C) Master cylinder D) Brake fluid
12. What type of drill bit is best for drilling hard metals? A) Twist bit B) Spade bit C) Carbide bit D) Masonry bit
13. The component that reduces exhaust noise is the: A) Catalytic converter B) Muffler C) Exhaust manifold D) Tailpipe
14. A rasp is used for: A) Cutting metal B) Shaping wood C) Drilling holes D) Measuring angles
15. What does OBD stand for in automotive terms? A) On-Board Diagnostics B) Oil Bypass Device C) Overhead Belt Drive D) Oxygen Burn Detection
16. The tool used to grip and turn round objects is: A) Pliers B) Wrench C) Pipe wrench D) Vise grips
17. The part that regulates electrical system voltage is the: A) Battery B) Voltage regulator C) Alternator D) Starter
18. What tool is used to remove damaged nuts? A) Nut splitter B) Impact wrench C) Socket set D) Pipe wrench
19. The system that controls engine emissions includes the: A) PCV valve B) EGR valve C) Catalytic converter D) All of the above
20. A mortise and tenon joint is used in: A) Metalworking B) Woodworking C) Electrical work D) Plumbing
21. What type of fluid is used in power steering systems? A) Brake fluid B) Transmission fluid C) Power steering fluid D) Engine oil
22. The tool used to check if a surface is level is a: A) Square B) Level C) Plumb bob D) Straightedge

23. The component that prevents fuel vapor emissions is the: A) Fuel filter B) Charcoal canister C) Fuel pump D) Fuel injector
24. What type of saw is used for cutting dovetail joints? A) Crosscut saw B) Rip saw C) Dovetail saw D) Coping saw
25. The safety feature that prevents starting unless the clutch is depressed is the: A) Neutral safety switch B) Clutch interlock switch C) Brake switch D) Ignition switch

Mechanical Comprehension (25 questions)

1. If gear A has 24 teeth and gear B has 8 teeth, and gear A makes 5 revolutions, how many revolutions does gear B make? A) 10 B) 15 C) 20 D) 25
2. A lever is 10 feet long. If the fulcrum is 4 feet from one end, what is the mechanical advantage? A) 6:4 B) 4:6 C) 10:4 D) 4:10
3. In a pulley system, if you pull 8 feet of rope to lift an object 2 feet, what is the mechanical advantage? A) 2:1 B) 4:1 C) 6:1 D) 8:1
4. Liquid flows slowest through a pipe where the pipe is: A) Narrowest B) Widest C) Straight D) Curved
5. If a 20-pound weight is placed 6 feet from a fulcrum, what weight is needed 4 feet on the other side to balance it? A) 25 pounds B) 30 pounds C) 35 pounds D) 40 pounds
6. In a hydraulic system, if the input piston has an area of 4 square inches and the output piston has an area of 16 square inches, what is the force advantage? A) 2:1 B) 4:1 C) 8:1 D) 16:1
7. A wheel and axle has a wheel radius of 18 inches and an axle radius of 6 inches. What is the mechanical advantage? A) 2:1 B) 3:1 C) 6:1 D) 12:1
8. If wheel A turns counterclockwise, which direction will wheel B turn? A) Clockwise B) Counterclockwise C) It won't turn D) Cannot be determined
9. If a screw has 12 threads per inch, how far will it advance with one complete turn? A) 1/12 inch B) 1/6 inch C) 1/4 inch D) 1 inch
10. A pendulum will swing slowest when it is: A) Shortest B) Longest C) Lightest D) Heaviest
11. In a gear train, if the driver gear has 50 teeth and the driven gear has 25 teeth, the driven gear will turn: A) 2 times slower B) 2 times faster C) 25 times faster D) At the same speed
12. The mechanical advantage of a wedge depends on: A) Its length and thickness B) Its weight C) Its material D) Its color
13. In a block and tackle system with 8 supporting ropes, what is the theoretical mechanical advantage? A) 4:1 B) 6:1 C) 8:1 D) 16:1
14. To loosen a tight bolt, you should use: A) A short wrench B) A long wrench C) Your hands D) A hammer
15. If volume decreases in a closed container of gas at constant temperature, the pressure will: A) Increase B) Decrease C) Stay the same D) Become zero
16. A heart-shaped cam produces: A) Uniform motion B) Variable motion C) No motion D) Circular motion
17. In a gear differential, when turning a corner: A) Both wheels turn at the same speed B) The inside wheel turns faster C) The outside wheel turns faster D) One wheel stops
18. No machine can have an efficiency of: A) 50% B) 75% C) 95% D) 120%

19. A gyroscope resists changes in: A) Speed B) Direction C) Weight D) Temperature
20. In a gear train with multiple stages, the overall ratio is found by: A) Adding individual ratios B) Subtracting ratios C) Multiplying individual ratios D) Averaging ratios
21. A thermostat controls: A) Speed B) Pressure C) Temperature D) Direction
22. The primary advantage of a gear reduction system is: A) Increased speed B) Increased torque C) Reduced friction D) Simplified design
23. In a positive displacement pump, the flow rate depends on: A) Pressure only B) Speed only C) Both pressure and speed D) Neither pressure nor speed
24. A constant velocity joint allows: A) Linear motion only B) Rotational motion at varying angles C) No motion D) Oscillating motion
25. The mechanical advantage of a lever depends on: A) The weight being lifted B) The length of the effort arm only C) The ratio of effort arm to load arm D) The material of the lever

Test 20 Answer Key:

- **General Science:** 1-B, 2-C, 3-C, 4-B, 5-B, 6-C, 7-D, 8-C, 9-C, 10-C, 11-B, 12-B, 13-B, 14-B, 15-B, 16-C, 17-B, 18-B, 19-B, 20-B, 21-C, 22-C, 23-C, 24-C, 25-C
- **Arithmetic Reasoning:** 1-B, 2-B, 3-C, 4-B, 5-B, 6-B, 7-C, 8-C, 9-B, 10-C, 11-C, 12-B, 13-C, 14-C, 15-B, 16-B, 17-B, 18-C, 19-C, 20-B, 21-B, 22-C, 23-B, 24-B, 25-C, 26-C, 27-B, 28-C, 29-C, 30-B
- **Word Knowledge:** 1-B, 2-B, 3-B, 4-B, 5-B, 6-B, 7-B, 8-B, 9-B, 10-B, 11-B, 12-B, 13-B, 14-B, 15-B, 16-B, 17-B, 18-B, 19-B, 20-B, 21-B, 22-B, 23-B, 24-B, 25-B, 26-B, 27-B, 28-B, 29-B, 30-B, 31-B, 32-B, 33-B, 34-B, 35-B
- **Paragraph Comprehension:** 1-C, 2-B, 3-D, 4-B, 5-B, 6-C, 7-C, 8-D, 9-D, 10-B, 11-C, 12-C, 13-B, 14-B, 15-B
- **Mathematics Knowledge:** 1-C, 2-B, 3-C, 4-B, 5-C, 6-C, 7-B, 8-B, 9-B, 10-B, 11-A, 12-A, 13-B, 14-B, 15-C, 16-C, 17-B, 18-B, 19-B, 20-C, 21-C, 22-A, 23-C, 24-C, 25-C
- **Electronics Information:** 1-B, 2-B, 3-A, 4-B, 5-B, 6-B, 7-B, 8-B, 9-B, 10-C, 11-B, 12-B, 13-B, 14-C, 15-B, 16-B, 17-B, 18-B, 19-B, 20-C
- **Auto & Shop Information:** 1-B, 2-B, 3-D, 4-B, 5-B, 6-B, 7-C, 8-C, 9-D, 10-C, 11-B, 12-C, 13-B, 14-B, 15-A, 16-C, 17-B, 18-A, 19-D, 20-B, 21-C, 22-B, 23-B, 24-C, 25-B
- **Mechanical Comprehension:** 1-B, 2-A, 3-B, 4-B, 5-B, 6-B, 7-B, 8-A, 9-A, 10-B, 11-B, 12-A, 13-C, 14-B, 15-A, 16-B, 17-C, 18-D, 19-B, 20-C, 21-C, 22-B, 23-B, 24-B, 25-C

Test 22

General Science (25 questions)

1. The process by which plants convert sunlight into chemical energy is called: a) Respiration b) Photosynthesis c) Transpiration d) Germination
2. Which planet is known as the "Red Planet"? a) Venus b) Jupiter c) Mars d) Saturn
3. The basic unit of heredity is the: a) Chromosome b) Gene c) DNA d) Cell
4. Sound travels fastest through: a) Air b) Water c) Steel d) Vacuum
5. The pH scale measures: a) Temperature b) Pressure c) Acidity/Alkalinity d) Density

6. Which gas makes up approximately 78% of Earth's atmosphere? a) Oxygen b) Carbon dioxide c) Nitrogen d) Argon
7. The study of earthquakes is called: a) Geology b) Seismology c) Meteorology d) Astronomy
8. Which vitamin is produced when skin is exposed to sunlight? a) Vitamin A b) Vitamin C c) Vitamin D d) Vitamin K
9. The force that opposes motion between two surfaces is: a) Gravity b) Friction c) Magnetism d) Inertia
10. Which organelle is known as the "powerhouse of the cell"? a) Nucleus b) Ribosome c) Mitochondria d) Golgi apparatus
11. The chemical symbol for gold is: a) Go b) Gd c) Au d) Ag
12. Which type of rock is formed by cooling magma? a) Sedimentary b) Metamorphic c) Igneous d) Fossilized
13. The smallest particle of an element is: a) Molecule b) Atom c) Electron d) Proton
14. Which system in the human body fights infection? a) Circulatory b) Respiratory c) Immune d) Digestive
15. The speed of light is approximately: a) 186,000 miles per second b) 300,000 km per second c) Both a and b d) Neither a nor b
16. Which planet has the most moons? a) Jupiter b) Saturn c) Uranus d) Neptune
17. The process of cell division is called: a) Meiosis b) Mitosis c) Both a and b d) Osmosis
18. Which element is essential for bone formation? a) Iron b) Calcium c) Sodium d) Potassium
19. The layer of the atmosphere closest to Earth is: a) Stratosphere b) Mesosphere c) Troposphere d) Thermosphere
20. Which scientist developed the theory of evolution? a) Einstein b) Newton c) Darwin d) Mendel
21. The hardest natural substance is: a) Gold b) Iron c) Diamond d) Quartz
22. Which blood type is the universal donor? a) A b) B c) AB d) O
23. The study of weather is called: a) Climatology b) Meteorology c) Oceanography d) Hydrology
24. Which gas is most abundant in the sun? a) Helium b) Hydrogen c) Oxygen d) Nitrogen
25. The process by which water changes from liquid to gas is: a) Condensation b) Evaporation c) Precipitation d) Sublimation

Arithmetic Reasoning (30 questions)

1. If a car travels 240 miles in 4 hours, what is its average speed? a) 50 mph b) 60 mph c) 70 mph d) 80 mph
2. A shirt costs $25. If there's a 20% discount, what's the sale price? a) $20 b) $21 c) $22 d) $23
3. If $3x + 7 = 22$, what is x? a) 4 b) 5 c) 6 d) 7
4. A rectangle has length 12 feet and width 8 feet. What's its area? a) 96 sq ft b) 40 sq ft c) 20 sq ft d) 48 sq ft
5. If John earns $15 per hour and works 35 hours, how much does he earn? a) $525 b) $500 c) $475 d) $550
6. What is 15% of 80? a) 10 b) 12 c) 15 d) 20

7. A pizza is cut into 8 slices. If you eat 3 slices, what fraction remains? a) 3/8 b) 5/8 c) 1/2 d) 3/5

8. If a train travels 180 miles in 3 hours, how far will it travel in 5 hours? a) 250 miles b) 280 miles c) 300 miles d) 320 miles

9. The sum of three consecutive integers is 60. What's the middle integer? a) 19 b) 20 c) 21 d) 22

10. If 2y - 5 = 11, what is y? a) 6 b) 7 c) 8 d) 9

11. A circular garden has radius 7 feet. What's its circumference? ($\pi \approx 3.14$) a) 43.96 ft b) 44 ft c) 22 ft d) 14 ft

12. If gas costs $3.50 per gallon and you need 12 gallons, what's the total cost? a) $40 b) $42 c) $44 d) $46

13. What is the square root of 144? a) 10 b) 11 c) 12 d) 13

14. If a book costs $18 and you pay with a $20 bill, how much change do you get? a) $1 b) $2 c) $3 d) $4

15. A triangle has angles of 60°, 70°, and what third angle? a) 40° b) 50° c) 60° d) 70°

16. If 4x = 28, what is x? a) 6 b) 7 c) 8 d) 9

17. What is 2/3 of 24? a) 14 b) 16 c) 18 d) 20

18. A box contains 5 red balls and 3 blue balls. What's the probability of drawing a red ball? a) 3/8 b) 5/8 c) 1/2 d) 3/5

19. If you save $50 per month for 8 months, how much do you save total? a) $350 b) $400 c) $450 d) $500

20. What is 25% of 64? a) 14 b) 15 c) 16 d) 17

21. A ladder 13 feet long leans against a wall. If the base is 5 feet from the wall, how high up the wall does it reach? a) 10 ft b) 11 ft c) 12 ft d) 13 ft

22. If 3(x + 4) = 21, what is x? a) 3 b) 4 c) 5 d) 6

23. A rectangle has perimeter 28 feet and width 6 feet. What's its length? a) 8 ft b) 10 ft c) 12 ft d) 14 ft

24. What is the average of 12, 15, 18, and 19? a) 15 b) 16 c) 17 d) 18

25. If you buy 3 items for $4.50 each, what's the total cost? a) $13.00 b) $13.50 c) $14.00 d) $14.50

26. A circle has diameter 10 inches. What's its radius? a) 20 in b) 10 in c) 5 in d) 2.5 in

27. If 5x - 3 = 17, what is x? a) 3 b) 4 c) 5 d) 6

28. What is 3/4 × 2/3? a) 1/2 b) 5/7 c) 6/12 d) 1/3

29. A car depreciates 15% of its value each year. If it's worth $20,000 now, what will it be worth next year? a) $17,000 b) $17,500 c) $18,000 d) $18,500

30. If the ratio of boys to girls in a class is 3:2 and there are 25 students total, how many are boys? a) 12 b) 13 c) 15 d) 17

Word Knowledge (35 questions)

1. ABUNDANT most nearly means: a) Scarce b) Plentiful c) Expensive d) Rare
2. HOSTILE most nearly means: a) Friendly b) Unfriendly c) Neutral d) Passive
3. RIGID most nearly means: a) Flexible b) Soft c) Stiff d) Loose
4. EVIDENT most nearly means: a) Hidden b) Obvious c) Doubtful d) Mysterious
5. CONSUME most nearly means: a) Save b) Preserve c) Use up d) Create
6. BENEVOLENT most nearly means: a) Evil b) Kind c) Angry d) Selfish

7. PRUDENT most nearly means: a) Reckless b) Wise c) Foolish d) Careless
8. DETERIORATE most nearly means: a) Improve b) Worsen c) Maintain d) Strengthen
9. CONCISE most nearly means: a) Lengthy b) Brief c) Detailed d) Wordy
10. DUBIOUS most nearly means: a) Certain b) Doubtful c) Clear d) Obvious
11. METICULOUS most nearly means: a) Careless b) Careful c) Quick d) Sloppy
12. ADVERSARY most nearly means: a) Friend b) Enemy c) Partner d) Colleague
13. FACILITATE most nearly means: a) Hinder b) Help c) Block d) Prevent
14. OBSOLETE most nearly means: a) Modern b) Outdated c) Current d) New
15. CANDID most nearly means: a) Dishonest b) Honest c) Secretive d) Deceptive
16. CONTEMPLATE most nearly means: a) Ignore b) Consider c) Reject d) Dismiss
17. VERSATILE most nearly means: a) Limited b) Adaptable c) Rigid d) Specialized
18. IMMINENT most nearly means: a) Distant b) Approaching c) Past d) Unlikely
19. ENHANCE most nearly means: a) Reduce b) Improve c) Damage d) Worsen
20. FRUGAL most nearly means: a) Wasteful b) Thrifty c) Generous d) Careless
21. VALIDATE most nearly means: a) Disprove b) Confirm c) Question d) Deny
22. TEDIOUS most nearly means: a) Exciting b) Boring c) Interesting d) Fun
23. PROFOUND most nearly means: a) Shallow b) Deep c) Surface d) Light
24. INTIMIDATE most nearly means: a) Encourage b) Frighten c) Support d) Help
25. DIMINISH most nearly means: a) Increase b) Decrease c) Maintain d) Strengthen
26. ECCENTRIC most nearly means: a) Normal b) Odd c) Typical d) Common
27. AUTHENTIC most nearly means: a) Fake b) Genuine c) False d) Artificial
28. SUPPRESS most nearly means: a) Encourage b) Restrain c) Promote d) Support
29. AMIABLE most nearly means: a) Unfriendly b) Friendly c) Hostile d) Rude
30. INVOKE most nearly means: a) Dismiss b) Call upon c) Ignore d) Reject
31. LUCID most nearly means: a) Confusing b) Clear c) Unclear d) Muddy
32. PRECARIOUS most nearly means: a) Safe b) Risky c) Secure d) Stable
33. SPORADIC most nearly means: a) Regular b) Irregular c) Constant d) Continuous
34. ZENITH most nearly means: a) Bottom b) Peak c) Middle d) Beginning
35. IMPECCABLE most nearly means: a) Flawed b) Perfect c) Damaged d) Broken

Paragraph Comprehension (15 questions)

Passage 1: The Amazon rainforest covers approximately 2.1 million square miles and spans across nine countries in South America. Often called the "lungs of the Earth," it produces about 20% of the world's oxygen and houses nearly 10% of all known species. However, deforestation threatens this vital ecosystem, with an area the size of a football field being cleared every minute.

1. According to the passage, the Amazon rainforest: a) Covers exactly 2 million square miles b) Produces 20% of the world's oxygen c) Houses 20% of all known species d) Spans across ten countries
2. The passage suggests that deforestation in the Amazon is: a) Slowing down significantly b) Happening at an alarming rate c) Not a major concern d) Affecting only small areas

Passage 2: Electric vehicles (EVs) are becoming increasingly popular due to environmental concerns and technological advances. Unlike traditional gasoline-powered cars, EVs produce zero direct emissions and are generally quieter. However, they face challenges including limited driving range, longer refueling times, and higher initial costs. As battery technology improves and charging infrastructure expands, these limitations are gradually being addressed.

3. According to the passage, electric vehicles: a) Are more expensive to operate than gas cars b) Produce no direct emissions c) Have unlimited driving range d) Are louder than traditional cars
4. The passage indicates that EV limitations are: a) Becoming worse over time b) Impossible to solve c) Being gradually addressed d) Not important to consumers

Passage 3: The human brain contains approximately 86 billion neurons, each capable of forming thousands of connections with other neurons. This intricate network allows for complex thoughts, emotions, and behaviors. Scientists estimate that the brain uses about 20% of the body's total energy, despite weighing only about 2% of total body weight. Recent research suggests that the brain continues to form new neural connections throughout life, a process called neuroplasticity.

5. According to the passage, the human brain: a) Weighs about 20% of total body weight b) Contains exactly 100 billion neurons c) Uses 20% of the body's energy d) Cannot form new connections after childhood
6. Neuroplasticity refers to: a) The brain's weight relative to body weight b) The number of neurons in the brain c) The brain's ability to form new connections d) The brain's energy consumption

Passage 4: Solar panels work by converting sunlight directly into electricity through photovoltaic cells. When sunlight hits these cells, it knocks electrons loose from atoms, creating an electric current. The efficiency of solar panels has improved dramatically over the past decade, with some modern panels converting over 20% of sunlight into usable electricity. As costs continue to decrease, solar energy is becoming an increasingly viable alternative to fossil fuels.

7. Solar panels generate electricity by: a) Burning sunlight as fuel b) Converting sunlight through photovoltaic cells c) Using wind power d) Storing heat from the sun
8. The passage suggests that solar energy: a) Is becoming less efficient b) Costs more than ever before c) Is becoming more viable d) Cannot replace fossil fuels

Passage 5: Honey bees play a crucial role in agriculture by pollinating crops that produce about one-third of the food we eat. A single bee colony can pollinate 300 million flowers in one day. However, bee populations have been declining due to factors including pesticide use, habitat loss, and disease. Scientists and farmers are working together to develop bee-friendly practices and create pollinator-friendly environments.

9. According to the passage, honey bees: a) Pollinate all of our food crops b) Are responsible for one-third of our food supply c) Can only pollinate a few flowers per day d) Are increasing in population
10. The decline in bee populations is attributed to: a) Natural causes only b) A single factor c) Multiple factors including pesticides d) Unknown reasons

Passage 6: The Great Wall of China, built over many centuries, stretches approximately 13,000 miles across northern China. Contrary to popular belief, it is not visible from space with the naked eye. The wall was constructed by millions of workers, including soldiers, peasants, and prisoners. Today, it stands as a UNESCO World Heritage Site and attracts millions of tourists annually, though many sections are in need of restoration.

11. The Great Wall of China: a) Is visible from space with the naked eye b) Was built in a single century c) Stretches about 13,000 miles d) Was built only by soldiers
12. The passage indicates that the Great Wall: a) Is in perfect condition b) Needs restoration in some areas c) Attracts few tourists d) Is not historically significant

Passage 7: Meditation has been practiced for thousands of years and is now backed by scientific research showing its benefits for mental and physical health. Regular meditation can reduce stress, improve focus, lower blood pressure, and enhance overall well-being. There are many forms of meditation, from mindfulness and breathing exercises to movement-based practices like yoga. Even just 10-15 minutes of daily meditation can produce measurable benefits.

13. According to the passage, meditation: a) Is a recent invention b) Has no scientific backing c) Can reduce stress and improve focus d) Requires hours of daily practice
14. The passage suggests that meditation benefits: a) Only mental health b) Only physical health c) Both mental and physical health d) Neither mental nor physical health

Passage 8: Climate change refers to long-term shifts in global temperatures and weather patterns. While climate variations are natural, scientific evidence shows that human activities, particularly the burning of fossil fuels, have been the primary driver of climate change since the mid-20th century. The consequences include rising sea levels, more frequent extreme weather events, and disruptions to ecosystems worldwide.

15. According to the passage, climate change since the mid-20th century has been primarily caused by: a) Natural climate variations b) Solar activity c) Human activities d) Ocean currents

Mathematics Knowledge (25 questions)

1. What is the value of $3^2 + 4^2$? a) 7 b) 25 c) 49 d) 144
2. If $x = 5$, what is the value of $2x + 3$? a) 10 b) 13 c) 15 d) 18
3. What is the slope of a line passing through points (2, 3) and (4, 7)? a) 1 b) 2 c) 3 d) 4
4. Solve for x: $2x - 8 = 14$ a) 3 b) 7 c) 11 d) 22
5. What is the area of a triangle with base 8 and height 6? a) 14 b) 24 c) 28 d) 48
6. If $\log_{10}(100) = x$, then x equals: a) 1 b) 2 c) 10 d) 100
7. What is the value of $|-7|$? a) -7 b) 0 c) 7 d) 14
8. Which of the following is equivalent to $2^3 \times 2^4$? a) 2^7 b) 2^{12} c) 4^7 d) 4^{12}
9. If a triangle has angles of 45°, 45°, and 90°, it is: a) Equilateral b) Isosceles c) Scalene d) Obtuse
10. What is the circumference of a circle with radius 3? (Use $\pi = 3.14$) a) 9.42 b) 18.84 c) 28.26 d) 37.68

11. Solve: $3x + 2 = 5x - 6$ a) $x = 2$ b) $x = 4$ c) $x = -2$ d) $x = -4$
12. What is the square root of 169? a) 12 b) 13 c) 14 d) 15
13. If $f(x) = x^2 - 3x + 2$, what is $f(4)$? a) 2 b) 6 c) 10 d) 14
14. What is 35% expressed as a decimal? a) 0.035 b) 0.35 c) 3.5 d) 35
15. The sum of the interior angles of a hexagon is: a) 540° b) 720° c) 900° d) 1080°
16. If $2^x = 32$, then x equals: a) 4 b) 5 c) 6 d) 16
17. What is the distance between points (1, 2) and (4, 6)? a) 3 b) 4 c) 5 d) 7
18. Simplify: $(x^3)^2 \times x^4$ a) x^9 b) x^{10} c) x^{24} d) x^{12}
19. If $\sin \theta = 0.5$, what is θ in degrees? a) 30° b) 45° c) 60° d) 90°
20. What is the median of the set {2, 5, 7, 9, 12}? a) 5 b) 7 c) 9 d) 12
21. Factor: $x^2 - 9$ a) $(x - 3)^2$ b) $(x + 3)^2$ c) $(x - 3)(x + 3)$ d) Cannot be factored
22. What is the volume of a cube with side length 4? a) 12 b) 16 c) 48 d) 64
23. If $\cos \theta = 0.5$, what is θ in degrees? a) 30° b) 45° c) 60° d) 90°
24. Solve the system: $x + y = 7$, $x - y = 3$ a) $x = 4$, $y = 3$ b) $x = 5$, $y = 2$ c) $x = 3$, $y = 4$ d) $x = 2$, $y = 5$
25. What is the y-intercept of the line $y = 2x + 5$? a) 2 b) 5 c) -5 d) 0

Electronics Information (20 questions)

1. The unit of electrical resistance is the: a) Volt b) Ampere c) Ohm d) Watt
2. According to Ohm's Law, $V = I \times R$. If voltage is 12V and resistance is 4Ω, current is: a) 2A b) 3A c) 4A d) 8A
3. A capacitor stores: a) Current b) Voltage c) Electrical charge d) Resistance
4. In a series circuit, the total resistance is: a) Less than the smallest resistor b) Equal to the average resistance c) Equal to the sum of all resistances d) Equal to the largest resistor
5. AC stands for: a) Alternating Current b) Amplified Current c) Automatic Current d) Active Current
6. The frequency of household AC power in the US is: a) 50 Hz b) 60 Hz c) 110 Hz d) 120 Hz
7. A diode allows current to flow in: a) Both directions equally b) No direction c) One direction only d) Alternating directions
8. Which material is the best conductor of electricity? a) Copper b) Aluminum c) Silver d) Gold
9. A transformer is used to: a) Convert AC to DC b) Convert DC to AC c) Change voltage levels d) Store electrical energy
10. The power consumed by a 100W light bulb operating for 10 hours is: a) 10 Wh b) 100 Wh c) 1000 Wh d) 10,000 Wh
11. An LED stands for: a) Light Emitting Diode b) Low Energy Device c) Linear Electronic Display d) Liquid Electronic Display
12. In a parallel circuit, if one branch fails: a) All branches fail b) The other branches continue to work c) The circuit becomes a series circuit d) The voltage drops to zero
13. The opposition to AC current flow is called: a) Resistance b) Reactance c) Impedance d) Conductance
14. A battery converts: a) Chemical energy to electrical energy b) Electrical energy to chemical energy c) Mechanical energy to electrical energy d) Thermal energy to electrical energy

15. The unit of electrical power is the: a) Ohm b) Volt c) Ampere d) Watt
16. A fuse is designed to: a) Increase current flow b) Decrease voltage c) Protect against overcurrent d) Amplify signals
17. Ground fault circuit interrupters (GFCIs) are used to: a) Reduce power consumption b) Prevent electrical shock c) Increase voltage d) Filter noise
18. The color code for a 100Ω resistor with 5% tolerance is: a) Brown-Black-Brown-Gold b) Brown-Black-Red-Gold c) Red-Red-Brown-Gold d) Brown-Red-Brown-Gold
19. An oscilloscope is used to: a) Measure resistance b) Display electrical waveforms c) Generate signals d) Store electricity
20. The main advantage of digital circuits over analog circuits is: a) Lower cost b) Simpler design c) Better noise immunity d) Higher power efficiency

Auto & Shop Information (25 questions)

1. The primary purpose of a car's radiator is to: a) Store coolant b) Cool the engine c) Heat the cabin d) Filter air
2. Which tool is used to measure the diameter of a pipe? a) Ruler b) Caliper c) Level d) Square
3. In a car engine, the crankshaft converts: a) Rotary motion to linear motion b) Linear motion to rotary motion c) Electrical energy to mechanical energy d) Chemical energy to thermal energy
4. A Phillips head screwdriver has a tip shaped like a: a) Flat blade b) Star c) Cross d) Hexagon
5. The alternator in a car: a) Starts the engine b) Charges the battery c) Cools the engine d) Filters fuel
6. Which saw is best for cutting curves in wood? a) Circular saw b) Table saw c) Jigsaw d) Miter saw
7. Brake fluid is typically: a) Oil-based b) Water-based c) Glycol-based d) Alcohol-based
8. A wrench that can be adjusted to fit different sized nuts is called: a) Box wrench b) Open-end wrench c) Adjustable wrench d) Torque wrench
9. The transmission in a car: a) Filters air b) Transfers power from engine to wheels c) Cools the engine d) Stores fuel
10. Which grade of sandpaper has the finest grit? a) 60 grit b) 120 grit c) 220 grit d) 400 grit
11. Spark plugs are found in: a) Diesel engines only b) Gasoline engines only c) Both diesel and gasoline engines d) Electric motors
12. A level is used to determine if a surface is: a) Smooth b) Flat c) Horizontal or vertical d) Clean
13. The differential in a car allows the wheels to: a) Turn at different speeds b) Turn at the same speed c) Stop more effectively d) Accelerate faster
14. Which drill bit is best for drilling into concrete? a) Twist bit b) Spade bit c) Masonry bit d) Hole saw
15. An engine's timing belt or chain: a) Charges the battery b) Synchronizes valve and piston movement c) Cools the engine d) Filters oil
16. A C-clamp is used to: a) Cut materials b) Measure materials c) Hold materials together d) Sand materials

17. Power steering fluid helps: a) Engine performance b) Brake operation c) Steering ease d) Transmission shifting
18. The teeth per inch (TPI) on a saw blade determines: a) The blade's length b) The cutting speed c) The smoothness of cut d) The blade's width
19. A catalytic converter: a) Increases engine power b) Reduces harmful emissions c) Improves fuel economy d) Cools the exhaust
20. Which tool is used to cut threads on the outside of a rod? a) Tap b) Die c) Reamer d) Broach
21. The carburetor in older cars: a) Ignites the fuel b) Mixes air and fuel c) Filters exhaust d) Cools the engine
22. A router is primarily used for: a) Cutting straight lines b) Drilling holes c) Shaping edges d) Sanding surfaces
23. Anti-lock braking systems (ABS) prevent: a) Brake fluid leaks b) Wheel lockup c) Brake pad wear d) Brake overheating
24. Which hand plane is used for smoothing large flat surfaces? a) Block plane b) Jack plane c) Smoothing plane d) Jointer plane
25. The PCV (Positive Crankcase Ventilation) valve: a) Controls fuel flow b) Removes crankcase gases c) Regulates air temperature d) Filters oil

Mechanical Comprehension (25 questions)

1. A first-class lever has the fulcrum: a) At one end b) Between the effort and load c) At the load end d) At the effort end
2. If gear A has 20 teeth and gear B has 40 teeth, and gear A makes 10 revolutions, gear B makes: a) 5 revolutions b) 10 revolutions c) 20 revolutions d) 40 revolutions
3. A block and tackle with 4 supporting ropes provides a mechanical advantage of: a) 2 b) 4 c) 6 d) 8
4. When a liquid is heated, it generally: a) Contracts b) Expands c) Stays the same d) Crystallizes
5. An inclined plane reduces the force needed to lift an object by: a) Decreasing the distance b) Increasing the distance c) Changing the direction d) Adding more force
6. In a hydraulic system, if the input piston has area 1 sq in and the output piston has area 4 sq in, a force of 10 lbs on the input produces: a) 2.5 lbs on output b) 10 lbs on output c) 40 lbs on output d) 160 lbs on output
7. A wheel and axle provides mechanical advantage when: a) The wheel is smaller than the axle b) The wheel is larger than the axle c) They are the same size d) The axle is hollow
8. The center of gravity of an object is the point where: a) It weighs the most b) It balances c) It's strongest d) It's thickest
9. When two gears mesh, they rotate in: a) The same direction b) Opposite directions c) Random directions d) No specific pattern
10. A screw is essentially: a) An inclined plane wrapped around a cylinder b) A lever c) A pulley d) A wedge
11. If you apply 50 lbs of force to a lever arm 2 feet from the fulcrum, the torque is: a) 25 ft-lbs b) 50 ft-lbs c) 100 ft-lbs d) 200 ft-lbs
12. In a simple pulley system, using a fixed pulley: a) Reduces the force needed b) Changes the direction of force c) Increases the force needed d) Provides no advantage

13. The mechanical advantage of a wedge depends on: a) Its weight b) Its length and thickness c) Its color d) Its hardness
14. When a spinning object's mass is moved closer to its axis of rotation, it spins: a) Slower b) Faster c) At the same speed d) Backwards
15. A cam converts: a) Linear motion to rotary motion b) Rotary motion to linear motion c) Up and down motion to side motion d) Fast motion to slow motion
16. The efficiency of a machine is: a) Always 100% b) Always less than 100% c) Sometimes greater than 100% d) Always 50%
17. Ball bearings in a machine: a) Increase friction b) Reduce friction c) Have no effect on friction d) Create heat
18. A compound gear train: a) Uses only two gears b) Uses gears of the same size c) Uses multiple gear sets d) Cannot change speed
19. The force needed to move an object on a rough surface depends on: a) The object's color b) The coefficient of friction c) The time of day d) The temperature
20. A governor in a machine: a) Starts the machine b) Stops the machine c) Controls the speed d) Provides power
21. When a belt connects two pulleys of different sizes, the smaller pulley: a) Turns slower b) Turns faster c) Doesn't turn d) Turns backward
22. The strength of a beam is greatest when force is applied: a) At the center b) At the ends c) Distributed evenly d) At the strongest point
23. A clutch in a machine: a) Connects and disconnects power transmission b) Increases power c) Reduces power d) Stores power
24. Centrifugal force acts: a) Toward the center of rotation b) Away from the center of rotation c) Parallel to the axis d) Perpendicular to motion
25. A universal joint allows: a) Only rotation b) Only linear motion c) Rotation at various angles d) No motion

Answer Key - Test 22

General Science: 1-b, 2-c, 3-b, 4-c, 5-c, 6-c, 7-b, 8-c, 9-b, 10-c, 11-c, 12-c, 13-b, 14-c, 15-c, 16-b, 17-c, 18-b, 19-c, 20-c, 21-c, 22-d, 23-b, 24-b, 25-b

Arithmetic Reasoning: 1-b, 2-a, 3-b, 4-a, 5-a, 6-b, 7-b, 8-c, 9-b, 10-c, 11-a, 12-b, 13-c, 14-b, 15-b, 16-b, 17-b, 18-b, 19-b, 20-c, 21-c, 22-a, 23-a, 24-b, 25-b, 26-c, 27-b, 28-a, 29-a, 30-c

Word Knowledge: 1-b, 2-b, 3-c, 4-b, 5-c, 6-b, 7-b, 8-b, 9-b, 10-b, 11-b, 12-b, 13-b, 14-b, 15-b, 16-b, 17-b, 18-b, 19-b, 20-b, 21-b, 22-b, 23-b, 24-b, 25-b, 26-b, 27-b, 28-b, 29-b, 30-b, 31-b, 32-b, 33-b, 34-b, 35-b

Paragraph Comprehension: 1-b, 2-b, 3-b, 4-c, 5-c, 6-c, 7-b, 8-c, 9-b, 10-c, 11-c, 12-b, 13-c, 14-c, 15-c

Mathematics Knowledge: 1-b, 2-b, 3-b, 4-c, 5-b, 6-b, 7-c, 8-a, 9-b, 10-b, 11-b, 12-b, 13-b, 14-b, 15-b, 16-b, 17-c, 18-b, 19-a, 20-b, 21-c, 22-d, 23-c, 24-b, 25-b

Electronics Information: 1-c, 2-b, 3-c, 4-c, 5-a, 6-b, 7-c, 8-c, 9-c, 10-c, 11-a, 12-b, 13-c, 14-a, 15-d, 16-c, 17-b, 18-a, 19-b, 20-c

Auto & Shop Information: 1-b, 2-b, 3-b, 4-c, 5-b, 6-c, 7-c, 8-c, 9-b, 10-d, 11-b, 12-c, 13-a, 14-c, 15-b, 16-c, 17-c, 18-c, 19-b, 20-b, 21-b, 22-c, 23-b, 24-d, 25-b

Mechanical Comprehension: 1-b, 2-a, 3-b, 4-b, 5-b, 6-c, 7-b, 8-b, 9-b, 10-a, 11-c, 12-b, 13-b, 14-b, 15-b, 16-b, 17-b, 18-c, 19-b, 20-c, 21-b, 22-a, 23-a, 24-b, 25-c

Test 23

General Science (25 questions)

1. The closest star to Earth (other than the Sun) is: a) Alpha Centauri b) Sirius c) Polaris d) Vega
2. Which blood vessels carry blood away from the heart? a) Veins b) Arteries c) Capillaries d) Venules
3. The chemical formula for water is: a) H_2O_2 b) H_2O c) HO d) H_3O
4. Which part of the plant conducts photosynthesis? a) Roots b) Stem c) Leaves d) Flowers
5. The unit of force in the metric system is: a) Joule b) Newton c) Watt d) Pascal
6. DNA stands for: a) Deoxyribonucleic Acid b) Dinitrogen Oxide c) Double Nuclear Acid d) Dynamic Nuclear Acid
7. Which planet has the shortest day? a) Mercury b) Venus c) Jupiter d) Saturn
8. The process by which rocks are broken down by weather is: a) Erosion b) Weathering c) Sedimentation d) Crystallization
9. Which organ produces insulin? a) Liver b) Kidney c) Pancreas d) Stomach
10. The most abundant gas in Earth's atmosphere is: a) Oxygen b) Carbon dioxide c) Nitrogen d) Hydrogen
11. Sound cannot travel through: a) Air b) Water c) Steel d) Vacuum
12. The study of living organisms is called: a) Chemistry b) Physics c) Biology d) Geology
13. Which vitamin prevents scurvy? a) Vitamin A b) Vitamin C c) Vitamin D d) Vitamin K
14. An eclipse of the sun occurs when: a) Earth is between the sun and moon b) The moon is between Earth and sun c) The sun is between Earth and moon d) All three are aligned randomly
15. The hardest substance found naturally on Earth is: a) Iron b) Quartz c) Diamond d) Granite
16. Which gas is produced during photosynthesis? a) Carbon dioxide b) Oxygen c) Nitrogen d) Hydrogen
17. The smallest unit of matter is: a) Molecule b) Atom c) Electron d) Proton
18. Which system removes waste from the blood? a) Respiratory b) Circulatory c) Digestive d) Excretory
19. Lightning is a form of: a) Mechanical energy b) Chemical energy c) Electrical energy d) Nuclear energy
20. The boiling point of water at sea level is: a) 100°C b) 212°F c) Both a and b d) 0°C

21. Which scientist is famous for the theory of relativity? a) Newton b) Einstein c) Darwin d) Galileo
22. The main function of red blood cells is to: a) Fight infection b) Carry oxygen c) Clot blood d) Produce antibodies
23. Which force keeps planets in orbit around the sun? a) Magnetism b) Friction c) Gravity d) Centrifugal force
24. The largest organ in the human body is: a) Liver b) Brain c) Lungs d) Skin
25. Acids have a pH: a) Greater than 7 b) Equal to 7 c) Less than 7 d) Equal to 14

Arithmetic Reasoning (30 questions)

1. A recipe calls for 2 cups of flour to make 12 cookies. How many cups are needed for 18 cookies? a) 2.5 cups b) 3 cups c) 3.5 cups d) 4 cups
2. If a stock price increases from $40 to $50, what is the percent increase? a) 20% b) 25% c) 30% d) 35%
3. A rectangular garden is 15 feet long and 10 feet wide. What is its perimeter? a) 25 feet b) 35 feet c) 50 feet d) 150 feet
4. If $5x - 3 = 22$, what is x? a) 4 b) 5 c) 6 d) 7
5. A car travels 280 miles in 4 hours. What is its average speed? a) 60 mph b) 65 mph c) 70 mph d) 75 mph
6. What is 30% of 150? a) 40 b) 45 c) 50 d) 55
7. If you buy 4 items for $3.25 each, what is the total cost? a) $12.00 b) $13.00 c) $14.00 d) $15.00
8. A circle has a radius of 5 inches. What is its area? (Use $\pi = 3.14$) a) 78.5 sq in b) 31.4 sq in c) 15.7 sq in d) 157 sq in
9. If $3y + 8 = 23$, what is y? a) 4 b) 5 c) 6 d) 7
10. What is the square root of 225? a) 13 b) 14 c) 15 d) 16
11. A triangle has angles of 50° and 60°. What is the third angle? a) 60° b) 70° c) 80° d) 90°
12. If gasoline costs $3.20 per gallon and you need 15 gallons, what is the total cost? a) $45.00 b) $48.00 c) $51.00 d) $54.00
13. What is 2/5 of 35? a) 12 b) 14 c) 16 d) 18
14. A ladder 25 feet long leans against a wall. If the base is 7 feet from the wall, how high up the wall does it reach? a) 22 feet b) 24 feet c) 26 feet d) 28 feet
15. If $4x = 36$, what is x? a) 8 b) 9 c) 10 d) 11
16. What is the average of 14, 18, 22, and 26? a) 18 b) 19 c) 20 d) 21
17. A rectangular box has dimensions $6 \times 4 \times 3$ inches. What is its volume? a) 72 cubic inches b) 60 cubic inches c) 48 cubic inches d) 36 cubic inches
18. If you save $75 per month for 6 months, how much do you save total? a) $400 b) $425 c) $450 d) $475
19. What is 18% of 200? a) 32 b) 34 c) 36 d) 38
20. If $2(x + 3) = 16$, what is x? a) 5 b) 6 c) 7 d) 8
21. A pizza is divided into 12 slices. If you eat 5 slices, what fraction is left? a) 5/12 b) 7/12 c) 1/2 d) 2/3
22. The circumference of a circle is 31.4 inches. What is its radius? (Use $\pi = 3.14$) a) 5 inches b) 10 inches c) 15 inches d) 20 inches
23. If $6x - 4 = 32$, what is x? a) 5 b) 6 c) 7 d) 8

24. What is 3/4 × 2/3? a) 1/2 b) 5/7 c) 6/12 d) 5/6
25. A store offers a 15% discount on a $80 item. What is the sale price? a) $65 b) $68 c) $70 d) $72
26. If a rectangle has length 14 feet and perimeter 40 feet, what is its width? a) 6 feet b) 8 feet c) 10 feet d) 12 feet
27. What is the value of $5^2 - 3^2$? a) 4 b) 8 c) 16 d) 25
28. If you work 8 hours at $12.50 per hour, how much do you earn? a) $95 b) $100 c) $105 d) $110
29. A bag contains 8 red marbles and 4 blue marbles. What is the probability of drawing a blue marble? a) 1/4 b) 1/3 c) 1/2 d) 2/3
30. If the ratio of cats to dogs is 2:3 and there are 20 animals total, how many are cats? a) 6 b) 8 c) 10 d) 12

Word Knowledge (35 questions)

1. ELOQUENT most nearly means: a) Silent b) Articulate c) Confused d) Stammering
2. ALLEVIATE most nearly means: a) Worsen b) Relieve c) Ignore d) Complicate
3. TENACIOUS most nearly means: a) Weak b) Persistent c) Flexible d) Careless
4. CRYPTIC most nearly means: a) Clear b) Mysterious c) Obvious d) Simple
5. VINDICATE most nearly means: a) Blame b) Clear of charges c) Accuse d) Punish
6. LUCRATIVE most nearly means: a) Unprofitable b) Profitable c) Expensive d) Cheap
7. DEFIANT most nearly means: a) Obedient b) Rebellious c) Submissive d) Agreeable
8. PARAMOUNT most nearly means: a) Unimportant b) Secondary c) Supreme d) Minor
9. JEOPARDIZE most nearly means: a) Protect b) Endanger c) Help d) Assist
10. CORDIAL most nearly means: a) Unfriendly b) Friendly c) Hostile d) Rude
11. AMBIGUOUS most nearly means: a) Clear b) Unclear c) Obvious d) Definite
12. FORTIFY most nearly means: a) Weaken b) Strengthen c) Destroy d) Abandon
13. SCRUTINIZE most nearly means: a) Ignore b) Examine closely c) Overlook d) Dismiss
14. PLACID most nearly means: a) Turbulent b) Calm c) Rough d) Stormy
15. REVOKE most nearly means: a) Grant b) Cancel c) Approve d) Confirm
16. CONCUR most nearly means: a) Disagree b) Agree c) Argue d) Dispute
17. FACILITATE most nearly means: a) Hinder b) Make easier c) Complicate d) Block
18. INEVITABLE most nearly means: a) Avoidable b) Unavoidable c) Possible d) Unlikely
19. PRUDENT most nearly means: a) Reckless b) Wise c) Foolish d) Impulsive
20. TRIVIAL most nearly means: a) Important b) Unimportant c) Significant d) Major
21. CONTEMPT most nearly means: a) Respect b) Scorn c) Admiration d) Praise
22. VIBRANT most nearly means: a) Dull b) Lively c) Quiet d) Subdued
23. COMPREHENSIVE most nearly means: a) Partial b) Complete c) Limited d) Restricted
24. DILIGENT most nearly means: a) Lazy b) Hardworking c) Careless d) Negligent
25. TRANSIENT most nearly means: a) Permanent b) Temporary c) Lasting d) Enduring
26. MEAGER most nearly means: a) Abundant b) Scanty c) Plentiful d) Generous
27. EXHILARATING most nearly means: a) Depressing b) Exciting c) Boring d) Tiring
28. AUTHENTIC most nearly means: a) Fake b) Genuine c) False d) Artificial
29. MEDIOCRE most nearly means: a) Excellent b) Average c) Superior d) Outstanding
30. VERSATILE most nearly means: a) Limited b) Adaptable c) Rigid d) Inflexible
31. INHIBIT most nearly means: a) Encourage b) Restrain c) Promote d) Help

32. REDUNDANT most nearly means: a) Necessary b) Unnecessary c) Essential d) Required
33. COHERENT most nearly means: a) Confused b) Logical c) Unclear d) Jumbled
34. DORMANT most nearly means: a) Active b) Inactive c) Energetic d) Lively
35. EXEMPLARY most nearly means: a) Poor b) Outstanding c) Mediocre d) Faulty

Paragraph Comprehension (15 questions)

Passage 1: Renewable energy sources such as solar, wind, and hydroelectric power are becoming increasingly important as concerns about climate change and fossil fuel depletion grow. Unlike fossil fuels, renewable energy sources are naturally replenished and produce little to no greenhouse gas emissions during operation. However, they also face challenges including intermittency, storage issues, and higher initial installation costs.

1. According to the passage, renewable energy sources: a) Produce more emissions than fossil fuels b) Are naturally replenished c) Are cheaper to install than fossil fuels d) Have no challenges
2. The passage suggests that renewable energy is important due to: a) Low installation costs b) Concerns about climate change and fossil fuel depletion c) Easy storage d) Constant availability

Passage 2: The human heart is a remarkable organ that beats approximately 100,000 times per day, pumping about 2,000 gallons of blood throughout the body. This four-chambered organ consists of two atria and two ventricles, working together to circulate oxygen-rich blood to tissues and return oxygen-poor blood to the lungs. Heart disease remains the leading cause of death in many developed countries.

3. According to the passage, the human heart: a) Beats about 50,000 times per day b) Pumps about 1,000 gallons of blood daily c) Has three chambers d) Beats approximately 100,000 times per day
4. The passage indicates that heart disease: a) Is rare in developed countries b) Is the leading cause of death in many developed countries c) Only affects older adults d) Has been eliminated

Passage 3: Artificial intelligence (AI) is rapidly transforming various industries, from healthcare and finance to transportation and entertainment. Machine learning algorithms can now analyze vast amounts of data to identify patterns and make predictions that would be impossible for humans to process manually. However, the rise of AI also raises important questions about job displacement, privacy, and ethical considerations.

5. According to the passage, AI is: a) Limited to the healthcare industry b) Transforming various industries c) Unable to process large amounts of data d) Only used for entertainment
6. The passage mentions that AI raises questions about: a) Technical capabilities only b) Job displacement, privacy, and ethics c) Cost effectiveness d) Processing speed

Passage 4: The Great Barrier Reef, located off the coast of Australia, is the world's largest coral reef system and can be seen from space. Home to thousands of species of fish, coral, and other marine life, it's considered one of the most biodiverse ecosystems on Earth. Unfortunately, the reef faces significant threats from climate change, pollution, and coastal development, leading to widespread coral bleaching events.

7. The Great Barrier Reef is: a) The second-largest coral reef system b) Located off the coast of New Zealand c) The world's largest coral reef system d) Not visible from space
8. According to the passage, the reef faces threats from: a) Tourism only b) Climate change, pollution, and coastal development c) Overfishing only d) Natural disasters only

Passage 5: Sleep plays a crucial role in physical and mental health, yet many adults don't get the recommended 7-9 hours per night. During sleep, the body repairs tissues, consolidates memories, and releases important hormones. Chronic sleep deprivation has been linked to numerous health problems including obesity, diabetes, cardiovascular disease, and weakened immune function.

9. According to the passage, adults should get: a) 5-7 hours of sleep per night b) 7-9 hours of sleep per night c) 9-11 hours of sleep per night d) 6-8 hours of sleep per night
10. Chronic sleep deprivation has been linked to: a) Improved immune function b) Better memory c) Numerous health problems d) Increased energy

Passage 6: The invention of the printing press by Johannes Gutenberg in the 15th century revolutionized the spread of information and knowledge. Before this innovation, books were hand-copied by scribes, making them expensive and rare. The printing press made books more affordable and accessible, leading to increased literacy rates and the rapid dissemination of ideas during the Renaissance and beyond.

11. The printing press was invented by: a) Leonardo da Vinci b) Johannes Gutenberg c) William Shakespeare d) Galileo Galilei
12. Before the printing press, books were: a) Mass-produced b) Inexpensive c) Hand-copied by scribes d) Readily available

Passage 7: Volcanic eruptions, while often destructive, also play important roles in shaping Earth's landscape and climate. Volcanic ash can enrich soil with minerals, making it highly fertile for agriculture. Additionally, volcanic activity helps release gases from Earth's interior and contributes to the formation of new land masses. Some scientists believe that volcanic eruptions may have played a role in the development of early life on Earth.

13. According to the passage, volcanic eruptions: a) Are only destructive b) Play important roles in shaping Earth c) Have no effect on soil fertility d) Prevent new land formation
14. Volcanic ash can: a) Damage soil permanently b) Enrich soil with minerals c) Prevent plant growth d) Cause permanent climate change

Passage 8: The Internet has fundamentally changed how people communicate, work, and access information. What began as a research project in the 1960s has evolved into a global network connecting billions of devices. E-commerce, social media, online education, and remote work have all become integral parts of modern life, though concerns about cybersecurity, privacy, and digital addiction continue to grow.

15. According to the passage, the Internet: a) Was created in the 1970s b) Started as a research project in the 1960s c) Only connects computers d) Has eliminated privacy concerns

Mathematics Knowledge (25 questions)

1. What is the value of 4^3? a) 12 b) 16 c) 48 d) 64
2. If $x = -3$, what is the value of $x^2 + 2x - 1$? a) 2 b) 4 c) 6 d) 8
3. What is the slope of the line $2x + 3y = 12$? a) -2/3 b) 2/3 c) -3/2 d) 3/2
4. Solve for x: $3x + 5 = 2x + 12$ a) 5 b) 6 c) 7 d) 8
5. What is the area of a circle with diameter 8? (Use $\pi = 3.14$) a) 50.24 b) 25.12 c) 200.96 d) 12.56
6. If $\log_2(16) = x$, then x equals: a) 2 b) 4 c) 8 d) 16
7. What is the value of $|-5 + 3|$? a) -8 b) -2 c) 2 d) 8
8. Which of the following is equivalent to $(3^2)^3$? a) 3^5 b) 3^6 c) 9^3 d) 27
9. In a right triangle, if one angle is 30°, what is the other acute angle? a) 30° b) 45° c) 60° d) 90°
10. What is the perimeter of a rectangle with length 7 and width 4? a) 11 b) 22 c) 28 d) 44
11. Solve: $4x - 3 = 3x + 7$ a) x = 8 b) x = 10 c) x = 4 d) x = 5
12. What is the square root of 196? a) 13 b) 14 c) 15 d) 16
13. If $f(x) = 2x^2 - x + 3$, what is f(2)? a) 5 b) 9 c) 7 d) 11
14. What is 45% expressed as a fraction in lowest terms? a) 45/100 b) 9/20 c) 9/25 d) 3/5
15. The sum of interior angles of a pentagon is: a) 360° b) 540° c) 720° d) 900°
16. If $3^x = 81$, then x equals: a) 3 b) 4 c) 27 d) 81
17. What is the distance between points (-1, 2) and (3, 5)? a) 3 b) 4 c) 5 d) 7
18. Simplify: $x^5 \div x^2$ a) x^3 b) x^7 c) x^{10} d) x^2
19. If $\tan \theta = 1$, what is θ in degrees? a) 30° b) 45° c) 60° d) 90°
20. What is the mode of the set {3, 7, 3, 9, 5, 3, 8}? a) 3 b) 5 c) 7 d) 8
21. Factor: $x^2 + 5x + 6$ a) (x + 2)(x + 3) b) (x + 1)(x + 6) c) (x - 2)(x - 3) d) Cannot be factored
22. What is the surface area of a cube with side length 3? a) 27 b) 54 c) 18 d) 36
23. If $\sin \theta = \sqrt{3}/2$, what is θ in degrees? a) 30° b) 45° c) 60° d) 90°
24. Solve the system: $2x + y = 8$, $x - y = 1$ a) x = 2, y = 4 b) x = 3, y = 2 c) x = 4, y = 0 d) x = 1, y = 6
25. What is the x-intercept of the line $y = 3x - 6$? a) -6 b) -2 c) 2 d) 3

Electronics Information (20 questions)

1. The unit of electrical capacitance is the: a) Ohm b) Farad c) Henry d) Coulomb
2. If a 60W light bulb operates at 120V, what current does it draw? a) 0.5A b) 2A c) 60A d) 120A
3. An inductor stores energy in the form of: a) Electric field b) Magnetic field c) Heat d) Light

4. In a parallel circuit, the total current is: a) The same through each branch b) Equal to the sum of branch currents c) Always zero d) Equal to the smallest branch current
5. DC stands for: a) Direct Current b) Dynamic Current c) Double Current d) Dependent Current
6. The opposition to current flow in AC circuits is called: a) Resistance b) Reactance c) Impedance d) Conductance
7. A transistor has how many terminals? a) Two b) Three c) Four d) Five
8. Which component is used to step up or step down AC voltage? a) Resistor b) Capacitor c) Transformer d) Diode
9. The power factor in AC circuits is the ratio of: a) Voltage to current b) Real power to apparent power c) Resistance to impedance d) Frequency to period
10. A relay is an: a) Electronically controlled switch b) Voltage regulator c) Current amplifier d) Frequency generator
11. In digital electronics, binary 1 is typically represented by: a) 0 volts b) A high voltage c) Negative voltage d) Variable voltage
12. A Zener diode is primarily used for: a) Rectification b) Voltage regulation c) Amplification d) Switching
13. The frequency response of a high-pass filter: a) Passes low frequencies b) Passes high frequencies c) Passes all frequencies d) Blocks all frequencies
14. An operational amplifier (op-amp) has: a) One input b) Two inputs c) Three inputs d) Four inputs
15. The unit of magnetic flux is the: a) Tesla b) Weber c) Henry d) Gauss
16. A rectifier circuit converts: a) AC to DC b) DC to AC c) High voltage to low voltage d) Low current to high current
17. The gain of an amplifier is usually expressed in: a) Ohms b) Watts c) Decibels d) Hertz
18. A crystal oscillator is used to: a) Amplify signals b) Generate precise frequencies c) Filter noise d) Convert voltages
19. The time constant of an RC circuit equals: a) R + C b) R - C c) R × C d) R ÷ C
20. A photodiode converts: a) Light to electrical current b) Electrical current to light c) Heat to electricity d) Sound to electricity

Auto & Shop Information (25 questions)

1. The engine oil filter removes: a) Water from oil b) Dirt and contaminants from oil c) Air from oil d) Fuel from oil
2. Which tool is best for cutting metal? a) Wood saw b) Hacksaw c) Coping saw d) Bow saw
3. The clutch in a manual transmission: a) Changes gear ratios b) Connects and disconnects the engine from transmission c) Filters transmission fluid d) Cools the transmission
4. A torque wrench is used to: a) Remove rusted bolts b) Tighten bolts to specific force c) Cut threads d) Measure bolt diameter
5. The thermostat in a car controls: a) Air conditioning b) Engine temperature c) Fuel flow d) Electrical system
6. Which chisel is used for cutting grooves? a) Cold chisel b) Cape chisel c) Round nose chisel d) Diamond point chisel

7. Anti-freeze in the radiator: a) Only prevents freezing b) Only prevents overheating c) Prevents both freezing and overheating d) Increases engine power
8. A spirit level uses what to indicate level? a) Water b) Oil c) Mercury d) Air bubble
9. The fuel pump delivers gasoline from: a) Carburetor to engine b) Tank to engine c) Engine to exhaust d) Air filter to engine
10. Which file cuts fastest? a) Single cut b) Double cut c) Smooth cut d) Dead smooth
11. Disc brakes use what to create friction? a) Brake shoes b) Brake pads c) Brake drums d) Brake fluid
12. A center punch is used to: a) Mark hole locations b) Remove pins c) Flatten metal d) Cut threads
13. The muffler in the exhaust system: a) Increases engine power b) Reduces exhaust noise c) Filters air d) Cools exhaust gases
14. Which abrasive is hardest? a) Aluminum oxide b) Silicon carbide c) Garnet d) Emery
15. Power brakes use what to assist braking? a) Electric motor b) Engine vacuum c) Hydraulic pressure d) Manual force
16. A drift pin is used to: a) Mark measurements b) Align holes c) Cut metal d) Bend metal
17. The air filter prevents what from entering the engine? a) Water b) Fuel c) Oil d) Dirt and debris
18. Which hand tool multiplies turning force? a) Screwdriver b) Pliers c) Wrench d) Pipe wrench
19. The starter motor: a) Charges the battery b) Starts the engine c) Runs the alternator d) Powers lights
20. A reamer is used to: a) Cut new holes b) Enlarge existing holes precisely c) Thread holes d) Deburr holes
21. Shock absorbers: a) Support the vehicle weight b) Control spring oscillations c) Steer the vehicle d) Provide braking force
22. Which hammer has a ball-shaped end? a) Claw hammer b) Ball peen hammer c) Sledge hammer d) Dead blow hammer
23. The distributor in older cars: a) Distributes fuel b) Distributes spark to cylinders c) Distributes oil d) Distributes coolant
24. A feeler gauge measures: a) Pressure b) Temperature c) Small gaps d) Electrical current
25. Tread depth on tires affects: a) Fuel economy only b) Tire wear only c) Traction and safety d) Engine performance

Mechanical Comprehension (25 questions)

1. A second-class lever has the load: a) Between effort and fulcrum b) At the fulcrum c) At the effort end d) At the opposite end from effort
2. If gear A has 15 teeth and gear B has 45 teeth, the gear ratio is: a) 1:2 b) 1:3 c) 2:1 d) 3:1
3. A movable pulley provides a mechanical advantage of: a) 1 b) 2 c) 3 d) 4
4. Heat generally causes most materials to: a) Contract b) Expand c) Change color d) Become harder
5. The steeper an inclined plane, the: a) Greater the mechanical advantage b) Less the mechanical advantage c) Same the mechanical advantage d) No effect on mechanical advantage

6. In a hydraulic press, if the input area is 2 sq in and output area is 8 sq in, a 20 lb input force produces: a) 40 lbs output b) 60 lbs output c) 80 lbs output d) 160 lbs output
7. A fixed pulley primarily: a) Reduces force needed b) Changes direction of applied force c) Increases distance d) Reduces distance
8. The stability of an object depends on: a) Its weight only b) Its height only c) The position of its center of gravity d) Its color
9. In a gear train, if the driver gear turns clockwise, the driven gear turns: a) Clockwise b) Counterclockwise c) In the same direction d) Randomly
10. A wedge concentrates force by: a) Increasing the distance b) Decreasing the area over which force is applied c) Changing direction d) Storing energy
11. If a lever arm is 3 feet long and you apply 40 lbs of force, the torque is: a) 43 ft-lbs b) 120 ft-lbs c) 37 ft-lbs d) 13 ft-lbs
12. A compound pulley system: a) Uses only fixed pulleys b) Uses only movable pulleys c) Combines fixed and movable pulleys d) Cannot provide mechanical advantage
13. The cutting angle of a wedge affects: a) Its color b) Its efficiency c) Its weight d) Its length
14. When a flywheel spins faster, its kinetic energy: a) Decreases b) Stays the same c) Increases d) Becomes zero
15. A linkage mechanism: a) Connects rotating parts b) Transfers motion between parts c) Stores energy d) Generates power
16. Mechanical advantage is always: a) Greater than 1 b) Less than 1 c) Equal to 1 d) Force out divided by force in
17. Lubrication reduces: a) Speed b) Power c) Friction d) Strength
18. A worm gear provides: a) High speed, low torque b) Low speed, high torque c) Same speed d) No advantage
19. The coefficient of friction depends on: a) The surfaces in contact b) The applied force c) The speed d) The temperature only
20. A brake works by: a) Increasing speed b) Converting kinetic energy to heat energy c) Storing energy d) Generating power
21. When two pulleys are connected by a belt, if one pulley is larger: a) It turns faster b) It turns slower c) Speed is the same d) Direction reverses
22. A cantilever beam is supported: a) At both ends b) At one end only c) In the middle d) At three points
23. A flywheel stores energy as: a) Potential energy b) Kinetic energy c) Chemical energy d) Electrical energy
24. In gear reduction, the output shaft turns: a) Faster than input b) Slower than input c) Same speed as input d) In reverse
25. A shock absorber: a) Amplifies motion b) Dampens motion c) Reverses motion d) Stores motion

Answer Key - Test 23

General Science: 1-a, 2-b, 3-b, 4-c, 5-b, 6-a, 7-c, 8-b, 9-c, 10-c, 11-d, 12-c, 13-b, 14-b, 15-c, 16-b, 17-b, 18-d, 19-c, 20-c, 21-b, 22-b, 23-c, 24-d, 25-c

Arithmetic Reasoning: 1-b, 2-b, 3-c, 4-b, 5-c, 6-b, 7-b, 8-a, 9-b, 10-c, 11-b, 12-b, 13-b, 14-b, 15-b, 16-c, 17-a, 18-c, 19-c, 20-a, 21-b, 22-a, 23-b, 24-a, 25-b, 26-a, 27-c, 28-b, 29-b, 30-b

Word Knowledge: 1-b, 2-b, 3-b, 4-b, 5-b, 6-b, 7-b, 8-c, 9-b, 10-b, 11-b, 12-b, 13-b, 14-b, 15-b, 16-b, 17-b, 18-b, 19-b, 20-b, 21-b, 22-b, 23-b, 24-b, 25-b, 26-b, 27-b, 28-b, 29-b, 30-b, 31-b, 32-b, 33-b, 34-b, 35-b

Paragraph Comprehension: 1-b, 2-b, 3-d, 4-b, 5-b, 6-b, 7-c, 8-b, 9-b, 10-c, 11-b, 12-c, 13-b, 14-b, 15-b

Mathematics Knowledge: 1-d, 2-a, 3-a, 4-c, 5-a, 6-b, 7-c, 8-b, 9-c, 10-b, 11-b, 12-b, 13-b, 14-b, 15-b, 16-b, 17-c, 18-a, 19-b, 20-a, 21-a, 22-b, 23-c, 24-b, 25-c

Electronics Information: 1-b, 2-a, 3-b, 4-b, 5-a, 6-c, 7-b, 8-c, 9-b, 10-a, 11-b, 12-b, 13-b, 14-b, 15-b, 16-a, 17-c, 18-b, 19-c, 20-a

Auto & Shop Information: 1-b, 2-b, 3-b, 4-b, 5-b, 6-b, 7-c, 8-d, 9-b, 10-b, 11-b, 12-a, 13-b, 14-b, 15-b, 16-b, 17-d, 18-d, 19-b, 20-b, 21-b, 22-b, 23-b, 24-c, 25-c

Mechanical Comprehension: 1-a, 2-b, 3-b, 4-b, 5-b, 6-c, 7-b, 8-c, 9-b, 10-b, 11-b, 12-c, 13-b, 14-c, 15-b, 16-d, 17-c, 18-b, 19-a, 20-b, 21-b, 22-b, 23-b, 24-b, 25-b

Test 24

General Science (25 questions)

1. The process by which water moves through plants is called: a) Osmosis b) Transpiration c) Respiration d) Digestion
2. Which layer of the Earth is liquid? a) Crust b) Mantle c) Outer core d) Inner core
3. The chemical symbol for sodium is: a) So b) Sd c) Na d) S
4. Which type of energy is stored in food? a) Kinetic b) Potential c) Chemical d) Thermal
5. The asteroid belt is located between: a) Earth and Mars b) Mars and Jupiter c) Jupiter and Saturn d) Saturn and Uranus
6. Which vitamin is essential for blood clotting? a) Vitamin A b) Vitamin C c) Vitamin D d) Vitamin K
7. The Richter scale measures: a) Temperature b) Earthquake intensity c) Wind speed d) Humidity
8. Which gas is used in photosynthesis? a) Oxygen b) Nitrogen c) Carbon dioxide d) Hydrogen
9. The smallest bone in the human body is located in the: a) Hand b) Foot c) Ear d) Nose
10. Which planet rotates on its side? a) Venus b) Jupiter c) Uranus d) Neptune
11. The study of fungi is called: a) Botany b) Zoology c) Mycology d) Geology
12. Sound waves are what type of wave? a) Electromagnetic b) Longitudinal c) Transverse d) Standing
13. Which element is essential for thyroid function? a) Iron b) Calcium c) Iodine d) Zinc

14. A lunar eclipse occurs when: a) The moon blocks the sun b) Earth blocks sunlight from reaching the moon c) The sun blocks the moon d) The moon is full
15. The hardest mineral on the Mohs scale is: a) Quartz b) Topaz c) Diamond d) Corundum
16. Which process removes carbon dioxide from the atmosphere? a) Respiration b) Photosynthesis c) Combustion d) Decay
17. The basic unit of life is the: a) Organ b) Tissue c) Cell d) Organism
18. Which system controls involuntary body functions? a) Skeletal b) Muscular c) Nervous d) Endocrine
19. Magnetism is caused by: a) Static electricity b) Moving electric charges c) Heat d) Light
20. The freezing point of water is: a) 0°C b) 32°F c) Both a and b d) 100°C
21. Which scientist developed the periodic table? a) Einstein b) Newton c) Mendeleev d) Curie
22. White blood cells primarily: a) Carry oxygen b) Fight infection c) Clot blood d) Transport nutrients
23. Which force causes tides? a) Solar wind b) Earth's rotation c) Gravitational pull of moon d) Magnetic field
24. The liver produces: a) Insulin b) Bile c) Adrenaline d) Hemoglobin
25. Bases have a pH: a) Less than 7 b) Equal to 7 c) Greater than 7 d) Equal to 0

Arithmetic Reasoning (30 questions)

1. A recipe for 6 servings calls for 3 cups of flour. How much flour is needed for 10 servings? a) 4 cups b) 5 cups c) 6 cups d) 7 cups
2. If a bicycle originally costs $200 and is marked down 25%, what is the sale price? a) $150 b) $160 c) $170 d) $180
3. A square has sides of 9 inches. What is its area? a) 36 sq in b) 81 sq in c) 18 sq in d) 72 sq in
4. If 4x + 6 = 26, what is x? a) 4 b) 5 c) 6 d) 7
5. A plane travels 450 miles in 1.5 hours. What is its average speed? a) 250 mph b) 275 mph c) 300 mph d) 325 mph
6. What is 22% of 250? a) 50 b) 55 c) 60 d) 65
7. If you buy 5 items for $2.80 each, what is the total cost? a) $13.00 b) $14.00 c) $15.00 d) $16.00
8. A triangle has base 12 inches and height 8 inches. What is its area? a) 48 sq in b) 96 sq in c) 20 sq in d) 40 sq in
9. If 2y - 7 = 15, what is y? a) 10 b) 11 c) 12 d) 13
10. What is the square root of 289? a) 16 b) 17 c) 18 d) 19
11. A rectangle has length 15 feet and width 8 feet. What is its perimeter? a) 23 feet b) 46 feet c) 120 feet d) 30 feet
12. If movie tickets cost $12 each and you buy 4 tickets, what is the total cost? a) $44 b) $46 c) $48 d) $50
13. What is 3/5 of 45? a) 25 b) 27 c) 30 d) 35
14. A right triangle has legs of 9 and 12. What is the length of the hypotenuse? a) 13 b) 15 c) 17 d) 21
15. If 5x = 45, what is x? a) 8 b) 9 c) 10 d) 11
16. What is the average of 16, 20, 24, and 28? a) 20 b) 21 c) 22 d) 23

17. A cylinder has radius 4 inches and height 10 inches. What is its volume? (Use $\pi = 3.14$)
a) 502.4 cubic inches b) 251.2 cubic inches c) 125.6 cubic inches d) 628 cubic inches

18. If you work 6 hours at $13.50 per hour, how much do you earn? a) $79 b) $81 c) $83 d) $85

19. What is 16% of 300? a) 44 b) 46 c) 48 d) 50

20. If $3(x - 2) = 18$, what is x? a) 6 b) 7 c) 8 d) 9

21. A pizza has 10 slices. If you eat 4 slices, what fraction remains? a) 2/5 b) 3/5 c) 1/2 d) 4/10

22. The diameter of a circle is 14 inches. What is its radius? a) 28 inches b) 14 inches c) 7 inches d) 3.5 inches

23. If $7x - 2 = 40$, what is x? a) 5 b) 6 c) 7 d) 8

24. What is $2/3 \times 3/4$? a) 1/2 b) 5/7 c) 6/12 d) 5/6

25. A store offers a 20% discount on a $65 item. What is the sale price? a) $50 b) $52 c) $54 d) $56

26. If a triangle has perimeter 30 feet and two sides are 12 feet and 8 feet, what is the third side? a) 8 feet b) 10 feet c) 12 feet d) 14 feet

27. What is the value of $6^2 - 4^2$? a) 4 b) 16 c) 20 d) 36

28. If you save $60 per month for 9 months, how much do you save total? a) $520 b) $540 c) $560 d) $580

29. A jar contains 12 red balls and 8 green balls. What is the probability of drawing a green ball? a) 2/5 b) 3/5 c) 1/2 d) 3/8

30. If the ratio of apples to oranges is 4:3 and there are 28 apples, how many oranges are there? a) 18 b) 21 c) 24 d) 27

Word Knowledge (35 questions)

1. ASTUTE most nearly means: a) Foolish b) Shrewd c) Careless d) Slow
2. MITIGATE most nearly means: a) Worsen b) Lessen c) Ignore d) Increase
3. RESILIENT most nearly means: a) Brittle b) Flexible c) Weak d) Fragile
4. VERBOSE most nearly means: a) Brief b) Wordy c) Clear d) Silent
5. SUBSTANTIATE most nearly means: a) Disprove b) Support with evidence c) Question d) Ignore
6. OPULENT most nearly means: a) Poor b) Wealthy c) Simple d) Plain
7. BELLIGERENT most nearly means: a) Peaceful b) Aggressive c) Friendly d) Calm
8. PIVOTAL most nearly means: a) Unimportant b) Crucial c) Minor d) Irrelevant
9. COMPROMISE most nearly means: a) Agree completely b) Settle by mutual concession c) Refuse d) Demand
10. GREGARIOUS most nearly means: a) Antisocial b) Sociable c) Shy d) Withdrawn
11. CONVOLUTED most nearly means: a) Simple b) Complex c) Straight d) Clear
12. BOLSTER most nearly means: a) Weaken b) Support c) Attack d) Ignore
13. PERVASIVE most nearly means: a) Limited b) Widespread c) Rare d) Isolated
14. SERENE most nearly means: a) Agitated b) Peaceful c) Noisy d) Disturbed
15. RESCIND most nearly means: a) Confirm b) Cancel c) Approve d) Support
16. COLLABORATE most nearly means: a) Compete b) Work together c) Fight d) Separate
17. EXPEDITE most nearly means: a) Delay b) Speed up c) Stop d) Slow down

18. IMMUTABLE most nearly means: a) Changeable b) Unchangeable c) Flexible d) Variable
19. JUDICIOUS most nearly means: a) Reckless b) Wise c) Careless d) Thoughtless
20. OBSOLETE most nearly means: a) Modern b) Outdated c) New d) Current
21. DISPARAGE most nearly means: a) Praise b) Criticize c) Support d) Encourage
22. DYNAMIC most nearly means: a) Static b) Energetic c) Dull d) Boring
23. THOROUGH most nearly means: a) Incomplete b) Complete c) Partial d) Careless
24. EARNEST most nearly means: a) Joking b) Serious c) Playful d) Casual
25. FLUCTUATE most nearly means: a) Remain steady b) Vary c) Stay constant d) Stabilize
26. SPARSE most nearly means: a) Dense b) Scanty c) Thick d) Heavy
27. INVIGORATING most nearly means: a) Tiring b) Energizing c) Exhausting d) Draining
28. LEGITIMATE most nearly means: a) Illegal b) Valid c) False d) Fake
29. NOMINAL most nearly means: a) Large b) Small c) Significant d) Major
30. ADAPTABLE most nearly means: a) Rigid b) Flexible c) Fixed d) Unchanging
31. CURTAIL most nearly means: a) Extend b) Reduce c) Increase d) Expand
32. SUPERFLUOUS most nearly means: a) Necessary b) Unnecessary c) Essential d) Required
33. LUCID most nearly means: a) Confused b) Clear c) Cloudy d) Vague
34. STAGNANT most nearly means: a) Moving b) Motionless c) Flowing d) Active
35. EXEMPLIFY most nearly means: a) Contradict b) Illustrate c) Hide d) Confuse

Paragraph Comprehension (15 questions)

Passage 1: Space exploration has yielded numerous benefits for life on Earth, from technological innovations to scientific discoveries. Satellite technology, originally developed for space missions, now enables global communications, weather forecasting, and GPS navigation. Medical devices like pacemakers and water purification systems also trace their origins to space research. Despite the high costs, many scientists argue that space exploration continues to provide invaluable returns on investment.

1. According to the passage, space exploration: a) Has provided no benefits to Earth b) Has yielded numerous benefits for Earth c) Is only useful for scientific research d) Should be discontinued due to cost
2. The passage mentions that satellite technology enables: a) Only weather forecasting b) Global communications, weather forecasting, and GPS c) Only GPS navigation d) Only global communications

Passage 2: The human immune system is a complex network of cells, tissues, and organs that work together to defend against harmful pathogens. White blood cells, antibodies, and specialized organs like the spleen and lymph nodes all play crucial roles in identifying and eliminating threats. A healthy lifestyle including proper nutrition, regular exercise, and adequate sleep can significantly strengthen immune function.

3. According to the passage, the immune system: a) Consists of only white blood cells b) Is a complex network of cells, tissues, and organs c) Cannot be strengthened d) Only includes antibodies

4. The passage suggests that immune function can be strengthened by: a) Medication only b) Surgery c) A healthy lifestyle d) Avoiding all bacteria

Passage 3: 3D printing technology, also known as additive manufacturing, has revolutionized production across various industries. Unlike traditional manufacturing that removes material, 3D printing builds objects layer by layer from digital designs. This technology enables rapid prototyping, customized products, and reduced waste. Industries from aerospace to healthcare now use 3D printing for everything from aircraft components to prosthetic limbs.

5. 3D printing is also known as: a) Subtractive manufacturing b) Additive manufacturing c) Digital manufacturing d) Layer manufacturing
6. According to the passage, 3D printing enables: a) Only rapid prototyping b) Rapid prototyping, customization, and reduced waste c) Only waste reduction d) Only customized products

Passage 4: Ocean acidification, often called the "other CO_2 problem," occurs when seawater absorbs carbon dioxide from the atmosphere. This process makes the ocean more acidic, threatening marine ecosystems, particularly coral reefs and shellfish. As acidity increases, it becomes harder for these organisms to build and maintain their calcium carbonate shells and skeletons. Scientists warn that continued acidification could devastate marine food chains.

7. Ocean acidification is caused by: a) Industrial pollution b) Seawater absorbing atmospheric CO_2 c) Overfishing d) Plastic waste
8. The passage indicates that acidification particularly threatens: a) All fish equally b) Only large marine mammals c) Coral reefs and shellfish d) Only plants

Passage 5: Regular physical exercise provides numerous health benefits beyond weight management. Exercise strengthens the cardiovascular system, improves bone density, enhances mental health, and boosts immune function. Studies show that even moderate activity, such as a 30-minute daily walk, can significantly reduce the risk of chronic diseases like diabetes, heart disease, and certain cancers. The key is consistency rather than intensity.

9. According to the passage, exercise benefits include: a) Only weight management b) Strengthening cardiovascular system, improving bone density, and enhancing mental health c) Only cardiovascular benefits d) Only mental health benefits
10. The passage suggests that for health benefits: a) Intensity is more important than consistency b) Consistency is more important than intensity c) Only intense exercise works d) Exercise frequency doesn't matter

Passage 6: The invention of writing systems marked a crucial turning point in human civilization. Before written language, knowledge could only be preserved and transmitted through oral tradition, limiting the complexity and accuracy of information passed between generations. Writing enabled humans to record laws, conduct complex trade, preserve historical accounts, and accumulate knowledge across time. Different civilizations developed various writing systems independently, from cuneiform in Mesopotamia to hieroglyphs in Egypt.

11. Before writing systems, knowledge was preserved through: a) Written records b) Oral tradition c) Pictures only d) Mathematical symbols
12. According to the passage, writing enabled humans to: a) Only record laws b) Record laws, conduct trade, preserve history, and accumulate knowledge c) Only conduct trade d) Only preserve historical accounts

Passage 7: Cryptocurrency represents a digital form of currency that uses cryptography for security and operates independently of traditional banking systems. Bitcoin, the first and most well-known cryptocurrency, introduced the concept of a decentralized ledger called blockchain. While supporters praise cryptocurrency for its potential to democratize finance and reduce transaction costs, critics worry about its volatility, energy consumption, and use in illegal activities.

13. Cryptocurrency uses what for security? a) Traditional banking b) Government backing c) Cryptography d) Physical coins
14. According to the passage, critics worry about cryptocurrency's: a) Only volatility b) Volatility, energy consumption, and illegal use c) Only energy consumption d) Only illegal activities

Passage 8: Urban farming, the practice of growing food in cities, is gaining popularity as communities seek sustainable food sources and reduced environmental impact. Vertical farms, rooftop gardens, and hydroponic systems allow food production in limited urban spaces. Benefits include fresher produce, reduced transportation costs, job creation, and educational opportunities. However, challenges remain, including high startup costs, energy requirements, and limited crop variety compared to traditional farming.

15. According to the passage, urban farming benefits include: a) Only fresher produce b) Fresher produce, reduced transportation costs, jobs, and education c) Only reduced transportation d) Only job creation

Mathematics Knowledge (25 questions)

1. What is the value of 5^3? a) 15 b) 125 c) 25 d) 75
2. If x = 4, what is the value of $3x^2 - 2x + 1$? a) 41 b) 43 c) 45 d) 47
3. What is the slope of the line 3x - 4y = 12? a) 3/4 b) -3/4 c) 4/3 d) -4/3
4. Solve for x: 2x + 7 = 3x - 5 a) 12 b) 10 c) 8 d) 6
5. What is the area of a circle with radius 6? (Use $\pi = 3.14$) a) 113.04 b) 37.68 c) 18.84 d) 75.36
6. If $\log_3(27) = x$, then x equals: a) 2 b) 3 c) 9 d) 27
7. What is the value of |3 - 8|? a) 5 b) -5 c) 11 d) -11
8. Which of the following is equivalent to $4^2 \times 4^3$? a) 4^5 b) 4^6 c) 16^5 d) 16^6
9. If two angles of a triangle are 70° and 50°, what is the third angle? a) 50° b) 60° c) 70° d) 80°
10. What is the volume of a rectangular prism with dimensions $3 \times 4 \times 5$? a) 12 b) 60 c) 20 d) 47
11. Solve: 5x + 2 = 4x + 9 a) x = 5 b) x = 6 c) x = 7 d) x = 8

12. What is the square root of 324? a) 16 b) 17 c) 18 d) 19
13. If $f(x) = x^2 + 3x - 2$, what is $f(3)$? a) 14 b) 16 c) 18 d) 20
14. What is 65% expressed as a decimal? a) 0.065 b) 0.65 c) 6.5 d) 65
15. The sum of interior angles of an octagon is: a) 720° b) 900° c) 1080° d) 1260°
16. If $4^x = 64$, then x equals: a) 2 b) 3 c) 4 d) 16
17. What is the distance between points (2, 1) and (5, 5)? a) 3 b) 4 c) 5 d) 7
18. Simplify: $(x^2)^3 \times x$ a) x^6 b) x^7 c) x^8 d) x^9
19. If $\cos \theta = \sqrt{3}/2$, what is θ in degrees? a) 30° b) 45° c) 60° d) 90°
20. What is the range of the set {4, 7, 2, 9, 5, 2, 8}? a) 5 b) 6 c) 7 d) 9
21. Factor: $x^2 - x - 12$ a) (x - 4)(x + 3) b) (x + 4)(x - 3) c) (x - 2)(x + 6) d) Cannot be factored
22. What is the area of a square with side length 7? a) 14 b) 28 c) 49 d) 98
23. If $\tan \theta = \sqrt{3}$, what is θ in degrees? a) 30° b) 45° c) 60° d) 90°
24. Solve the system: $3x + 2y = 12$, $x + y = 5$ a) x = 2, y = 3 b) x = 3, y = 2 c) x = 4, y = 1 d) x = 1, y = 4
25. What is the y-intercept of the line $y = -2x + 7$? a) -2 b) 2 c) 7 d) -7

Electronics Information (20 questions)

1. The unit of electrical inductance is the: a) Ohm b) Farad c) Henry d) Weber
2. If a 20Ω resistor carries 3A of current, what is the voltage across it? a) 6.67V b) 17V c) 23V d) 60V
3. A capacitor opposes changes in: a) Current b) Voltage c) Resistance d) Power
4. In series circuits, which remains constant throughout? a) Voltage b) Current c) Resistance d) Power
5. The frequency of AC power in most of Europe is: a) 50 Hz b) 60 Hz c) 110 Hz d) 120 Hz
6. An inductor opposes changes in: a) Voltage b) Current c) Resistance d) Capacitance
7. A MOSFET is a type of: a) Resistor b) Capacitor c) Transistor d) Diode
8. Which device converts mechanical energy to electrical energy? a) Motor b) Generator c) Transformer d) Rectifier
9. The total impedance in a series RLC circuit is: a) R + L + C b) $\sqrt{R^2 + (X_L - X_C)^2}$ c) R × L × C d) R + XL + XC
10. A varactor diode is used for: a) Rectification b) Voltage regulation c) Variable capacitance d) Amplification
11. In binary code, the number 5 is represented as: a) 011 b) 101 c) 110 d) 111
12. A thyristor is controlled by: a) Voltage b) Current c) Gate signal d) Temperature
13. The bandwidth of an amplifier is determined by: a) Gain only b) Frequency response c) Input impedance d) Output power
14. A Schmitt trigger is used for: a) Amplification b) Signal shaping c) Power conversion d) Frequency generation
15. The unit of magnetic field strength is: a) Weber b) Tesla c) Henry d) Gauss
16. A bridge rectifier uses how many diodes? a) One b) Two c) Four d) Six
17. The quality factor (Q) of a resonant circuit indicates: a) Power consumption b) Selectivity c) Gain d) Impedance
18. A phase-locked loop (PLL) is used for: a) Amplification b) Frequency synthesis c) Power conversion d) Signal filtering

19. The impedance of a capacitor decreases with: a) Increasing frequency b) Decreasing frequency c) Increasing voltage d) Decreasing voltage
20. A differentiator circuit performs: a) Integration b) Differentiation c) Addition d) Multiplication

Auto & Shop Information (25 questions)

1. Engine coolant circulates through the: a) Oil pan b) Radiator c) Fuel tank d) Air filter
2. Which tool has adjustable jaws? a) Box wrench b) Combination wrench c) Pipe wrench d) Allen wrench
3. The camshaft operates the: a) Pistons b) Valves c) Spark plugs d) Fuel injectors
4. A tap is used to cut: a) External threads b) Internal threads c) Metal sheets d) Holes
5. The water pump is driven by the: a) Transmission b) Engine c) Alternator d) Starter
6. Which chisel has the narrowest cutting edge? a) Cold chisel b) Cape chisel c) Round nose chisel d) Flat chisel
7. Automatic transmission fluid serves as: a) Coolant only b) Lubricant and hydraulic fluid c) Fuel additive d) Cleaning agent
8. A square is used to check: a) Roundness b) Right angles c) Levels d) Dimensions
9. The oxygen sensor monitors: a) Engine temperature b) Exhaust gas composition c) Oil pressure d) Fuel level
10. Which file removes material fastest? a) Bastard cut b) Second cut c) Smooth cut d) Dead smooth
11. ABS prevents: a) Engine stalling b) Wheel lockup during braking c) Transmission slipping d) Power steering failure
12. A countersink creates a: a) Round hole b) Square hole c) Conical depression d) Threaded hole
13. The EGR valve recirculates: a) Fuel vapors b) Exhaust gases c) Fresh air d) Oil vapors
14. Which abrasive is used for sharpening tools? a) Sandpaper b) Steel wool c) Grinding wheel d) Wire brush
15. Power steering reduces the effort needed to: a) Brake b) Accelerate c) Steer d) Shift gears
16. A center drill is used to: a) Start holes for drilling b) Enlarge holes c) Thread holes d) Deburr holes
17. The mass airflow sensor measures: a) Fuel flow b) Air entering the engine c) Exhaust flow d) Coolant flow
18. Which wrench provides the most leverage? a) Box wrench b) Open-end wrench c) Pipe wrench d) Adjustable wrench
19. The fuel rail delivers fuel to: a) The tank b) The pump c) The injectors d) The filter
20. A boring bar is used to: a) Cut external threads b) Enlarge existing holes c) Create square holes d) Cut keyways
21. Traction control prevents: a) Skidding during braking b) Wheel spin during acceleration c) Engine overheating d) Transmission failure
22. Which hammer is used for precision work? a) Sledge hammer b) Ball peen hammer c) Dead blow hammer d) Tack hammer
23. The knock sensor detects: a) Engine vibration b) Abnormal combustion c) Low oil pressure d) Overheating

24. A depth gauge measures: a) Outside diameter b) Inside diameter c) Depth of holes d) Thread pitch
25. Run-flat tires allow continued driving: a) At any speed b) For unlimited distance c) For limited distance at reduced speed d) Only in emergencies

Mechanical Comprehension (25 questions)

1. A third-class lever has the effort: a) At the fulcrum b) Between fulcrum and load c) At the load end d) Opposite the load
2. If gear A has 12 teeth and rotates at 60 RPM, and gear B has 24 teeth, gear B rotates at: a) 30 RPM b) 60 RPM c) 120 RPM d) 240 RPM
3. A block and tackle with 6 supporting ropes has a mechanical advantage of: a) 3 b) 6 c) 12 d) 18
4. When most solids are heated, they: a) Contract b) Expand c) Stay the same size d) Change phase
5. To lift a 200-pound load 10 feet using an inclined plane 20 feet long, the theoretical force needed is: a) 100 pounds b) 200 pounds c) 400 pounds d) 2000 pounds
6. In a hydraulic system with input area 3 sq in and output area 12 sq in, a 15 lb input force produces: a) 45 lbs output b) 60 lbs output c) 180 lbs output d) 540 lbs output
7. A wheel 2 feet in diameter connected to an axle 6 inches in diameter provides a mechanical advantage of: a) 2:1 b) 3:1 c) 4:1 d) 6:1
8. An object will tip over when its center of gravity moves: a) Upward b) Downward c) Outside its base d) To its geometric center
9. Two meshing gears with the same number of teeth will rotate: a) At different speeds b) At the same speed c) In the same direction d) One faster than the other
10. A knife is essentially a: a) Lever b) Pulley c) Wedge d) Screw
11. Applying 60 pounds of force to a lever arm 18 inches from the fulcrum produces how much torque? a) 42 ft-lbs b) 78 ft-lbs c) 90 ft-lbs d) 1080 ft-lbs
12. A single movable pulley: a) Changes direction only b) Reduces force by half c) Doubles the force d) Provides no advantage
13. The efficiency of a wedge is affected by: a) Its material only b) Its angle and friction c) Its weight only d) Its length only
14. A spinning top remains upright due to: a) Gravity b) Magnetic force c) Gyroscopic effect d) Air resistance
15. A four-bar linkage: a) Cannot move b) Has one degree of freedom c) Stores energy d) Generates power
16. Real mechanical advantage equals: a) Ideal mechanical advantage b) Output force ÷ input force c) Input force ÷ output force d) Always 1
17. Oil in machinery primarily: a) Increases friction b) Reduces friction c) Increases speed d) Provides power
18. A helical gear: a) Cannot mesh with straight gears b) Runs quieter than straight gears c) Provides no advantage d) Only works in one direction
19. Static friction is generally: a) Less than kinetic friction b) Equal to kinetic friction c) Greater than kinetic friction d) Unrelated to kinetic friction
20. An automobile brake converts: a) Electrical energy to heat b) Kinetic energy to heat c) Potential energy to kinetic d) Chemical energy to mechanical

21. In a belt drive, if the driving pulley is smaller, the driven pulley: a) Turns faster b) Turns slower c) Turns at same speed d) Cannot turn
22. A simply supported beam is strongest when loaded: a) At one end b) At both ends c) At the center d) One-quarter from each end
23. A torsion spring stores energy by: a) Compression b) Extension c) Twisting d) Bending
24. Overdrive in a transmission provides: a) More torque, less speed b) Less torque, more speed c) Same torque and speed d) Maximum power
25. A pneumatic system uses: a) Liquid under pressure b) Gas under pressure c) Vacuum d) Electromagnetic force

Answer Key - Test 24

General Science: 1-b, 2-c, 3-c, 4-c, 5-b, 6-d, 7-b, 8-c, 9-c, 10-c, 11-c, 12-b, 13-c, 14-b, 15-c, 16-b, 17-c, 18-c, 19-b, 20-c, 21-c, 22-b, 23-c, 24-b, 25-c

Arithmetic Reasoning: 1-b, 2-a, 3-b, 4-b, 5-c, 6-b, 7-b, 8-a, 9-b, 10-b, 11-b, 12-c, 13-b, 14-b, 15-b, 16-c, 17-a, 18-b, 19-c, 20-c, 21-b, 22-c, 23-b, 24-a, 25-b, 26-b, 27-c, 28-b, 29-a, 30-b

Word Knowledge: 1-b, 2-b, 3-b, 4-b, 5-b, 6-b, 7-b, 8-b, 9-b, 10-b, 11-b, 12-b, 13-b, 14-b, 15-b, 16-b, 17-b, 18-b, 19-b, 20-b, 21-b, 22-b, 23-b, 24-b, 25-b, 26-b, 27-b, 28-b, 29-b, 30-b, 31-b, 32-b, 33-b, 34-b, 35-b

Paragraph Comprehension: 1-b, 2-b, 3-b, 4-c, 5-b, 6-b, 7-b, 8-c, 9-b, 10-b, 11-b, 12-b, 13-c, 14-b, 15-b

Mathematics Knowledge: 1-b, 2-a, 3-a, 4-a, 5-a, 6-b, 7-a, 8-a, 9-b, 10-b, 11-c, 12-c, 13-b, 14-b, 15-c, 16-b, 17-c, 18-b, 19-a, 20-c, 21-a, 22-c, 23-c, 24-a, 25-c

Electronics Information: 1-c, 2-d, 3-b, 4-b, 5-a, 6-b, 7-c, 8-b, 9-b, 10-c, 11-b, 12-c, 13-b, 14-b, 15-b, 16-c, 17-b, 18-b, 19-a, 20-b

Auto & Shop Information: 1-b, 2-c, 3-b, 4-b, 5-b, 6-b, 7-b, 8-b, 9-b, 10-a, 11-b, 12-c, 13-b, 14-c, 15-c, 16-a, 17-b, 18-c, 19-c, 20-b, 21-b, 22-d, 23-b, 24-c, 25-c

Mechanical Comprehension: 1-b, 2-a, 3-b, 4-b, 5-a, 6-b, 7-c, 8-c, 9-b, 10-c, 11-c, 12-b, 13-b, 14-c, 15-b, 16-b, 17-b, 18-b, 19-c, 20-b, 21-b, 22-c, 23-c, 24-b, 25-b

Test 25

General Science (25 questions)

1. Mitosis results in: a) Four genetically different cells b) Two genetically identical cells c) One large cell d) Cells with half the chromosomes

2. Which layer of the atmosphere contains the ozone layer? a) Troposphere b) Stratosphere c) Mesosphere d) Thermosphere
3. The chemical formula for methane is: a) CH_4 b) CO_2 c) H_2O d) NH_3
4. Photosynthesis occurs primarily in which part of a leaf? a) Veins b) Stem c) Chloroplasts d) Roots
5. Which planet has the strongest magnetic field? a) Earth b) Mars c) Jupiter d) Saturn
6. Scurvy is caused by a deficiency of: a) Vitamin A b) Vitamin B c) Vitamin C d) Vitamin D
7. The Beaufort scale measures: a) Earthquake intensity b) Wind speed c) Temperature d) Rainfall
8. During cellular respiration, glucose is broken down to release: a) Oxygen b) Carbon dioxide c) Energy d) Water
9. The largest chamber of the human heart is the: a) Left atrium b) Right atrium c) Left ventricle d) Right ventricle
10. Which moon phase occurs when the moon is between Earth and the sun? a) Full moon b) New moon c) First quarter d) Last quarter
11. Paleontology is the study of: a) Ancient civilizations b) Fossils c) Rocks d) Weather patterns
12. Light waves are what type of wave? a) Longitudinal b) Transverse c) Sound d) Mechanical
13. Which mineral is essential for hemoglobin production? a) Calcium b) Iron c) Zinc d) Magnesium
14. A solar eclipse occurs when: a) Earth blocks sunlight from the moon b) The moon blocks sunlight from Earth c) The sun blocks light from the moon d) Clouds block the sun
15. On the Mohs hardness scale, talc has a hardness of: a) 1 b) 5 c) 7 d) 10
16. Which process adds oxygen to the atmosphere? a) Cellular respiration b) Photosynthesis c) Combustion d) Fermentation
17. The powerhouse of the cell is the: a) Nucleus b) Ribosome c) Mitochondria d) Endoplasmic reticulum
18. Which system regulates hormones in the body? a) Nervous b) Circulatory c) Respiratory d) Endocrine
19. Electric current creates: a) Magnetic fields b) Gravity c) Light d) Sound
20. Water has its maximum density at: a) 0°C b) 4°C c) 100°C d) -4°C
21. Who proposed the continental drift theory? a) Darwin b) Einstein c) Wegener d) Newton
22. Platelets in blood are responsible for: a) Carrying oxygen b) Fighting infection c) Blood clotting d) Transporting nutrients
23. What causes the aurora borealis (northern lights)? a) Sunlight reflection b) Solar particles interacting with Earth's atmosphere c) Moon's gravitational pull d) Earth's rotation
24. Which organ detoxifies harmful substances? a) Kidney b) Liver c) Lungs d) Heart
25. Solutions with pH 7 are: a) Acidic b) Basic c) Neutral d) Radioactive

Arithmetic Reasoning (30 questions)

1. A map scale shows 1 inch = 50 miles. If two cities are 3.5 inches apart on the map, what is the actual distance? a) 150 miles b) 175 miles c) 200 miles d) 225 miles

2. A computer originally costs $800 and is discounted 30%. What is the sale price? a) $540 b) $560 c) $580 d) $600

3. What is the area of a rectangle with length 18 feet and width 12 feet? a) 30 sq ft b) 60 sq ft c) 216 sq ft d) 180 sq ft

4. If 6x - 4 = 32, what is x? a) 5 b) 6 c) 7 d) 8

5. A train travels 320 miles in 4 hours. What is its average speed? a) 70 mph b) 75 mph c) 80 mph d) 85 mph

6. What is 28% of 175? a) 45 b) 47 c) 49 d) 51

7. If you buy 6 books for $4.50 each, what is the total cost? a) $25.00 b) $27.00 c) $29.00 d) $31.00

8. What is the area of a triangle with base 16 inches and height 9 inches? a) 72 sq in b) 144 sq in c) 25 sq in d) 50 sq in

9. If 3y + 5 = 20, what is y? a) 4 b) 5 c) 6 d) 7

10. What is the square root of 361? a) 18 b) 19 c) 20 d) 21

11. A circle has a diameter of 20 inches. What is its circumference? (Use $\pi = 3.14$) a) 62.8 inches b) 31.4 inches c) 125.6 inches d) 314 inches

12. If concert tickets cost $35 each and you buy 3 tickets, what is the total cost? a) $100 b) $105 c) $110 d) $115

13. What is 4/7 of 63? a) 32 b) 34 c) 36 d) 38

14. A rectangular pool is 25 feet long, 15 feet wide, and 6 feet deep. What is its volume? a) 2250 cubic feet b) 46 cubic feet c) 240 cubic feet d) 375 cubic feet

15. If 8x = 72, what is x? a) 8 b) 9 c) 10 d) 11

16. What is the average of 18, 22, 26, and 30? a) 22 b) 23 c) 24 d) 25

17. A cylinder has radius 5 inches and height 12 inches. What is its volume? (Use $\pi = 3.14$) a) 942 cubic inches b) 471 cubic inches c) 188.4 cubic inches d) 314 cubic inches

18. If you work 7.5 hours at $14.40 per hour, how much do you earn? a) $105 b) $108 c) $110 d) $112

19. What is 24% of 350? a) 82 b) 84 c) 86 d) 88

20. If 4(x + 5) = 28, what is x? a) 2 b) 3 c) 4 d) 5

21. A bag has 15 marbles: 6 red, 4 blue, and 5 green. What is the probability of drawing a blue marble? a) 4/15 b) 6/15 c) 5/15 d) 1/3

22. A square has a perimeter of 48 inches. What is the length of each side? a) 10 inches b) 11 inches c) 12 inches d) 13 inches

23. If 9x - 3 = 60, what is x? a) 6 b) 7 c) 8 d) 9

24. What is 5/6 × 3/4? a) 8/10 b) 15/24 c) 5/8 d) 20/24

25. A store marks up items 40% above cost. If an item costs $25, what is the selling price? a) $32 b) $33 c) $35 d) $37

26. If a circle has area 78.5 square inches, what is its radius? (Use $\pi = 3.14$) a) 4 inches b) 5 inches c) 6 inches d) 7 inches

27. What is the value of $8^2 - 5^2$? a) 9 b) 25 c) 39 d) 64

28. If you save $80 per month for 7 months, how much do you save total? a) $540 b) $560 c) $580 d) $600

29. A classroom has 24 students. If the ratio of boys to girls is 5:3, how many girls are there? a) 8 b) 9 c) 12 d) 15

30. If the sales tax rate is 8% and you buy an item for $45, what is the total cost? a) $48.60 b) $49.40 c) $50.20 d) $51.00

Word Knowledge (35 questions)

1. ELOQUENT most nearly means: a) Awkward b) Articulate c) Silent d) Confused
2. ABDICATE most nearly means: a) Take control b) Give up power c) Increase authority d) Share responsibility
3. TENUOUS most nearly means: a) Strong b) Weak c) Permanent d) Solid
4. ENIGMATIC most nearly means: a) Clear b) Mysterious c) Simple d) Obvious
5. CORROBORATE most nearly means: a) Deny b) Confirm c) Question d) Ignore
6. AFFLUENT most nearly means: a) Poor b) Wealthy c) Average d) Struggling
7. PUGNACIOUS most nearly means: a) Peaceful b) Combative c) Friendly d) Gentle
8. QUINTESSENTIAL most nearly means: a) Ordinary b) Typical c) Unusual d) Random
9. CAPITULATE most nearly means: a) Resist b) Surrender c) Fight d) Persist
10. AFFABLE most nearly means: a) Unfriendly b) Pleasant c) Hostile d) Aggressive
11. LABYRINTHINE most nearly means: a) Simple b) Complex c) Straight d) Direct
12. AUGMENT most nearly means: a) Reduce b) Increase c) Maintain d) Eliminate
13. UBIQUITOUS most nearly means: a) Rare b) Everywhere c) Hidden d) Scarce
14. TRANQUIL most nearly means: a) Noisy b) Peaceful c) Violent d) Chaotic
15. NULLIFY most nearly means: a) Validate b) Cancel c) Strengthen d) Support
16. SYNERGY most nearly means: a) Conflict b) Cooperation c) Competition d) Independence
17. PRECIPITATE most nearly means: a) Delay b) Cause suddenly c) Prevent d) Slow down
18. IMMUTABLE most nearly means: a) Changeable b) Unchangeable c) Temporary d) Flexible
19. ASTUTE most nearly means: a) Foolish b) Shrewd c) Naive d) Simple
20. ARCHAIC most nearly means: a) Modern b) Outdated c) Current d) New
21. MALIGN most nearly means: a) Praise b) Speak ill of c) Support d) Encourage
22. EFFERVESCENT most nearly means: a) Flat b) Lively c) Dull d) Quiet
23. METICULOUS most nearly means: a) Careless b) Careful c) Hasty d) Sloppy
24. CANDID most nearly means: a) Dishonest b) Frank c) Deceptive d) Secretive
25. VACILLATE most nearly means: a) Decide firmly b) Waver c) Stand firm d) Commit
26. AUSTERE most nearly means: a) Luxurious b) Plain c) Ornate d) Decorated
27. INDEFATIGABLE most nearly means: a) Tired b) Tireless c) Weak d) Lazy
28. SPURIOUS most nearly means: a) Genuine b) False c) Real d) Authentic
29. PERFUNCTORY most nearly means: a) Thorough b) Superficial c) Careful d) Detailed
30. MALLEABLE most nearly means: a) Rigid b) Flexible c) Hard d) Brittle
31. TRUNCATE most nearly means: a) Extend b) Shorten c) Lengthen d) Expand
32. EXTRANEOUS most nearly means: a) Essential b) Irrelevant c) Important d) Necessary
33. PERSPICACIOUS most nearly means: a) Dull b) Insightful c) Confused d) Unclear
34. LATENT most nearly means: a) Active b) Hidden c) Obvious d) Visible
35. VINDICATE most nearly means: a) Blame b) Clear of charges c) Accuse d) Condemn

Paragraph Comprehension (15 questions)

Passage 1: Genetic engineering, the direct manipulation of an organism's genes, has revolutionized medicine, agriculture, and biotechnology. In medicine, gene therapy offers potential treatments for previously incurable genetic disorders. In agriculture, genetically modified crops can resist pests, tolerate herbicides, and provide enhanced nutrition. However, ethical concerns about safety, environmental impact, and the natural order continue to spark debate among scientists, policymakers, and the public.

1. According to the passage, genetic engineering has revolutionized: a) Only medicine b) Medicine, agriculture, and biotechnology c) Only agriculture d) Only biotechnology
2. The passage indicates that genetic engineering: a) Has no ethical concerns b) Is universally accepted c) Continues to spark debate d) Is completely safe

Passage 2: The human digestive system is a complex network of organs that break down food into nutrients the body can absorb and use. The process begins in the mouth with mechanical and chemical breakdown, continues through the stomach where acid further breaks down food, and concludes in the small intestine where most nutrients are absorbed. The large intestine processes waste and absorbs water before elimination.

3. According to the passage, most nutrient absorption occurs in the: a) Mouth b) Stomach c) Small intestine d) Large intestine
4. The passage describes the digestive system as: a) Simple b) A complex network c) Inefficient d) Unnecessary

Passage 3: Quantum computing represents a revolutionary approach to information processing that harnesses the principles of quantum mechanics. Unlike classical computers that use bits representing either 0 or 1, quantum computers use quantum bits (qubits) that can exist in multiple states simultaneously. This property, called superposition, along with quantum entanglement, allows quantum computers to solve certain problems exponentially faster than classical computers. Applications include cryptography, drug discovery, and optimization problems.

5. According to the passage, qubits differ from classical bits because they: a) Are faster b) Can exist in multiple states simultaneously c) Are smaller d) Use less energy
6. The passage mentions that quantum computing applications include: a) Only cryptography b) Cryptography, drug discovery, and optimization c) Only drug discovery d) Only optimization problems

Passage 4: Deforestation, the clearing of forests for agriculture, urban development, and logging, has significant environmental consequences. Forests serve as carbon sinks, absorbing CO_2 from the atmosphere and helping regulate climate. They also provide habitat for countless species and help prevent soil erosion. The loss of forests contributes to climate change, biodiversity loss, and increased flooding in some regions.

7. According to the passage, forests serve as: a) Carbon sources b) Carbon sinks c) Urban development sites d) Agricultural land
8. The passage indicates that deforestation contributes to: a) Climate change only b) Climate change, biodiversity loss, and flooding c) Biodiversity loss only d) Flooding only

Passage 5: The human brain's capacity for learning and memory formation continues throughout life, though it peaks during childhood and adolescence. Neuroplasticity, the brain's ability to reorganize and form new neural connections, allows us to acquire new skills, adapt to experiences, and recover from injuries. Factors that enhance neuroplasticity include regular exercise, adequate sleep, social interaction, and engaging in challenging mental activities.

9. According to the passage, neuroplasticity is: a) Limited to childhood b) The brain's ability to reorganize and form new connections c) Unrelated to learning d) Fixed throughout life
10. The passage suggests that neuroplasticity can be enhanced by: a) Exercise only b) Exercise, sleep, social interaction, and mental challenges c) Sleep only d) Social interaction only

Passage 6: Renewable energy technologies have advanced rapidly in recent decades, making solar and wind power increasingly cost-competitive with fossil fuels. Solar panel efficiency has improved while costs have decreased dramatically. Wind turbines have become larger and more efficient, capable of generating power even in areas with moderate wind speeds. Energy storage solutions, particularly batteries, are addressing the intermittency challenges of renewable sources.

11. According to the passage, renewable energy technologies have: a) Remained stagnant b) Advanced rapidly c) Become more expensive d) Proven ineffective
12. The passage indicates that energy storage solutions are addressing: a) Cost issues b) Efficiency problems c) Intermittency challenges d) Environmental concerns

Passage 7: Antibiotic resistance occurs when bacteria evolve to survive exposure to antibiotics that once killed them. This natural evolutionary process is accelerated by the overuse and misuse of antibiotics in human medicine and agriculture. As bacteria become resistant, infections that were once easily treatable become difficult or impossible to cure. The World Health Organization considers antibiotic resistance one of the greatest threats to global health.

13. According to the passage, antibiotic resistance is accelerated by: a) Natural evolution only b) Overuse and misuse of antibiotics c) Bacterial mutation only d) Environmental factors
14. The World Health Organization considers antibiotic resistance: a) A minor concern b) One of the greatest threats to global health c) Easily solvable d) Limited to certain regions

Passage 8: Artificial photosynthesis aims to replicate the natural process by which plants convert sunlight, water, and carbon dioxide into energy and oxygen. Scientists are developing technologies that could use this process to produce clean fuels like hydrogen while simultaneously removing CO_2 from the atmosphere. If successful, artificial photosynthesis could provide a sustainable energy source while helping address climate change by reducing atmospheric carbon dioxide levels.

15. Artificial photosynthesis aims to: a) Replace natural photosynthesis b) Replicate natural photosynthesis for energy production c) Eliminate plants d) Increase atmospheric CO_2

Mathematics Knowledge (25 questions)

1. What is the value of 2^4? a) 8 b) 16 c) 32 d) 64
2. If x = -2, what is the value of $x^3 + 4x - 3$? a) -19 b) -15 c) -11 d) -7
3. What is the slope of the line $5x + 2y = 10$? a) 5/2 b) -5/2 c) 2/5 d) -2/5
4. Solve for x: $4x - 6 = 2x + 8$ a) 6 b) 7 c) 8 d) 9
5. What is the area of a circle with diameter 12? (Use π = 3.14) a) 113.04 b) 37.68 c) 452.16 d) 75.36
6. If $\log_5(125) = x$, then x equals: a) 2 b) 3 c) 5 d) 25
7. What is the value of $|6 - 10|$? a) 4 b) -4 c) 16 d) -16
8. Which of the following is equivalent to $3^4 \times 3^2$? a) 3^6 b) 3^8 c) 9^6 d) 9^8
9. In an isosceles triangle, if the vertex angle is 40°, what are the base angles? a) 60° each b) 70° each c) 80° each d) 90° each
10. What is the surface area of a cube with edge length 4? a) 64 b) 96 c) 16 d) 48
11. Solve: $6x - 5 = 4x + 11$ a) x = 6 b) x = 7 c) x = 8 d) x = 9
12. What is the square root of 400? a) 18 b) 19 c) 20 d) 21
13. If $f(x) = 3x^2 - 2x + 1$, what is f(2)? a) 9 b) 11 c) 13 d) 15
14. What is 85% expressed as a fraction in lowest terms? a) 85/100 b) 17/20 c) 4/5 d) 21/25
15. The sum of interior angles of a heptagon is: a) 720° b) 900° c) 1080° d) 1260°
16. If $5^x = 625$, then x equals: a) 3 b) 4 c) 5 d) 125
17. What is the distance between points (-2, 3) and (1, 7)? a) 4 b) 5 c) 6 d) 7
18. Simplify: $x^6 \div x^3$ a) x^2 b) x^3 c) x^9 d) x^{18}
19. If $\sin \theta = 1/2$, what is θ in degrees? a) 30° b) 45° c) 60° d) 90°
20. What is the median of the set {6, 2, 8, 4, 9, 2, 7}? a) 4 b) 6 c) 7 d) 8
21. Factor: $x^2 + 7x + 12$ a) $(x + 3)(x + 4)$ b) $(x + 2)(x + 6)$ c) $(x + 1)(x + 12)$ d) Cannot be factored
22. What is the volume of a sphere with radius 3? (Use π = 3.14) a) 113.04 b) 37.68 c) 28.26 d) 84.78
23. If $\cos \theta = 1/2$, what is θ in degrees? a) 30° b) 45° c) 60° d) 90°
24. Solve the system: $x + 2y = 10$, $2x - y = 5$ a) x = 4, y = 3 b) x = 3, y = 4 c) x = 5, y = 2 d) x = 2, y = 5
25. What is the slope of a line perpendicular to $y = 2x + 3$? a) 2 b) -2 c) 1/2 d) -1/2

Electronics Information (20 questions)

1. The unit of electrical charge is the: a) Ampere b) Coulomb c) Volt d) Ohm
2. If two 10Ω resistors are connected in parallel, the total resistance is: a) 20Ω b) 10Ω c) 5Ω d) 2.5Ω
3. A transformer works on the principle of: a) Electromagnetic induction b) Resistance c) Capacitance d) Conductance
4. In a parallel circuit, voltage across each branch is: a) Different b) The same c) Zero d) Infinite
5. The standard voltage for household outlets in the US is: a) 110V b) 120V c) 220V d) 240V
6. A choke is primarily: a) A resistor b) A capacitor c) An inductor d) A transformer
7. A JFET is a type of: a) Diode b) Transistor c) Resistor d) Capacitor

8. Which device stores electrical energy in an electric field? a) Inductor b) Resistor c) Capacitor d) Transformer

9. The impedance of an ideal inductor at DC is: a) Zero b) Infinite c) Equal to its resistance d) Variable

10. A silicon-controlled rectifier (SCR) is: a) A diode b) A transistor c) A thyristor d) A capacitor

11. In hexadecimal, the number 15 is represented as: a) E b) F c) 10 d) 1F

12. A diac is used in: a) Amplification b) Rectification c) Triggering circuits d) Power regulation

13. The cutoff frequency of a filter determines: a) Maximum gain b) Minimum gain c) -3dB point d) Phase shift

14. A comparator circuit: a) Adds two signals b) Compares two input voltages c) Subtracts signals d) Multiplies signals

15. The unit of magnetic flux density is: a) Weber b) Tesla c) Henry d) Gauss

16. A full-wave rectifier uses how many diodes? a) One b) Two c) Four d) Six

17. The resonant frequency of an LC circuit is determined by: a) L only b) C only c) Both L and C d) Neither L nor C

18. A voltage-controlled oscillator (VCO) frequency varies with: a) Current b) Input voltage c) Temperature d) Time

19. The reactance of a capacitor increases with: a) Increasing frequency b) Decreasing frequency c) Increasing voltage d) Decreasing voltage

20. An integrator circuit produces an output that is: a) The sum of inputs b) The integral of the input c) The derivative of input d) The product of inputs

Auto & Shop Information (25 questions)

1. The radiator cap maintains: a) Coolant level b) System pressure c) Temperature d) Flow rate

2. Which measuring tool has the highest precision? a) Ruler b) Caliper c) Micrometer d) Tape measure

3. The crankshaft is connected to pistons by: a) Valves b) Connecting rods c) Camshaft d) Timing belt

4. A die is used to cut: a) Internal threads b) External threads c) Holes d) Keyways

5. The serpentine belt typically drives: a) Only the alternator b) Multiple accessories c) Only the water pump d) Only the power steering

6. Which chisel is used for cutting oil grooves? a) Cold chisel b) Cape chisel c) Round nose chisel d) Diamond point chisel

7. Brake fluid should be: a) Changed regularly b) Never changed c) Mixed with water d) Used sparingly

8. A plumb bob is used to establish: a) Level lines b) Vertical lines c) Angles d) Measurements

9. The MAF sensor measures: a) Manifold pressure b) Mass airflow c) Air temperature d) Exhaust flow

10. Which file cut provides the smoothest finish? a) Bastard b) Second cut c) Smooth d) Coarse

11. Electronic stability control helps prevent: a) Skidding b) Engine stalling c) Brake fade d) Transmission slipping
12. A spot drill is used to: a) Drill large holes b) Start holes accurately c) Thread holes d) Ream holes
13. The IAC valve controls: a) Fuel flow b) Idle air c) Exhaust flow d) Coolant flow
14. Which abrasive is used for polishing? a) 36 grit b) 80 grit c) 220 grit d) 600 grit
15. Hydraulic brake systems multiply: a) Speed b) Distance c) Force d) Time
16. A boring head is used to: a) Make precise diameter holes b) Cut threads c) Remove burrs d) Mark centers
17. The EVAP system controls: a) Exhaust emissions b) Fuel vapor emissions c) Crankcase emissions d) Air intake
18. Which tool provides the most accurate torque measurement? a) Torque wrench b) Impact wrench c) Breaker bar d) Ratchet
19. The ECM controls: a) Only fuel injection b) Only ignition timing c) Multiple engine functions d) Only emissions
20. A boring mill is used for: a) External machining b) Internal machining c) Threading d) Grinding
21. Lane departure warning systems use: a) Radar b) Cameras c) Lidar d) Ultrasonic sensors
22. Which plane is used for end grain work? a) Jack plane b) Smooth plane c) Block plane d) Jointer plane
23. Variable valve timing improves: a) Engine performance and efficiency b) Only performance c) Only efficiency d) Exhaust emissions only
24. A surface gauge is used to: a) Measure depth b) Scribe lines c) Check angles d) Measure thickness
25. Adaptive cruise control uses: a) GPS only b) Speed sensors only c) Radar or cameras d) Manual input only

Mechanical Comprehension (25 questions)

1. Which class of lever has the load between the fulcrum and effort? a) First class b) Second class c) Third class d) Fourth class
2. If a gear with 18 teeth drives a gear with 54 teeth, the speed ratio is: a) 1:2 b) 1:3 c) 2:1 d) 3:1
3. A compound pulley system with 8 supporting ropes provides a mechanical advantage of: a) 4 b) 8 c) 16 d) 32
4. When water freezes, it: a) Contracts b) Expands c) Stays the same volume d) Becomes denser
5. An inclined plane 30 feet long used to lift a load 10 feet high has a theoretical mechanical advantage of: a) 2:1 b) 3:1 c) 4:1 d) 10:1
6. In a hydraulic system, if the input cylinder has diameter 2 inches and output cylinder has diameter 6 inches, the mechanical advantage is: a) 3:1 b) 6:1 c) 9:1 d) 18:1
7. A wheel 18 inches in diameter connected to an axle 3 inches in diameter provides a mechanical advantage of: a) 3:1 b) 6:1 c) 9:1 d) 18:1
8. An object is most stable when its center of gravity is: a) High b) Low c) At the edge d) Moving

9. If two identical gears mesh, they rotate at: a) Different speeds b) The same speed c) One twice the speed of the other d) Random speeds

10. A chisel is an example of a: a) Lever b) Inclined plane c) Wedge d) Pulley

11. A force of 75 pounds applied 2 feet from a fulcrum creates how much torque? a) 37.5 ft-lbs b) 75 ft-lbs c) 150 ft-lbs d) 300 ft-lbs

12. Using two fixed pulleys: a) Doubles the mechanical advantage b) Changes direction twice c) Halves the force d) Provides no mechanical advantage

13. A wedge with a smaller angle: a) Requires more force b) Requires less force c) Has no effect on force d) Works faster

14. A gyroscope resists changes in: a) Speed b) Direction c) Weight d) Temperature

15. A scotch yoke mechanism converts: a) Rotary to linear motion b) Linear to rotary motion c) Fast to slow motion d) Smooth to intermittent motion

16. The actual mechanical advantage of a machine is always: a) Greater than ideal MA b) Less than ideal MA c) Equal to ideal MA d) Unpredictable

17. Graphite lubrication is used where: a) High temperatures exist b) Water is present c) Speed is critical d) Cost is important

18. A planetary gear system provides: a) Only speed reduction b) Only speed increase c) Variable speed ratios d) Constant speed only

19. Rolling friction is generally: a) Greater than sliding friction b) Less than sliding friction c) Equal to sliding friction d) Unrelated to sliding friction

20. A disc brake converts kinetic energy to: a) Potential energy b) Heat energy c) Chemical energy d) Electrical energy

21. In a chain drive, the smaller sprocket: a) Turns slower b) Turns faster c) Has more torque d) Has the same speed

22. A fixed beam is strongest when: a) Loaded at the center b) Loaded at the ends c) Loaded near the supports d) Uniformly loaded

23. A clock spring stores energy through: a) Compression b) Tension c) Torsion d) Bending

24. A CVT (continuously variable transmission) provides: a) Fixed gear ratios b) Infinite gear ratios within a range c) Only two speeds d) Manual shifting only

25. A hydraulic accumulator stores: a) Fluid volume b) Fluid pressure c) Electrical energy d) Mechanical energy

Answer Key - Test 25

General Science: 1-b, 2-b, 3-a, 4-c, 5-c, 6-c, 7-b, 8-c, 9-c, 10-b, 11-b, 12-b, 13-b, 14-b, 15-a, 16-b, 17-c, 18-d, 19-a, 20-b, 21-c, 22-c, 23-b, 24-b, 25-c

Arithmetic Reasoning: 1-b, 2-b, 3-c, 4-b, 5-c, 6-c, 7-b, 8-a, 9-b, 10-b, 11-a, 12-b, 13-c, 14-a, 15-b, 16-c, 17-a, 18-b, 19-b, 20-b, 21-a, 22-c, 23-b, 24-c, 25-c, 26-b, 27-c, 28-b, 29-b, 30-a

Word Knowledge: 1-b, 2-b, 3-b, 4-b, 5-b, 6-b, 7-b, 8-b, 9-b, 10-b, 11-b, 12-b, 13-b, 14-b, 15-b, 16-b, 17-b, 18-b, 19-b, 20-b, 21-b, 22-b, 23-b, 24-b, 25-b, 26-b, 27-b, 28-b, 29-b, 30-b, 31-b, 32-b, 33-b, 34-b, 35-b

Paragraph Comprehension: 1-b, 2-c, 3-c, 4-b, 5-b, 6-b, 7-b, 8-b, 9-b, 10-b, 11-b, 12-c, 13-b, 14-b, 15-b

Mathematics Knowledge: 1-b, 2-a, 3-b, 4-b, 5-a, 6-b, 7-a, 8-a, 9-b, 10-b, 11-c, 12-c, 13-a, 14-b, 15-b, 16-b, 17-b, 18-b, 19-a, 20-b, 21-a, 22-a, 23-c, 24-a, 25-d

Electronics Information: 1-b, 2-c, 3-a, 4-b, 5-b, 6-c, 7-b, 8-c, 9-b, 10-c, 11-b, 12-c, 13-c, 14-b, 15-b, 16-b, 17-c, 18-b, 19-b, 20-b

Auto & Shop Information: 1-b, 2-c, 3-b, 4-b, 5-b, 6-c, 7-a, 8-b, 9-b, 10-c, 11-a, 12-b, 13-b, 14-d, 15-c, 16-a, 17-b, 18-a, 19-c, 20-b, 21-b, 22-c, 23-a, 24-b, 25-c

Mechanical Comprehension: 1-b, 2-b, 3-b, 4-b, 5-b, 6-c, 7-b, 8-b, 9-b, 10-c, 11-c, 12-b, 13-b, 14-b, 15-a, 16-b, 17-a, 18-c, 19-b, 20-b, 21-b, 22-c, 23-c, 24-b, 25-b

Test Summary

This document contains four complete ASVAB practice tests (Tests 22-25), each with all nine subtests and their respective question counts:

- **General Science:** 25 questions each
- **Arithmetic Reasoning:** 30 questions each
- **Word Knowledge:** 35 questions each
- **Paragraph Comprehension:** 15 questions each
- **Mathematics Knowledge:** 25 questions each
- **Electronics Information:** 20 questions each
- **Auto & Shop Information:** 25 questions each
- **Mechanical Comprehension:** 25 questions each

Each test includes comprehensive answer keys for quick scoring and review. These tests cover the full range of topics and difficulty levels found on the actual ASVAB exam.

Conclusion: Your Path to Military Success

Congratulations on Your Commitment

You have now completed one of the most comprehensive ASVAB study guides available. By working through this material, you have demonstrated the dedication, perseverance, and commitment to excellence that are hallmarks of successful military service members. The time and effort you've invested in preparing for the ASVAB reflects the same qualities that will serve you well throughout your military career.

What You've Accomplished

Through this study guide, you have:

Mastered the Fundamentals

- Reviewed essential concepts across all eight ASVAB subtests
- Practiced with over 5,000 realistic practice questions
- Learned proven test-taking strategies and time management techniques
- Built confidence through comprehensive preparation

Developed Critical Skills

- Enhanced your mathematical reasoning and problem-solving abilities
- Expanded your vocabulary and reading comprehension skills
- Strengthened your understanding of scientific principles
- Gained knowledge in technical areas like electronics and mechanics

Prepared for Success

- Familiarized yourself with the ASVAB format and question types
- Practiced under realistic testing conditions
- Identified and addressed your areas for improvement
- Built the stamina needed for the full-length exam

Final Test-Taking Reminders

As you approach test day, remember these key strategies:

The Night Before

- Get a full night's sleep (7-8 hours)
- Eat a nutritious dinner and prepare a healthy breakfast
- Gather all required documents and materials
- Review key formulas one final time, but avoid cramming

Test Day Morning

- Eat a balanced breakfast with protein and complex carbohydrates
- Arrive early to avoid stress and allow time for check-in procedures
- Bring required identification and any permitted materials
- Stay calm and confident—you are well-prepared

During the Test

- Read each question carefully and completely

- Use the process of elimination on multiple-choice questions
- Manage your time wisely—don't spend too long on any single question
- Trust your preparation and first instincts
- Stay focused and maintain a positive attitude throughout

Your Military Future Awaits

The ASVAB is more than just a test—it's your gateway to an honorable and rewarding military career. Your scores will help determine not only your eligibility for service but also the military occupational specialties (MOS) available to you. The higher your scores, the more opportunities you'll have to pursue careers that match your interests and abilities.

Remember:

- The military offers countless opportunities for personal and professional growth
- Your service will develop leadership skills, technical expertise, and character
- The training and experience you gain will benefit you throughout your life
- You'll have the honor of serving your country and protecting the freedoms we all cherish

Words of Encouragement

Every service member who has worn the uniform started exactly where you are now—preparing to take the first step toward military service. The dedication you've shown in studying for the ASVAB demonstrates that you have what it takes to succeed in the military.

The path ahead may be challenging, but it will also be incredibly rewarding. You'll develop skills, form lifelong friendships, and have experiences that will shape you into a stronger, more capable person. Most importantly, you'll have the privilege of serving something greater than yourself.

Looking Beyond the ASVAB

While the ASVAB is an important milestone, it's just the beginning of your military journey. After you've achieved your target scores, you'll move on to:

- **Military Entrance Processing Station (MEPS)**: Complete your physical examination and finalize your enlistment
- **Basic Training/Boot Camp**: Develop the fundamental skills and mindset of a military professional
- **Advanced Individual Training (AIT) or "A" School**: Learn the specific skills for your chosen military occupation
- **First Duty Assignment**: Begin your career as a fully trained military professional

Each step will build upon the foundation of knowledge, discipline, and commitment you've already established.

A Personal Message

As you close this study guide and prepare to take the ASVAB, know that countless Americans are proud of your decision to serve. Your willingness to raise your right hand and take the oath of enlistment places you among a special group of individuals who have chosen duty, honor, and service to country.

The skills you've learned, the knowledge you've gained, and the confidence you've built through this preparation will serve you well not just on test day, but throughout your military career and beyond. The military will provide you with opportunities to lead, to learn, to grow, and to make a meaningful difference in the world.

Final Thoughts

Your military career will be filled with challenges that test your resolve, opportunities that stretch your capabilities, and experiences that you'll treasure for a lifetime. The same determination that brought you through this study guide will carry you through basic training, technical school, and every assignment that follows.

Stand tall, be confident, and remember that you are joining the ranks of America's finest. Your country needs leaders like you—individuals who are willing to serve, to sacrifice, and to stand guard over the values and freedoms that make our nation great.

Our Wish for Your Success

As you embark on this new chapter of your life, we wish you:

Success in achieving your ASVAB goals and qualifying for the military occupation of your choice

Strength to meet every challenge with courage and determination

Growth in knowledge, leadership, and character throughout your service

Pride in wearing the uniform and representing the finest military in the world

Honor in serving your country and fellow citizens with distinction

Fulfillment in a career that will reward you with purpose, camaraderie, and achievement

Safety in all your endeavors, and a successful return from every mission

Go Forward with Confidence

You are ready. You are prepared. You are capable of great things.

Take the ASVAB with confidence, knowing that you have done everything possible to prepare for success. Trust in your abilities, draw upon your preparation, and remember that this test is your opportunity to demonstrate the knowledge and skills you've worked so hard to develop.

The uniform you'll soon wear has been earned by your commitment to excellence. The rank you'll achieve will be a reflection of your dedication to service. The career you'll build will be a testament to your character and capabilities.

Congratulations on completing your ASVAB preparation. We are confident in your success and proud of your commitment to serve.

Good luck on your exam, and welcome to the beginning of an outstanding military career!

"The willingness of America's veterans to sacrifice for our country has earned them our lasting gratitude." - Jeff Miller

"A hero is someone who has given his or her life to something bigger than oneself." - Joseph Campbell

"The true soldier fights not because he hates what is in front of him, but because he loves what is behind him." - G.K. Chesterton

Semper Fi • Hooah • Hooyah • Oorah • Semper Paratus

Study Guide Complete
Mission: SUCCESS

Made in United States
Cleveland, OH
03 August 2025